Praise for *Business Modeling with Spreadsheets*

HP's Strategic Planning and Modeling team has done analytic modeling work in Excel for more than 19 years. Two years ago, we began offering spreadsheet modeling training to HP employees, which has been very much appreciated by attendees, and enthusiastically supported by our company's management. Strong spreadsheet skills are critical to many job functions in today's business environment. I'm very impressed with the Singapore Management University's Computer as an Analysis Tool course. It provides exactly the types of skills I would like to see in new recruits. Good job by SMU.

Congratulations! I'm glad your work will now be available to more people, and I expect the benefits to your readers will be substantial.

Mr. Brian Cargille
Asia-Pacific Manager
Strategic Planning and Modeling (SPaM)
Hewlett Packard

All round excellent case studies, simple to use, and students should enjoy going through the subject matter.

Mr. Robert Yap
Senior Vice President
Worldwide Shared Services Centre & Trading Division
Information Technology Division
DFS Group Limited

Reading this book is absolutely the best way for anyone new to the subject to learn about building models for making better business decisions. Importantly, through considered use of case studies, it shows the reader how to think about modeling, rather than just the mechanics of how to drive a spreadsheet. It is also littered with useful tips and hints that the authors have acquired through years of experience, building models across a diverse range of industries including finance, marketing, and operations.

Mr. Richard Ayres
Co-founder & Principal
Maroon Analytics Pte. Ltd.

I found the book clearly focused on its stated objective which is to get spreadsheet users to the next higher level of spreadsheet use – from simply computation to using spreadsheets to solve business problems. Given the many business problems faced where structure is absent, this may be a very good way to start to unravel the underlying basic drivers of the problem.

Mr. Venky Krishnakumar
Former COO
Citibank
Asia Pacific

The book offers a wealth of real challenges to explore and ample opportunity to learn by doing. It will test the student's ability to conceptualize problems from the very mundane to the more exotic, and will bring a taste of the real world into the classroom.

Mr. Peter Borup
Group Senior Vice President
NORDEN Shipping

This gem of a book will help you discover the power of spreadsheets intelligently applied. It provides tools to uncover problems and explore them imaginatively in a quantitative way. Interactive solutions will be easier to find with the techniques this book uses.

Professor Pang Eng Fong
Professor of Management Practice
Former Dean, Lee Kong Chian School of Business
Singapore Management University

Anyone who has to find solutions to a problem that involves numbers will benefit from this book. It elicits many useful techniques in thinking and spreadsheet modelling that is not typical of many books on modelling or Excel spreadsheet.

Professor Tsui Kai Chong
Provost & Professor
SIM University

THIRD EDITION

BUSINESS MODELING WITH SPREADSHEETS

Problems, Principles, and Practice

Thin-Yin LEONG
SIM University

Michelle L.F. CHEONG
Singapore Management University

McGraw Hill Education

BUSINESS MODELING WITH SPREADSHEETS 3E
PROBLEMS, PRINCIPLES, AND PRACTICE

Cover image © Violka08/iStock

10 9 8 7 6 5 4 3
CTP SLP
20 18 17

When ordering this title, use **ISBN 978-981-4595-15-5** or **MHID 981-4595-15-2**

To Mee Huan, Jonathan, Daniel, and Zanna

~ Thin-Yin LEONG

To Chuan Leong, Sherwyn, Mum, and Dad

~ Michelle CHEONG

CONTENTS

CONTENTS

CHAPTER 3 — DATA LOOKUP AND LINKUP   69

CHAPTER 4

FUNCTIONS AND RELATIONSHIPS 101

CHAPTER 7

PROCESSES AND TIME   **201**

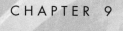

CHAPTER 9

CONTENTS

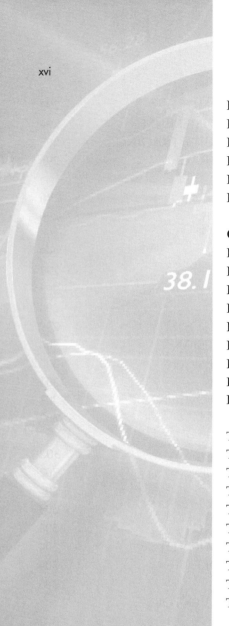

PREFACE

First Edition

Many people with some recent exposure to spreadsheets will quickly attest to how useful a tool it is. They usually want to learn more, to help them improve their performance at work or even at play. You probably would want to do the same. Unfortunately, picking up a book on Excel™ (or for that matter, your favorite spreadsheet application) or attending a spreadsheet course has thus far left many rather frustrated. No doubt, these books and courses, which meet the intent of their writers, course designers, and instructors, are extremely helpful for learning spreadsheet computational features. However, going through such manuals and courses can be as dry and challenging as learning a new language by studying its grammar. Whatever is assimilated this way can be rather superficial. Unless a language is effectively applied and internalized, no further progress will be made and all that is learned will soon go to waste. We believe this to be true for spreadsheets as well.

The best way we found to acquire competency in spreadsheets is really to use them, and we mean to apply them to real problems. There are other books which are also problem driven in pedagogical approach, using the spreadsheet as a medium of problem expression. They, however, are model-centric and not modeling-centric, using the spreadsheet mainly as a computing tool. The models they cover are for problems in statistical analysis, optimization, simulation, or decision support. These problems can be quite remote from what most people typically use spreadsheets for. What then is the essential basic set of spreadsheet skills that we are promoting in this book? It is exploratory modeling. By this, we mean the ability to think through issues on a spreadsheet, and not merely to compute the results of a model derived principally by other means. Working on a spreadsheet has many advantages over analyzing graphically or mathematically on paper as it is particularly suited for experimentation and has widespread acceptance.

We have assembled in this book a broad variety of problem contexts to help you develop this spreadsheet exploratory modeling capability. Instead of the more complex, structured problems found in tertiary textbooks and academic settings, we want to assist you in dealing with simpler unstructured problems, the kind that you and others in the business community have to work with on a regular basis. The models in themselves are not as important as the modeling and thinking processes we want to guide you through. This book arises from our extensive experience teaching spreadsheet modeling in an undergraduate *Computer as an Analysis Tool* course, a master's *Spreadsheet Modeling for Technology and Operations Decisions* course, and another master's *Financial Modeling* course at the Singapore Management University. These courses are considered tough, but are nonetheless highly rated by students. A large team of professors continues to teach them using our class exercises, which form the basis of this book.

This is not a *how-to* book, though we explain the use of key spreadsheet features in the appendices for your easy reference. Neither is this a *case* book, in that, beyond the interesting problem contexts, we provide in our exercises process guidance in modeling, and well-formatted and documented spreadsheet solutions (in the accompanying CD). These spreadsheet workbooks are the primary artifacts of the book and should not be mistaken for secondary supplementary material. You want to open each spreadsheet workbook in your personal computer and work along with this book in hand. Do not, however, expect from the text detailed step-by-step procedures on how to construct the workbook models, as this will run counter to the exploratory modeling spirit.

Our wide application scope covers business, finance, operations, and technology management areas. We want you to experientially learn the art of modeling for business analysis, as if you are alongside with us as business consultants. You will learn how to identify the key aspects of business situations, analyze decision trade-offs and sensitivities, and explore the implications of uncertainties and risks. The concerns studied are deliberately toned down to be less challenging than those in an introductory management science course, which would be a natural follow-on pursuit. You should question, create, and adjust spreadsheet models, and learn to use them as a communication medium in modeling. Test this approach out on real clients, people who are interested in the results of the models rather than the models themselves. We will prompt you to examine how you could effectively implement the solutions recommended by your analysis.

Thousands of students have gone through the many challenging exercises and tools presented in this book and have found them to be extremely useful and enriching to their learning. Many can apply rather effectively what they have learned to their internship work assignments or regular jobs upon graduation, improving their job performance. We hope the same would be true for you as you start this interesting learning journey with us. It is important to note that we do only a small portion of the exercises in our courses; usually no more than two exercises or tools are collectively worked on in a three-hour class session. About two or three other exercises are additionally highlighted to students in each session for them to work on their own time outside of class.

If you are using this book on your own, then likewise just attempt one or two exercises from each chapter, progressing from Chapters 1 to 8 roughly in that order. You can return to the other exercises in the earlier chapters later to review and practice what you have learned. It is not necessary to attempt every exercise in the book as some of them may be beyond what most people can handle. This is especially true for those labeled as tools. Read and reflect on the tips given at the end of most chapters. Just imagine that you are there in class listening to us saying them to you.

Second Edition

The feedback we got for the first edition was very encouraging. While our colleagues and students using the book as a course textbook found the first edition extremely useful, others reading the book on their own outside of the courses we teach commented that they needed more help. Modeling is already difficult to do within the context of a course with an instructor demonstrating and facilitating students in the modeling process. Without the instructor alongside, it is perhaps intimidating to the uninitiated and more detailed steps should be given. It is, however, quite contrary to the spirit of modeling to show all the steps since half the fun and most of the learning come from self-discovery.

We revised the book to better order the exercises in each chapter and notes in the appendices. New exercises and appendices notes were added to give a wider range of topic coverage, and, most importantly as a concession, we selected an exercise per chapter for which detailed workings were shown. Exercises and tools now totaled 101, an increase of 29 from the first edition. A lot more than before, there were now 51 tips. The tips from the last edition were totally reorganized and new ones added. Some of the larger tips given before were split into smaller bite sizes so that the individual ideas were separated and more accessible. The ordering of the tips better fit the way they were delivered in our classes alongside the exercises.

The appendix notes were also rearranged to better fit the learning process, and Appendix A was split into Appendices A-1, A-2, and A-3, with each covering the spreadsheet features and functions of Excel 2007, Excel 2003 (and older versions) and OpenOffice.org Calc, respectively. We put in a lot of work to fully include Calc as we felt the need to generalize spreadsheet work beyond Microsoft Excel™. The challenges come from the minor differences in the names of spreadsheet features and major learning of the dissimilar way OOo deals with spreadsheet objects in their BASIC macro language. Appendix B which dealt with the Basic programming language and macros was similarly split into Appendices B-1 and B-2. Other than more exercises, tools, and tips, the book was also made thicker by the overlap in materials in these sub-appendices. However, that made it easier for learners to focus on their particular version of spreadsheet application without distracting references to the others.

To extend the modeling learning further, a new chapter (Chapter 9) and 14 additional accompanying workbooks were also added as examples of completed student projects. Also presented were many more project challenges that learners could develop as their own projects. However, we only provided the business scenarios, not their workbooks, project concepts, and workings comments. A total of 101 projects (inclusive of example projects) were provided. To further assist you, we made available, some "template" and tool workbooks, such as New Exercise, New Project, and Modeling Tools, to name a few. They were provided to help you construct your project and make the work easier.

Finally, our advice remained the same: modeling can only be learned by doing. So persevere and try to clock at least 1,000 hours of spreadsheet modeling within the next few years, to work towards becoming an expert in this valuable art. Work hard and have fun!

Third Edition: What's New

Excel 2010/2011. The introduction of new Excel versions compeled us to start working on another edition of this book. We have tried as much as possible to keep the main text free from Excel version specific information but alas, new appendices have to be released to give more direct help to weaker students using the new Excel versions. We had earlier released supplementary Appendices A-4 on Excel 2010 and A-5 on Mac Excel 2011 to avert introducing a new version so soon after the publication of the second edition. Appendix A-5 is particularly special since this is the first time we address the Mac audience.

Excel 2013 is the latest version released by Microsoft at the time of this writing. The menu system and features of Excel 2010 is retained in this new release in Microsoft Windows. Therefore, Appendix A-4 will now cover both Excel 2010 and Excel 2013; no additional appendix is added. There are of course new and more powerful features in Excel 2013 not found in Excel 2010. They however do not substantially alter the business modeling and basic spreadsheet skills learning presented in our book, and we as such leave it to the reader to explore them on their own. To further simplify the book structure, trimming it by a quarter in thickness, only Excel 2010-2013 materials and Excel VBA are retained in the book proper of this edition, as Appendix A and Appendix B respectively. All other appendices are moved as pdf files for users' reference into the *Online Learning Center* that accompanies this book.

Mac Excel. Excel workbooks released in previous editions of this book do not all work in the Mac OS environment. Functionally, they generally perform satisfactorily in Mac Excel. However, we discovered through our students that worksheets and tables designed to fit neatly into pages in Windows do not necessarily fit in their Macs. A possible solution is to view and print at 92% magnification. Fonts more compatible to work on both Windows and Mac PCs are now used to avert the problem, together with some adjustments to columns widths. Due to technological limitations, this however still does not guarantee that workbooks designed in one environment will look the same in another. Another issue was some workbooks with macros that open and close files could not work in the Mac environment, namely *RenameFiles, TextDataImportExport*, and *UsefulMacros*. The problem we now identified is in the different separators used in the file path notations of MS Windows and Mac OS: "/" vs ":". The macros in there now corrected will auto-detect and adapt to the two operating systems. Other workbooks that use forms, such as *Binomial Option, Black–Scholes*, and *InvestmentJournal*, still may not work in Mac Excel. Other exercise and tool workbooks should now be Mac-compliant.

LibreOffice Calc. Appendices A and B associated with Calc are now pdf files in the accompanying *Online Learning Center*. This allows us to make them freely available to the open source community. Our OpenOffice.org (now OpenOffice) Calc 3 workbook files from the second edition are also in the *Online Learning Center*. We have sinced adopted LibreOffice Calc 4, reviewed and updated the workbooks and Appendix A, taking in revisions and new features. A new Appendix A on LibreOffice Calc and associated new files are also in the *Online Learning Center*. Notable new features are worksheet tabs with colors, better Conditional Formatting, and advanced functions such as AVERAGEIF, COUNTIFS and SUMIFS. However, not all attempts to incorporate new features into the LO Calc 4 workbooks have been successful. The notes comparing Excel and Calc have been updated in Appendices A for Excel 2003, 2007, 2010–2013, LibreOffice Calc, and OpenOffice Calc.

Discovery Points. Though helpful to support modeling, *Tips* presented in each chapter are process-oriented and technical; they do not assist the uninitiated in the exploratory modeling of business content and its problem structure. To better support underlying thinking and give pointers to guide business problem exploration, we added a new section called *Discovery Points* and placed about five points in each chapter. More general than the comments in the *Concept* sub-section of exercises, they are ideas many experienced modelers use intuitively. By listing them at the start of each chapter, we believe it will help consolidate the learning for seasoned modelers, and make it easier for instructors to impart the art of modeling to students. Use them for self-discovery, class discussion, and project team deliberations. The themes in the points can be applied to various settings and exercises found in this book.

Problem Sets. It seems strange that a book with 101 spreadsheet exercises and tools should need to have problem sets. However, it is a reality of academia that students need to be given homework and tested to ensure that learning has taken place at the correct pace. Students found the exercises in the book rather challenging and as extensive as assignments and tests. Professors seeking to adopt this book as their course text requested separate question sets for assignments, quizzes, and examinations. For this reason, we added at the end of each chapter, simpler and more defined problems for students to practice and be evaluated on their spreadsheet skills. The questions with given data are generally easier. Harder questions are marked with an asterisk (*).

Thin-Yin LEONG (tyleong@unisim.edu.sg)
Michelle CHEONG (michcheong@smu.edu.sg)

To access the Online Learning Center, please visit www.mheducation.asia/olc/leong.

ACKNOWLEDGMENTS

This book was developed over many years of teaching thousands of undergraduate and graduate students, and its exercises are derived from decades of accumulated industry working experience as well as interactions with students and colleagues in the universities. We are grateful to numerous people who have inspired us to cultivate and advance our art of spreadsheet modeling. Our special thanks go to all our colleagues who use our material in their class sections.

Particularly noteworthy are the adjunct professors who took valuable time off from their professional jobs to share their experiences in teaching many class sections of our courses. We express our sincere appreciation to them all for their dedication and relentless pursuit of excellence and thereby helping us to verify and validate many of the exercises, which in turn brought greater clarity to how they should be used in class.

We would also like to thank our past batches of Singapore Management University students who have worked on the exercises and provided us with constructive feedback to improve their subject content and design. Finally, our sincere gratitude goes to the many people who had (some unknowingly) contributed help and suggestions, ideas for new exercises, and who encouraged us along the way. We always welcome more contributions and comments. Instructors using this book will no doubt create more exercises of their own to use in class. We encourage you to share them with all of us too. Let us know also how our exercises have worked out for you.

ABOUT THE AUTHORS

Thin-Yin LEONG (PhD, Massachusetts Institute of Technology)

Dr. Leong is currently Associate Professor at the SIM University in Singapore. He was Associate Dean (Strategic Planning and Initiatives) and a faculty member at the School of Information Systems, Singapore Management University, for 10 years. Before that, he was a faculty member at the National University of Singapore's Business School for 10 years. Over two decades, he has designed and taught many courses in operations management, logistics, and supply chain management, and business spreadsheet modeling in undergraduate, MBA, and executive programs. In between academia, Dr. Leong spent more than a decade in the industry and served as Vice-President (Operations Planning & Research) and Senior Vice-President (Information Technology) with the port operator that runs the world's busiest container terminal, where he spearheaded its operations improvements, and systems and technology development. He also provided many models that supported management decisions in strategy, capacity development, operational planning and scheduling, and financial and tax issues. One of his current pet teaching and research interests is spreadsheet modeling and analysis, leveraging his past experience for research as well as industry applications. Although in academia, he remains active in business consulting and has worked with many multinational corporations and local companies, particularly those in the electronics, petrochemical, medical, hospitality, banking, cargo logistics, passenger transport, and government sectors.

Michelle CHEONG (PhD, Nanyang Technological University Singapore-MIT Alliance, Innovations in Manufacturing Systems and Technology Program)

Dr. Cheong is Associate Professor of Information Systems (Practice) at the Singapore Management University (SMU) and Associate Dean of the School of Information System's (SIS) Postgraduate Professional Programs, where she is in charge of two masters programs and Continuing Education & Training. Dr. Cheong has worked eight years in the industry developing and implementing enterprise IT solutions for manufacturing companies. She has led teams to develop complex IT systems which were implemented enterprise-wide covering business functions from sales to engineering, inventory management, planning, production, and distribution. She consulted for precision engineering, printing, aerospace, and brewery companies in business process reengineering for IT solutions implementation. Upon obtaining her PhD in Operations Management, she joined SMU in 2005 where she teaches the Business Modeling with Spreadsheets course at the undergraduate level. She also teaches different variants of spreadsheet modeling courses in three different masters programs at SMU, covering different domains, including financial modeling, innovation modeling, and IT project management. She also designed and delivered an Operations Analytics and Applications course for the Master of IT in Business (Analytics) program at SIS.

Case Study and Spreadsheet Modeling

LEARNING OUTCOMES

- Able to explain how spreadsheet modeling is effective for solving business problems
- Able to apply simple spreadsheet models for business case study analysis

INTRODUCTION

Personal computers are important tools in most business executives' day-to-day work, and increasingly so too, with improved portability, wireless network access, and more easy-to-use new software applications. The truth, however, is that their tremendous potential is only marginally harnessed, leaving a significant gap between what technology has to offer and its actual use in addressing business concerns. Linking the two is a challenge: not so well-defined concerns have to be translated into mental models, and correct techniques appropriately used to present these models in forms amenable for analysis by stakeholders. This could be just a client or a project team with diverse backgrounds.

In this book, we limit the use of mathematical notations and programming codes language to employ the spreadsheet as a modeling and thinking tool. Your attention will be directed to simple day-to-day business contexts, rather than formulation and programming technicalities. The exercises here are designed to integrate what you already know, both in analytical thinking and common business concepts. The contexts build up progressively, with partial overlaps in the use of spreadsheet features between successive exercises and between consecutive chapters to help reinforce your learning. Through self-experimentation, and preferably with some technical coaching and guided self-learning, you should be able to learn a lot and retain that learning. If you are taking up a spreadsheet modeling course, look for instructors with business consulting experience and not just someone who knows a lot about spreadsheets.

As you read and practice along with this book, you will learn Microsoft Excel™ or another spreadsheet software of your choice. But that is not all. Most importantly, this book, in supporting the course you are taking, will help you in an experiential and interactive manner to learn the effective use of spreadsheets as an exploratory modeling tool to analyze and solve business problems. You can then take that further to improve your credibility in business judgment and responsiveness in addressing workplace challenges.

This introductory chapter aims at opening your eyes to the possibilities. The exercises are simple, but you should think about what the problem to solve is, where data can be found, what the link between the variables is, and so on. The first exercise, *Achilles and the Tortoise,* will be worked on step by step to demonstrate how a simple spreadsheet model can unravel a paradox that once stumped the great philosophers. The remaining exercises will present other challenges, discussing the concepts behind them, and offering working suggestions. *Community Water Tank* and *Palibalo Ferry* are two other easier exercises to start you on the modeling journey. Like the first exercise, they will make you think about the simple mathematical relationships among the variables.

Slightly more challenging, the *Alex Processing* exercise highlights an effective model extracted from real practice on capital asset acquisition planning. *Data Center Assets,* similar to *Alex Processing* in concept, compares and contrasts various ways of projecting future equipment needs and suggests that the most effective solution may not be powerful mathematical computations. The same problem structure is found in *Financial Statement,* as an application to corporate finance and in understanding the drivers of a business concern. These three exercises make use of ratios to provide the answers to their underlying questions.

The last three exercises in this chapter, namely, *Group Trip Expenses, 100 Meters in 9 Seconds,* and *Gini Index,* explore the issue of how to make the results more visual and intuitive. This is done using the formatting and charting features available in spreadsheets.

Remember to work with the exercise workbook displayed on your personal computer screen. In each workbook, move sequentially from the first to the last worksheet, working one worksheet at a time and progressing to the next only when you are satisfied that you have already tried your best on the current worksheet.

DISCOVERY POINTS

Counting 28 haphazardly placed items requires 28 steps. You can quickly arrange the same items in four rows of sevens. Multiplying 4 times 7 gives 28. Doing arithmetic like this is faster than tedious counting. Though still concrete, it is inflexible. Now, $4 \times 7 = 28$ can be generalized to algebraic $a \times b = c$ for any a and b. Algebra, in this way, is abstract but flexible. As illustrations of analytical flexibility, you can set another value for a and vary b to keep the same c or find the smallest perimeter $(2a + 2b)$ for the same area (c).

> **Concrete versus abstract**

Simple modeling usually works with numbers. In physical modeling particularly, numbers are scaled down to reduce construction cost and time, and to allow better model manipulation. Instead of completing an actual building as an experiment, a 1:1000 scale model can be constructed at possibly 1/1000 of cost and time. Adjustments to preliminary designs can be made and the model refined along the way. Working with numbers, physical modeling is still concrete and inflexible.

Computer modeling using digital information technology, on the other hand, is based on algebra and other advanced mathematics. It is extremely flexible, though their programming codes are abstract. A clear exception is the spreadsheet. It is an interesting form of computer modeling that emulates working on a sheet of paper. As a user, you enter numbers into cells and set up arithmetic-like relationships between these numbers. Not perceptible to many, you are not actually working with numbers but rather cells as algebraic variables.

Absolute numbers are only meaningful within their given contexts. Say you earn $1000. Is that high or low, good or bad? $1000 per day is probably good, as compared to the same per month or per year. This is an example in a (single) time context. Now if your income last period was $2000, then $1000 this period is a 50% per period reduction. This is a multiple time or dynamic context. If your peer earns $700, then you are doing better than him, as an ad hoc paired comparison.

> **Ratio and relativity**

Across your school cohort, your pay may only be in the 10th percentile. That is low then. This context is statistical comparison over a population. Finally, your net income of $1000 is obtained by selling $4000 worth of goods. Then, your sales revenue is ($4000 + $1000 =) $5000 with cost of goods sold/sales ratio of ($4000/$5000 =) 0.8 and margin of ($1000/$5000 =) 20%. Or, your $1000 can only buy a sofa set or pay a week of rent. These are relative contexts. We generalize better by using ratios and relative values. A useful side application is when data is not available; you can simply estimate the value of unknown data relative to known data.

Point 3

Projection versus targeting

Scientific projection extrapolates the past to the future. It assumes that the future is a continuation of the past. The actual outcome is at best a probabilistic distribution about the projected trend line. No matter how elaborate and rigorous the projection approach is, such a forecast cannot be accurate. It can be simply argued that the projected is but an expected point or mean trend line. Theory tells us that the probability of a single point in a distribution is zero and as such, good forecasts should be confidence intervals rather than points.

It is however still useful as a basis for targeting since as a mean, underestimation approximately balances overestimation. The linear extrapolations are often moderated down with claims that trends tend to slow down, saturate or reach maturity. However, as a targeting exercise, it may also be ramped up by managerial choice and investor requirement. For example, your company had been growing at 10% per year in the last decade and more recently at 8%. Trending forward, you want to put forth a growth rate estimation of 5% to your management board. The board's chairperson may counter, using the 9% growth rate of a close competitor as a benchmark, requiring you to put up plans to show how the company can aggressively grow at an annual rate of 12%. This means that it is not business as usual. You have to work against your company's momentum and create new market potential.

Point 4

Questions and givens

At school, your teachers pose assignment and test questions to evaluate whether you have learned and are able to apply specific methods taught. In the real world and in higher-level jobs, you manage a situation under your charge. The questions to be solved, data and solving approaches to be used, must come from you. Young executives rely on their seniors and bosses to provide guidance, and they tap on others' experiences using questions used in the past. As executives and managers living in a rapidly changing world, your job is not just to perpetuate the past but also to create the future.

In *Point 3*, I have already started the discussion on this, particularly to use the past only as a projection into the future. Other areas that need attention are where you put effort into and how you are organized. Typically, organizations are divided into functional areas and business areas. Each area tries to identify its own problems as it has always done, and solves them using past approaches. Following this pattern, new areas will not be found and things that fall in between the cracks will not be addressed. You therefore must take charge and think anew.

Point 5

Case study and analysis

A globally well-received way of learning how to examine and solve business organizational concerns is the case study. This approach is commonly used in law and medical schools to train future professionals by exposing them to past precedences. Cases describe problem situations or scenarios, rather than the problems directly. Business students in case studies are asked to put themselves into the shoes of analysts and decision makers. They are to raise and examine possible questions, to ask what are the central concerns, how to go about uncovering specific problems, how to get and sort through the data, how to do the analyses, and what conclusions and actions can be drawn.

Case studies put the burden of asking the questions and answering them on the students. The process of struggling through case studies helps students develop real-world experiences without having to leave the classroom much. Along the way, they learn how to put up quick analysis, make decisive choices, link and apply theoretical concepts to reality, work within a small group and resolve conflicts if any, and communicate their observations, analyses and recommendations to a larger audience of stakeholders and management.

Case study first involves individual preparation, reviewing the case as an overview as well as drilling down selected details. It also typically involves team members in a study group, who may be from different backgrounds and having a variety of skills. The power of the team is to be able to draw upon each other's strengths in evaluating the case and looking out for blind spots in each other's arguments and proposals. The need for collaboration calls for tools that allow everyone to work concurrently in an expedient fashion, rather than sequentially. Look out for new platforms such as files and folder sharing on the cloud and web-based office software such as Office 360 and Google Docs.

EXERCISES

ACHILLES AND THE TORTOISE   Worked Example

Challenge   Among the many paradoxes given by ancient Greek philosopher Zeno (of Elea; 490–425 BC) is the story of Achilles and the tortoise. According to this story, Achilles and a tortoise decided to have a race. Achilles gave the tortoise a head start since he could run twice as fast as the tortoise.

Zeno argued that by the time Achilles reached the tortoise's starting point, the tortoise would have moved by half the distance of the head start given it. Next, by the time Achilles reached that point, the tortoise would have moved further by half the distance that was between them previously, and so on and so forth.

Therefore, it appears that Achilles can never catch up with the tortoise. But surely this cannot be right. Achilles, being twice as fast as the tortoise, must eventually win the race. But is this always so?

Concept   This simple exercise introduces to you the basic Excel features like menu items, toolbars, workbook, worksheets, sheet tabs, and cell format, as you work on an interesting problem. You will learn that a table is defined as a rectangular block of values with empty cells surrounding it. By putting the cursor anywhere in the table, Excel will automatically identify the table and form a graph when you click **Insert/Charts** in the menu for one of the chart types. (Users of Excel 2003 need to select the **Chart Wizard** in the standard toolbar and follow the steps given.) Of course, you have to decide which chart type is the most appropriate to use for presenting your data.

How have you and people you know been using spreadsheets? There are, in fact, quite a few possibilities. Some people would use them to store and organize values and text data. They often do the needed computations using external means, like calculators. Working through this exercise, you will see that problems far more complex than those you have managed so far can be solved using a spreadsheet, and usually with relative ease too. In particular, by charting the information in graphs, the so-called paradox can be visually unravelled and explained. The truth can now be more clearly seen in such a way that even a nontechnical audience will be convinced.

Working (Detailed)   Before we start exploring the problem, let us open the workbook and go through some spreadsheet basics.

a.   The workbook has several worksheets. To move from one sheet to the next, click on the sheet tabs. In each sheet, there will be many cells where we can type text or numbers. Of course, the usefulness of a spreadsheet lies in its ability to do computations with mathematical formulas and functions.

b. The first sheet of this workbook, as in all the other workbooks provided in this book, is the *Home* sheet. We will use the *Home* sheet to describe the problem. The description notes can be in a textbox object or directly in the cells.

c. The second sheet is the *Scratch* sheet. We encourage you to start modeling the given problem context from this blank worksheet. Many students have told us that the most difficult part in modeling is starting from a blank sheet. When you are given a completed model, the solution to the business challenge always seems so easy.

d. The third sheet is the *Proto* sheet, where a skeleton model is provided as an intermediate step to guide you through the modeling process.

e. The fourth sheet is the *Model* sheet, which contains the complete solution.

To model a problem, we first postulate the type of end result we want to compute. In this exercise, we would like to know if Achilles would overtake the tortoise. Several performance measures will address this, such as:

a. Distance covered. The total distance individually covered by Achilles and the tortoise will increase with time, and as soon as the total distance covered by Achilles exceeds that of the tortoise, Achilles would have overtaken the tortoise.

b. Time taken. Alternatively, we can compute the time taken for each of them to cover any given distance. In this exercise, the distance to cover at each iteration is the distance between Achilles and the tortoise, as we would want to illustrate the logical argument given by the Greek philosopher. As he travels further from the starting point, the distance between Achilles and the tortoise becomes increasingly smaller. At the point where the distance between them is zero, Achilles can begin to overtake the tortoise.

Mathematically, it is easier to compute part a than part b. We will present both approaches to solve the paradox.

Having clarified the desired end result, we then determine the required inputs for the exercise. These should be the headstart distance and the speeds of Achilles and the tortoise.

The steps for the simple solution approach (see *Figure 1-1*) are as follows:

a. Select the *Proto* sheet. Identify two cells to store the speeds of Achilles and the tortoise. We will use cell C4 for Achilles' speed and cell D4 for the tortoise's speed.

    i. Since the exact speeds are not known, it would suffice to let the tortoise's speed be 1, and set Achilles' speed to 2, twice that of the tortoise. It is a good practice in general to use relative values as absolute values require more effort to find and maintain.

Figure 1-1

Simple
Solution for
Achilles and
the Tortoise

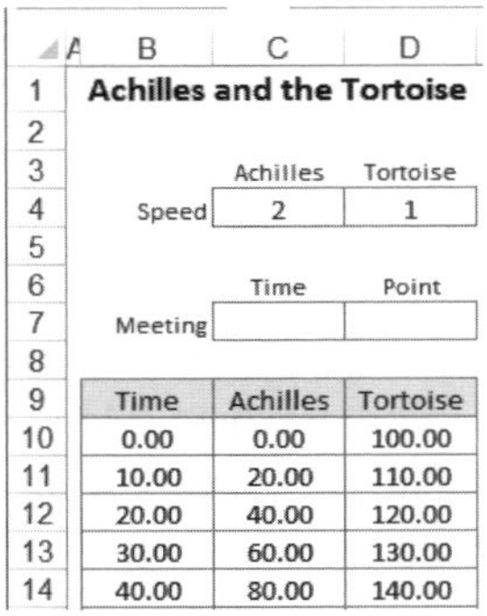

◢A	B	C	D
1	**Achilles and the Tortoise**		
2			
3		Achilles	Tortoise
4	Speed	2	1
5			
6		Time	Point
7	Meeting		
8			
9	Time	Achilles	Tortoise
10	0.00	0.00	100.00
11	10.00	20.00	110.00
12	20.00	40.00	120.00
13	30.00	60.00	130.00
14	40.00	80.00	140.00

    ii.   Also, it is better to enter the value 1 into cell D4 and =2*D4 into cell C4. This offers flexibility by allowing Achilles' speed to be inferred should the tortoise's actual speed be known.

b.   To determine the absolute distance covered, we will need to formulate the mathematical relation that links the speed inputs to the distance outputs: Distance = Speed * Time.

    i.   Prepare cells B9:B43 to store the elapsed time.

    ii.   Prepare cells C9:C43 to store Achilles' total distance.

    iii.   Prepare cells D9:D43 to store the tortoise's total distance.

    iv.   Enter the value 0 into cell B10 and the value 10 into cell B11. Select both cells B10 and B11, move the cursor to the lower-right corner of the selection until the white cross cursor becomes a black cross cursor and then drag the cursor to cell B30. Now, you have completed a **Fill** operation, under which values are linearly extrapolated from your selection to the empty cells. With this done, cell B30 should have the value 200.

    v.   Enter the value 0 into cell C10, which marks the starting point for Achilles at time 0.

    vi.   Enter the value 100 into cell D10 as the arbitrary head-start distance for the tortoise.

    vii.   Enter in cell C11 the formula =B11*C$4, which states that Achilles' total distance = Time traveled * Achilles' speed.

    viii.   Enter into cell D11 the formula =B11*D$4+D$10, which states that the tortoise's total distance = Time * Tortoise's speed + Head start.

    ix.   Select cells C11 and D11 and complete the **Fill** operation to row 30. This operation copies the formulas in the selected cells in row 11 of columns C and D and pastes them in the empty cells below. The relative referencing behavior of the formulas would correctly complete the model.

c. The meeting time and distance point, which can be computed mathematically as well, can be visually inspected from the table of results.

   i. Visually inspecting the table, we can see that Achilles and the tortoise meet at time 100 when they are at a distance of 200 from Achilles' starting point.

   ii. Mathematically, the meeting time C7 = D10/(C4–D4) (i.e., Head start/ Difference between Achilles' and the tortoise's speeds).

   iii. Similarly, meeting point D7 = C7*C4 (i.e., Meeting time * Achilles' speed), or D7 = C7*D4+D10 (i.e., Meeting time * Tortoise's speed + Head start).

   This model is not flexible enough. To illustrate, assume Achilles can travel at 2.5 times the tortoise's speed. We now set C4 = 2.5 or, more accurately, 2.5*D4. From the revised results, we can no longer visually inspect the exact meeting time and point. The table only roughly tells us that the meeting time is somewhere between 60 and 70, and the meeting point is between 160 and 170.

The advanced solution approach (see *Figure 1-2*) determines the time taken for Achilles to come closer to the tortoise as he tries to reach the point where the tortoise was last at, mimicking the argument presented by the Greek philosopher Zeno. For this, we set Achilles' total distance traveled to be equal to the tortoise's previous total distance, and then compute the time that must elapse between his last location and this. With the elapsed time, we can compute the tortoise's next total distance. At each iteration, the difference in their total distances becomes increasingly smaller. They will meet when the distance difference becomes zero. The difference, however, will not reach zero in such a process. It only approaches zero.

a. Select the *Proto* sheet. Identify two cells to store the speeds for Achilles and the tortoise. We will use cell C4 for Achilles' speed and cell D4 for the tortoise's speed.

   i. Since the exact speeds are not known, it would suffice to let the Tortoise's speed be 1, set Achilles' speed to 2, twice that of the tortoise. It is a good practice in general to use relative values as absolute values require more effort to find and maintain.

   ii. Also, it would be better to enter the value 1 into cell D4, and =2*D4 into cell C4. This offers flexibility by allowing Archilles' speed to be inferred should the tortoise's actual speed be known.

b. To determine the meeting point, we will use the mathematical relationship that the tortoise's new distance = Head start + Elapsed time * Tortoise's speed.

   i. Prepare cells B9:B43 to store the elapsed time.

   ii. Prepare cells C9:C43 to store Achilles' total distance.

   iii. Prepare cells D9:D43 to store the tortoise's total distance.

Figure 1-2

Advanced
Solution for
*Achilles and
the Tortoise*

◢ A	B	C	D	I
1	**Achilles and the Tortoise**			
2				
3		Achilles	Tortoise	
4	Speed	2	1	
5				
6		Time	Point	
7	Meeting	100	200	
8				
9	Time	Achilles	Tortoise	
10	0.00	0.00	100.00	
11	50.00	100.00	150.00	
12	75.00	150.00	175.00	
13	87.50	175.00	187.50	
14	93.75	187.50	193.75	
15	96.88	193.75	196.88	
16	98.44	196.88	198.44	
17	99.22	198.44	199.22	
18	99.61	199.22	199.61	
19	99.80	199.61	199.80	
20	99.90	199.80	199.90	
21	99.95	199.90	199.95	
22	99.98	199.95	199.98	
23	99.99	199.98	199.99	
24	99.99	199.99	199.99	
25	100.00	199.99	200.00	
26	100.00	200.00	200.00	
27	110.00	220.00	210.00	
28	120.00	240.00	220.00	

iv. Enter the value 0 into cell B10 to represent the starting time.

v. Enter the value 0 into cell C10, as the starting point of Achilles at time 0.

vi. Enter the value 100 into cell D10, as the arbitrary head-start distance for the tortoise.

vii. Enter into cell C11 the formula =D10 (i.e., Achilles' total distance = Tortoise's previous total distance).

viii. Enter into cell B11 the formula =C11/C$4 (i.e., Time = Achilles' total distance/Achilles' speed).

ix. Enter into cell D11 the formula =D10+(B11-B10)*D$4 (i.e., Tortoise's total distance = Head start + Elapsed time * Tortoise's speed).

x. Select cells B11 through D11 concurrently and complete the **Fill** operation to row 30. The **Fill** operation in this case copies the formulas in the selected cells in row 11 of columns C and D and pastes them into the empty cells below. The relative referencing behavior of the formulas would correctly complete the model. You should be able to observe that Achilles is getting closer to the tortoise.

c. The meeting time and point, which can be computed mathematically as well, can be visually inspected from the table of results.

    i. Visually inspecting the table, we can see that Achilles and the tortoise meet at time 100 when they both are at a distance of 200 from Achilles' starting point. The cells still provide valid results when you change the input values for head start or the speeds of Achilles and the tortoise. In *Figure 1-2*, change Achilles' speed to three times that of the tortoise. The meeting time is now changed to 50, and the meeting point is changed to 150.

    ii. Mathematically, meeting time C7 = D10/(C4–D4) (i.e., Head start/ Difference between Achilles' and the tortoise's speeds).

    iii. Meeting point D7 = C7*C4 (i.e., Meeting time * Achilles' speed) or D7 = C7*D4+D10 (i.e., Meeting time * Tortoise's speed + Head start).

d. After the meeting point, the race will behave as if both Achilles and the tortoise have just begun a new race from a common starting point. From here onwards, the distance traveled by both will simply be computed as Time * Speed.

    i. As cell B26 takes the value of the meeting time, we increment cells B27 onwards by 10 with each row down.

    ii. Enter into cell C26 the formula =$B26*C$4 (i.e., Achilles' distance = Time * Achilles' speed).

    iii. Enter into cell D26 the formula =D$10+$B26*D$4 (i.e., Tortoise's distance = Head start + Time * Tortoise's speed).

    iv. Select both C26 and D26 and apply the **Fill** operation to copy their equations down to rows beyond 30. These values can be used to plot the portion of the chart beyond the meeting point.

How is it that in the first place, we can be led to believe that Achilles would never overtake the tortoise? Following Zeno's argument, given enough time, the distance between Achilles and the tortoise grows to be infinitesimally small, making it impossible for Achilles to overtake the tortoise. However, the time increments between iterations also become infinitesimally small. These elapsed time increments do add up to a finite value. This means that keeping to the iterations so specified, you only observe time values just short of the meeting point. To go beyond, Achilles must be allowed to run free and not be restrained to reaching the meeting point only.

Using the results obtained from the advanced solution approach, we can learn to plot a chart (see *Figure 1-3*) to show the distances covered by Achilles and the tortoise against time. Ensure that Achilles' speed in cell C4 is set as two times that of the tortoise's speed.

a.   Put your cursor anywhere in the table (cell range B9:D43) that shows the distances covered by Achilles and the tortoise over time. Select **Insert/Charts/Scatter with Straight Lines** from the Excel menu.

b.   You can change the chart type, data series, and chart formats. To do this, click on the chart to select it and then select from the options available in the **Design, Layout**, and **Format** tabs in the menu. These three tabs will only appear if a chart is selected.

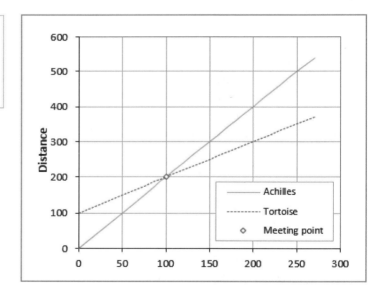

Figure 1-3

Chart for
*Achilles and
the Tortoise*

COMMUNITY WATER TANK

Exercise 2

Challenge

Sammy is planning a new community water tank for the village. An open-top, rectangular concrete tank to hold 30 cubic meters (cbm) of water is to be constructed. Given the site constraints, the width of the tank will be 2 meters. Building the tank costs $10 per square meter (sqm) for the base and $5 per square meter for the sides.

Concept

The focus of this exercise is to recapture the imagination of the modeler for basic mathematical formulas and show how they are applied in the real world. The volume of a cuboid is well defined as the product of its length, width, and height, and total surface of the cuboid would be the sum of the products of "length" and "width" of each flat surface (appropriately defined in each case). Without giving reference to these formulas, you should be able to deftly work with them to determine the required results.

Working

For any given volume and width of the tank, the length of the tank can be found for different tank heights. These results have to be first tabulated for comparisons. With the remaining dimensions computed, you can compute the surface areas of the base and the sides. The two areas are separately computed because the base is more costly to construct than the sides. The total construction can now be computed.

The variation of the tank heights allows us to compare the cost of different ways of configuring the tank. The results can be plotted to provide a more visual way to interpret the findings. It appears that the tank construction cost decreases as the tank height increases. On closer inspection, the result actually suggests that there is an optimum height of about 4 meters, after which the construction cost would increase again, though only minimally.

It is possible to get a more accurate determination of the optimal height; either by using finer height variations closer to 4 meters or better still, using **Solver**. However, this is not necessary since the change in the total cost with variation of tank height when the height is about 4 meters is really very small.

PALIBALO FERRY

Exercise 3

Challenge

At river Palibalo, a ferry service operates between the north and south banks. In this service, one ferry vessel sails continuously pendulum-wise between two jetties that are located directly opposite each other. The schedule indicates that the ferry arrives at a jetty every 60 minutes, each time staying 15 minutes for passengers and cargo to be unloaded and then loaded. This means that in each round trip, the vessel spends 30 minutes in total unloading and loading, and 30 minutes in total on the move. The ferry's average speed between the jetties is 15 km per hour.

To cater to growth in passenger traffic, the service operator is considering whether to replace the current ferry vessel with a larger one or get an additional vessel.

Concept

The formula to apply in this exercise is less obvious. You may want to sketch the scene out in a blank spreadsheet or on a piece of paper. The focus here is to deal fittingly with time, distance, and speed. You should already know that speed is equal to distance divided by time. The added complexity would be the addition of another vessel. The point to remember is that the ferry vessel moves in a continuous "circuit" and so offering the service with more than one vessel would be best done with the vessels evenly spaced in this "circuit."

Working

Always set up the formulas as simply as possible. This would mean to let the direct component variables be inputs and the obvious required results be outputs. If the "result" is an input variable, use **Goal Seek** to find the required answer. In this exercise, one such exercise is the width of the river, which is not *a priori* given.

Increasing the number of ferry vessels will improve the frequency of the ferry service and this is typically preferred by passengers. Having two ferries will also make it easier to keep the service operating even when one vessel is out for maintenance or has broken down. However, more ferries would require more sets of crew and may have other cost disadvantages. On the other hand, a larger ferry may require the jetty to be upgraded to cater to the larger size of the vessel. The concluding recommendations would be based on a balancing of a host of such considerations.

Exercise 4

ALEX PROCESSING

Challenge

Alex Processing Inc. produces a line of food products that are used as key ingredients in mass-produced meals. The CEO, who recently hired you as his assistant, requested that you prepare an equipment acquisition plan.

After consulting Sam English, the executive engineer, you are able to tabulate the equipment holding, the last 10 years' annual aggregate throughputs, and the next 10 years' expected annual aggregate demands.

Some advice had earlier been given by others in the company. This is listed as follows:

- Past forecasts and acquisition plans were very crude, though they were adequate in the fast business growth phase.
- Demand growth rate has slowed significantly, and from here on, such rough planning may lead to buying equipment too early and even possible expensive over-purchase mistakes.
- Productivity will continue to improve but its change rate will eventually approach saturation.

Concept

In this exercise, you will learn that it does not require a complex model to come up with really powerful and practical results. But first, you have to learn not to be too easily distracted by all the additional cautionary and complicated comments. Do start slowly and easily with a small model, and deal with one issue at a time. It would help if you ask the most important questions first. What do we really want to find? Why do we need to evaluate this problem at all? Build a simple model, however incomplete it may first appear. Grow that model as you query and test the objectives and assumptions raised with each marginal adjustment.

This is a good time to find out about functions and try out on the data some simple ones such as **AVERAGE, MAX, MIN, IF, TREND, and GROWTH**. Also learn about the **Fill** operation. **Fill** is extremely handy for extending table values such as serial running numbers (i.e., 1, 2, . . . or 1.0, 1.1, 1.2, . . .) and dates (e.g., days of the week and months of the year). It does not, however, extend any two adjacent cells with the letter *a* in one cell and *b* in the other cell to list the letters in the English alphabet. This can be corrected by adding your own custom list.

Extrapolating the equipment holding numbers to future years is but one of the possible considerations in extending the model to work with the data. Every time such an idea surfaces, ask yourself these questions:

- What actual calculations are made to arrive at the results? Plot them out to see for yourself if the response is true.
- Are the computations intuitively correct?
  - If yes, why? If no, why?
  - If correct, do the results look realistic?
  - Then keep modifying the model ever so slightly to improve it. When do we stop refining the model? It certainly should not be when it is perfect because that is not attainable. Maybe, it should be when it is useful, that is, at least good enough.

Working

Without data, there can be no analysis. It is, however, difficult to know what data to fetch without first doing some analysis. So you may have to do a little of both concurrently. As you get the data, you will probably need to figure out how they are related to each other. The *Scratch* worksheet is provided for that purpose, for you to visually think through. Expressing your thoughts explicitly helps you, and also those around you working on the problem, to share ideas, develop consensus, and cultivate ownership. The tools for doing this more effectively will be learned in subsequent exercises. For now, experiment and learn from your mistakes. The *Proto* worksheet gives the skeleton of the final model with which you can compare the work you have done so far. You can use this worksheet to further develop the model, the suggested solution of which is in the *Model* worksheet. This is the convention that will be applied to all the other exercises as well.

It is almost effortless to use **Fill** to project the equipment numbers to complete the table. How do these results relate to the past quantities of equipment held? You should realize that the given projected demand does not seem to have any bearing on the projected equipment quantities. In short, no matter how the projected demand changes, the required equipment projection stays the same. Can this be correct?

One way to link the equipment numbers to aggregate demand is to compute the throughput to equipment quantity ratios. Future required equipment numbers can be found by multiplying the aggregate throughput per equipment for each equipment type by the projected demand. Ask yourself these questions when you are working on the model:

- Do you think you can compute the past aggregate throughput per equipment ratios?
- How would you project future equipment throughput performance ratios from past throughput performance ratios?
  - Is there more than one way?
  - What are the ways?
  - How do they differ and which is most appropriate for our situation?
  - Is there an easier way of doing the same calculations?

Now examine the cautionary comments. Past equipment purchase decisions may not be well-informed. There should be some errors in these decisions.

- Can you identify where the mistakes are?
  - What should you do about them?
  - Will they affect our projections of equipment throughput performance ratios?
- Can throughput performance ratio changes be due to the business volumes, extent of time the machines have been operating, number of machines in operation, or even changes in product mix?
  - Which one of these would be more appropriate?

- How do you use the projected throughput performance ratios to compute the future required equipment quantities?
- How do you translate the equipment quantities required for each year into an equipment purchase plan? Note that there is lead time between purchasing and receiving the equipment.

Think through the implementation plan. What other things are there to consider?

- Would the conceived plan be well received?
- Who would object or support it?
- Is it possible to avoid having to worry about this equipment acquisition planning problem in the first place?
  o That is, why do we need an equipment acquisition plan?
  o If it is indeed useful to develop the plan, how far ahead should this plan cover?
  o What is the basis for each of your decisions?

We are sure you are getting the idea now. Modeling is hard work, but it can also be fun. There are lots of questions to ask, although you do not really have to be an expert to do this. While experience and checklists help, it is not possible to have all the questions ready ahead of time for every instance of such challenges. Just put yourself in the shoes of the person doing the job and patiently apply common sense.

DATA CENTER ASSETS

Exercise 5

Challenge

The CEO of SAM Bank, who recently hired you as his assistant, requested that you examine the bank's IT asset capacity and prepare a simple analysis report on the strengths and weaknesses of its data center's assets.

After consulting the key senior IT staff, you are able to tabulate the bank's annual business volume and head count for the last 10 years, and the corresponding IT asset holding quantities. Contingent to getting the projected business volume and organization size for the next five years, you think you can put up the bank's future IT asset capacity plan.

While more complex tools are available to model systems and network performance, and to monitor actual performance metrics of individual equipment, such as utilization level, input/output rates and response times, to help determine when and how much additional capacities are needed, the CEO wanted something simple that he can also use to examine if new software applications are indeed able to share current computing hardware and to project future IT capacity requirements for the next few years.

Concept   If you do not know what a data center is, then maybe it is time to find out. Try searching the Internet to familiarize yourself with what it is and the physical assets it holds. What you find out does not really matter to the modeling. The modeling approach and problem-solving thinking in this exercise are similar to *Alex Processing*, or for that matter any other problems on capital asset planning. Read the notes there, if you have not already done so.

From the modeling perspective, we are simply dealing with a setup that uses assets to support business operations. It is likely that with a higher business volume, more of these assets are needed. Decide and define the variables to use for your model. A common variable (productivity) is needed to link the two weakly related variables (namely demand volume and holding quantities of each asset type). They are weakly related because a plot of aggregate demand against equipment holding quantities will yield a scatter of points that are elongated in the north-easterly direction and not a straight line or curve.

Try to recognize the difference between demand forecast and sales target. Which of these should rightly be the input of your model? Discuss with others why past decisions are not necessarily good information to use to project the future. What then are the key characteristics of good information to use?

Working   Use **Fill**. Double-clicking the right-bottom corner box of a cell in a partially filled table will help speed up work in completing the tables.

You want to be careful how you formulate the equations using relative, absolute, or mixed cell referencing where appropriate. What happens when you try to **Fill** from cells that contain formulas instead of data values to other cells?

Ponder over the following questions when you work on the model:

- What are the ways to improve productivity?
- What if the so-called productivity improvement really arises from previous equipment overpurchases, changes in relative equipment use, or improvement in the capabilities of newer equipment models?
- Past business volume performance and future expansion may be limited by bottlenecks in the IT systems. How can you identify these bottlenecks?

Whether to drill down further to determine more accurately the productivities depends on the magnitude of machine acquisition costs. There is no point in spending too much effort if the acquisition cost is low, or is there?

FINANCIAL STATEMENT

The financial statement is the standard corporate financial management tool. Studying past data, we can extract performance ratios and movement trends relative to sales or time. We can study these to determine how the firm has been doing and what actions to take to improve the firm's future performance.

Financial statements of firms are often given as a table of values. This practice continued from the days when the statements were in paper document form. Even with computerization, electronic financial statement tables are still not yet interactive. However with spreadsheets, the situation is drastically changed. For example, *tax, before-tax profit, after-tax profit, total assets,* and *total liabilities* cells in a spreadsheet can contain formulas instead of precalculated values. Updating the other independent variable values would automatically change the results of these dependent variables. These results can therefore be treated as outputs of the model, and are no longer inputs like the rest.

We will use functional relationships, relative to sales and other line items, and management policies as bases for computing all the items in the financial statement. This way, the future values of these variables can be projected. Some of these values are derived from ratios to sales because sales volume is usually the major driver behind them. For example, cost would generally increase with sales. This increase can be reasonably assumed to be linear within small ranges of change in sales. Similarly, given their ratios to sales and sales value, you can easily estimate most of the other variable values. The same also applies to those variables which may be derived from their ratios to other financial items.

Other variables can be derived from management policy decisions. One example would be the dividend payout. With the *dividend to after-tax profit* ratio determined, the dividend payout can be computed as a product of this ratio and the profit after tax. Finally, some assumptions have to be made about how sales would change over time. Usually, this would be given as annual percentage growth rates, which makes future sales dependent upon the immediate past period's sales. Future sales can then be projected sequentially from current sales. The growth rate can be a constant or it can follow some known pattern of change such as the lifecycle of products or the maturity of the firm or industry.

The logic underlying the various relationships between the variables will result in circular computation among the variables. Normally, this would be a problem. However in spreadsheets, the difficulty is resolved by letting the spreadsheet software do the iterative calculation.

Working   You should first tabulate the past financial numbers, covering the major items in the income statement and balance sheet. Some variables are really dependent on the other variables. The values in the cells containing these dependent variables should first be converted to formulas. These formulas are generally applicable for all time periods, past, present, and future. You need to set the iterative calculation option if it is not already done.

When entering data values, be careful to adopt a consistent sign convention. If negative numbers, which may be formatted with brackets in accordance with accounting convention, are used for costs, they have to be added to, not subtracted from, sales to give the gross operating income.

In accordance with accounting principles, *total assets* should be equal to *total liabilities*. Any difference between the two will have to be made up by having either excess cash which will end up as additional *cash and marketable securities*, or more debt, which will be recorded as increases in debt. There are other considerations, and this topic is best considered in the *Financial Projection* exercise. For the time being, you can set the debt to be a constant and let the value be large enough to have some cash left over. You will have to pay interest on the debt and at the same time earn short-term returns on the excess cash. Refer to the *Charity Donation* exercise to learn more about iterative computation.

Values of relevant variables can next be divided by sales to give their performance ratios. These ratios should be computed for as many periods in the past as there are data. With sufficient historical ratio values, you can study how they have varied over time. Some of them may be trending up or down and others simply gyrating with fixed or uncertain periodicity. Knowing their properties, you can project future ratio values. One way of extending the ratios into the future is to use the **Fill** operation. You would notice that using **Fill** to extend cells with formulas in this case would result in computational errors in the filled cells. This is because filling from cells with formulas to other cells is the same as copying from the source cells and pasting them into the other cells. As it is now, the cells referenced in the filled cells are empty.

To **Fill** the historical ratio values into the other cells, you will first need to convert the ratio formulas into data values using **Copy** and **PasteSpecial Values**. Once that is done, the cells containing the ratio values (not formulas now) can be filled forward. What does **Fill** do with these data values to give the future projection? You may want to plot the data in a **Chart** to examine the effect. Are there other ways to project the future financial ratios? Should the future be mere extrapolation of the past?

Assuming for the time being you are willing to accept the projected financial ratio values, you can use these values to help compute the line item values for the future periods. With this done, you can examine the result of your computation and do some analysis.

- What is the key performance indicator that should be of primary interest?
- What are the other important variables?
- Examine how these values change with changes in future ratio values.
- How does management will and determination play in bringing the company forward?
- How would you use the financial statement constructed thus far to support management decisions?

GROUP TRIP EXPENSES **Exercise 7**

Challenge

Carl, Jonson, Sally, and Emily will be taking a vacation trip together again. From their past experiences of traveling together, they know that it will not be easy to manage their expenses. On previous trips, they had most meals together and shared many expenses as a group. However, sometimes one person or another wanted something special, in which case it would not be fair to split the cost. They have learned that it is neither good nor convenient to have only one person holding all the cash in foreign currencies to make payments. It is also impractical to share the expenses at each and every juncture.

They need to devise a simple way to record, for each item, what is spent, how much each person contributes (if any) to the payment, and how the expenses are shared among them. It will be assumed that the data can be entered at suitable times into an electronic spreadsheet. With the consolidated information at the end of the trip, each person will know how much he or she has spent on the trip and how much he or she owes the others.

Concept

To create a simple user-friendly spreadsheet is not an easy task. Spreadsheets should be practical and intuitive to use. At the same time, it must check and verify that input values are correct and consistent. Finally, the way it presents the results must be visually clear and appealing. All these can be done using the available formatting and charting features.

Working

Devise a layout that will present all the information required, both inputs and outputs, in a table that will fit the width of the screen and standard size paper. The few main formulas would compute for each person the total amount paid, due and net payable, all in a base currency. These are the essential required results. Other formulas would be needed to convert the expenses in their original currency to the base currency and also to allocate the expenses to the individuals.

Since the allocation approach is not uniform across the various expenses, it would not be sensible to put in the fixed formulas for this. This means that the user must enter the inputs in two places, one as the cost of the expense item and then again as subproportioned amounts allocated to each person. Also, the inputs may be formulas, working on values and cell references, rather than mere values.

There is also the need to record which individual has paid for the expense item. Sometimes, more than one person may contribute towards paying for the item. For example, one person uses his credit card to pay the bill while another person contributes the tip for the waiter. To avoid using too many columns in the table, this can be presented as a second row of the entry. This means that there are now two rows per entry record.

Finally, it is necessary to check that the total allocated amounts and total contributed amounts both are equal to the cost of the expense item. Without adding too many columns, the checking can be done more subtly using formulas in **Conditional Formatting**, rather than overtly in the cells.

| Exercise 8 | **100 METERS IN 9 SECONDS** |

Challenge

The world records for sports events like the 100-meter sprint for men have been re-written year after year. Is there no limit to what athletes can achieve? It was not too long ago when we wondered if a person could break the 10-second barrier in the 100-meter sprint or a sub-5-minute mile. Now, dare we wonder if someone can break the 9-second limit and when that will likely happen?

Concept

The future can be projected using data of the immediate past. The underlying assumption is that the past momentum will be sustained forward, usually linearly or in some simple manner such as polynomial or exponential extrapolation. The possibilities can be further extended by the choice of how far back in history the projection should be based upon. These possibilities can provide a projection "cone," which may be more appropriate than a single thin line or curve into the future.

Working

There are only data values and no formulas in this spreadsheet model. The input data are plotted in a chart to present the pattern of record-breaking performances. Use the **Add Trendline** feature in the chart to provide the projections, and where available, the supporting information and statistics.

Further analysis can be done as follows:

- How can you better assure that the future projections are sufficiently accurate?
- Can you compute the errors of past projections and characterize the errors?

GINI INDEX   **Exercise 9**

Challenge

Italian statistician Corrado Gini created this index in 1912 as a measure of income or wealth inequality. Its values range from 0 to 1, with 0 being perfect equality and 1 perfect inequality. It is mathematically defined as 1 – the ratio of the area under the empirical cumulative distribution curve to that under the uniform (perfect equality) distribution curve.

The Gini indices of developed countries have historically been low, meaning their incomes are well distributed with the existence of a large middle class in their populations. Underdeveloped countries have notorious income and wealth inequalities and thus large Gini indices.

In recent years, however, the Gini indices of almost every country have been increasing. The Gini indices of the United States are now larger than those of the poor Latin American countries. This is matter of grave concern which may lead to economic disasters and political unrest.

What trends, correlations, and inferences can you draw from the Gini and other socio-economic indicators? What are the likely root causes for their changes? How can the situation be improved? What is the most desirable equilibrium state?

Concept

The Gini index provides a way of understanding the distribution of a variable. There are other ways of understanding this, such as using the standard deviation and the ratio of standard deviation to the mean (or the coefficient of variation). Which measure to use depends on the setting. In this case, the concern is about how unequal income distribution is or, more specifically, how rich the wealthy are relative to the poor. A simpler, but not necessarily more effective, measure is the ratio of the lowest income of the top 10% over the highest income of the bottom 10%.

Working

Lest you get distracted from the main agenda, this exercise is to examine income distributions among countries and not the effectiveness of the Gini index as a measure of income inequality. It would be good to first sort the countries and rank them according to their Gini indices. The relative frequency can be obtained from the count of nations, and this is plotted against the Gini index.

Further extensions to explore:

- Can you further extend the model to examine how the Gini index varies with population size?
- Can you come up with more ideas to understand the global Gini index distribution better?
- How do they help you better understand related socio-economic and development problems?

MODELING TIPS

Enter data only once

Every piece of data should only be entered once. This means that if its value is changed, it only needs to be amended in a single cell. This cell should of course be appropriately placed and formatted. It should also be properly labeled so that users know what the value is for. Formulas would therefore only have to refer to this cell if there is a need to use that variable value. If the value has to be displayed in another place, just link the destination cell to the cell that stores the value. Remember to follow a standard color code so that the user knows which cells to update. We have an icon placed in the right-hand corner of the *Home* sheet of our workbooks that denotes our color code. If you use a format different from the one we recommend, have the legend of your color code prominently displayed in your workbook so that new users of your spreadsheet can easily refer to it and have no difficulty understanding your model.

Hard-coding

Formulas should contain only cell references, operators (^, /, *, +, −, &), and functions. Check all your formulas to see if there are any values in them. If there are, then you are hard-coding! As a general rule, values in formulas should rightly be placed individually in separate cells and the formulas refer to these input cells. This makes it easier to change the input values and see their impact on formulas in the output cells. Hard-coding mingles inputs with outputs. It makes the model difficult to understand and subsequently more demanding to maintain. So, please avoid hard-coding if possible. There are of course exceptions to this rule. But be very careful if you want to break the rule. You never know; even universal constants (one of the exceptions) can change with time, and unusual provisions such as 13 months in a year and five days in a week appear from time to time.

Another very subtle and more severe form of hard-coding is when calculations are done outside of the spreadsheet, either mentally or using a calculator, and the results of which are entered into the spreadsheet model. These results are not linked in any way to the input values entered in other cells. Therefore, ensure as far as possible that all dependent values in your spreadsheet models are obtained using formulas.

Data, model, view

Conceptually, keeping data separate makes model maintenance easier. The substance of the work is in the model while view deals with communication, working the modeling, and explaining the results to the client. More simply, one could say data, model, and view are about information, insight, and impression respectively.

There should be a clear separation between data, model, and view elements in your spreadsheet. Data are better managed if they are only entered once and definitely not hidden inside any formula. The cells containing values constitute the *Data* and collectively cells with formulas form the *Model*. The third aspect *View* refers to how you format, layout, and display the data and model to make it easier for analysis and use. This would cover cell number format, font and shading color, table layout, and graphical chart features.

Be careful, what you see in a cell is sometimes not what it actually contains. If a cell shows 2, the underlying number can be any real number larger or equal to 1.5 and less than 2.5 when it is formatted with zero decimal places. If this number is multiplied by the whole number 4, the answer can range from slightly larger than 6 to just short of 10. Therefore if you want to, you can make 2×4 to erroneously equal to 6, 7, 8, 9, or 10.

A good practice is to key **Ctrl + `** every so often during the modeling. This operation toggles the spreadsheet view between showing all values and showing all formulas in the cells. In the cells with formulas, you check for hard-coding (i.e., the presence of values). For cells with data, you can see the values displayed in their full raw form, without the sometimes misleading effect arising from **Cell Number Format**.

Tip 4 Computer as an analysis tool

There are lots of things to pick up when learning a software application like the Excel spreadsheet. One can spend years trying to master all the technicalities of spreadsheets in general and the innuendos of Excel, in particular. There will also be new versions released every few years and even alternative offerings of the same software type. However, you must remember that the main purpose in learning the software application is not so much to be an expert in the software but to apply it. Therefore, you must not limit your learning to just technical features of spreadsheets or any kind of software, but develop a deep understanding of enduring concepts that will outlive the specific software or even a class of software.

In spreadsheets for example, you should be developing the art of modeling and analysis of business contexts and challenges. If you can effectively use the spreadsheet in the exploratory discovery of a situation, you will learn a lot more about the situation. Your competency development should not be restricted to the use of the spreadsheet features, but include acquiring and creating ways to build models. Do not be satisfied with knowing how to put numbers in and get numbers out. Use instead the process of working on the problem using spreadsheets as a tool to develop deeper insights into the nature of the problem.

Finally, also remember that software products are changing at a rapid rate and the only way to keep up with the changes is to learn-to-learn. As you hone your skills on modeling issues, keep a lookout also for changes on the technical front and keep learning and applying.

Smart guessing

Tip 5

Not all problems can be synthesized into a model straightaway. For example, it would not be easy to determine how many piano tuners there are in your city. If the data can be searched, either by calling upon people or surfing the Internet, then there is no need to build a model. That is, if you care only for the current answer. Often the questions posed are those for which there are no known answers in the first place, such as making projections into the future. Without resorting to wild guesses, we can build a model to do some *smart guessing*. To build a model to answer any question, start with what you already know, such as how many people live in your city, what is the size of the average family, what percentage of families own a piano, how often and how long it takes to tune a piano, and so on. It has been found that such an approach, often referred to as *Fermi questions* named after Nobel laureate Dr. Enrico Fermi, of stating assumptions and better known facts, and layering them, can generate fairly accurate results to the original question posed.

FURTHER REFERENCES

- Barnfield and Walkenbach, 2010. *Excel 2010 for Dummies: Quick Reference*, Wiley.
- Leong, 2014. Spreadsheet Modeling Resources
  - http://isotope.unisim.edu.sg/users/tyleong/SpreadsheetModeling.htm
  - http://dl.dropboxusercontent.com/u/19228704/SpreadsheetModeling.htm
- Leong and Cheong, 2008. "Spreadsheet Modeling of Equipment Acquisition Plan," *Decision Sciences Journal of Innovative Education* 6(2): 357–366.
- Leong and Cheong, 2008. "Teaching Business Modeling using Spreadsheets," *INFORMS Transactions on Education* 9(1): 20–34.
- Leong and Cheong, 2009. "Essential Spreadsheet Modeling Course for Business," *ORMS Today*, August, 36(4).
- Powell and Baker, 2007. *Management Science: The Art of Modeling with Spreadsheets, Second edition,* Chapters 1 and 2, Wiley.
- Walkenbach, 2004. *Excel VBA Programming for Dummies*, Wiley.
- Walkenbach and Banfield, 2007. *Excel 2007 for Dummies: Quick Reference*, Wiley.

- Keywords. Relevant topics to search in Google and Wikipedia
  - *Data model view . Spreadsheet hardcoding . Spreadsheet modeling . Linear extrapolation . Ratio . Projection forecast . Target setting*

PROBLEM SET 1

* Hard problems   † Solutions provided

Qn 1.01

Jogging. You are a regular jogger. After each run, you record the distance covered in kilometers and the time taken in minutes and seconds. This information is in a small paper notebook. Looking at the data, it is difficult to evaluate how your performance has changed over time.

a. Transfer the data to a spreadsheet and start tabulating them to compute other information, such as speed in kilometers per hour.

b. As you enter more data, you notice some of the earlier runs have distances recorded in miles and time recorded in minutes (in 1 or 2 decimal places). For completeness, you want to capture these data as well. So you add columns for entering the data in the different dimensions, convert them into standardized units and provide speed information in miles per hours as well. A mile is 1.60934 kilometers, 60 seconds makes a minute, and 60 minutes make an hour.

Qn 1.02

Physical health. As a parent of a few children, you want to keep close track of their physical health. You record at birthdays, their heights and body weight. For the sake of overseas relatives and friends, with whom you share news of your children, the height and weight information have to be in meters and kilograms as well as feet and inches and pounds. To those not familiar with the different measures, one meter equals 39.3701 inches, one kilogram equals 2.20462 pounds, 12 inches is a foot, and 16 ounces is a pound. You recently learned that healthcare professionals use the *Body Mass Index (BMI)* to gauge whether a person is under or over weight. *BMI* is computed by dividing the person's body weight in kilograms by the square of his or her height in meters. *BMI Prime* is defined as the ratio of *BMI* to the maximum healthy *BMI*, currently set at 25. A healthy person should have a *BMI* between 18.5 and 25, or a *BMI Prime* of 0.74 to 1.00.

a. Construct a spreadsheet for recording the children's information over time.

b. Provide a table of *BMI* values for heights of 0.8 to 1.4 meters (31 to 55 inches) and weight of 10 to 55 kilograms (22 to 122 ounces).

Qn 1.03†

Windchill. Temperatures are affected by wind. This is particularly important to residents of cold countries with sub-freezing weather. Scientists have determined a way to correct temperatures taken using a thermometer in still air to account for the chilling effect of the wind. In the metric system, this is given by the formula: $Tw = 13.12 + 0.6215 \times T - 11.37 \times V^{0.16} + 0.3965 \times T \times V^{0.16}$, where Tw is the windchill temperature in degree Celsius, T is the air temperature in degree Celsius and V is the wind velocity in kilometers per hour (kmph), taken at 10 meters height. For those preferring the imperial system, using measurements in degree F and miles per hour (mph), the formula is $Tw = 35.74 + 0.6215 \times T - 35.75 \times V^{0.16} + 0.4275 \times T \times V^{0.16}$.

a. Construct a spreadsheet model for either the metric or imperial system that gives the windchill temperature for any possible air temperature and wind velocity.

b. Provide a table of windchill temperatures for ranges of air temperatures and wind velocities. Windchill temperature is only defined for air temperatures at or below 10 degrees C or 50 degrees F and wind velocity greater than 4.8 kmph or 3.0 mph.

Foreign currency. You are about to travel to an exotic country. The currency of the nation you are residing in is not universally convertible and at your destination, there are few banks and automatic teller machines. Therefore, you want to have sufficient foreign currency before leaving home. As your local money changer will not have enough foreign currency, you need to carry some amounts in United States Dollar (USD), European Euro, British Pound, or Japanese Yen, in case you run out of cash during the trip.

Qn 1.04⁺

a. Construct a spreadsheet model to compute the equivalents in your destination currency and these internationally convertible currencies.

b. You want to convert about USD 2400's worth of your currency to the destination currency, subject to what is available. For the remaining amount, you would convert equally to USD, Euro, Pound, and Yen.

c. Make your model flexible so that you can vary the allocation proportions. Remember your local money changer does not carry small notes and loose change in foreign currencies.

Time sheet. A marine shipyard employs hourly-wage workers to do odd jobs. Every four weeks, the shipyard grades these workers on their punctuality, skills, and work quality. According to their grading score, the workers are each assigned their hourly pay rates. Worked hours are clocked each day and recorded. At the end of the week, the workers' pay are tabulated and paid out. The government requires the employer to withhold as income tax 22% of each worker's gross pay. The shipyard also deducts on behalf of the house union $8 per worker each week as union fees.

Qn 1.05⁺

a. Construct a spreadsheet for the above. Enter the data for a few simulated workers: hours worked for each day of the week and individualized hourly rates. Use a variety of input values.

b. Compute the total worked hours for the week, gross pay, tax, union fees and net pay.

c. The spreadsheet should be pleasing to the eye, and easy to understand and use even for a large shipyard with many workers.

Qn 1.06   **Retail rice**. The International Rice Research Institute (IRRI) keeps excellent data on rice production and trade. Visit their website to learn what they do and download data using their online query form and analyze them. A set of data taken from IRRI is on page 31. It shows the milled rice retail price from years 2000 to 2009 for the top 10 rice producing countries.

a. Using only years 2000 to 2004 data, construct a spreadsheet model to forecast by linear extrapolation the retail rice prices for years 2005 to 2009.

b. Compare your forecasted prices against the actual prices. This back-testing approach is often used to evaluate forecasting methods. By doing so, you can know the accuracy of the methods without having to wait many years to find out.

Qn 1.07[†]   **Sprocket hub**. The *Sprocket* production line requires 10,000 *Sprocket* hubs per year. Purchasing estimated that processing each order costs them $15.00 in manpower and computing cost. In stock, hubs cost $15.00 per unit per year in space, damage, loss, and insurance costs. Your job as a logistic planner is to calculate how many hubs should be ordered at each replenishment request. If you order 200 hubs, deliveries will be arriving almost weekly with very low carry costs. If you order at one go the whole annual requirement of 10,000 hubs, the purchase order cost is lowest but carry cost will be highest. The *Economic Order Quantity* (*EOQ*) is the order amount that minimizes the sum of order and carry costs. It is given by the formula $EOQ = (2DO/C)^{0.5}$, where D is the annual demand quantity, O is the cost per order, and C is the unit carry cost per year.

a. Construct a spreadsheet model that shows the *EOQ* for any input values and test it on the above data as base case.

b. Compute the annual order and inventory carry costs. Assume the hub stock is drawn out evenly over time by the production line and typically ordered early enough for its level to be at just above 10% of the order size when new stocks arrive.

c. If the demand for sprockets increases dramatically to require 20,000 hubs per year as input material, what is the optimal quantity of hubs to order each time?

Qn 1.08*[†]   **Paper Products**. *Paper Products* is a traditional maker of customized stationery. Their handcrafted cards and envelopes are popular for corporate offices, weddings and other special occasions. To expand their production capacity to meet rapidly growing demand and shorter turnaround time, the owner is studying the possibility of using more machinery on some product lines. Mechanization can be crudely divided

Country	Output '000 ton 2011	Milled retail rice at '000 local currency/ton									
		2000	2001	2002	2003	2004	2005	2006	2007	2008	2009
China	202,600	1.323	1.422	1.580	1.637	2.362	2.225	2.174	2.430	2.400	3.930
India	105,700	11.84	10.85	10.73	10.59	10.92	11.41	11.92	13.38	16.56	17.96
Indonesia	65,700	2778	2851	3389	3202	3317	3318	3381	3445	3510	
Bangladesh	50,600	13.34	13.25	14.21	14.49	16.34	15.96	16.44	20.60	29.79	20.71
Vietnam	42,300	2783	2510	3423	3455	3665	4316	4463	5765	9336	8908
Thailand	34,500										
Myanmar	32,800	46.26	47.00	98.00			155.80	217.28	259.41	352.34	340.92
Philippines	16,600	19.45	19.43	19.98	20.20	21.04	22.88	23.56	24.72	32.71	34.12
Brazil	13,500										
Pakistan	9,200	16.57	16.62	16.59	18.69				20.73	31.00	43.36

Source: http://ricestat.irri.org:8080/wrs

† Prices are rounded to 4 significant digits

into three levels: manual with electric hand tools, semi-automated machinery, and fully automated mass production. Their cost structures are low-fixed high-variable, mid-fixed mid-variable, and high-fixed low-variable respectively. Considering the substantial initial financial outlays, she wonders at what sales volumes would the automation investments break even for each mechanization level.

She decided to focus on one product line at a time. Their envelopes are now priced at about $0.30 each and current sales volume is 50,000 per year. From the various equipment suppliers' quotations and internal production costing, they estimated that the (fixed, variable) costs combinations available are ($10,000, $0.23), ($20,000, $0.18), and ($50,000, $0.15).

a. Construct a spreadsheet model for this problem.
b. Which level of technology should she implement? Can there be a hybrid solution?
c. What if the sales volume fails to meet up?
d. What if the variable cost estimates are incorrect?

Qn 1.09*   **Plan-track.** Construct a spreadsheet to help a university student analyze how she spends her time on various weekly activities. These include attending classes and studying, sleeping and napping, eating meals and tea breaks, exercising, reading newspapers and non-academic materials, watching television, and playing computer games.

a. The student should be able to view each activity laid out against the days of the week.
b. Use the spreadsheet to sketch out a plan for better allocation of her time. To test the plan, to see how effective it is, record her actual behavior and compare this against the plan.
c. Enter some data into your spreadsheet and compute basic statistics such as average, maximum, and distribution. Type in short comments as analysis of the situation.

Qn 1.10*   **Largest countries.** The top 10 largest countries in the world according to the 2012 population data are China, 1,343,239,923; India, 1,205,073,612; United States, 313,847,465; Indonesia, 248,645,008; Brazil, 193,946,886; Pakistan, 190,291,129; Nigeria, 170,123,740; Bangladesh, 161,083,804; Russia, 142,517,670; and Japan, 127,368,088. The top 10 largest countries by square kilometer land area are Russia, 17,075,400; Canada, 9,984,670; United States, 9,826,675; China, 9,598,094; Brazil, 8,514,877; Australia, 7,617,930; India, 3,287,263; Argentina, 2,766,890; Kazakhstan, 2,724,900; and Sudan, 2,505,813. In the year 2012, the world's population was 7,017,846,922 and land area was 148,940,000 square km.

a. Tabulate the data provided in a spreadsheet. Add more columns to present information derived from the data that may be helpful to the user. For example, show the population and area of each country as percentages of the top 10 countries and of the world.

b. Your information should anticipate questions the user may ask about the top 10 countries, such as which country is smallest or largest, what is their average population and land area of the group, and how much of the world's population or area is accounted for by the top 1, 2, . . . , 10 countries.

Problem Solving and Spreadsheet Engineering

LEARNING OUTCOMES

- Able to compose systematically a spreadsheet model for any business challenge
- Able to implement *Trade-off analysis and Sensitivity analysis* on a spreadsheet model

INTRODUCTION

Modeling a problem provides a platform to discuss the issues faced, and to refine collective understanding to arrive at solutions. Problem solving has not always been as scientific as it is now. Some trace the history of analytical problem solving to operations research teams formed during World War II by the United States and British governments to help solve real military operations problems. These interdisciplinary teams, comprising people from various academic fields, proved to be very effective. Many of their approaches continue to this day, but are more broadly applied beyond the armed forces to industries and businesses.

The key to solving problems is to take an approach that is based on data and logic, and along with it a strong dose of common sense and understanding of human behavior. Defining the problem, determining the end goals, and enumerating the alternative options are but some of the steps. The pervasive rigorous approach in modeling business problems, taking a page from scientific research, specifies them in mathematical formulations. Hopefully, these models are good enough to represent the problem, but primarily they have to be simple enough to yield tractable analytical results. Usually, their derived mathematical formulas are either too difficult or time-consuming to be solved by hand, and need to be programmed into electronic computers.

As powerful as they are, mathematical formulas, algorithms, and computer programs are not easy for developers to construct and for average users to understand and accept. They represent the form of the problem rather than the solution. The advent of spreadsheets brings a totally new and wonderful freshness to the modeling experience. It is very intuitive and has a point-and-shoot simplicity. A cell in a spreadsheet is more than just a space to put a value or a formula, it is in fact a variable that may be linked to other variables, and they dynamically interact with one another. The developer can therefore jointly construct the model with users, one looking at the formulas and the other concurrently looking at the generated solution values. The results can be charted into graphs where they are more easily interpreted. This actually makes putting together a spreadsheet model somewhat easy and fun.

The exercises in this chapter guide you through a systematic process of developing a spreadsheet model, which is referred to as spreadsheet engineering. This involves understanding problem solving as both an art and a science. The *F1 Night City Race* exercise teaches us how to use the *Influence* and *Black-box* diagrams to graphically derive the model, which includes approximating the relationship between two variables, namely demand volume and product price, and also how to determine the prices that will generate the target and best profits. *Inkjet Printer* has a similar problem structure except it now involves pricing two interrelated products. In addition to using graphical methods, asking relevant questions is very important in model building.

You can also use the *Financial Projection, Web Store, Casino Hotel, Village Coffee,* and *Invest In Education* exercises to help develop your modeling and questioning skills. In fact, the art of modeling is more about asking the right questions rather than finding the right answers. True leaders in life are the people who present us with the most intriguing questions, the ones that impactfully changed the world. Finally, the *Stopped Watch* exercise makes the timely reminder that in modeling you need to be careful of how you specify the criteria of success.

DISCOVERY POINTS

Exploratory modeling uses the process of building a computer model to learn about the given situation, identify its key concerns, and generate resolution possibilities. During the modeling, participants will discover information that they *a priori* did not know. They also acquire implicit learning and insights about the structure of the studied situation. Where the learning can be made explicit, it can be documented for future reference. Thorough documentation may prove to be difficult. A viable alternative is to keep the modeling ongoing with periodic situation reviews and model revisions. This will involve an ever-changing landscape of people and circumstances. It retains the institutionalized learning and keeps it fresh. Discovering the evolving situation is possibly the most important reason for modeling.

This modeling format usually starts from scratch, not knowing what the real questions are, where the data are coming from, and how one variable relates to another. Simpler sub-models are built along the way, and analyses are done on these interim portions to gather insights to guide further model consolidation and improvement. Experiments that can be performed include *What-if*, *Trade-off*, *Sensitivity*, and *Validity* analyses. Such analyses are also done on a computational model after it is completed to get results. In exploratory modeling however, these analyses (actual and simulated play, gaming, and deliberation) provide inputs to the development and modification of interim models.

The ultimate end of the exploration, if there is even such a thing, may not be one "completed" complex computational model, but rather a set of interrelated, not necessarily tightly coupled, "semi-finished" simpler exploratory models. They provide different domain perspectives, alternative competing views, and possible solution approaches to be used to supplement real-world experience in decision making. Model building as a learning process extends user experience, and application of the models enhances, supports, and not supplants human thinking. It brings a new rigorous meaning to business case study, as we now know. With constructed models and experience acquired during modeling, analyst and business case owners can ask richer *what-if* questions and evaluate more alternatives.

Point 7

| Linear approximation |

In modeling, the relationship between variables is often unknown. What is known is whether a dependent output variable generally increases or decreases with increases in the independent input variable. This relationship is often non-linear and non-monotonic, that is, it does not keep increasing (or decreasing) but reverses direction as the input values get larger. To get out of this bind, you can assume a simple linear relationship between the variables over a short range of input values. Approximate slope and intercept values may be used in the initial modeling.

After completing this initial model, the discovery process begins with various *What-if* and *What's-best* analyses. The validity of the linear assumption is then tested in two ways: whether the solution discovered 1) stays within the range of the input values, and 2) remains insensitive to sufficiently large variations in the slope and intercept values. Where a larger range of input values is needed to support wider analyses of different aspects such as *break-even* points (where profit equals zero) and maximum profit point, a *piecewise-linear* approach may be used. This means you need to have a few linear relationships, each covering non-overlapping ranges.

Point 8

| What-if, trade-off and sensitivity |

What-if analysis generally asks what happens to the outputs when the inputs are changed. There are two broad kinds of inputs, those the decision maker can change arbitrarily and those given. Given parameters can be further divided into unchangeables, for example, data from the past, and negotiables, which are usually data provided by others such as goals, targets, and return rates. Negotiables can be changed but with great effort working with the source of the inputs, who may be your bosses, customers, suppliers, markets, or business environment. We therefore separate *What-if* analyses into two types, one type dealing with changing decision variables and another dealing with changing parametric variables. The first we call *Trade-off* analysis (TA) and the second, *Sensitivity* analysis (SA).

In TA, you seek out the break-even, maximum, and minimum points of your performance indicators. The first occurs at where the performance indicator function intercepts the decision variable axis, and the latter two where the slopes of their functions equal zero. It is reasonable to assert that slopes in the neighborhood near maximas and minimas are close to zero. Optimas are therefore usually insensitive to their decision variables' changes. Thus, TA which evaluates changes in output variables against changes in decision variables should give fairly robust optimas. This means that it is quite unnecessary to spend too much effort to get precise optimal decision variable values. The same cannot be said of break-even points though.

SA on the other hand, is not about varying decision variables but, rather, about changes in parameter values. This step is often missed in modeling and analysis. Why bother with SA? It seems frivolous since parameter values are givens and thus cannot be changed by the decision maker. Well, the answers are 1) the decision maker doesn't have to take givens as unchangeables and can spend additional effort seeking alternative givens, either by negotiation or restructuring their situations to need less of those inputs, or not at all, and more importantly, 2) givens are market or externally imposed and the external world can change without needing our concurrence.

Point 9

Validity, pros and cons

The final test of a model is whether it applies in the real-world situation it represents. Validity analysis therefore asks for any given set of actual inputs if the outputs of the model tally with what is actually happening. It then goes further to check that when the inputs are varied slightly beyond the actual in a particular direction, whether outputs of the model also move in the direction intuitively expected in the real situation. This is to check the applicability of the model for possible future settings. Only after these tests is the model able to be confidently used in practice, for deriving actionable recommendations and subsequently, monitoring change implementation.

When effecting a change, we usually persuade by explaining why the existing is no longer adequate and that the new way to be implemented is significantly better. Good public communication principles dictate we keep the message simple. Arguably, this common approach is as simple as it can get. Trimming it further will make it less convincing.

This approach, unfortunately, is inappropriate for exploratory modeling. Each way has its advantages and disadvantages. So the new way proposed will surely have its pros and cons. The current way also has pros and cons. When the new way is introduced, you should look not just at the new advantages it brings, but also any adverse side effects it may have. At the same time, abandoning the current also means that you are not just getting rid of its cons but also all the benefits it is endowed with. Are these benefits also found in the new? If yes, all of them? What measures can be taken to mitigate against the cons of the new way?

Be careful not to base your comparisons just on the number of pros and cons. Pros and cons cannot be of equal worth. Some advantages are substantial and of greater value. These are the ones that change the pace of growth, increase market share, improve revenue, or drastically cut cost. Others, less valuable, include those that make doing the work easier or more convenient for the operators with no impact on the customers.

Point 10

Business excellence

The Malcolm Baldrige National Quality Award of the United States of America has been used to measure the performance of organizations on a broader basis, rather than just their profitability. Other countries have similarly adapted the framework for use to recognize excellence in organizations and businesses. The basic framework comprises a set of drivers, systems, and outcomes common to all organizations. In the *Business Excellence* framework presented by SPRING Singapore, there are seven categories: *Leadership, Planning, Information, People, Processes, Customers,* and *Results*.

The business is first evaluated on their infrastructural drivers of leadership, planning, and information. Leadership covers the strength of their senior leadership in leading the development of the mission, vision, values, and ethics of the organization; the development of organizational culture in relation to their policies, structures, practices, and programs; and their contribution to society through participation in community and environmental projects. Planning covers the development and deployment of strategy, both short- and long-term. Information covers the organization's management of information and knowledge, and their use to improve processes.

It is then evaluated on the executional systems of people, processes, and customers. People covers the development of strategies and plans for human resource planning, employee engagement, employee learning and development, employee well-being and satisfaction, and employee performance and recognition. Processes cover their ability to get innovative ideas for new product and services, and efforts to better manage and improve processes. Customers cover their ability to determine market requirements, the ease to conduct business with the company, and the ability in gathering information on customer satisfaction and retention.

Finally, all these cumulate into results. The framework's multi-attribute scorecard elements cover customer, financial and market, people, and operational results.

Examples of the elements include customer satisfaction and retention; financial trends and target achievements in magnitude and in comparison against competitors and benchmarks; employee engagement, learning, well-being, and satisfaction; and operational trends and target achievements for business processes, suppliers and partners, and in comparison to others and benchmarks.

EXERCISES

F1 NIGHT CITY RACE   Worked Example

Challenge

The Formula 1 race is coming to town. This is the first time the race is held in a city street at night. The annual event helps to boost tourism for a short while and increase the city's global visibility. To help defray the massive costs in hosting the race, the city's tourism authority is going to levy a 30% service charge on all hotel rooms for the 5-day duration before and during the race. The overall estimation is that hotels can charge up to three times their usual rate for each room and still see full occupancy.

Hotel general manager Tom Hawkes wants to understand the situation better before he makes the decision on pricing. He is skeptical that room occupancy will be full at such high room rates. Maybe he has to throw in some extras, like wine, cheese, and fruits, to make his hotel rooms more attractive.

Concept

Working through these worksheets, you will learn how to systematically build a spreadsheet model to analyze a business problem. The most basic business model, in which revenue and cost interact to yield profit, is introduced. The main decision to be made is the price to sell the rooms. Easy as it seems, a clear process is needed in approaching the problem or for that matter any problem.

Using the *Influence* diagram, the variables identified in an open discussion may be organized to show their relationships. You should be clear which of the variables are inputs and outputs; and of the inputs, which ones you must decide on and which ones are given; and of the outputs, which ones are key performance indicators and which ones are intermediate variables.

Where the relationship between variables (e.g., demand and price) is not given, a simple relationship should be first established and then evaluated to see if it needs to be improved further.

Working

You can work on the problem starting from the *Scratch* worksheet to establish the *Influence* diagram. Though it is possible to start with getting the *Black-box* diagram first and then expanding it to produce the *Influence* diagram, our preference is to brainstorm first to work out the *Influence* diagram and then summarizing and confirming the findings as a *Black-box* diagram. This approach is more amenable to a wider range of problems, where it may not be evident from the start which variables are the inputs and outputs.

a. Building the *Influence* diagram

The purpose of an *Influence* diagram is to show the interrelationship among all the variables in the challenge. Through the pair-wise connection between any two variables, the overall picture shows how the exogenous variables (known and given input variables) lead to the performance measures (output variables). The steps in building an *Influence* diagram are as follows:

   i. Start with the performance measure. If there are more than one, begin with the most critical one and then continue with the rest.
   ii. Decompose the performance measure into two or more intermediate variables from which it is mathematically derived.
   iii. Similarly, further decompose each intermediate variable into more intermediate variables until the input decision variable is reached.

For this exercise, we will start with *Profit* as the performance measure and decompose it to obtain intermediate variables *Total Revenue* and *Total Cost*, and then repeat this process until the input decision variable *Room Rate* is reached.

   Select the *Working* sheet and you will see the components of the *Influence* diagram we have prepared for you. When tackling an open problem, such components have to be identified by going through the systematic steps defined earlier. With the broad relationship between the variables diagrammed, we next work out the mathematical formulas connecting the variables. They are:

   i. *Profit = Total revenue − Total cost*
   ii. *Total revenue = Room revenue + Other revenue*
   iii. *Room revenue = Room rate * Room occupancy*
   iv. *Room rate* affects *Room demand*, which in turn is translated into *Room sales* and *Room occupancy. Room occupancy = Room sales / Room capacity.*
   v. *Total Cost = Fixed Cost + Variable Cost * Room Occupancy.*

The completed *Influence* diagram we constructed for your reference can be revealed by unhiding the *Influence* worksheet. To do this, right-click on any sheet tab and select **Unhide**, and then select the appropriate choice.

b. Creating the *Black-box* model diagram

    A *Black-box* model is a simple diagram that summarizes the input and output variables, hiding the "spider web" of relationships among the variables into the "black" box. The variables can be classified as follows:

    i. Decisions are controllable input variables, the values of which are to be decided by the user.
    ii. Parameters are uncontrollable input variables with values given by external parties.
    iii. Consequence variables are output variables and their values are produced by mathematical calculations.
    iv. Performance measures are output variables and their values are of key interest to the user, answering to the main objective of building the model.

    The completed *Black-box* model is provided in the *Black-box* sheet and you can view it by unhiding this worksheet.

c. Modeling the problem

It is not difficult, even with minimal prior experience, to compute the profit from values of the parameters given. You can work on the model using the *Proto* sheet. With this model, you can compare the profit per room at different room rates. Here are the steps:

  i. Enter the data values for the input variables

- *Room rate* (in cell C6) = $200.
- *Fixed cost* (in cell C10) = $100.
- *Variable cost* (in cell C11) = $10.
- *Room occupancy* (in cell C14) = 70%.

  ii. Compute the intermediate variables and performance measure values

- Enter into cell C17 the formula =C6*C14 (i.e., *Room revenue = Room rate * Room occupancy*).
- Enter into cell C18 the formula =C10+C11*C14 (i.e., *Total room cost = Fixed cost + Variable cost * Room occupancy*).
- Enter into cell C19 the formula =C17-C18 (i.e., *Room profit = Room revenue – Room cost*).
- Enter into cell C20 the formula =C19/C17 (i.e., *Profit margin = Room profit/ Room revenue*). You will notice that the answer for cell C20 is $0. This is because the format for the cell is set to currency rather than percentage. To display percentage, select cell C20, right-click and select **Format Cells**. In the dialog box, select **Percentage** under the **Number** tab and define the number of decimal places desired. The result should appear as 24%.

  iii. Now, we change the room rate to $250 and then $300. Notice that the profit margin keeps increasing from 24% to 39%, and then 49%. Which room rate would you prefer and why? From the increasing profit margin, it is easy to understand that a larger room rate is preferred. In fact, an infinite room rate will bring infinite profit! This is great news to the hotel! But why this incredible result? The model has not taken into account the relationship between room rate and occupancy. We know that when room rate increases, room occupancy should decrease. We will determine this missing relationship in part e and add the relationship into the model in part f.

d. Using **Solver** and **Goal Seek**

Before we correct the model to incorporate the *Room rate* vs. *Occupancy* relationship, let us use the incomplete model to determine the room rates that will give us the maximum profit and break-even point, using **Solver** and **Goal Seek**.

  i. Using **Solver** to determine the room rate that gives the highest profit,

- Select from the Excel menu, **Data/Solver** and the **Solver Parameters** dialog will appear (see *Figure 2-1*).

- Specify **Set Target Cell** as C19 (i.e., *Profit*).
- Select **Equal To** as Max.
- Set **By Changing Cells** as C6 (i.e., *Room rate*).
- What we have defined here is a setting for the **Solver** tool to iteratively change the value in C6 to achieve a maximum profit in C9.
- Click the **Solve** button. The result obtained is "The Set Cell Values do not converge." This shows that the solution is unable to converge. Since the model is incomplete, **Solver** can essentially go through a very large number of iterations to set room rate to an exceedingly large number and generate an exceedingly large profit. The iteration is aborted due to stopping criteria defined under **Solver** options.

ii. Using **Goal Seek** to determine the room rate to achieve breakeven
- Select from the Excel menu, **Data/What-If Analysis/Goal Seek** and the **Goal Seek** window will appear (see *Figure 2-2*).
- Put C19 (i.e., *Profit*) as the **Set cell**.
- Set **To value** as 0 (since break-even is obtained when profit = 0).
- Set **By changing cell** as C6 (i.e., *Room rate*).

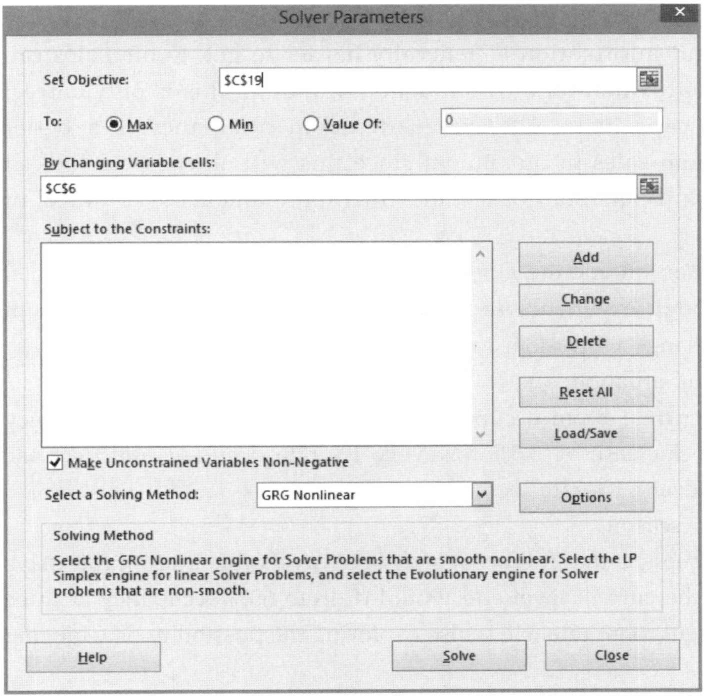

Figure 2-1

Using Solver to Maximize Profit by Changing Room Rate

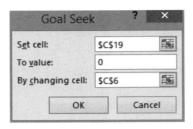

Figure 2-2
_____

Using Goal
to Determine
Break-even
Room Rate

- With these settings, the **Goal Seek** tool will iteratively change the value in cell C6 to achieve a profit of 0 in C9.
- Click the **OK** button to start the **Goal Seek** operation. The break-even room rate of $152.86 should be found.
- In fact, the **Solver** tool can also be used to perform break-even analysis by setting the **Equal To** option to the value of 0. **Solver** is a more sophisticated tool than **Goal Seek**. It is able to perform operations that **Goal Seek** is unable to, primarily maximizing or minimizing a target cell, changing several input cells (**Goal Seek** only allows you to enter one input cell to change values), and allowing the inclusion of constraints on the feasible range of changing values.

e.   Determining the _Room rate_ vs. _Occupancy_ relationship

How would you relate room demand to room rate? Would it be better to relate room occupancy to room rate?

Room demand information is generally harder to get. Room sales can be used as an approximation of room demand, though this is only correct when the hotel capacity is not exceeded. Room occupancy is a better measure than room sales in our model since this will allow us to look at the problem from a per room basis, and thus more amenable to hotels of different sizes.

To work further, unhide the _Demand_ sheet. We assume here that the hotel manager has enough experience to exercise judgment about how the room occupancy will change with room rates.

i.   For the current situation

At $200, the current room occupancy is about 70%. The room occupancy is expected to increase by 0.5% for every 1% rate decrease, and decrease by 0.45% for every 1% rate increase.

ii.   During the F1 season

Tom's initial guess is that full occupancy is only possible if room rate stays at two times the current level and would drop to 65% occupancy at three times the current room rate. He is also exploring the possibility of achieving

80% occupancy at three times the current room rate by throwing in some complimentary wine and cheese.

Using the preceding information, we hope to determine the room rate vs. occupancy relationship for the current situation and during the F1 season.

i. For the current situation
- The current occupancy at room rate of $200 is entered as 70% in cell C17.
- To determine the occupancy at a lower room rate, we use the room rate of $100 and compute the occupancy. In cell C15, the formula to compute the corresponding occupancy is entered as =(1+0.5*(B17-B15)/B17)*C17.
- To determine the occupancy at a higher room rate, we use the room rate of $400 and compute the occupancy. In cell C21, the formula to compute the corresponding occupancy is entered as =(1-0.45*(B21-B17)/B17)*C17.
- Note that both formulas determine the percentage change in room rate with respect to $200 (in cell B17) and then use the result to compute the change in occupancy with respect to the occupancy of 70% (in cell C17).
- Plot these three points using an XY scatter plot. Right-click on the data to add a trend line. Check the **Equation** box to show the equation of the best fit line. From the chart, we see that the slope of the straight line is –0.0016 and the y-intercept is 1.0325.

ii. During the F1 season
- The expected occupancy at room rate of $400 is entered as 100% in cell D21.
- The expected occupancy at room rate of $600 is entered as 65% in cell D25. This value can be changed to a higher value like 80% when the hotel throws in complimentary wine and cheese.
- Plot these two points again in a XY scatter plot. Similarly, add a trend line. The slope of this trend line is –0.00175 and the y-intercept is 1.7.

f. Adding the *Room rate* vs. *Occupancy* relationship

Let us add the missing relationship into the model in the *Proto(2)* sheet.

i. For the current situation
- Enter into cell F5 the formula = –0.0016*B5+1.0325 (i.e., Occupancy = –0.0016 * Room rate + 1.0325; this is the *Room rate* vs. *Occupancy* relationship).
- Enter into cell G5 the formula =B5*F5 (i.e., *Revenue per room = Room rate * Occupancy*).

- Enter into cell H5 the formula =C5+F5*D5+E5*G5 (i.e., *Total cost per room = Fixed cost + Variable cost * Occupancy + Government levy * Revenue*).
- Enter into cell I5 the formula =G5-H5 (i.e., *Profit per room = Revenue – Cost*).
- Enter into cell J5 the formula =I5/G5 (i.e., *Profit% = Profit/Revenue*).
- Test the model with different values of room rate in cell B5 to observe the change in the profit.

ii. During the F1 season
- The model provides three possible scenarios for occupancy rate (65%, 73%, and 80%) at room rate = $600.
- To determine the intercept and slope for the three scenarios,
  o Enter into cell B16 the formula =INTERCEPT(C19:C20,B19:B20).
  o Enter into cell C16 the formula =SLOPE(C19:C20,B19:B20).
  o Copy the formulas in cells B16:C16 and paste into E16:F16 and H16:I16. By pasting, we would have filled the same formulas for computing intercept and slope for the remaining two scenarios.
- Enter room rate = $600 into cells B24:B26.
- Enter fixed cost = $100 into cells C24:C26.
- Enter government levy = 30% into cells E24:E26.
- Enter different variable costs to account for including extras to boost occupancy. We can enter variable cost = $10, $15, and $20 into cells D24:D26 to correspond to occupancy of 60%, 73%, and 80%, respectively.
- Enter the *Room rate* vs. *Occupancy* relationship
  o Enter into cell F24 the formula =C16*B24+B16.
  o Enter into cell F25 the formula =F16*B25+E16.
  o Enter into cell F26 the formula =I16*B26+H16.
- Copy the formulas in cells G5:J5 and paste into G24:J24, G25:J25, and G26:J26. By pasting the formulas, we would have filled the same formulas for computing revenue, cost, profit, and profit margin for all three scenarios.

g. Tabulating the profits for different room rates
To show all the results for the different room rates at one go, we can expand the model to include multiple columns. Are you able to simplify the model to avoid multiple entries of the same values?
- Unhide the *Analysis* sheet.
- The model shows the profit and profit margin for different room rates for the current situation.

- Notice that the profit margin increases from 27% to 39% when room rate increases from $300 to $500. After that, the profit margin starts to decrease. The maximum profit occurs when the room rate is $500.

h. Charting the profits for different room rates

The same results can also be observed on a chart.

- Unhide the *Trade-off* sheet. This chart shows the trade-off between room rate and cost, revenue, and profit. A trade-off analysis is used to study the effect of changing the value of the decision variable (e.g., *Room rate*) on the performance measure (e.g., *Profit*). Look at the chart and answer the following questions:
    - o What is the best rate that Tom should set for the deluxe rooms? What if he deviates from the best rate? Is the rate that brings in the most profit per room necessarily the best rate?
    - o What is Tom's business objective? Maximize profit or maximize market share?
    - o How does the room rate of one type of room affect the rest?
    - o How could Tom continue to use the model after the F1 race is over?

If Tom has another new product such as a pie or a wedding banquet he wants to analyze, further questions can be asked:

- Can he use the same approach to price it?
- Can he test the market by setting it low (or high) first and then increasing (or decreasing) it later?
- What is the implication of setting a price and then later having to adjust it?
- Is it better to adjust it up or down? What is the best way to do this?
- If you were Tom, what other information or decision suggestions would you want from the model?

i. Sensitivity analysis of the model

Sensitivity analysis is used to study the effect of changing the value of an uncontrollable parameter (e.g., slope of the *Room rate* vs. *Occupancy* relationship) on the performance measure (e.g., *Profit*).

- Unhide the *Analysis(2)* sheet.
- A two-dimensional **DataTable** is shown with the room rate as the first variable listed down column C, and the Occupancy slope as the second variable listed across row 8. The resulting profit is computed in the table.
- As can be seen from the table, there are some regions with positive profits and some regions with negative profits.

j. Charting the sensitivity analysis curves

From the DataTable in part i, it is not easy to observe the effect of *Occupancy slope* on profit. The effect is better observed by plotting the profit vs. room rate for different occupancy slope values.

- Unhide the *Sensitivity* sheet.
- Several curves representing different occupancy slope are charted.
- From the curves, we can observe that profit is very sensitive to occupancy slope at high room rates, and is totally insensitive to occupancy slope at room rate that is less than or equal to $400.
- What it tells us is that our model would be more reliable at lower room rates even if we have predicted the occupancy slope inaccurately.

Exercise 11   INKJET PRINTER

Challenge

Seiko Epson Corporation, Canon Inc., Lexmark International Inc., and Hewlett-Packard Company – each produces a range of printers that uses ink as the print medium. Their ink cartridges employ proprietary technology and therefore can only be purchased from their respective companies. Prices of inkjet printers have been dropping, even as their print quality continues to improve, so much so that they are now almost as good as laser printers. It is hard to believe how the manufacturers can produce such excellent products at costs low enough for them to be sold at such competitive prices that they are practically ubiquitous in every office. Can there be reasons other than a low printer production cost?

Concept

The focus of this exercise is to determine the price for a product, namely the inkjet printer. Since the demand for ink cartridges is dependent on the number of printers sold, both products become inevitably linked. The printers cannot use cartridges intended for printers produced by other companies. This further strengthens the linkage. The analysis must therefore determine the prices of the printer and the cartridge together, which could help us to understand why printers may even be sold below cost. Lower priced usable cartridge imitations or substitutes are starting to appear in the market. These cartridges are produced using alternative poorer quality technology or simply by refilling existing cartridges. The impact of consumers choosing not to buy original cartridges should be of great concern to printer manufacturers.

Working

You need not know from the onset which variables are inputs and which are outputs, and what the objective of the modeling exercise is. The picture becomes clearer after completing the *Influence* diagram and then the *Black-box* diagram.

You can continue, using your own common sense, by working out the formula to determine the profit for the printer. After completing the table, compare the profit made from sales at the other printers' suggested prices. State which of the three prices is preferable. Of course, the profit can be made even larger if the printer price is further increased. Why?

You may want to establish the relationship between printer demand and printer price. Start with a straight line approximation. You can decide later if a nonlinear function is really needed.

We have yet to establish the ink cartridge price. How would you go about doing that? It may be reasonable to assume that the cartridge price cannot be larger than some fraction of the printer price, since a high cartridge price relative to the printer price may dissuade consumers from buying the printer in the first place. Now you are beginning to link the cartridge to the printer, and hopefully with more thinking you will be able to establish the prices of both printer and cartridge.

FINANCIAL PROJECTION

Exercise 12

Challenge

Financial statement projection is the "bread-and-butter" component of corporate financial analysis. It forms the basis for valuations and credit analysis. We can use it to project a firm's future financing needs: additional debt or equity. This is not a single model but a family of models to modify from to fit your particular situation and can be extended to handle more complex cases. Have fun!

Concept

This exercise is about projecting the financial statement of a firm where a limited amount of data is available. This may be a yet-to-be-established, new, or very private company. It demonstrates the use of a systematic approach in framing a business model and extending it. The main technique employed here is in asking questions to identify the variables and then establishing loosely the interrelationships between pairs of them. Collectively, they can be represented in an *Influence* diagram. And then you can discover from among these variables, which are the inputs and outputs. The best way to present this result is a *Black-box* diagram.

The main concept commonly practiced is to use sales as the main driver for most of the other variables. Variables like sales, debt, and equity may be assumed to either remain constant or to be growing at some fixed or variable per period growth rate. There are still other variables that have future values governed by management policies, which set them as values with given relative magnitudes to other variables. For example, dividend payout may be set as a fixed ratio of the after-tax profit or in the case of a more complex relationship where there is no dividend payout until the debt is below some level, set at a fixed ratio to a combination of variable values like sales revenue and profit.

The amount of funds available may not be sufficient to operate the business, and therefore debt may be incurred to tie over many time periods until there is enough net earnings to completely pay the debt off. With debt, come interest payments, which in turn reduce profit further, thus possibly incurring more debt. Tax, however, is also reduced in the process. There is thus some circular computation here.

The *plug* is the discretionary funding needed (DFN) to balance *total assets* and *total liabilities*. If the *debt* is set as a reasonably large constant over all the periods, then the *plug* would be the additional *cash and marketable securities* asset values. The *plug* may also be debt, which is most applicable when the firm is short of funds. The firm may want to keep some fixed level of *cash and marketable securities*, thereby inflating the debt slightly. The third possibility is to set the *debt-to-equity* ratio to some target value or series of values for the time periods. *Equity* is defined as the sum of *stock* and *retained earnings*. This means that if *debt* needs to be increased to meet business needs, new *stock* may have to be raised. *Equity* is therefore the *plug* in this third instance. Other constraints may be applied such as no *dividends* until *debt* is paid up, paying up within a given time limit, and no new *equity* is permitted before a fixed time.

Working To build the model from scratch, you first have to identify all the variables and build up the *Influence* diagram. Here, we are taking a fairly high-level management perspective that does not involve very specific business parameters such as products and their prices, sales volumes, and production costs. To determine the *cost of goods sold*, you can multiply a fraction to the total dollar *sales*. This fraction would be the *cost of goods sold to sales* ratio. In most businesses, the ratio is fairly constant over a wide range of sales volume. Management may want to target the ratio to decrease over time to reflect the economy of scale in production or purchasing, or learning with time effect. There may also be more strategic moves like changing directions in product offerings or growing market share in geographic markets. These can be captured in the ratio value choices.

Using the basic values given, assuming that the given ratios are constants applicable to the planning horizon, you can work out the values of all the line items. The ratios are assumed constant over the whole planning merely as a modeling convenience. This makes it easy to change their values and study their impact on the key performance indicators. If their values can vary over time, this may be done as a secondary step after the main impact of the base value changes has been sufficiently studied. You can now determine the effectiveness of using the different *plugs* and examine when they are applicable.

You can do further analysis by examining the impact of changing one ratio value at a time to see how one variable value is a trade-off against another. This is commonly referred to as *Trade-off* or *What-if* analysis. You should only do this on those variables that you can change in reality, which are known in short as controllable or decision variables. There are also other variables that you cannot change which are a consequence of the external environment. You can still change their values in the model to study how key performance indicators and decision choices may be affected by them. This is referred to as *Sensitivity* analysis. The **DataTable** operation may be used to collect the key output values for varying values of *sales growth rate*, *cost of goods sold to sales* ratio, *debt-to-equity* ratio, and others.

Many of the worksheets in this workbook are hidden. You may need to unhide them one at a time to work on the exercise. There is also another way to quickly unhide all of them. Ask your instructor for assistance on how to do this. How does this approach work?

WEB STORE | **Exercise 13**

Challenge

Hilbert runs a web service selling novelty soft toys. He buys selected toys in bulk from his supplier and puts them up for sale on his website. The cost of a toy to him depends on how many he buys at a time. The more he buys the less he pays for each soft toy. If he buys ahead, he can store a limited number of units in his home for free. For a larger number of units, he needs to store the extra quantity in a rented room in a nearby warehouse and pay a daily rental.

Concept

The focus of this exercise is to determine the most economical quantity to order, taking into consideration quantity discounts and storage space constraints. The demand for the toys can be assumed to be fairly elastic since they are sold on the web and other sellers can easily obtain stock from the same supplier. However, Hilbert can leverage the user-friendliness of his website, and the reliability and responsiveness of his service to his advantage.

Working

Though the price-quantity relationship is nonlinear, it can be classified as piecewise-linear. To compute the total price as a function of the order quantity, you need to work out the three linear formulas. For any order quantity, it can be easily deduced from the graph that the total price would be the smallest of the results of the three formulas.

Applying this to the model is easy, but do be careful about the capacity limits given. Also, it will always be prudent to ship out the toys stored in the warehouse first since cost is incurred there. This is an implicit but very reasonable assumption.

- What conclusion can you draw from the analysis?
- If Hilbert wants to expand his business, what would you suggest he do?

Exercise 14   CASINO HOTEL

Challenge

An integrated resort hotel is to be built in a newly approved project location. Potential guests expected range from slot machine players to high rollers. They have different revenue and cost profiles. The hotel owner hopes to get the best guest mix, one that would maximize the hotel's net income. The hotel management needs to determine what this desired guest mix is so that they can provide the final inputs to the building design architect to finalize the construction blueprint.

Concept

The design of a hotel depends on the guest mix that it wants to cater to, which in turn is based on a combination of market demand and decision choices that seeks to maximize overall profit. This exercise begins with the understanding that the revenue or yield of the hotel can be better managed.

As simplifying modeling assumptions, demand for the different customer types are only restricted to within given minimum and maximum values. The probabilistic aspect of the problem is postponed until the base model is constructed and analyzed. The capacity of the hotel is not defined by the number of rooms but by floor space, and minimum and maximum occupancy, the last being specified by fire safety and possibly aesthetic reasons.

The profit changes with the guest mix. To find the maximum profit, you will have to experiment with the different possible guest mix values and compare them. A better approach is to use the optimization software called **Solver**, available in the spreadsheet application or add-in.

Working

List the guest count and space usage related parameters, and then the expenses and revenue related parameters. Organize the information such that the final key inputs, the guest mix values, are at the top. The constraint limits should be near the values that they are compared against. The general layout of the spreadsheet model is such that the user can work from top left to the bottom right.

Apply Solver to find the optimal solution. Before running Solver, remember that decision variable values need to be appropriately set since the solution depends on what was initially provided. This is particularly important when there are multiple local optimum solutions. In such a case, how would you know that you have the global optimum solution?

The guest mix found gives at best the desired relative proportions. The execution of the results would be subject on a daily basis to the request orders coming in. The orders could be for the same day or a day many months later. This continued streaming of orders gives rise to new challenges. Some of them are as follows:

- Are there revenue differences between guests who booked early and those who booked late?
- Are there seasonal changes in the room booking demands?
- How will seasonal changes in guest mix affect the overall design decision?

VILLAGE COFFEE   **Exercise 15**

Challenge

High-quality Arabica coffee plants grow practically wild on the upper slopes of the foothills behind a village in East Timor. International prices for green Arabica coffee beans have recently plummeted, moving from over $3.50 per kg in 1998 to about $0.50 per kg in 2006. As a result, the villagers have abandoned the coffee plantations to focus on subsistence farming to feed their families. The village chief is deciding if he should marshal the villagers to return to the plantations again.

Concept

The exercise demonstrates the logical thinking steps in framing a business model and extending it. The main technique employed here is in asking questions, the appropriate questions, followed by more questions.

Some comments on typical students' solutions to this exercise are listed below:

- Still need to work on their relative and absolute referencing.
- Logical reasoning can be improved. More practice on real-world problems would be helpful. Stop depending on standard formulas and canned thinking.
- Still not able to distinguish between parametric versus decision inputs. You cannot decide on the prices of coffee, a commodity traded in the world markets.
- Also need to understand when decisions can be made. Here only once, some time before the season to get an advance contract and commitment to buy before expending the cost to maintain. Like all crops, coffee is harvested within a short period to sell and is not produced period by period like factory products.

Working

The data though given were supposedly to be determined. The point here is to be able to come up with the right questions to know what data to get.

- Are the data really so clear-cut or easy to get?
- If not, how to guesstimate them?

After that, the next step is to come up with the right questions to work out the model. What are some of the questions you can ask?

Remember also to ask:

- Are these questions complete?
- Where do the data included in the questions come from?

INVEST IN EDUCATION

Social entrepreneurs seek new solutions to existing society issues and none is as interesting as investing in people and education. For example, micro financing schemes provide small loans as additional capital to help villagers start or expand their business or improve their agricultural productivity. The social organizations that give out the loans operate like banks, with their base capital provided by their founders and partners from more wealthy communities. The loans are to be paid back by borrowers with interests.

Capital contributors can expect financial returns. However, many partners do contribute their money as donations, rather than investments. There are indeed risks associated with lending money to the poor, and justification and monitoring devices are needed to ensure effective disbursement of the funds. Generally, borrowers have to explain their business model, disclose what they would do with the borrowed money, and how profit can be made to repay the loan. The loan durations are generally short, spanning a few weeks to less than a year.

A new and more ambitious scheme is to invest in the education of children and youths. Again, instead of a straight handout to sponsor the educational needs of the young in the community, social organizations can fund the education of individuals as they would finance business ventures. The returns from such an investment would be a predetermined percentage of the salary stream of the sponsored person, for a given duration of time upon his or her graduation.

Investing in people is very different from investing in machines or businesses. The opportunities for abuse are high and monitoring is extremely difficult. The success of the investment depends on many factors that go beyond giving the student the financial means to take up the learning opportunity. Therefore, the need to find the correct alignment of interest between the sponsored student and the investor is much stronger.

It is just as difficult to find an appropriate way to represent the overall challenge. There are many possible issues to examine. The one chosen for this exercise is the allocation of the available investment funds to students at different levels of schooling. Presumably, it would be cheaper to support a primary school student than a tertiary student. A student supported at lower levels should continue to receive support if he or she progresses into higher education.

List and explore the different education levels available. For each level, estimate the investment required and, subject to the specific payback formula to be devised, the expected returns achievable. Assume that each sponsored student completes the program supported and then starts to generate the returns to the investor. The case of a student applying to go on to the next level, thus not generating immediate return and needs additional funding support, is postponed for further modeling and analysis.

Working

The duration of studies for each level is different. The total number of students to support has to be divided by the duration years to determine how many new recipients of support can be given each year. If the program is expected to receive new funding support, further adjustments can be made in the allocation on a yearly basis.

There should be provisions for defaulting students. Further refinements of the model can be considered:

- How would you cater for the time lag between the investment outlay and subsequent payback returns?
- Any there any other possible refinements and considerations?

STOPPED WATCH   **Exercise 17**

What kind of watches are the most accurate? Surely, it must be a chronograph (commonly known as a stopwatch), or more precisely (no pun intended) a chronometer.

Challenge

The term "chronometer" is the status a watch can attain only after a series of severe tests. The Official Swiss Chronometer Testing Institute (COSC) strictly prescribes the protocols. The rules have become increasingly stringent over the years. For simple reference, one 1973 specification for a mechanical chronometer is that it must not deviate by more than $-4/+6$ seconds per day. This is done against an atomic clock, which by the way is in a totally different league in precision.

The correct answer to the question above depends on how we define accuracy. If clock accuracy is defined by the number of times in any given period (say 100 years) that a clock tells the exact time, then a watch of any kind that has stopped working would be the most accurate. Chew on this.

This exercise provides a lesson that involves some mathematical thinking, which for some of us may be a little rusty. No difficult spreadsheet skill is expressively

Concept

pursued here. The primary intention of the model is to examine the importance of clarifying the objective of any modeling exercise. A wrong specification can cause a very accurate model that is totally useless, if not comical, to be built. Also, it may not be necessary or even practical to get the most correct model to represent any situation, just as you would not expect to get a totally accurate clock with only minimal investment in terms of time, money, or other resources. This is an important start to appreciate the value of "quick-and-dirty" modeling and analysis, and in particular why spreadsheet modeling is not something to be trifled with.

Working   Discuss the following questions:

- What should be the correct goals in any spreadsheet business modeling and analysis exercise?
- How would one assure that the level of modeling precision is right for the effort one is prepared to spend?
- How can the stopped watch model be further simplified for the mathematically challenged?

MODELING TIPS

_____ **Systemic view**

Tip 6

Before taking on any modeling assignment, you may want to ask these five key sets of questions:

- First, ask the "why bother?" questions. Many a time, you do not need to model or do any analysis, but if needed, ensure that your goal is worthy and clear.
- Secondly, keeping the goal in mind. Find out if the approach you have chosen is the right one.
- There may be more than one right way, in which case you may want to find the most or more efficient ones in the third set of questions. Sometimes, you may want to compromise on what is correct for the sake of expediency.
- Fourthly, whichever way you adopt, ask how people would respond. No matter how good the intention or how excellent and efficient the approach, it will all come to naught if people react negatively to it. The term "people" here refers to all stakeholders, including all those who need to operate and maintain the models.
- With all these in mind, the final questions are the "so what?" questions. Analysis without action is daydreaming. The real work is not in the modeling and analysis, but in using your model to understand the situation and implement the actions necessary to achieve the desired results.

_____ **Systematic modeling**

Tip 7

While having the systemic view is to try to "do the right thing," taking systematic steps attempts to "do the thing right." To model systematically, adopt the following sequence: define problem, collect data, identify variables, formulate model, evaluate model, recommend solution, implement solution, collect feedback, and evaluate feedback. It does not always have to be so linear. You may have to loop and re-loop some subset of the steps, refining the model as you go along. The _Influence_ and _Black-box_ diagrams are excellent tools to support this process. In modeling the situation, the problem becomes better understood and may even lead to the point of having it redefined or redirected to other stakeholders.

_____ **Black-box diagram**

Tip 8

The first thing in modeling is to get a good handle on the variables and data values that you may be interested in. A quick check of available reference documents, talking with clients, and then brainstorming among project team members will soon generate a long list of variables and data values. Learn to group them, categorizing them into logical clusters before proceeding further. One grouping of variables is as inputs versus outputs. If this is clear from the start, put up a *Black-box* diagram with all the inputs going into a large box as arrows from the left and outputs leaving the box as arrows to the right. The box represents the computations that are at this point undetermined, hence the black box. If it is not clear yet what the input and output variables are, build up an *Influence* diagram first and then organize the *Black-box* diagram from it.

Tip 9

Influence diagram

A group modeling session can easily get bogged down with disagreements over many things. It is therefore best to postpone what need not be defined until later. The simplest first step would be to list the variables. Do not be in a hurry to relate the variables to one another, set assumptions, or work out formulas. Use small boxes to represent the variables and then use arrow connectors to link them to map out their broad relationships. All these can be done in the spreadsheet itself using the drawing features available.

Use different font colors to separate inputs from outputs. Input variables are boxes that have only arrows going out of them and outputs are boxes with only arrows coming into them. With the *Influence* diagram constructed, you can then proceed to capture the model in cells with values and formulas. You may first want to follow the *Influence* diagram layout and later **Cut** and **Paste** cells to organize the model into tables. It would be good to take a moment to work out the *Black-box* diagram if it is not already done. This will be the simplest form of the model you can use to explain the situation to your client. Sometimes, the *Influence* diagram may need to be reorganized into not one but many *Black-box* diagrams.

Tip 10

Affinity diagram

While doing the initial steps to develop the *Influence* diagram, you may begin to realize that there are more variables and issues than can be easily handled. In such cases, you may choose to continue to gather the variables and not to proceed with linking them with arrow connectors yet. After the variables are sufficiently found, the study team can now take an additional intermediate step of clustering the variables. Do this by putting together variables that have close "affinity" with each other. Affinities need not be clearly defined or specified. As long as there is a vague hint of a reason why one variable should be with a group of variables, it is added there. In this process, new variables may still be discovered and added to the general pool or to a group of variables. Each group should be small, with about three to seven variables.

The next step is to examine each clustered group in turn to find what the common theme among its constituents is. The common theme becomes the name of the group and the group is now a variable. After this is done, the total number of variables is reduced by a factor of 5. The reduction process can continue by clustering groups with other groups to form higher-order groups. When the total number of higher-order groups is small enough, say about 3 to 7, you can stop the clustering. Show the affinity relationship between any pair of highest order groups using a simple line; precedence or cause-effect relationship is not defined in this relationship and thus no arrowhead is used. Repeat the affinity relationship within each higher-order group with its constituent members and then continue further into lower-order groups.

Similarly, *Mind maps* are used to represent information in a nonlinear graphic form. The difference between *Mind map* and *Affinity diagram* lies both in their starting point and final form. Mind mapping starts with a goal or focus, depicted as a center core. It first seeks to identify first-order dependents, drawing them out as thick branches from the center. Progressively, secondary, tertiary, and higher-order dependents as thinner lines. It is drawn as a memory aide for collating data and as explained using a top-down rather than the bottom-up approach used in *Affinity* diagrams. Mind maps are structurally hierarchical with one root node (i.e., a tree as defined in Computer Science) whereas an *Affinity* diagram is primarily a data-clustering tool. The clusters are presented with their association to each other in nested networks.

Summarizing, the *Affinity* diagram

- Is more primitive and precedes *Influence* and *Black-box* diagrams
- Does not need cause-effect relationships
- Is useful for breaking large problems into many smaller problems
- Can be applied in System Dynamics analysis

_____**Vitals at the top** | **Tip 11**

When laying out a spreadsheet model, try to partition the cells into three separate distinct areas: the inputs, key outputs, and workings. It is most logical to put the inputs at the very top of the model so that the user can intuitively work from top to bottom and also from left to right. Color coding of input cells is particularly helpful, especially for reasons of user-friendliness and interactivity; certain input cells as an exception are placed directly into tables. Working tables should be kept at the bottom, still within the viewing screen where possible.

Commonly, table totals are in the right-most columns and bottom-most rows. However, it may be more user-friendly in spreadsheets to put them in left-most columns and rows above the table headers. This makes the results more readily visible to users, especially when the tables are large. It also makes it easier to add even more rows and columns, which usually happens as the model is extended. In order to keep the total formulas correct, insertions should be done at any point within the table, say before the last row or column. An additional last row and column may be marked out, usually with a shorter * label, to indicated this. The **SUM** formulas will automatically extend when new rows or columns are inserted within their current referenced cell ranges.

Tip 12

Color coding

The convention we recommend involves keeping all non-changeable cell values and formulas or **Fill** generated values in a dark or black font. That way, they look printed and official. Important results can be further shaded with a fill color ranging from light beige to bright yellow, as if they have been highlighted. A good rule is to make the shade progressively brighter for results with higher importance. Input data values should be in a blue font (as if penned in by hand with blue ink). Their cells when empty should be filled with a light blue color, an effect easily achieved using **Conditional Formatting**. Other font colors that we used include green for historical data and purple for parameters. Again, conditional format the cells to display a light shade of the same color when the cells are empty. We try not to use too many colors as it will not be easy for the user to remember. This color-coding convention is summarized in the legend icon found in the *Home* sheet of all our workbooks.

FURTHER REFERENCES

- Grossman, 2001. "Causes of the Decline of the Business School Management Science Course," *INFORMS Transactions on Education* 1(2).
  - http://archive.ite.journal.informs.org/Vol1No2/Grossman/Grossman.pdf
- Grossman, 2002. "Spreadsheet Engineering: A Research Framework," *European Spreadsheet Risks Interest Group Symposium*, Cardiff, Wales.
  - http://sprig.section.informs.org/sprigfiles/Spreadsheet_Engineering_A_ Research_ Framework_by_ThomasGrossman_HaskayneSchool.pdf
- Leong, 2014. Spreadsheet Modeling Resources
  - http://isotope.unisim.edu.sg/users/tyleong/SpreadsheetModeling.htm# Education
  - http://isotope.unisim.edu.sg/users/tyleong/SpreadsheetModeling.htm# Practice

- o http://dl.dropboxusercontent.com/u/19228704/SpreadsheetModeling.htm# Education
  - o http://dl.dropboxusercontent.com/u/19228704/SpreadsheetModeling.htm# Practice
- Leong and Lee, 2010. "Spreadsheet Modeling to Determine the Optimum Hotel Room Rate for a Short High-demand," *INFORMS Transactions on Education* 11(1): 35–42.
- Leong and Ma, 2011. "Inkjet Printer Pricing," *INFORMS Transactions on Education* 11(3): 132–135.
- Powell, 2001a. "Teaching Modeling in Management Science," *INFORMS Transactions on Education* 1(2).
  - o http://archive.ite.journal.informs.org/Vol1No2/Powell/Powell.pdf
- Powell, 2001b. "Introduction to the Special Issue: Teaching Management with Spreadsheets Workshop," *INFORMS Transactions on Education* 1(1).
  - o http://archive.ite.journal.informs.org/Vol1No1/Others/Introduction.pdf
- Powell and Baker, 2007. *Management Science: The Art of Modeling with Spreadsheets, Second edition*, Chapters 1 and 2, Wiley.

- Keywords. Relevant topics to search in Google and Wikipedia
  - o *Exploratory modeling . Fermi problem . Spreadsheet engineering . Affinity diagram . Blackbox diagram . Influence diagram . Cost-volume-profit analysis . Interpolation . Linear approximation . Management . Organizing (Management)*

PROBLEM SET 2

* Hard problems   + Solutions provided

Qn 2.01   **Furniture store.** The store sets furniture prices at 175% of wholesale cost plus $120 for administrative overheads. When a customer bargains on the price, the shop can drop the price as much as 25%.
a. Construct a spreadsheet model to support the store's sales personnel in managing the ad hoc discounts they give. Sketch out the *Influence* diagram of your model.
b. The model should show the list and best-discounted prices.
c. Try your model on a selection of furniture with various wholesale prices from $200 to $2000.

Qn 2.02   **Lawn mowing.** John's father has a motorized lawn mower. He borrowed it to earn extra money during the summer mowing the neighbors' front yards. He charges $18 for each front yard and employs a classmate at $7 a day to help. He can do at most 8 yards in a day. His competitor, Melvin, uses a manual mower. He charges $20 a yard and can do at most 5 yards a day.
a. Construct a spreadsheet model to evaluate the situation. Sketch out the *Influence* diagram of your model.
b. Based on the given data only, who do you think would do better? Who do you think would do better in real life?
c. Elaborate how your model may be further improved to support your argument.

Qn 2.03   **Rent a car.** The two popular rental car companies in town are Goldee and Supreme. Goldee charges $195.99 per day plus $0.85 per kilometer, and Supreme charges $175.99 a day plus $1.29 per kilometer. You are taking a trip upcountry and will need to rent a car.
a. Construct a spreadsheet model to analyze the two choices. Sketch the *Influence* diagram of your model.
b. It is likely that this trip will span 3 to 5 days and involve a significant amount of driving. Which company should you go with? Explain your choice.
c. At what travel distances will you be indifferent to either rental company? If the trip is longer than 5 days, will the indifferent distance be longer or shorter?

Qn 2.04   **Donut.** Michela wants to get some donuts for the family. She found a coupon in today's paper for Wunkin' Donuts. Their donuts are normally sold for $2.60 each. With each coupon, the store refunds the customer $5.00 if she buys a dozen or more donuts. On reaching the store, Michela found that donuts are on sale this week for $27.99 per dozen, but the coupon cannot be concurrently used with this sales price. Odd quantities are sold at the normal (per donut) price.

a. Construct a spreadsheet model to analyze this case. Sketch the *Influence* diagram of your model.
b. Should Michela use the coupon for her purchase? Why?
c. What if the coupon is worth only $3.00?

Qn 2.05

Tan family. Last year, the Tan household spent $11,000 on food, $5,900 on trans-port- ation, and $7,200 on other expenses. The cost increases per year by official estimates for food is 4.5%, transportation is 6.2%, and others are 8%. The family's total income in the previous year was $24,500. This is expected to grow per year by only 3.2%. Their bank balance at the start of last year was $2,000.

a. Construct a spreadsheet model to evaluate for this year and two more years ahead. Sketch the *Influence* diagram of your model.
b. Provide answers to various pertinent questions: What proportion of income was and will be spent on the various expenses? What do the current and projected savings and bank balances look like?
c. What should be their minimum income growth rates to ensure the family's i) bank balances stay above 0, ii) incomes keep up with expenses, and iii) bank balances stay above $2,000?
d. What if they tighten their belt and control cost growth for food to 4%, transport-ation to 5%, and others to 6%? What again would the minimum income growth rates need to be?

Qn 2.06

Population. Corol has a population of 2,674,362 people, with an average birth rate of 1.7% and death rate of 0.5%. This island nation with an emerging economy requires many foreign talents to lead new industrial developments, while at the same time, many citizens are leaving to countries with less hectic lifestyles. Last year, 4,608 people immigrated in and 4,245 people emigrated out. This is expected to stay relatively stable for the years ahead.

a. Construct a spreadsheet model of the population of Corol for the next 10 years. Sketch the *Influence* diagram of your model. The population balance equation is: next population = current population + birth – death + immigration – emigration.
b. What if birth rate drops to 1.5% and death rate rises to 0.6%?
c. The Minister of Population plans to take Corol's population to 3,500,000 by the end of year 10. Show how this can be achieved – changing birth, death, and immigration and emigration rates. Remember, it is difficult to alter the rates too drastically.

Qn 2.07*   **Saving.** Having just collected your first paycheck after graduating from college, you decide to be more deliberate in saving for your future. Your annual income is now $32,000, and this is expected to increase at about 3% per year. Your bank balance is practically zero and the plan is to start growing it by saving 10% of your income. Bank interest is now 1% per annum, but after five years, you should have enough money and knowledge to want to invest your money into bonds and stocks, to get return rates of at least 3.5%. Large expenses expected along the way, namely cars, an apartment, a wedding, babies, vacation trips, children's education and college, should give you a lot to think about but you intend to just focus on the savings and watch first how their balances grow.

a. Without factoring the large expenses, construct a spreadsheet model of your savings for the next 20 years. Sketch the *Influence* diagram of your model.

b. What if your income grows at 2% and savings at 8% of income?

c. What if the interest rate drops to 0.5% and the investment return rate is only 2.5%?

d. You intend to bring the year-end saving balances to at least $45,000 at year 10, $80,000 at year 15 and $150,000 at year 20. Work out three combinations of saving, interest and return rates, one for each goal, that you can realistically apply.

Qn 2.08   **Pop shop.** The shop sells small popular movie collectibles and memorabilia. Since the launch of their new shopping website last year, the number of visits is growing at 4.5% per month. Last month, there were 2.3 million visits and 3,910 of these visits or 1.7% have at least one order. Of these visits with sales, the average sales amount was $32.50. Sales revenue is growing at 7.7% per month.

a. Construct a spreadsheet model of the website's visits and sales for the next 12 months. It should provide the relevant proportion and growth results. Sketch the *Influence* diagram of your model.

b. What if the number of visits grows at 5% per month? What if the proportion of visits that results in sales is 2%? What if the sales growth rate is 8%?

c. Comment on how the results change with time and how their growth rates are related to the input growth rates.

Qn 2.09*   **Class grade.** The course has three assignments (each 10%), two tests (each 5%), class participation (15%), a term paper (30%) and a final examination (30%). The total 100% is obtained by taking the sum of the better two assignments, the better of the two tests, and the other components. All assessments are graded upon 100 marks. The basic criteria for letter grades of component assessments and weighted total are given as follows: A, 80% and above; B, 70 to 79.9%; C, 60 to 69.9%; D, 50 to 59.9%; and F, below 50%. The students however cannot get final letter grades higher than that of their individual term paper's grade.

a. Construct a spreadsheet model for a class of 15 simulated students. Sketch the *Influence* diagram of your model.
b. Compute the lowest, highest, average, and standard deviation marks, and letter grade of each component assessment.
c. Highlight students with the highest, second highest, lowest, and second lowest marks of each assessment and final total.

Goat farm. Goats are very productive animals to breed and can be easily raised on a farm for their meat. Female goats (does) reach sexual maturity at 11 months old, reproduce a kid crop after five months gestation, nurse for 3 months and then start again. This means a doe produces 3 kid crops every 2 years. First time does usually have one-kid crops and thereafter, they yield 2 kids per crop. On the average, every kid born is equally likely to be male or female. Only a few stronger males are selected as herd sires (breeding bucks). The others are neutered to yield better meat quality. Kids weigh about 2 kg at birth and grow to be 35 kg full-size at 56 months old, at which point they are usually sold. Meat goats are marketable at a younger age, from 32 months when they weigh about 20 kg.

Qn 2.10*

a. Construct a spreadsheet model for a goat farm, with two bucks and two does, all at 11 months old. Sketch the *Influence* diagram of your model. Show how many goats are on the farm at the start of every 8-month period for 12 years.
b. Record the number of goats sold at each period if they are sold at 56 months old, and goats sold in total after 15 years.
c. Comment on what should be done if the farm cannot hold more than 500 goats at any time.

Data Lookup and Linkup

INTRODUCTION

Models run on data, much like vehicles need fuel to operate. Users typically enter data as input values into models by hand. Due to human involvement in this data entry process, lots of things can go wrong. In fact, most spreadsheets used in corporations and businesses have been found to have errors, and many of these errors are due to incorrect or inconsistent data, most likely arising from slip-ups in data entry and updating. A good error avoidance practice would be to ensure that every piece of data need only be entered once and to link them to formulas that need them, a habit which is not yet common among spreadsheet users. Further, the **Data Validation** operation can be used to check the correctness of data as they are being entered, and also the use of worksheet protection can block accidental tampering of formula cells by naïve users. Read the tips at the end of Chapter 1 and other chapters for more useful suggestions like these.

With standardization in computer technology and the availability of more open platforms, data stored in other applications, databases, networks, or websites can now be extracted and electronically entered into spreadsheets. This takes the human out of the loop and reduces data entry errors. In fact, Excel allows the user to refresh the data at will or specify the time intervals for automatic updates. After the data are found, entered, and regularly refreshed, there is still the problem

of getting spreadsheet models to work with them. For example, companies have large product catalogues, and associated with each product are many prices. The prices of a product can vary according to purchase volume, delivery destination, or shipping terms. We can use the lookup family of functions to extract data, without the need for human users to refer to product catalogues and price lists, and find the price values for the specified conditions.

In this chapter, the *Echo Office Supplies* exercise shows how lookup can be used to extract prices for a situation with quantity discounts and then evaluate how the current price list may be revised in view of competitive pressures. The *Transport Cost* exercise examines how the cost of transportation between multiple city pairs may be estimated and then applied to other models. Data for this exercise are extracted from a posted post office air parcel rates, which may be linked to the spreadsheet using one of the many **Data Import** operations. The *CCH Kindergarten* exercise, in addition to helping to compare expenses against budget, illustrates the value of formatting and layout in improving readability of worksheets. Additional exercises that use lookups in other business contexts are *Chop Seng Provisions*, *Ocean Shipping*, *Weight Management*, and *Topix Weights*.

DISCOVERY POINTS

Point 11

Business functions

Small business ventures are often managed by very few managers. In large, more established organizations, problem solving and decision making are distributed into specialized areas, each led by a functional head. These functions include administration, finance, human resource, information technology, operations, product development, and sales and marketing. Refer to *Discovery Points 37* to *45* for further descriptions of some areas. Each area has the expertise and resources to perform their tasks, and is measured by its achievement of functional goals.

Briefly, sales and marketing are responsible for increasing sales and finding new markets. Their effort needs the support of IT to provide timely information and reliable systems to ensure smooth sales logging and inventory tracking. Production must meet product quality and shipping delivery requirements. Human resource ensures that the company has sufficient, well-trained employees to do the work and organizes for their professional development. Achievement of functional goals should help the organization achieve its overall goals. This may not be true, particularly when functional areas sub-optimize corporate goals by pushing their area goals too far.

Traditional demarcation of departments often runs into difficulties when problems fall into the cracks. Some organizations use matrix structures, which give functional staff additional project team affiliations. Others have cross-functional structures. For example, supply chain management takes responsibility for the flow of material and serves to resolve internal conflicts and derive synergies among affected functions. So, for example, instead of continually looking for better ways to produce a part cheaper, maybe it is better to purchase it from external suppliers.

Point 12

Plans are just plans

The main goal of the intellectual exercise of building a model is to discover and diagnose the situation, that is, to understand what is happening. To be useful, the model should be analyzed to yield actionable plans. The key point to remember is that plans are only recommendations, not royal edicts. Plans should not be rigidly followed, but rather serve as guides and starting points for further adjustments from other "inputs" such as gut feelings and implicit managerial experience. If implementation takes time, you will need to adapt the recommendations to the progressive reaction of other stakeholders of and participants in the plan, as it rolls out. There is of course the danger of plans flip-flopping in execution. Plans must therefore be guided by a set of unwavering policies, together with tracking and control measures. The discovery process is therefore ongoing and adaptive.

Point 13

Price differentiation

The price of a product can be changed to coax more demand. Reducing prices generally increases demand and, conversely, increasing it decreases demand. The contrary exception applies to ostentatious goods where the buyer derives status signaling benefits from higher prices and therefore attracts more purchase with price increases. It may be said that demand decreases monotonically with prices until a point, after which it starts to increase again. Prices can be further varied by purchase volume, order time, delivery time and buyer attributes. Usually, reputable buyers who order large quantities early for a lull demand period gets the best price. Companies may not apply all these features. The most common feature applied has to be quantity discounts.

Point 14

Discount and rebate

Discount based on a schedule of purchase quantities can be given each time a purchase is made. Such price schedules tend to give prices that decrease with purchase volume, where a price applies over a sub-range of volumes. The observant modeler will note the weird behavior just after each price interval change points: buying an extra quantity actually reduces the total charge. You may want to explore how this anomaly may be corrected. Or, consider whether you should just leave it alone.

Gifts are another form of immediate discounts, just given in kind. Other than these, cash vouchers can also be given to offset future purchases. They usually come with expiration dates to coax the prospective purchase response. Alternatively, rebates can be applied retrospectively to past purchases. They can apply for a customer for all receipts in a day, week, month, sales season, calendar season, quarter, or year. Sales tracking and accumulation, for individuals as well as corporate clients, are expediently done using information systems. For cash flow and other reasons, customers may not like to wait until the end of the year to collect their rebates. Some forms of progressive disbursing of rebates can be done to mitigate this problem. Discuss with your team or instructor what the various possible ways to do this are.

Search and iteration

What's-best solutions can be found using "myopic" neighborhood search. This means changing the decision variables' current values slightly in different ways and selecting the best among the set evaluated as an intermediate solution. Keep iterating by repeating the process from this solution until no better solution can be found. This is analogous to finding the highest or lowest point in a geographical area by a visually challenged person with a walking stick. This person points her stick around her to find a better point nearby and moves towards it. She keeps doing this until no better point can be found.

Search also applies to finding a target output variable value by varying the input variable values. The approach is similar, except now it terminates when the target value is found. More aggressive and faster approaches use slope of the output function to give a point for the next iteration that is much further than myopic search. These iterations are automated in spreadsheets in **Goal-Seek** and **Solver** operations. Manual attempts to find the required solutions may yield findings that automation cannot.

In both *What's-best* and *Goal-seek* operations, the starting solution of the search is important, especially when there is more than one final solution. Starting solutions may be seeded randomly or in a stratified manner by dividing the input variables' value ranges into equal-sized regions and sampling from them. The optimal solution found from each initial solution gives a local optima. The best among the local optimas may be considered the global optima.

EXERCISES

Exercise 18   **ECHO OFFICE SUPPLIES**   Worked Example

Challenge   The marketing department has just completed the projected sales demand for next year. Though the projection shows a healthy increase in demand for Echo's products, the managing director (MD) is very concerned about the aggressive change in the recent competitive landscape. While he still believes the projected sales quantities are achievable, he expects the need to drop prices to prevent en bloc customer defection to new competitors.

In particular, all the five big customers would want Echo's prices to fall by at least 8% from their perspective. Overall, the MD said that they may have to reduce projected revenue from big customers as a group by as much as 9%, and 5% (or more) for other customers collectively.

Concept   The intent of this exercise is to examine how to reward customers for their loyalty and encourage them to buy more. For this reason, the unit price of products usually decreases with purchase quantity. This may apply to each purchase order the customer puts up to the company or alternatively be applied to the overall annual volume of purchase. In the latter case, the price reduction can be effected as a rebate on the total business volume done at year-end. The rebate is computed by taking the difference between the total prices paid computed at standard prices and the total price when the quantity-discounted prices are applied. Unless the discounted price list and rebate structure are made known at the start of the year, the customer's purchase behavior may not be influenced at all during the year. So prior planning is required to establish the discounted price list, and more likely than not some adjustments to the price list within the year may be necessary.

With new competitors entering the market, management needs to be extra careful about how their prices are set. This usually entails some unitary price-cutting to discourage the competition from stealing the company's customers. However, you probably can do better than just lowering the product prices evenly across the board. You can take a more selective approach to fine-tune the price changes. Customer account managers will no doubt argue their cases to influence the change in their favor. Hence you will need to assess what would be best for the company as a whole. Your spreadsheet application software should have a **Solver** operation that can determine, for such complex situations, the best prices for the given objective, subject to specified constraints. The constraints, not always explicitly given, may need to be inferred. The solution determined by **Solver** may not be totally acceptable to the price revision committee, but it will certainly provide a useful starting point for further deliberation.

Before we explore the problem, let us first learn how to extract the price of *Widgets* for any specified purchase quantity.

**Working
(Detailed)**

i. Select the *Widgets* sheet. We can apply one of the **Lookup** functions on the price list there.

ii. The price list for different units of widgets is shown in cells B4:C9. This table however cannot be used since it is not a table of values, but rather of text strings.

iii. We need to separate the two numbers in the first column of this given price list and posit one value in each cell. They will represent the lower and upper limit of the price interval. However, the upper bound value is really redundant since it should be one less than the next lower bound value. Therefore, only one column of the lower limit values is needed. The revised table is as shown in cells B14:C19.

iv. Practice a simple example.

  • Enter into cell F19 the number of widgets. You can add a drop-down list using **Data Validation** on this cell so that data entry would be less error prone.

  • Enter into cell G19 the formula =VLOOKUP(F19,B14:C19,2). This function will compare the value in F19 with the left-most column of the **table array** in B14:C19. The value 2 in the formula denotes that the returned value will be taken from the specified second column of the **table array**. You should also later learn how to use other **Lookup** functions to achieve the same result. For now, try entering different input values to examine if the prices are correctly extracted.

  • Enter into cell H19 the formula =F19*G19. This formula will compute the total charge as the product of quantity and price.

v. To tabulate the total charge for different quantities of widgets, we can expand the previous working to many rows after you correctly adjust the cell references to the correct referencing type. Alternatively, you can use a one-dimensional **DataTable**. This is a very powerful feature that allows you to compile the results of a base model for the various required input values. We can use this table to examine what happens to the total charge as the purchase quantity increases.

- Copy the column of quantity values from cells F25:F37 to cells F43:F55. These values correspond to the points before and at the price changes.
- Enter into cell G42 the formula =G19. This is equivalent to duplicating the formula in G19 to cell G42. This approach is preferred since any change in the formula in G19 is automatically updated in G42, avoiding a potential spreadsheet maintenance error.
- Enter into cell H42 the formula =H19, to similarly bring the formula in H19 to bear in cell H42.
- Select cells F42:H55 and activate the **DataTable** operations by selecting **Data/What-If Analysis/Data Table**.
- Identify the **Column Input Cell** as F19. F19 is selected because it contains the value for the quantity of widgets that is used in the formulas in cells G19 and H19.
- Examine the total charges at 200, 500, 2000, and so on. Notice that though the total charge increases with the purchased quantity, it is cheaper to buy one more widget at these values. In fact, this phenomenon, as shown in the chart, persists for quite a few units more. This effect arises because unit prices of widgets decrease with an increase in the quantity purchased.

vi. This leads us to ponder on some related questions.
  - How do you correct this abnormal total charge behavior?
  - Would it be necessary to correct it at all?
  - What if the prices instead increase with volume?
  - Under what circumstances does this "increasing price structure" apply?
  - Can you generalize the formula so that the user can specify the price structure type?

Now we are ready to return to our main business challenge, to apply what you have learned to compute the projected sales figures for Echo's different products. We would then like to revise the price list to satisfy the customers' request for price reduction subject to constraints specified by management. The modeling effort should include three basic steps:

i. Compute the projected sales revenue before price revision using the original price list.

ii. Compute the projected sales revenue using a revised price list.

iii. Compute the percentage drop in revenue from each customer groups and ensure that they satisfy the minimum reduction criteria. Compute the percentage drop in total revenue for the company and ensure that it is minimized.

With three products and six different quantity ranges, you have to essentially reset 18 prices to achieve the desired results. Testing out the different variations of price changes manually will be too difficult and also contentious with the different stakeholders seeking to better their individual interests. In addition, it will be difficult to establish if the result would indeed be causing the least amount of potential revenue loss. So, what shall we do? This is where a tool like **Solver** would be really handy.

a. Compute the projected sales revenue based on the original price list.
   i. Select the *Proto* sheet.
   ii. Enter into cell H21 the formula D21*VLOOKUP(D21,$G$5:$J$10,2) (i.e., *Projected revenue = Unit price * Quantity* for the first customer and first product).
   iii. Fill the formula in cell H21 into cells I21:J21 to compute the projected revenue for the next two products. Take care to change the **Column Index Number** from 2 to 3 and 4, respectively. You can use other lookup functions to achieve the same results.
   iv. Enter into cell G21 the formula =SUM(H21:J21) to sum the projected sales revenue for the first customer.
   v. Fill the formulas in cells G21:J21 for all the remaining 49 customers.
   vi. Fill the formulas in cells F13:F15 into cells G13:J15 to compute total projected sales revenue for the two customer groups and overall total.
   vii. For easy monitoring, we will add additional lookup functions into cells G17:J17 to retrieve for the selected customer in cell B17 the corresponding projected sales revenue.
      - Enter into cell G17 the formula =INDEX($G21:$J70,MATCH ($B17,$B21:$B70,0),MATCH(G20,$G20:$J20,0)). This formula will retrieve the corresponding project sales for widgets for the selected customer by matching the customer name with the column of customer names in B21:B70 to give the row number, and matching the header with the row of headers in G20:J20 to give the column number.
      - Fill the formula in cell G17 into cells H17:J17. These formulas will retrieve the projected sales revenue for product Sprocket and Gizmos.
      - Alternatively, you can explore using array formula to achieve the same result. Select cell G17 and enter the formula =INDEX(G21:G70,MATCH($B17,$B21:$B70,0)).

b. Compute the projected sales revenue based on the revised price list.
   i.   Select the *Proto(2)* sheet.
   ii. The same computations for projected sales revenue based on the original price list are already replicated in columns G to J.
   iii. A new price list is prepared in cells K5:N10. Note that the prices here are for the time being the same as those in the original price list. These prices will be changed by **Solver** in part d.
   iv. Enter into cell L21 the formula =D21*VLOOKUP(D21,$K$5:$N$10,2) which uses the new price list in cells K5:N10.
   v.   Fill the formula in cell L21 into cells M21:N21 to compute the projected revenue for the next two products. Take care to change the **Column Index Number** from 2 to 3 and 4, respectively.
   vi. Enter into cell K21 the formula =SUM(L21:N21) to sum the projected sales revenue for the first customer.
   vii. Fill the formulas in cells K21:N21 for all the remaining 49 customers.
   viii. Fill the formulas in cells J13:J15 into cells K13:N15 to compute total projected sales revenue for the two customer groups and overall total.
   ix. To retrieve the corresponding projected sales revenue into cells K17:N17, for the selected customer in cell B17, select cell K17 and enter the formula =INDEX(K21:K70,MATCH($B17,$B21:$B70,0)) and fill into cells L17:M17.

c. Determine the percentage drop in revenue.
   i.   Enter into cell P13 the formula =(G13-K13)/G13*100 (i.e., *Percentage drop in revenue = Change in revenue/Original revenue*). This is the percentage drop in revenue from the big customer group.
   ii. Fill the formula in cell P13 to cells P14:P15. P14 will reflect the percentage drop in revenue from the other customer group. P15 will reflect the total percentage drop in revenue for the company.
   iii. Try to reduce the prices in cells L5:N10 to see the drop in revenue in cells P13:P15.

d. Prepare the model for **Solver.**
   i.   Prepare cells to store the *Left-hand-side* (LHS) formulas and *Right-hand-side* (RHS) values for the constraints in Solver.
       • Enter into cell R13 the value 9. This will be the RHS value of the constraint to ensure that revenue reduction from the big customer group will be 9% or more. The LHS of this constraint is already in cell P13.

- Enter into cell R14 the value 5. This will be the RHS of the constraint to ensure that revenue reduction from the other customer group will be 5% or more. The LHS of this constraint is already in cell P14.
- The last constraint states that the price reduction% for each big customer must be at least 8. This constraint is needed to ensure that the price reduction is not too unevenly distributed to benefit some big customers at the expense of the others and that every one of the big customers gets at least the 8% reduction in their cost.
- Copy the formula in cell P13 and paste into cells P21:P70. These formulas will compute the reduction in revenue from each of the big (and other) customers to form the LHS of the constraint.
- Enter into cells R21:R25 the value 8 as the RHS values.

ii. Identify the objective function.
- The objective is to minimize the reduction in total revenue for the company.
- This reduction value is already computed in cell P15, and this will be used as the objective function cell.

iii. Set up Solver.
- Select **Data/Solver** and the **Solver Parameters** dialog (as shown in *Figure 3-1*) will appear.
- Set **Target Cell** as P15.
- Select **Equal To** as Min.
- Set **By Changing Cells** as L5:N10.
- Click **Add** to add constraints and the **Add Constraint** dialog (as shown in *Figure 3-2*) will appear.
- Select **Cell Reference** as L5:N10, "<=," **Constraint** as H5:J10, and click **Add**. This constraint ensures that every value in the new price list will be less than or equal to their corresponding value in the original price list.
- Select **Cell Reference** as L5:N9, ">=," **Constraint** as L6:N10, and click **Add**. This constraint ensures that quantity discount is still applied in the new price list.
- Select **Cell Reference** as P13:P14, ">=," **Constraint** as R13:R14, and click **Add**. This constraint ensures that the revenue reduction is satisfied for both customer groups.
- Select **Cell Reference** as P21:25, ">=," **Constraint** as R21:R25, and click **Add**. This constraint ensures that the price reduction for the big customers is satisfied.

Figure 3-1

Setting Up
Solver

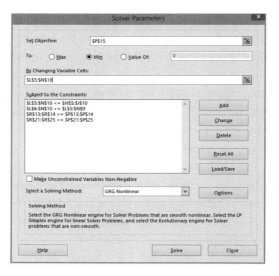

Figure 3-2

Adding
Constraint in
Solver

- Click **Cancel** to return to the **Solver Parameters** dialog.
- Finally, click **Solve** and Solver will iteratively change the prices in the new price list to minimize the reduction in total revenue while satisfying all the specified constraints.

The results obtained, reflecting targeted price reduction, will be more effective than if they were uniform "across the board" or even an ad-hoc selective reduction in prices. Note that there may be more than one set of revised prices that minimizes the given objective and satisfies the constraints in this problem. Each of the local optimal solutions is dependent on the initial new price list given before running Solver. One way to surface the various solutions is to vary the starting new price list. The final solution is the one, from among all the possible solutions, with the lowest total revenue reduction.

e. Automate the solving process.

Refer to Appendix B to apply the programming ideas here. Start with macro recording and editing, and later write your own subroutines from scratch. Expand your understanding and skill of **Excel VBA** or **LO Basic** macros with each subsequent exercise. If you put the Excel and **VB Editor** windows side by side, you will be able to see how the **VB** code is written as you record your macro. This is not possible for LO Basic, and so you have to remember the steps and compare them against the codes after you have completed recording. Do note the unnecessary recorded codes, such as window scrolling. These lines can be modified or deleted.

Try to "step" through your edited macro by keying **F8** with your cursor in the **Sub**. This again is best done with the spreadsheet and the Basic Editor windows appearing side by side on your computer screen. From this experience, learn to read the code and understand what each line and each key word means. Over time, and with frequent reference to the **VBA Object Library** (which is like a dictionary of all available key words for **VBA** codes), you will no doubt be able to write your own procedures like a seasoned programmer. LO Basic is more challenging because the recorded codes are not so readable, and you may want to learn to write the codes by studying Appendix B for LO Basic and looking at the examples provided in the other exercises.

i. To automate the Solver process to test different RHS values for the constraint, we can record simple macros.

ii. To record a macro to reset the new price list to the old price list's values in Excel,
   - Select **Developer/Record Macro** and the **Record Macro** window will appear. Provide a meaningful macro name and click **OK**.
   - Select cells H5:J10 and click **Copy** (or key **Ctrl + C**).
   - Select cell L5, right-click, and select **Paste Special/Values**.
   - Click **Esc** to release the copy selection.
   - Select **Developer/Stop Recording** to stop the macro recording.

iii. To record a macro to run Solver,
   - Select **Developer/Record Macro** and the **Record Macro** window will appear. Provide a meaningful macro name and click **OK**.
   - Select **Data/Solver** and click **Solve**.
   - Select **Developer/Stop Recording** to stop the macro recording.

iv. To assign the macros to buttons,
   - Select **Insert/Shapes**, pick any shape and form it on the spreadsheet.
   - Right-click on the shape and select **Assign Macro**.
   - Select the macro to assign.

Exercise 19   **TRANSPORTATION COST**

Challenge   A major challenge in making decisions for physical distribution is getting and managing the required massive amount of transportation cost data. It may be a good idea to first try to understand how transportation rates are structured and then, instead of using specific pair-wise transportation rates, apply that knowledge in approximate functional forms to physical distribution decision support. A simple proxy source of basic transportation data is the local post office. These data, though not directly applicable, are openly available and therefore much easier to get than the many quotations from the various transportation service providers. The transportation cost for large shipping volumes would in general be cheaper per unit than post office parcel rates. With increasing use of the Internet as a distribution channel, the sizes of delivery packages are getting smaller, and correspondingly the number of orders is getting larger. It is therefore not so far-fetched to establish cost baselines from post office rates.

Concept   Service providers are only keen to provide price quotations if there is a reasonable chance of getting the business. Without data, it is not possible to make informed decisions on the choice of routes and service provider to use. We have here a classic "which comes first, chicken or egg?" situation. The United States post office airmail parcel rates, or your local office rates if they are also electronically posted, may be analyzed and modeled into mathematical functions.

The rates are of course conservative relative to the annual contracted rates service providers give for large aggregated volumes. The company can therefore use the rates computed from the derived formulas as the basis for negotiating better rates from freight service providers. What other situations can you think of where such an approach would be appropriate and useful?

Working   Visit the post office, in person or via the Internet, and try to understand the delivery rates information presented there. The amount of information available is rather large, and therefore you have to be selective about what subset of data you want to use for your analysis. You may also want to consider automating the data extraction so that updated data can continue to be used to revise the parameters in your model over time.

- What possible independent variables would the postal rates be dependent upon?
- How would you relate these variables one at a time to the postal rate?
- How can the results be integrated so that the postal rates can be expressed as a function of all the relevant significant dependent variables?

- What do you do if the correlation (*R-squared*) is low? Would removing outliers help?

CCH Kindergarten's current expenses are recorded in a notebook. It is difficult to ensure that the entries are accurate, and more importantly, expenses tend to exceed the allocated budget when they are reviewed at the end of the year. Hence, additional sources of funds have to be found each time to make up for the shortfall.

The kindergarten administrator has thought of using spreadsheets to solve the problem and has begun working on them. Look through the worksheets and see if you can understand how they work. It appears that the crude worksheets are extremely hard to understand and that they can be improved with better formatting and possibly layout changes.

Make a copy of the draft version of the workbook, and try your hand at cleaning it up. Start with the more obvious solutions like adding more defined headers to the tables and color coding the cell entries with appropriate font colors.

- What else can you think of that will transform the workbook into a spreadsheet-based information system?
- Compare your work with the solution offered. What have you missed and what have you done better?

For many years, Tan Heng Huat has been running the traditional provision shop that he inherited from his father. Business has been going downhill, with his customers defecting to the new air-conditioned mini-marts and neighborhood supermarkets. He is thinking about how to renovate and upgrade his shop to keep up with the competition. His friends have told him that it is not just about changing the hardware in the shop but also the management process.

Recently, he learned about the importance of merchandise layout from his associates in *Provision Shop United* (PSU), a nonprofit organization set up to help small and medium-sized enterprises in his trade. Heng Huat now tries to see if he really understands the importance of stock layout on his retail shelves. The notes from the PSU's handout read: "*Planograms* are shelf-management tools used by retailers to determine how best to allocate shelf spaces for displaying products in their stores. The key idea is that products with higher profit margins deserve better shelf space (e.g., eye level) to help promote higher sales." He tries to study the example given in the handout: design a new *planogram* for how merchandise should be placed on the 8'× 5' shelving unit to achieve the best results for the store.

Concept

Many management problems are applicable across a wide range of industries and settings, and so the methods proposed to solve a problem in one setting may also be useful for other settings. Organizing the layout of goods on the shelves is one of the typical problems. Marketing professionals have developed techniques to manage it, and they are usually deployed in large retail outlets and for more expensive goods. Will a tool like the *planogram* be applicable to smaller provision shops that sell household groceries and general merchandise?

Working

First, understand what a *planogram* is and then determine how best to use it in a spreadsheet Discuss the following:

- What are the limitations faced? Can you work on a three-dimensional model?
- Do you think *planograms* will work for Chop Seng Provisions? Why?
- What are the practical challenges in deploying the *planogram* concept to small shops?

Exercise 22   **OCEAN SHIPPING**

Challenge

Shipping cargo by ocean freight in small volumes less than container load (LCL) is usually done through a freight forwarder on LCL rates. When the volume is larger, it may be cheaper to ship directly through a shipping line's agent using full container loads (FCL). This may involve using 20-foot (FCL-20), 40-foot (FCL-40), or both kinds of container types. FCL does not mean that the containers have to be full, since shipping a partially-filled container on FCL rates may be cheaper than LCL rates.

Assuming that volume (not weight or other considerations) is the only constraint, the shipper, given the volume to ship from an origin to a destination, has to decide how many (if any) of each kind of containers to use. The volume that exceeds the capacity of the containers is assumed to be shipped as LCL.

If, in addition, there is a constraint on the cargo weight, the approach has to be modified. What would you do?

Concept

Given the price table stating minimum volume and cost, it is possible to determine the choice of container type that would be most cost efficient to ship the cargo. The same applies to air cargo except in air freight, weight rather than volume is more important. By sea or air, the shipper actually has more access to data and can deal directly with the shipping services rather than through middlemen when their total volume or weight is large. This gets a bit more complicated since there will be now a combination of containers in each shipping consignment and not just a single container. Sometimes, because of the nature of the cargo, both volume and weight need to be evaluated concurrently.

Working

First, assume that the price table given is correct. The table is already sorted in ascending order of minimum volume against their container combinations. You should be able to use a **LOOKUP** function to determine the recommended shipping container type or combination and the associated total cost. Try out your formula on a few possible shipping volumes, covering variations of volumes less than, equal to, and greater than the maximum volume of both the full 20-foot and 40-foot containers.

Now, consider the following questions:

• Do you know how to find the lowest shipping container combination and total cost for any given volume?

• Does your lookup formula give the same answer and lowest possible total cost?

Next, try to understand the structure of the price table. How would you create such a table, in particular determining the minimum volume and ordering the container combinations? The table you create should give the lowest cost solutions.

Once you understand the approach, you can easily change volume to weight and do the same for the weight-constrained cases. This would still be for ocean freight since air freight does not really have common container sizes: air containers are customized to each plane type and for different locations on the plane. Usually it is quite clear if the cargo by their commodity type is bulky or massive. Otherwise, you would have to try both approaches and apply the one that uses more containers since that would be the constraining attribute.

WEIGHT MANAGEMENT

Exercise 23

Challenge

Your body weight is determined by a combination of diet and the activity level of your life-style. If you take in more calories in food than the energy consumed in your daily life, you will progressively gain weight. This fortunately does not go on forever because as you grow heavier you expend more energy just moving yourself around.

To work out a weight control plan, use the *Harris–Benedict* formula to first compute your daily metabolic rate based on body dimensions and activity level, and compare that against your daily caloric input. You can gain or lose weight by changing your activity level or food intake, or both. Changing them too quickly is detrimental to your health. Their rates of change must therefore be kept within reasonable limits.

A quick estimation of how long it takes to achieve your target is to divide the desired weight change by the weight equivalent of the difference between target diet intake and activity level. A more rigorous approach would account for changes in metabolic rates with progressive daily weight changes. How far off is the quick estimate?

Concept

There is dynamic balance in many systems in that they move from one equilibrium state to another when their inputs are changed. Some of these inputs are determined by choice, others arise out of an accumulated consequence of choices, and yet others such as age and weather are totally beyond our control. Choices towards achieving the target do not have to be static. They can be made to adapt to the intermediate progress made. Remember also that a plan is just a plan. It is based on some standard formula which may not be applicable to every individual. And adaptive plans are often too difficult for the average person to use. A simpler rule of thumb is usually preferred. The key question is how effective these simple rules are.

Working

Look through the *Harris–Benedict* formula. Study its parameter values. If the formula is usable, then you should expect daily changes in weight, which would in turn change your metabolic rate. Since the values of parameters are dependent on your particulars and current state, entering the values by hand will be quite tedious. Looking up parameter values in the model will have to be automated. Do you know how to do this?

Work out a simple "quick estimate" static plan to see the change in weight over time for a weight control program with its target diet and activity level choices. Use a row for each day and then determine which day the target weight is achieved. Over a wide range of input values, compare the results of this more comprehensive approach against those from the static plan.

- How does the quick estimate of the days needed to reach the target weight differ from that of the comprehensive computation?
- Should the quick estimate be used?

TOPIX WEIGHTS

Challenge

The weights that are used to combine the prices of the various component stocks to form an index are given. The user is now interested in knowing what the equivalent industry weights are. The typical spreadsheet users would compute the sum of the relevant stock weights by manually selecting them. This is tedious and error prone. How else could you look up the individual stocks for each industry sector and sum their weights?

Concept

Lookup here takes a different form from those examined in the earlier exercises. Here we are interested in identifying the instances of a particular lookup value (i.e., the industry sector code) from among the stocks. There are of course multiple instances of them and the required outcome is not so much to denote the industry sector name against each stock, but rather to sum the weights of all the stocks of the same industry sector. This looks like the case of using logical functions to identify the stocks with the same sector codes and then summing their weights. Typically, this should involve macro programming. However, this has become easier with new spreadsheet functions.

Working

Improve the layout and format of the *Proto* sheet, clearly identifying which values are inputs and what kind (historical inputs, parameter values, or decision variables). The main objective is to be able to do a conditional sum of the weights of the stocks. Though it is not explicitly stated that you should count the number of stocks in the index that belongs to each industry sector, it will be user-friendly to do so.

Check out the relevant functions available in your spreadsheet to do **SUMIF** and **COUNTIF**. There are possibly other such spreadsheet functions. It would be good to review and be familiar with them for future use. You could also view the short list of stocks in each sector by filtering the list. Review also how you could do that.

Consider the following questions as you explore this spreadsheet model:

- If the list is filtered, say for a particular stock, would the formula that adds up the weights of all stocks now only show the sum of weights of the filtered stocks?
- If not, is there a way to do this?
- Is this approach better than using **SUMIF** and **COUNTIF**? Why?

Tool 1

List management

It is often confusing to work on a name list which is updated progressively over time. A lot of effort is needed to compare an old list with an updated one, to figure out which names have been dropped, added, or retained. Another difficulty encountered is how to avoid multiple entries within each list.

Two name lists (*A* and *B*) are given in the *Proto* worksheet. Try to use formulas to extract names into three columns according to their status: *A only*, *A and B*, and *B only*. Then, for ease of verification, color code the names in the original lists to reflect their status (*A only*, *A and B*, or *B only*). It would be easier to do this using **Conditional Formatting**. Think also of simple tricks using conditional formatting to avoid or detect multiple entries in each list.

Tool 2

My investment portfolio

Monitoring our investment in financial assets can be very time-consuming as the market changes rapidly. To be able to keep on top of things is crucial, as some would assert that beyond getting financial fundamentals correct, investing is all about timing the buying and selling. The portfolio can comprise stocks, bonds, and any other asset classes.

Tool 3

Forms and links

Various kinds of form features are available in spreadsheets for users to enter data. The entered data can then be linked across worksheets and workbooks to be used by formulas there.

- The *CellLink* worksheet demonstrates different direct and indirect methods to link across workbooks.
- The *HyperLink* worksheet demonstrates how to select the corresponding hyperlink from a list of preset hyperlinks.
- The *CourseList* worksheet shows the listing of courses for a selected course group, and the user can also add a selected course to a selected course list.
- The *LookUpMultiple* worksheet shows how different projects with different due dates can be automatically sorted according to their due dates.
- The *Survey* worksheet shows a simple survey form with six questions. The *Submit* button submits the values selected by the user to a separate sheet for recording purpose.
- The *Forms* worksheet shows how to apply some of the commonly used objects such as **Group Box**, **List Box**, **Combo Box**, **Scroll Bar**, **Spinner**, and **Button**.

- The *Dialog* worksheet shows how the image of dialog boxes can be captured so that they can be used in the spreadsheet and other applications to document working steps.

Study the many ideas provided here and apply them to your project to add interesting and useful capability to your workbooks. Which are the ones you find helpful? How can you make the more difficult ones simpler?

Data import

Tool 4

External data from the Internet and databases can be imported into spreadsheet workbooks for analysis and reporting in any of the following ways: **Copy** and **Paste** from websites, and use **Data/Import External Data**.

Go to the website where your data exist and download the data where the download feature is available. If the data are in a table on a webpage, you can copy and paste the data onto a worksheet. You may need to parse the data into columns (using **Data/Text to Column**).

Select **Data/Import External Data** in Excel 2003 and then select **Import Data** to link to existing query (*iqy*) files, **New Web query** to make a new web query by entering the website's URL and click on arrows, or **New Database query** to make SQL filter data from tables in a database. In Excel 2007 or later versions, select **Data/Get External Data** and, once in there, select the equivalent options.

Tip 13

Table headers

It is absolutely important to ensure that all tables have headers. The suggested convention is that the main table has a black or maroon-shaded header with labels in the white font. Above this main table are the inputs and key outputs, with the former above the latter. The input and output cells should have medium grey, thin single-line borders and just plain labels above them. The labels themselves, preferably in a smaller (8 or 9 point) font, should not have any shading or borders around them. This is to make these cells appear as appendages to the main table rather than separate tables on their own. This is to minimize the number of tables and concentrate the users' attention on the main table.

Secondary tables' headers can have other dark colors or even progressively lighter color shades. Just remember, light-shade headers should use a dark or black font for their labels and dark-shade headers should use a light colored font for their labels. Table cells and headers should all have the common medium grey, thin single-line borders as well. This way, no matter what colors are used for shading the headers, the lines are still clearly visible. This simple scheme makes it easy to make revision changes which happen a lot in the modeling process.

A further refinement may be to use headers that are of a green shade where the entries are more related to historical variables and blue shaded headers if they contain the main decision variables. Headers should not take more than one row (or column, for horizontal tables). Header row's height can be doubled or tripled to accommodate long header labels. If needed, use **Alt + Enter** to split the labels into separate lines. Finally, remember there should not be any blank row header and cell column (or blank column header and cell row) as this will split your table into multiple tables.

Tip 14

Switch off gridlines

While Excel and other spreadsheet applications by default display grid lines in the worksheets, it is a good idea to switch them off. Too many lines in a spreadsheet make it difficult to see where one table ends and another begins. Define all tables by uniformly applying medium grey, thin single-line borders for all their headers and cells. This way, applying **Fill** or **Copy** and **Paste** to extend the table rows or columns will not affect the cell border format. Since the recommended header format is either a light-shade fill with dark fonts or a dark-shade fill with light fonts, the medium grey borders are equally applicable. Remember to leave clear empty row and column cell spacing between tables. Where it may be visually helpful to break a table into partitions, a good practice is to change the header shading, possibly alternating between dark and light shades. Do not insert blank columns or rows into the table for that purpose as it would split the table. As far as possible, try not to change the table's cell border line color or style. Just keep it simple.

Worksheet protection

Tip 15

Most cells in spreadsheet models should not really be tampered with by the user. Other than clearly denoting input cells by color-coding them, it may be good to protect all non-input cells. Just select all cells in the worksheet and mark the cells to be locked. This can be done in Excel 2007 or later versions by selecting **Home/Cells/Format/Protection**; in Excel 2003, **Format/Cells/Protection**; or in Calc, **Format/Cells/Cell Protection**. And then, select all input cells and ensure that they are not marked locked. These steps only indicate which cells are to be locked or unlocked. They are not yet locked or unlocked until you activate the protection.

To activate or deactivate, select **Review/Protect Sheet** or **Unprotect Sheet** accordingly in Excel 2007 and similarly in later Excel versions. In Excel 2003, select **Tools/Protection/ProtectSheet** and **Tools/Protection/Unprotect Sheet**. In Calc, you can toggle the protection on and off in **Tools/Protect Document/Sheet**. Macros may not run in protected worksheets. The remedy is simple. Put `ActiveSheet.Unprotect` as the first line of active code in your Excel macro, and protect it back with `ActiveSheet.Protect` in the last line before `End Sub`.

Linking cells across workbooks

Tip 16

If a cell formula refers to a cell or cells in another workbook or other workbooks, the resulting value of the formula would still be continually and seamlessly updated when all the affected workbooks are opened. If the other workbooks are not opened when you open the first workbook, a dialog will appear to prompt you that there are external links and you will be given the choice to update cells in your workbook with values in the referred external cells. If you agree to update, the external workbook or workbooks on their own accord will be momentarily opened and then closed. This is sufficient for your workbook to be updated, except possibly when there are circular references between your workbook and the other workbooks.

Orderly workbook

Tip 17

The state of a workbook last saved is how it would look when you next open it. It is therefore a good habit to keep the workbook in neat order before saving it. First, bring the workbook to **Normal** mode if it is in the **Page Preview** mode. Second, do clear all cell selections (by keying **Esc**) and put the cursor to cell A1 (by keying **Ctrl + Home**). Do this for every worksheet in the workbook. You may want to hide the grid lines, and possibly also the row and column headers, in worksheets that are ready for actual use. For these worksheets, remember also to activate worksheet protection. Finally, select the *Home* sheet and then save the file.

Tip 18

Proper file names

Workbook and other kinds of files are stored in folders in personal computers. You will soon find that it is not easy to locate your files and distinguish which ones are the latest as you start having more files. The suggested solution is to start using appropriate names for your files. As a rule, the names should be short yet simple to understand. The name of a file may be broken into two or more subportions. For example, *February 2009 monthly report of Sales Department.xls* has three sub-portions: *February 2009*, *Monthly Report*, and *Sales Department*. It may be better to name the file as *MonthlyReport_200902.xls* and keep this file in the *SalesDepartment* subfolder.

Here, the blanks are removed and the words within each portion concatenated. Capitalizing the first letter of each word makes the file name easier to read. Separate each subportion by a single _ (underscore character) and rearrange the subportion labels with the more significant subportion preceding the less significant subportion. Date labels should also be formatted numerically with the most significant digits first. That is, label *200902* is preferred over *Feb2009* or *022009*. The sorted list of many files named as such in the folder is simpler to understand. Do not use a date label to record the revision date of your file. Your computer's operating system already date-time stamps the files when they are saved.

When the number of subportions is too large, you may want to consider using subfolders to help organize the files. The names of the subfolders would be those of subportions. In our example, the subfolder is named *SalesDepartment* and the monthly reports therein filed as *MonthlyReport_200901.xls*, *MonthlyReport_200902.xls*, and so on. Again, if *MonthlyReport* is more significant a label than *SalesDepartment*, the subfolder may be named *MonthlyReports*, and the files therein named *SalesDepartment_200901.xls*, *SalesDepartment_200902.xls*, etc.

Tip 19

Version control

In the process of developing a workbook or writing a file, draft versions may be circulated among the co-authors and reviewers. The drafts should be properly managed to facilitate better tracking and merging of the revisions made. Draft files should be named with suffixes indicating their versions. For example, *MonthlyReport_200901_v2.xls* is the second draft of the report. A discipline that we found useful is for the main author to manage the master and most current copy of the file, which is always named without the version suffix. On completing a version, the main author should save the master file (as it is) and also **Saved As** a copy with the version suffix, incrementing from the last version number.

The copy with the version suffix is then released to a co-author who in turn can make changes and return his revised copy with the version number incremented by one. So if a co-author receives workbook *MonthlyReport_200901_v2.xls*, he can return his amended copy to the main author as *MonthlyReport_200901_v3.xls*. The main author on reviewing draft version 3 can accept or reject the changes and then save the revised copy as the new master (still named as *MonthlyReport_200901.xls*). If there is another co-author or reviewer, a copy is made from the master again and this copy to be released is named *MonthlyReport_200901_v4.xls* before being sent to the next person. All draft versions can be saved in a subfolder (usually named *Archive*). The *Archive* subfolder may be deleted if the revision history is no longer of interest to anyone.

Concurrent editing   Tip 20

A refinement of the preceding *Version Control* tip is needed when there are concurrent co-authoring and review. We suggest in this case that only the main author increment the version numbers. All others receiving a version numbered copy can review and then return the edited copy (with revision notes) to the main author with workbook file name suffixed with the reviewer's initials. So if a co-author (with initials *abc*) receives workbook *MonthlyReport_200901_v2.xls*, he returns his revised copy as *MonthlyReport_200901_v2abc.xls*. Other co-authors and reviewers (with initials def, ghi, etc.) would at the same time return *MonthlyReport_200901_v2def.xls, MonthlyReport_200901_v2ghi.xls*, etc.

The main author on receiving all these reviewed copies of version 2 can accept or reject the changes and incorporate them into his master copy and save it as the new master (still named as *MonthlyReport_200901.xls*). The co-authoring and review process continues with the release of *MonthlyReport_200901_v3.xls* (taken as a direct copy of the latest *MonthlyReport_200901.xls* workbook) to all collaborators. Again, all draft versions are to be saved in the *Archive* subfolder. This subfolder may be deleted if the revision history is no longer of interest to anyone.

Unless new spreadsheet features are used, an additional suggestion, especially when it involves numerous and possibly unspecified reviewers, is to keep Excel workbooks in the older *xls* file format. The reviewers may not all have the latest version of Excel or may not be using Excel as their spreadsheet application in the first place. At this point in time, until open document standards live up to expectations, the older file format is more accessible and can be more easily opened or converted to the other formats.

FURTHER REFERENCES

- Howard, 2006. *Managing Spreadsheets*, Bloor Research.
- Leong, 2014. Spreadsheet Modeling Resources
  - http://isotope.unisim.edu.sg/users/tyleong/SpreadsheetModeling.htm# Errors
  - http://dl.dropboxusercontent.com/u/19228704/SpreadsheetModeling.htm# Errors
- Panko, 2008. "What We Know about Errors in Spreadsheet", *Journal of End User Computing*, Special issue on Scaling Up End User Development, Spring 1998, 10(2): 15–21, Revised.
- Powell, Baker, and Lawson, 2009. "Errors in Operational Spreadsheets," *Journal of Organizational and End User Computing*, July–September, 21(3): 24–36.
- Raffensperger, 2003. "New Guidelines for Spreadsheets," *International Journal of Business and Economics* 2(2): 141–154.

- Keywords. Relevant topics to search in Google and Wikipedia
  - *Data lookup . Data visualization . Spreadsheet data import . Spreadsheet errors . Managing spreadsheets*

PROBLEM SET 3

* Hard problems

Grades. The maximum total marks for all the assessments and tests in a class is 100. Students are awarded letter grades based on their attained total marks. The grade criteria are A+, 95 to 100; A, 90 to 94.9; A−, 85 to 89.9; B+, 80 to 84.9; B, 75 to 79.9; B−, 70 to 74.9; C+, 65 to 69.9; C, 60 to 64.9; C−, 55 to 59.9; D+, 50 to 54.9; D, 45 to 49.9; D−, 40 to 44.9; and F, 0 to 39.9.

Qn 3.01

a. Construct a spreadsheet to compute the letter grades for a class of 26 students.
b. Create your own input data to cover all possible cases to test your model.

Donors. To recognize the different contribution levels, a charitable organization awards specific titles to their donors: supporter, less than $500; friends, $500 to $999; patron, $1,000 to $4,999; and benefactor, $5,000 or more per year.

Qn 3.02

a. Construct a spreadsheet to assign level titles for some donors. Create your own input data to cover all the possible cases to test your model. Record the donations for a few years.
b. Some donors are not consistent in their donation amounts from year to year. To account for this, the charity decides to award the titles based on the average per year donation for the last three years.
c. For new donors with less than three years of donation record, the average is done over whatever data are there.

Speeding ticket. The traffic police issues speeding tickets to violators. The demerit points and fines depend on how much the speed limit is exceeded. A warning is given when the speed does not exceed the limit by more than 15 kmph. Exceeding the speed limit by 15 to 29 kmph, the demerit is 3 points and the fine is $25; by 30 to 49 kmph, 4 demerit points and $50 fine; and by 50 kmph or more, 6 demerit points and $100 fine.

Qn 3.03

a. Construct a spreadsheet to compute the penalties for some speed violators.
b. Create your own input data to cover a variety of cases to test your model.

Taxi fare. The flag-down fare inclusive of the first kilometer or less is $3 for normal taxi, $3.90 for limousine, and $5 for Chrysler. Every 400 m thereafter or less, up to 10 km is $0.22 for normal taxi, $0.25 for limousine, and $0.33 for Chrysler. Every 350 m thereafter or less after 10 km is $0.18 for normal taxi, $0.20 for limousine, and $0.28 for Chrysler. For all three taxi-types, there is an additional charge of $0.20 for every 45 s of waiting or less.

Qn 3.04

a. Construct a spreadsheet to compute the taxi fare for some customers.
b. Create your own input data to cover a variety of cases to test your model.

Qn 3.05   **Handy hardware**. The hardware store is popular among contractors and hobbyists alike for the large range of products it holds and discounts it gives for large total purchases. The price list for selected items and discounts for the total amount purchased are given below:

Hardware[+]	Price
Bolts	$2.76
Drill bits	$3.86
Hacksaw blades	$4.91
Connectors	$4.27
Pins	$3.93
Rivets	$3.98
Washers	$2.70
Screws	$3.27
Nuts	$1.13

From	To	Discount
$0.00	$19.99	5%
$20.00	$49.99	8%
$50.00	$99.99	10%
$100.00	$499.99	12%
$500.00		15%

+ In sealed packs of specified quantities

a. Construct a spreadsheet model for a receipt of 10 purchased items of various quantities.
b. Compute the total price before and after discount. The total price should be rounded to the nearest cent.

Qn 3.06   **AA café**. The café sells the best sandwiches and coffee in the neighborhood. The sandwiches and beverages come in three sizes – namely regular, large, and super – to better cater to the different appetites of the customers. The prices of items served there all end with 9, for example, a regular chicken fillet sandwich is $5.39 and a regular cup of iced coffee is $2.99. The popular items and their prices are shown below:

Sandwich / Drink	Regular	Large	Super
Chicken fillet	$5.39	$6.69	$7.79
Club sandwich	$6.29	$7.89	$9.09
Ham and cheese	$4.39	$5.49	$6.39
Pastrami delight	$5.29	$6.69	$7.69
Salami	$4.49	$5.59	$6.49
Hot tea	$2.79	$3.49	$4.09
Iced coffee	$2.99	$3.69	$4.39
Milk shake	$3.49	$4.39	$5.09
Root beer float	$3.45	$4.29	$4.99

The total bill is always rounded down to the nearest 10 cents to make it more convenient to pay and, of course, slightly smaller in the customers' favor. What if the bill is rounded down to the nearest 5 cents?

a. Construct a spreadsheet model that emulates a restaurant bill.
b. Show the total for both rounding methods.

Downtown theater. The theater's musical show tickets are priced as follows: for ages 16 and over, premier ticket $80, floor ticket $50, and balcony ticket $40; 35% discount for under 16; and $10 discount for seniors (65 and over). Discount amounts are always deducted first before applying discount percentages when they are both present. Listed prices and totals are to be rounded to the nearest 10 cents. In support of family bonding, the theater is offering a three-generation family discount of 15%. This 6-ticket package is for grandpa, grandma, dad, mom, and two children. Children here refer to family relationship rather than age.

Qn 3.07*

a. Construct a spreadsheet model for an extended family to evaluate its ticketing options. The family is composed of a grandfather (age 78), grandmother (76), father (45), mother (43), child 1 (17), and child 2 (15).
b. Design a separate table to show the overall costs with and without the family discount.
c. The spreadsheet should be flexible enough for the theater management to design and evaluate future discount packages.

Mobile plan. The phone company's four consumer mobile phone plans and their monthly subscription charges are *Lite*, $27.90; *Value*, $39.90; *Super*, $59.90; and *Plus*, $99.90. The plans' free outgoing call minutes, excess outgoing calls charge per minute (rounded up to the nearest minute), free local data and excess data charge per every 2 KB (rounded up to nearest 2 KB) are *Lite*, 100 min, $0.16, 100 KB, $0.010; *Value*, 200 min, $0.15, 2 GB, $0.009; *Super*, 300 min, $0.14, 3 GB, $0.008; and *Plus*, 500 min, $0.13, 4 GB, $0.007. All incoming calls and short messages are free. Overseas data are separately charged depending on location. GB means gigabyte or 10^9 bytes, MB means megabytes or 10^6 bytes, and KB means kilobytes or 10^3 bytes.

Qn 3.08*

a. Construct a spreadsheet model that shows the best plan for low to high usage users.
b. Work out as many boundary conditions as possible for the plans so that users looking at them can quickly choose the right plans for themselves.

Rental car. The company, with a largely business clientele, tries to encourage more car rentals over the weekends (on Friday, Saturday, and Sunday). Their main vehicle for rent is the Toyota Camry sedan. They have adjusted their prices for the sedan from a flat $240 per day rate to one that favors longer rentals and particularly those

Qn 3.09*

that span over the weekend. As most of their customers are executives on short work assignments, the bulk of their rental contracts are 2- to 3-weekday rentals (on Monday, Tuesday, Wednesday, and Thursday) now charged at the peak rate of $250 per day. To soak up unused weekday capacity, they introduced a low one-day weekday rate of $150. This has been highly popular, but it has created a lot of work for the staff. They hope to attract more weekenders to take up an extra weekday and business renters to extend their business stay by one or more days, possibly into the weekend. The weekday rate for 4 or more days (straddling a weekend) is $220 per day. Weekend rates are now $200 per day for 1 to 3 days and $180 per day for 4 to 6 days, over one or two weekends.

a. Construct a spreadsheet model to show how much is chargeable for customers with different rented weekday and weekend days. You can assume that each rental contract spans a contiguous number of days and not disjointed periods.

b. Comment on what are the possible responses of customers and how the company may further refine their rates.

Qn 3.10* **Income tax.** Income tax for all countries works on a progressive scale, under which those with higher incomes pay more, not just in absolute quantity but, also, percentagewise. This makes calculating the tax payable rather difficult for most people. As we can see from the income tax rate table taken from an Inland Revenue Authority shown below, one usually needs an accountant to help figure out this financial maze.

Chargeable Income	Rate (%)	Gross Tax Payable ($)
First $20,000	–	0
Next $10,000	2	200
First $30,000	–	200
Next $10,000	3.5	350
First $40,000	–	550
Next $40,000	7	2,800
First $80,000	–	3,350
Next $40,000	11.5	4,600
First $120,000	–	7,950
Next $ 40,000	15	6,000
First $160,000	–	13,950
Next $ 40,000	17	6,800
First $200,000	–	20,750
Next $120,000	18	21,600
First $320,000	–	42,350
Above $320,000	20	

a. To help others compute their personal income taxes, construct a spreadsheet model using the preceding rate table. Your spreadsheet should compute the tax payable and the effective tax rate. Do this for a sample of people with different annual incomes.

b. In addition, a personal tax rebate of 30% for taxpayers below 60 years of age and 50% for taxpayers 60 years of age and over has been announced, subject to a maximum rebate of $1,500. Work out also the rebate for the people on your list, and compute the tax payable after rebate and the after rebate effective tax rate.

4 Functions and Relationships

LEARNING OUTCOMES

- Able to build models with different functions and variable types
- Able to work with changes in the value of money across time
- Able to apply computations and functions to evaluate a financial situation
- Able to solve a problem with iterative, recursive computations

INTRODUCTION

The relationship between data values, where possible, should be synthesized into functional forms. The functions can then be applied more directly, rather than having to extract data from tables. Eliminating lookup tables makes models trimmer and more extensible. Mathematical, statistical, and financial studies have generated many functions. Many of these functions are available in the spreadsheet application. Conversely, as explained in the exercises in Chapter 3, you can quickly automate the construction of tables in spreadsheets to tabulate the results for various user-specific input value combinations to any model. Putting up tables of data, by hand or otherwise, is a way to deliberately hide the underlying formulations from users.

Though the rules learned in mathematics (e.g., (^ / * + –, commonly referred to as the *BODMAS* order of mathematical evaluation) still apply in general, there are new features and limitations in spreadsheets. For example, spreadsheet permits only the rounded parenthesis and none of the other forms, and parenthesis alone does not perform the multiplicative operation. Apart from these, applying the old rules should enable you to put up simple formulas. While doing so, study also how you may systematically evaluate the different computations in a cell formula

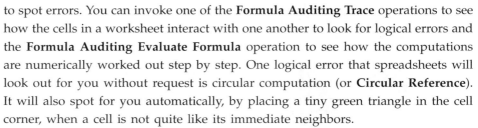

to spot errors. You can invoke one of the **Formula Auditing Trace** operations to see how the cells in a worksheet interact with one another to look for logical errors and the **Formula Auditing Evaluate Formula** operation to see how the computations are numerically worked out step by step. One logical error that spreadsheets will look out for you without request is circular computation (or **Circular Reference**). It will also spot for you automatically, by placing a tiny green triangle in the cell corner, when a cell is not quite like its immediate neighbors.

Of itself, circular computation is not always a mistake and in fact can be structured as iterative calculations to determine in a few cells, if it converges, the solution of very complex problems. Otherwise, such iterative computation may be achieved by using each row in the spreadsheet as an iteration step and then by using as many rows as needed to find the converged solution. Rows are often also used to represent a time period. Therefore, you can model problems with changes over many time periods by laying them out over the rows (or alternatively, over the columns). Finally, complex **If-Then-Else** relationships, which in the past were only possible in computer programs, can now be directly formed in a cell. These can even be used in a nested manner (i.e., putting an **If-Then-Else** formula within another **If-Then-Else** formula) to solve many rather challenging problems.

The first exercise in this chapter introduces the concept of time value of money and presents the various basic models and relevant spreadsheet financial functions. More interesting practical applications of this concept are found in the *Buy, Lease, or Rent*; *Flexible Loan*; *Home Loan in Crisis*; and *Lease and Buyback* exercises. The *Charity Donation* exercise shows how iterative computation may be easily handled in a spreadsheet. Such iterative concepts are needed in the financial valuation of firms, such as the situation presented in *Sothin and Sons*.

There are more complex business finance contexts such as option pricing. Two well-studied and structured ones are *Black–Scholes* and *Binomial Option*. An application of options to mitigate currency exchange rate fluctuations is found in *Foreign Investment*. Going back to more general settings, the *Game Scoring* and *Sailing* exercises require you to dig deeper into understanding the structural relationships among the various variables and presenting them as simply as you can.

DISCOVERY POINTS

When asked if one would prefer $100 today or the same in five years' time, almost everyone says today. This suggests that a dollar today is worth more than itself tomorrow. Why is this so? Some reasons encountered include:

Money over time

- Default. The giver may not honor, may be unable to honor, cannot be found, may or is dead when the amount is due.
- Urgency. The recipient wants to spend it on some immediate cravings.
- Insurance. The recipient prefers to hold it in case an emergency arises.
- Opportunity. The recipient does not want to miss opportunities to use the money when they arise.
- Inflation. Buying power of money depreciates over time.
- Exchange. Buying power of money may depreciate over currency rate changes.
- Interest. The recipient can put the money into a bank to earn interest.
- Investment. The recipient can invest the money for a good return.

The few contrarian voices say that they prefer someone else hold the money as they lack the discipline to save the money for future and better uses. Time value of money analysis in Finance focuses purely on investment. Other aspects may be incorporated indirectly into this pure concept.

An item (good or service) can be bought in a *spot* market. Not needed immediately, the item once purchased has to be stored at your cost and is subjected to possible damage and theft losses. The solution in this case is to delay the purchase until it is required. The risk in waiting is that the price may change over time. A price fall would be favorable, but then it could also rise.

Spot, future, and option

Another approach is to buy in the *future* market, signing a contract for the item to be delivered at the required date and locking in the price as offered. The price at the *future* market is not the same as that in the *spot* market. When the future date arrives, you must pay up and take possession of the item. If, in the meantime, need for the item has vaporized or its price in the spot market is lower than the contracted future price, you still have to complete the transaction.

The third approach, to mitigate against price and need changes, is to buy in the *option* market. In this market, you can buy a right to buy the item. You can also sell a right to buy, buy a right to sell, and sell a right to sell. To buy an option to buy, you pay a fee called the option price. This fee is like an insurance premium. The fee depends on the current item price and price volatility, risk-free rate, and exercise time and price. The exercise price is possibly the limit of the price you are willing to pay.

On the exercise day, with the option on hand you can choose to exercise or not. If the *spot* price then is higher than the exercise price, you should exercise and buy at the exercise price. If the current price is lower than the exercise price, you should just buy directly from the *spot* market. This then is the essential difference between a future contract and an option: the former is an obligation ("must buy") and latter is an option ("can buy").

Point 18

| Simple is hard; hard is simple |

Extracting a simple generalizable closed-form mathematical formulation of any challenge is hard work. An example of this is the *Black–Scholes Option* price formula. Researchers with excellent mathematical prowess worked at it with great effort and you are probably much less inclined to do so. Do you know that you can get an equivalent result simply by not insisting on reaching a closed-form formulation? Using a spreadsheet, you make hard simple by scattering the functional relationship between an output variable and its many input variables into many less complicated relationships over many cells. Thus, option prices can be obtained by either statistical evaluation or *Monte-Carlo* simulation.

On a different note, combinatorial mathematics and optimization are very hard. It is generally known that models with discrete variables are harder, much harder, than models with continuous variables to work with and solve. For example, it is easy to determine how much of different liquids can fill a bottle than how many items of various shapes can fit into a box. This *"knapsack"* problem has stumped many mathematicians, operation researchers, and industrial engineers. This suggests to us that we should avoid discreteness in our models by working with continuous approximations first before attempting to go further.

Similarly, planning models should be left as continuous models; it is unnecessary and incorrect to discretize its variable values. Take, for example, a project to estimate the future health services needs of a community. To determine how many nurses, doctors, clinics, and hospitals will be needed, you use the current population and resource numbers, and apply birth and death rates, migration patterns, and resource-to-population planning ratios. Working forward, you can calculate for each period what are the expected population sizes and how many of each resource will be required. A common mistake among students and young modelers is to round off these estimated population and resource numbers. Rounding makes the formulas more difficult and actually causes estimation errors.

Point 19

Graphic representation

There has been renewed interest in graphics, using the latest in information technology. Graphics are employed in analytical work to capture multi-dimensional attributes, relationships, and responses. More specifically, relationships are represented by relative placement of objects or links connecting them. Links can be arcs or arrows of different length, thickness, and color to show the strength of those relationships. Each object's attributes are depicted by its size, shape, and color. To better appreciate the multi-dimensional structure thus created, you can rotate and enlarge the whole, or stretch and distort portions of it. You can even traverse it, as if you were an insect, flying into and around the structure. Furthermore, relative movements and dynamic changes can also be incorporated, by varying with time the size, shape, color, location, and orientation of the objects and their links.

   Various interesting tricks have been employed to make visual analyses even more powerful. A simple one would be to change parameter values at a constant rate to see how the functional relationship changes. When the dynamic changes of one element are far smaller than others, another trick is to apply relative scaling to amplify one change magnitude over others. Consider a graph with bubbles representing the size of different economies and links representing the extent of trade between them. The bubbles will enlarge and the links thicken over time to show the changing size of these economies and trading volumes. Trading volume changes are small relative to the magnitude of economy size changes. Multiplying the trade changes by 100 and then making the graph display change with time to represent the years, you can better see the dynamic graphical representation and pick up the visual cues for analysis.

Point 20

Business strategy analyses

Diagrams have been used very effectively to represent relationships in business strategy analyses as well. Here, we learn that relationships are not just about variables only. Three popular diagrams are *SWOT*, *BCG* matrix, and Porter's *Five Forces* framework. Search the Internet for examples of these diagrams and save the ones you like for reference. Strategic analyses using the tools are customized to one of the three levels: corporate, business, and functional levels. SWOT (short for strengths, weaknesses, opportunities, and threats) is a situation analysis tool for the corporation as a whole, using a 2 × 2 matrix: internal (strengths and weaknesses) versus external (opportunities and threats). This tool reminds analysts not to look just at internal factors, or even just at external factors, but interactions between the two.

The Boston Consulting Group (BCG) matrix is used to evaluate the portfolio of the company's businesses by clustering businesses or product lines into two dimensions: market share and growth rate. Drawn again as a 2 × 2 matrix, items in the high market share, high growth rate quadrant are called *Stars*; those with high market share, low growth rate are *Cash cows*; low market share, high growth rate are *Question marks*; and low market share, low growth rate are *Dogs*. The company should invest in Stars using funds milked from Cash cows, cultivate Question marks to turn them to Stars, and divest as soon as possible the Dogs.

Lastly, the Five Forces framework shows the relationships among one business of a firm and its surroundings. In the inner circle is the business ringed in rivalry by competitors. To the right is a box representing buyers with an arrow pointing to the center for bargaining power of buyers; to the left is a box representing suppliers with an arrow pointing to the center, for bargaining power of suppliers; above is a box for potential entrants with an arrow pointing downwards, for threat of new entrants; and below is a box representing substitutes with an arrow pointing upwards, for threat of substitute products and services. As possible responses to interactions of the five forces, businesses can adopt one of three possible strategies: product differentiation, cost leadership, and market segmentation or focus by market or buyer group.

Worked Example   TIME VALUE   **Exercise 25**

Challenge

Time affects the value of money. If you are to choose between $100 today and the same amount five years from now, the obvious choice is to take the money now because you can always put the money in a bank and collect it back with interest in five years' time. However, it would be less obvious if the choice is between $100 now and $125 in five years. This would of course depend on what return rate you expect. Another question you can ask is what $100 in five years' time is worth today. There are more situations and factors to consider. What are they?

Concept

Spreadsheets have financial functions to help make work easier. The functions explored here can be divided into two groups: (1) **PMT**, **PV**, **FV**, **RATE**, and **NPER**; and (2) **NPV** and **IRR**. In the first group, any one of the five key variables can be computed, given the values of the other four. Each function, appropriately named, computes that value using the other values as inputs.

For the second group, given the discount rate, any series of monetary movements (in or out) for each successive time period over a time horizon can be converted to the equivalent of a single value today using the **NPV** function. Alternatively, we can seek the discount rate that will give a zero net present value (NPV). This rate, called the internal rate of return (IRR), can be computed using the **IRR** function.

- What is the difference between this rate and the discount rate? Do we need to compare the two?
- Other similar functions include **IPMT**, **PPMT**, and **XNPV**. How are they different from the earlier ones?

Working (Detailed)

Review the information in the *Explain* worksheet to fully understand the notation and convention adopted. Explore the financial functions introduced in the other worksheets, one at a time. For each situation posted, build two models, one using simple straightforward computations and the other with financial functions. Compare the two answers you found. They should be the same. If they are not, then find out why and resolve the discrepancy. Try various other ways that can yield other different results. This will help you understand the financial functions better.

Some mistakes often encountered include not understanding what entity is referred to when a money movement is said to be positive or negative, inconsistent choices of time units between the return rate and number of periods, and not being clear if a money movement should be made at the beginning or the end of the time periods.

Be sure to check out also the *Loan Calculator* workbook that comes as a standard template with the Excel application software. Do you know where to find this and other templates? See how user-friendly the workbook is and learn for your own adoption features that are useful. There are also other templates and spreadsheet workbooks available on the Internet, particularly for finance and accounting related problems. Look out for them as well.

It is important to understand the sign convention to help you manage the inputs and outputs used with the spreadsheet functions. A negative value is used when money is taken away from the specified point of reference, while a positive value is used when money is added to the point of reference. The point of reference can be you, your wallet, a bank account, a project, etc. It should be fixed to one entity for each evaluation of a formula.

Now, there are five variables:

i.   *pmt* = periodic payment (+ or −) of a common fixed value
ii. *pv* = present value or first amount (+ or −)
iii. *fv* = future value or last amount (+ or −)
iv. *rate* = interest rate per period (+)
v.   *nper* = number of periods (+)

One key thing to note is that *pmt*, *rate*, and *nper* must all be expressed in the same time units, whether weekly, monthly, or yearly. The values of these five variables must be consistent among themselves, in that given the values or any four of them, the fifth can be computed. Spreadsheets have therefore provided financial functions, appropriately named, that do exactly that. Let us now explore each of these functions.

a.   **PMT (rate, nper, pv, [fv], [type])**

- Returns the fixed periodic payment amount.
- fv and type are optional. If not specified, their values are set to zero.
- type allows you to set the payment type:
  - when payment is due at the end of the period, set type to 0 or omit.
  - when payment is due at the beginning of the period, set type to 1.

A simple example that examines the use of the PMT function is in the *PMT* worksheet. It also provides an alternative approach using only simple mathematical operators. This serves as a check of the correctness of the financial function and allows the two approaches to be compared in parallel. Select the *PMT* worksheet.

i.   Using PMT function
- Enter the *rate* value into cell B19 as 5%.
- Enter the *nper* value into cell C19 as 60.
- Enter the *pv* value into cell D19 as $140,000.

- Enter the *fv* value into cell E19 as -$10,000 (i.e., the future balloon payment is a single additional payment which will occur at the last period).
- Enter into cell F19 the formula =PMT(B19/12,C19,D19,E19). Here *type* is omitted since the payments are to occur at the end of the month.
- The PMT result of –$2,495 is obtained. The negative sign represents a payment from you.

ii. Using direct computation
- Enter into cell X15 an arbitrary payment amount of say $2,000. This arbitrary amount will be adjusted to fulfill the required conditions. Notice that the payment value is entered as a positive value since the direction of the monetary movement is already indicated by the *Payment* label. Entering it as a negative value here would be confusing as a negative payment would suggest a collection.
- Enter into cell X16 the formula =X$15. Fill the formula in cell X16 into all the cells below until cell X74. This will ensure that all the monthly payments have the same value as that found in cell X15.
- Enter into cell Y15 the formula =Y14*(1+$W$10/12)-X15 (i.e., *Residue loan in this period = Residue loan in the previous period*(1 + Period interest) – Periodic payment*).
- Fill the formula in cell Y15 into all the cells below until cell Y74.
- Enter into cell Y10 the formula =Y74. This will display the final residue loan amount at the top, eliminating the need to scroll down just to view the resulting value.
- The residue loan at the end of period 60, now at $43,658, should rightly be equal to $10,000, the final balloon payment amount. This is what the final balloon is there for.
- By implication, the monthly payment amount of $2,000 is therefore insufficient and needs to be increased to bring the residue loan to $10,000.
- We can manually, by trial and error, vary the monthly payment amount in cell X15, or use Goal Seek so that the desired end condition is satisfied. The monthly payment that fulfills this is the solution we are looking for.
- To use Goal Seek for this,
  - Click **Data/What-If Analysis/Goal Seek** to bring up the Goal Seek dialog.
  - Put Y10 (i.e., *Last residue*) as the **Set cell**.
  - Set **To value** as 10000 (the target last residue value). Notice a cell reference input is not permitted here. Ever wonder why this is so?

○   Set **By changing cell** as X15 (i.e., the *Payment* amount).

○   Click **OK** to start the Goal Seek operation. The monthly payment of $2,495 should be found. If you compare the two solutions, by entering =(X15=F19) in any empty cell, you will find that the two answers are not exactly the same. This is because Goal Seek applies an iterative search approach to converge towards the actual answer, within a small tolerance limit, and cannot compute the exact answer mathematically as in the PMT function.

b.   **PV (rate, nper, pmt, fv, [type])**

- Returns the present value of an investment based on fixed periodic payments, a single future amount, or both.
- To be meaningful, at least one of the two values (i.e., either the pmt value or the fv) should be provided.
- **type** sets the pmt payment type, as specified before in the PMT function.

i.   Using PV function

- Select the *PV* sheet.
- Enter the *rate* value into cell B19 as 3%.
- Enter the *nper* value into cell C19 as 9.
- Enter the *fv* value into cell E19 as -$600 (i.e., the final bank balance at the end of month 9 must be $600, which will be taken out to buy gifts).
- Enter the *pmt* value into cell F19 as -$3,500.
- Enter into cell D19 the formula =PV(B19/12,C19,D19,E19,1). The PV result of $31,774 is obtained.

ii.   Using direct computation

- Enter into cell Y14 an arbitrary starting bank balance of say $25,000. This arbitrary amount will be adjusted to fulfill the required conditions.
- The value in cell X$15 is given as $3,500.
- Enter into cell X16 the formula =X$15. Fill the formula in cell X16 into all the cells below until cell X23. This will ensure that all the monthly withdrawals are $3,500, as in cell X15.
- Enter into cell Y15 the formula =(Y14-X15)*(1+$W$10/12) [i.e., *Bank balance in this period = (Bank balance at the end of the previous period – Withdrawal)*(1 + Period interest)*].
- Fill the formula in cell Y15 into all the cells below until cell Y23.
- Enter into cell Y10 the formula =Y23. This will display the bank balance at the end of month 9.
- The bank balance at the end of month 9, now at –$6,328, should rightly be equal to $600, the amount left for gifts.

- By implication, the starting bank balance of $25,000 is insufficient to support the monthly expenses, let alone to have $600 left over for the gifts.
- We can manually, by trial and error, vary the bank balance amount in cell Y14, or use **Goal Seek** so that the desired end condition is satisfied. The starting bank balance that fulfills this is the solution we are looking for.
- To use Goal Seek for this,
  - Select **Data/What-If Analysis/Goal Seek** to bring up the Goal Seek dialog.
  - Put Y10 (i.e., *Last balance*) as the **Set cell**.
  - Set **To value** as 600 (the target last bank balance).
  - Set **By changing cell** as Y14 (i.e., *Starting bank balance*).
  - Click **OK** to start the Goal Seek operation. The monthly payment of $31,774 should be found.

c. **FV (rate, nper, pmt, pv, [type])**
- Returns the future value of an investment based on fixed periodic payments, a single investment today, or both.
- To be meaningful, at least one of the two values (i.e., either the pmt value or the pv) should be provided.
- **type** sets the pmt payment type, as specified before in the PMT function.

i. Using the FV function
- Select the *FV* sheet.
- Enter the *rate* value into cell B19 as 6.5%.
- Enter the *nper* value into cell C19 as 10.
- Enter the *pv* value into cell D19 as -$50,000 (i.e., an initial investment of $50,000).
- Enter the *pmt* value into cell F19 as -$8,000 (i.e., the yearly investment of $8,000 is invested at the end of each year).
- Enter into cell E19 the formula =FV(B19,C19,F19,D19). The FV result of $201,812 is obtained.

ii. Using direct computation
- The value in cell Y14 is given as $50,000, which is the initial investment.
- The value in cell X15 is given as $8,000, which is the yearly investment at the end of the year.
- Enter into cell X16 the formula =X$15. Fill the formula into cell X16 to all the cells below until cell X24. This will ensure that all the yearly investments are $8,000, as in cell X15.
- Enter into cell Y15 the formula =Y14*(1+$W$10)+X15 [i.e., *Total investment in this period = Total investment at the end of the previous period * (1 + Period interest) + Yearly investment*].

- Fill the formula in cell Y15 into all the cells below until cell Y24.
- Enter into cell Y10 the formula =Y24. This will display the total investment at the end of year 10.
- The total investment at the end of year 10 is $201,812. This value should be equal to the value found using the FV function.

d. **RATE (nper, pmt, pv, [fv], [type], [guess])**

- Returns the interest rate per period of an investment with fixed amount periodic payments, initial investment, future investments, or combinations thereof.
- RATE is calculated by iteration and can have zero or multiple solutions, though at most one is found.
- If after 20 iterations, the two consecutive RATE values still deviate by more than 0.0000001, #NUM! will be returned.
- To be meaningful, at least two of three (pmt, pv, and fv) values should be provided; fv is optional.
- **type** sets the pmt payment type, as specified before in the PMT function.
- **guess** is the initial guess for rate. If omitted, then Excel will use 10% as initial guess.

  i. Using RATE function
- Select the *RATE* sheet.
- Enter the *nper* value into cell C19 as 10.
- Enter the *pv* value into cell D19 as -$50,000 (i.e., an initial investment of $50,000).
- Enter the *fv* value into cell E19 as $250,000 (i.e., the future value of all the investments at the end of 10 years.)
- Enter the *pmt* value into cell F19 as -$8,000 (i.e., $8,000 is invested at the end of each year).
- Enter in cell B19 the formula =RATE(C19,F19,D19,E19). The RATE result of 9.6% is obtained.

  ii. Using direct computation
- Enter into cell W10 an arbitrary return rate of say 8%. This arbitrary amount will be adjusted to fulfil the required conditions.
- The value in cell Y14 is given as $50,000, which is the initial investment.
- The value in cell X$15 is given as $8,000, which is the yearly investment at the end of the year.
- Enter into cell X16 the formula =X$15. Fill the formula in cell X16 into all the cells below until cell X24. This will ensure that all the yearly investments are $8,000, as in cell X15.

- Enter into cell Y15 the formula =Y14*(1+$W$10)+X15 [i.e., *Total investment in this period = Total investment at the end of the previous period * (1 + Period interest) + Yearly investment*].
- Fill the formula into cell Y15 to all the cells below until cell Y24.
- Enter into cell Y10 the formula =Y24. This will display the total investment at the end of year 10.
- The total investment at the end of year 10, now at $223,839, is less than the target $250,000. This implies that the return rate of 8% is insufficient to grow the investment to the required size.
- We can manually, by trial and error, vary the return rate in cell W10, or use Goal Seek so that the desired end condition is satisfied. The return rate that fulfills this is the solution we are looking for.
- To use Goal Seek for this,
  - Select **Data/What-If Analysis/Goal Seek** to bring up the Goal Seek dialog.
  - Put Y10 (i.e., *End value*) as the **Set cell**.
  - Set **To value** as 250,000 (the target end value).
  - Set **By changing cell** as W10 (i.e., *Return rate*).
  - Click **OK** to start the Goal Seek operation. The return rate of 9.6% should be found.

e. **NPER (rate, pmt, pv, [fv], [type])**
  - Returns the number of periods for an investment with fixed amount periodic payments, initial investment, future investments, or combinations thereof, on a constant interest rate.
  - To be meaningful, at least two of three (pmt, pv, and fv) values should be provided; fv is optional.
  - **type** sets the pmt payment type, as specified before in the PMT function.

  i. Using NPER function
    - Select the *NPER* sheet.
    - Enter the *rate* value into cell B19 as 8%.
    - Enter the *pv* value into cell D19 as -$50,000 (i.e., an initial investment of $50,000).
    - Enter the *fv* value into cell E19 as $250,000 (i.e., the future value of all the investments at the end of 10 years).
    - Enter the *pmt* value into cell F19 as -$8,000 (i.e., the yearly investment of $8,000 is invested at the end of each year).
    - Enter into cell C19 the formula =NPER(B19,F19,D19,E19). The NPER result of 11 years is obtained.

ii. Using direct computation
- The value in cell Y14 is given as $50,000, which is the initial investment.
- The value in cell X15 is given as $8,000, which is the yearly investment at the end of the year.
- Enter into cell X16 the formula =X$15. Fill the formula in cell X16 into all the cells below until cell X34. This will ensure that all the yearly investments are $8,000, as in cell X15.
- Enter into cell Y15 the formula =Y14*(1+$W$10)+X15 [i.e., *Total investment in this period = Total investment at the end of the previous period * (1 + Period interest) + Yearly investment*].
- Fill the formula in cell Y15 into all the cells below until cell Y34.
- Enter into cell Y10 the formula =MATCH(X10,Y14:Y34,1) (i.e., $250,000 is approximately matched against the array of future investment values to return the relative position). The investment duration of 12 should be returned. By visual inspection, we can see in the table that by year 11, the total investment value will only grow to $249,746, which is still less than $250,000. Thus, by including the investment at year 0 (i.e., $50,000) in the array, we can be sure that the investment duration will be sufficient to grow the investment beyond $250,000.

f. **NPV (rate, value1, value2, ...)**
- Calculates the net present value of a series of future values, with payments in the negative and income in the positive, starting from period 1, for a given discount rate.
- *rate* is the discount rate applied to future values to compute the present worth, and must be expressed in the same periodic term as the values.
- Each value must be equally spaced in time and occur at the end of each period.

i. Using NPV function
- Select the *NPV* sheet.
- Enter the *rate* value into cell F10 as 8% (i.e., the yearly return rate is consistent with the cash flows).
- Enter into cell G10 the formula =NPV(F10,G15:G24)+G14. The cash flow value in G14 is not included in the NPV formula as it occurs in period 0. Thus, it will be added to the NPV result externally. The final result of $157,453 is obtained after formatting as currency.

ii. Using direct computation
- The value in cell W10 is given as 8%, which is the return rate.
- Enter into cell Y14 the formula =X14/(1+$W$10)^W14. [i.e., *Present value = Cash flow/(1 + Period interest)$^{Number\ of\ periods}$*]. This gives the present

value of the cash flow by discounting the cash flow according to the return rate and number of periods.

- Fill the formula in cell Y14 into all the cells below until cell Y24.
- Enter into cell Y10 the formula =SUM(Y14:Y24) (i.e., NPV = Sum of all the present values of all cash flows). The NPV of $157,453 should be found.

g. **IRR (*values*, [guess])**

- Returns the discount rate of return for a series of future values, with payments in the negative and income in the positive, starting from period 0, such that the NPV is zero.
- The cash flow values need not be the same but must be equally spaced in time and occur at the end of each period.
- To be meaningful, at least one value should be different in sign from the other values.
- IRR is calculated by iteration and can have zero or multiple solutions, though at most one is found.
- If after 20 iterations, the two consecutive IRR values still deviate by more than 0.0000001, #NUM! will be returned.
- If omitted, the guess value is assumed to be 0.1 (10%). Providing a good guess value may speed up the search.

i. Using **IRR** function

- Select the *IRR* sheet.
- Enter into cell G10 the formula =IRR(G14:G24). The IRR of 24.0% is obtained.

ii. Using direct computation

- Enter into cell W10 an arbitrary return rate of say 20%. This arbitrary value will be adjusted to fulfill the required conditions.
- Enter into cell Y14 the formula =X14/(1+$W$10)^W14. [i.e., *Present value = Cash flow/(1 + Period interest)$^{Number\ of\ periods}$*]. This gives the present value of the cash flow by discounting the cash flow according to the return rate and number of periods.
- Fill the formula in cell Y14 into all the cells below until cell Y24.
- Enter into cell Y10 the formula =SUM(Y14:Y24) (i.e., NPV = Sum of all the present values of all cash flows.) The NPV of $27,054 should be found.
- The NPV is not zero, which means that the return rate is not large enough to discount the cash flows to zero.
- We can manually, by trial and error, vary the return rate in cell W10, or use **Goal Seek** so that the desired end condition is satisfied. The return rate that fulfills this is the solution we are looking for.

- To use Goal Seek for this,
  - o Select **Data/What-If Analysis/Goal Seek** to bring up the Goal Seek dialog.
  - o Put Y10 (i.e., NPV) as the **Set cell**.
  - o Set **To value** as 0 (since IRR is the return rate that yields NPV = 0).
  - o Set **By changing cell** as W10 (i.e., *IRR*).
  - o Click **OK** to start the Goal Seek operation. The return rate of 24% should be found.

h. Tabulating the future value of money

To better understand how the future value of money will "change" over time at different return rates, we can tabulate the results for different time periods and rates.

  i. Select the *Model* sheet.
  - An initial cash value of $100 is given in cell C5.
  - The return rate of 3% is given in cell D5.
  - The period of four years is given in cell E5.
  - The future value is computed in cell F5 using =C5*(1+D5)^E5. This states that *Future value = Initial value *(1 + Interest)$^{Number\ of\ periods}$*.
  - This formula can be extended to =IF(COUNT(C5:E5)<3,"",C5*(1+D5)^E5). The **IF** function ensures that all the required values in cells C5:E5 are present, by using the **COUNT** function, before computing the required result. Otherwise, a blank ("") is returned.

  ii. Using mixed cell referencing, the table in C8:K28 shows the future values of $100 today for different time periods and return rates. Select cells D9:K28 and click **Conditional Formatting/Color Scales** to automatically shade the values with different color tones to reflect their relative magnitudes.

  iii. For practice, enter into cell R5 the formula =O5*(1+P5)^Q5. This gives the future value of $100 after four years at the interest rate of 3%. Apply a formula similar to the one described above to cell P9, and copy and paste that over to cells P9:W28.

  iv. Alternatively, to build the model as a two-dimensional **DataTable**
  - Enter into cell O8 the formula =R5.
  - Select cells O8:W28.
  - Select **Data/What-If Analysis/Data Table** to bring up the DataTable dialog.
  - Set cell P5 as **Row Input Cell**.
  - Set cell Q5 as **Column Input Cell**.

i. Tabulating the periodic payments

To compute the periodic payments for different number of periods and different return rates, we can tabulate the results.

    i. Select the *Model(2)* sheet
- The return rate of 4% is given in cell D5.
- The number of periods, that is 24, is given in cell E5.
- The present value of $80,000 is given in cell F5.
- The future value of –$10,000 is given in cell G5.
- The periodic payment is computed in cell H5 using =PMT(D5,E5, F5,G5).

    ii. The two-dimensional **DataTable** in C9:K19 shows the pmt results, for *pv* = $80,000, and *fv* = –$10,000, under different number of periods and different return rates.

    iii. To build the two-dimensional DataTable in the *Practice 1* area
- Copy cells D9:K9 into cells D23:K23. This copies the return rates.
- Copy cells C10:C19 into cells C24:C33. This copies the number of periods.
- Enter into cell C23 the formula =H5.
- Select cells C23:K33.
- Select **Data/What-If Analysis/Data Table** to bring up the DataTable dialog.
- Set cell D5 as **Row Input Cell**.
- Set cell E5 as **Column Input Cell**.

j. Exploring an *Interactive Model* using Event Triggered Procedure

Here, we explore using a simple VBA code to recompute the value of any of the variables when one or more (up to four) of the other inputs are changed. This VBA code is triggered to run when any of the cells in C5:G5 is changed. Such a triggering is termed as Event Triggered Procedure.

    i. Select the *Model(3)* sheet.
- Cells C5:G5 contain values for *rate* (4%), *nper* (24.0), *pv* ($80,000), *fv* (–$10,000), and *pmt* (–$4,999), Note: these cells do not contain any formulas.
- Select one or more of the cells and change the value. Once the cell value is changed, all the five cells will have their font color changed to blue and their cell shading is unfilled. For example, change the value for *pv* from $80,000 to $90,000.
- Select one of the cells to recompute by deleting the value in the cell, and the new value will be recomputed. The recomputed cell will have its font color changed to black and the cell shading changed to beige. For example, delete the value for rate, and the new value is recomputed as 2.95%.

ii. To understand the VBA codes

- Select **Developer/Visual Basic** (or key **Alt** + **F11**) to show the **Microsoft Visual Basic** Window. To understand more about **Visual Basic Editor**, refer to Appendix B.

- Double-click on *Sheet 12* [*Model(3)*] from the **Project Explorer** panel and the codes it contains will appear in the **Code** window.

- The codes are given below:

```
Private Sub Worksheet_Change(ByVal Target As Range)
If Intersect(Target, Range("C5:G5")) Is Nothing Then
  Exit Sub
Else
Range("C4:G4").Interior.ThemeColor = xlThemeColorLight2
Range("C4:G4").Interior.TintAndShade=0.799981688894314

Range("C5:G5").Interior.ColorIndex = xlNone
Range("C5:G5").Font.ColorIndex = 5 'Blue


  Call Update(Range("C5"))
  Call Update(Range("D5"))
  Call Update(Range("E5"))
  Call Update(Range("F5"))
  Call Update(Range("G5"))
End If
Application.CutCopyMode = False
End Sub

Private Sub Update(R As Range)
If R = "" And
Application.WorksheetFunction.Count(Range("C5:G5")) =
   4 Then
R.Offset(1, 0).Copy
  R.PasteSpecial Paste:=xlPasteValues
  R.Interior.ColorIndex = 19 'Light beige
  R.Font.ColorIndex = 1 'Black
'Light salmon header
R.Offset(-1,0).Interior.ThemeColor=xlThemeColorAccent6
R.Offset(-1,0).Interior.TintAndShade=0.799981688894314"
End If
End Sub
```

- `Private Sub Worksheet_Change(ByVal Target As Range)` describes the `Sub` procedure. `Worksheet_Change` is a VBA event subroutine name. This subroutine, as suggested by its name, will run whenever there is a change in the worksheet. The cell or cells changed are denoted by the name `Target`.

- `If Intersect(Target, Range("C5:G5")) Is Nothing Then` attempts to determine if `Target` is indeed one of the cells in C5:G5, by determining the intersection of `Target` and C5:G5. If the intersection is `Nothing` then the third line is executed.

- `Exit Sub` aborts the subroutine.

- The section between `Else` and `End If` will be executed when `Target` is indeed one of the cells within C5:G5.

- `Range("C4:G4").Interior.ThemeColor = xlThemeColorLight2`
  `Range("C4:G4").Interior.TintAndShade = 0.799981688894314`
  changes the header's fill to light blue shade, for cells C4:G4.
  `Range("C5:G5").Interior.ColorIndex = xlNone`
  `Range("C5:G5").Font.ColorIndex = 5 'Blue` clear the cells' fill colors and set their font colors to blue, for cells C5:G5."

- `Call Update(Range("C5"))` to `Call Update(Range("G5"))` calls another Sub procedure `Update` and feeds it with the cell name.

- `Private Sub Update(R As Range)` describes the `Sub` procedure with the input cell given the name R.

- `If R = "" And Application.WorksheetFunction.Count(Range("C5:G5")) = 4 Then` checks if the input cell R is empty and there are four other inputs with values.

- `R.Offset(1, 0).Copy` copies the value from the cell one row below R. This row contains the formulas for computing each of the corresponding variables stored in cells C5:G5. So, this code will copy the computed value from the cell below to replace the current value.

- `R.PasteSpecial Paste:=xlPasteValues` pastes the copied value into the empty cell R.

- `R.Interior.ColorIndex = 19 'Light beige` and `R.Font.ColorIndex = 1 'Black` change the cell color of cell R to light beige and its font color to black to denote it as the "output" cell.

- `R.Offset(-1, 0).Interior.ThemeColor =xlThemeColorAccent6`
  `R.Offset(-1, 0).Interior.TintAndShade = .799981688894314`
  change the header fill color to light beige to denote the "cell" below is the "output" cell.

| Exercise 26 | **BUY, LEASE, OR RENT** |

Challenge

The major hardware pieces in the data center are due for replacement. This will involve a fairly large capital outlay for your company in the next budget. Therefore, it will be prudent to examine the options available. You have discovered that you can either buy, lease, or rent equipment. Before setting out to get quotations, let us consider the options together to better understand how they would play out in our case and how the different parameters involved interact.

Concept

Now that you have been introduced to the concept of time value of money and the basic financial functions (**PMT**, **PV**, **FV**, **RATE**, **NPER**, **NPV**, and **IRR**) in more standard situations, it is time to evaluate other more flexible situations and learn to relate together some apparently disparate concepts.

For example, with principal repayments set to zero, the situation would be almost similar to renting, except for the provisions needed for periodic maintenance and accounting for final salvage value. Also, for freehold property assets, the salvage value may even be greater than the original purchase price, resulting in capital gain. This may be the reason why some rentals are so low; the owner of the property may just be waiting for the asset to increase in value. Similar ideas may be applied to leasing situations, where the future value of the asset may depreciate or appreciate.

Working

Look at the scenarios given and understand how they are related, taking in turn the buyer's and the seller's perspectives. Consider the case of a large airline which has an operating strategy of buying new planes to use for a short few years and then selling them. Their planes' salvage values are usually high, relative to other planes of the same model in the general used-planes market, because this airline is perceived to have done a good job in specifying its plane purchases and have excellent upkeep and technical maintenance programs. Why is this a successful strategy?

Suggest other real-life situations for analysis:

- What other situations can you think of that demonstrate how companies are able or fail to leverage its industry position in buying, renting, or leasing their capital assets?
- How would you leverage better information or understanding of the market to enhance asset returns?

FLEXIBLE LOAN

Challenge

Alphonso asked Timmy for a personal loan and promised to return the money in monthly installments over a few years. The monthly repayment amount to Timmy should rightly be about equal for ease of tracking.

Since Alphonso does not have a steady income and is not sure if he can meet all the planned (equal) payments, he asked to structure the payments such that he would pay the required amount as far as possible. If he is short of money, he must pay a fixed percentage of the projected planned payment, and if he has excess money, he can pay more than the planned payment.

The planned monthly payment amount for the remaining loan balance is always recomputed each month as if it is a fresh loan for the remaining number of months. They have agreed on the loan amount, payback period, and interest rate to charge for the loan and ask if you can put up a worksheet to support the tracking of the loan repayment.

Concept

The additional repayment conditions are set up to anticipate the possible deviations from the basic approach. The idea here is that base models may be extended without adding too many complications to cover practical considerations. In altering the base model, you are also able to better understand the financial functions and check what you have assumed about them is correct.

For instance, the proposed remaining loan balance computation approach is actually correct and is the same one used in spreadsheet financial functions. Another approach may be used if it is mutually agreeable to lender and borrower. Try to think of all the possibilities.

What is planned is often not what might transpire in reality. Spreadsheet models like those in the *Time Value* exercise only specify the loan repayment plan. When the repayment does not follow according to plan and where deviations are permitted, the spreadsheet model needs to be modified to capture the operational details and provide follow-up plans beyond the current time point. This would turn a planning model into an execution model.

Working

Set up the base financial model under which a constant repayment plan is used. Adjust the model, adding columns and cells to keep the values of variables that can change from period to period. Some variables will need three cells, one to hold the value when it is entered by the user, another to compute the value from formulas when it is not given, and the third to show appropriately one of these two values.

After you have completed your work, ask yourself the following questions:

- Can your model be used for both the base and extended cases?
- Is your model simple enough for the two parties to have faith in the results?
- What other complicating extensions can you think of that can be included?
- How would you minimally extend your model to address them?

HOME LOAN IN CRISIS

Challenge

Simon borrowed $400,000 from the local bank to finance the purchase of the condominium unit that his family now lives in. The loan duration is 20 years, at a fixed rate of 3.5% per annum, compounded monthly. Simon has already made 34 monthly payments to the bank and now the global financial turmoil boils up.

In view of the current economic crisis, the bank has announced that it can repackage Simon's loan such that all he has to do for the next 12 months (i.e., months 35 to 46) is to pay only the interest on the loan outstanding. Alternatively, the bank can soften the loan payments further by allowing Simon to resume after the crisis relief period with the original monthly payment amount. This means that the overall loan duration would thus be extended.

Help Simon evaluate the two options and offer suggestions on what should be done. Are there other possible options?

Concept

Once again, the idea here is that base models may be extended without adding too many complications to cover practical considerations. Paying only the interest implies that the outstanding loan principal balance remains the same. This outstanding principal can be repaid, after the 12-month crisis relief period, by using a newly calculated monthly repayment amount to end the loan without an extension of the initial completion date or the initial monthly repayment amount (comprising the interest and the repayment amounts) but now spread over the extended period of 12 months.

Working

First, set up the base financial model to cover the initial loan conditions. There should be columns to show the total monthly repayments, as well as the breakdown of this into the amounts for interest and loan principal repayment. Subtracting the loan repayment from the previous period's loan balance gives the next period's loan balance.

Adjust the model from the 35th month onwards for the 12 months in which only the interest repayment is made. From the 47th month onwards, construct first the case in which the loan must be repaid within the original 240-month loan duration. Then, construct the second case in which the total monthly repayment is reverted back to the initial repayment amount and extend the time horizon to determine the month that the loan would be fully paid. Do note that the last payment may not be the same as the other monthly payments.

After you have completed your work, ask yourself the following questions:

- Is your model simple enough for all parties to understand?
- Can the user easily compare one alternative against another?
- Are there other complicating extensions that can be included?
- How would you minimally extend your model to address them?

LEASE BUYBACK

Charlie bought his condominium unit new for $500,000 15 years ago. Since he has retired from his job, Charlie is considering the lease buyback scheme now offered by the original condominium project developer. Under the base option in this scheme, Charlie will receive a fixed monthly payout from the company for 20 years. In exchange, ownership of the property reverts to the company at the end of the 20 years. The developer intends to redevelop the whole project after that.

The current market price for his unit is $600,000. Considering the current global economic situation, Charlie thinks that this is below its true long-run trend valuation and thus should not be used as the basis for the scheme's calculation. He estimates that new condominium property prices should increase at an average of 3% per year and existing property prices depreciate "linearly" until they reach zero at the end of a 99-year tenure.

The scheme also allows property owners to take the offer up to 5 years later and for payback durations to be 15 or correspondingly lower years. Charlie is considering signing up for the scheme five years from now for the shorter 15-year payout duration.

Financial analysis is based on current parameters. If you believe these values will change in your favor, you may want to wait until they are realized before you act on it. Property prices in particular are easily affected by the current economic circumstances. Waiting it out before selling may be a good idea. However, your property would in the mean time depreciate in value, as its tenure is clocked down. The economic situation may improve later, which in turn brings up the prices of properties in general.

A benchmark to use is the prices of new properties (of the same size and equivalent location). You would have to correct for the remaining tenure of your property to convert the new property prices to get an estimate of your property's value. From this estimate, you can then convert its value into an annuity to determine the monthly payout you should at least expect from the developer. Of course, the developer may use a different approach and have a different estimate of the future. You will have a better deal if the developer's estimate is based on more promising prospects than yours.

Working

Start with a simple approach, tabulating the market price of your property for the past 15 years and estimate the price change rate. Compare the current annual change rate, as determined by the current price against the original price and the 15-year duration. Follow through with the notes given in the business challenge statements to estimate the property price for all the future years. From the future property price estimate, determine the monthly payout amount for a simple scenario. Adjust the scenario for possible complications and then different variations.

After you have completed your work, ask yourself the following questions:

- Is your model simple enough for you to explain to your family members and neighbors?
- What other approaches are there for estimating future prices of your property, one that your neighbor or the developer may use?
- How would you minimally extend your model to apply these alternative approaches?

Exercise 30

CHARITY DONATION

Challenge

Sam operates a small consulting business, which is expected to bring in about $180,000 in revenue. He has estimated the firm's total costs to be $108,500. Sam had earlier agreed with his wife to donate 10% of the firm's after-tax profit to charity. The corporate tax rate applicable to his firm should be about 25%. How much money would they be giving away?

Concept

Remember the following:

- Profit-before-tax can deduct Charity as a cost.
- Charity is to be a proportion of Profit-after-tax.

Isn't this a circular argument? How do we resolve this?

Though this challenge comes with a clear set of numerical inputs, it can equally apply to any other set of inputs. This should be the case since spreadsheet models are for *What-if* analysis. Moreover, there are many other problems with the same structure, such as the project financing and loan repayment schemes of some banks.

First, build the model without the charity donation component. Then include a fixed charity donation amount. You can keep changing the donation amount and through trial and error determine the amount that will give the required percentage relative to the after-tax profit.

Working

To make the computation more automatic, replace the charity donation amount with a formula, setting it to be a percentage of after-tax profit. This would result in a circular computation error. Check out what your spreadsheet online help has to say about resolving this kind of error and take the necessary corrective action.

To make the model more complete and useful for Sam, you should also extend it to answer this question: "What percentage of the before-tax-profit is given to charity?"

Now test if the model is always correct by varying the values of revenue and cost, and donation and tax rates.

- What happens if the company does not make any profit?
- What should logically be the correct outcome? Does your model still give the correct answer for this case?

SOTHIN AND SONS

Exercise 31

Challenge

The value of a firm can be inferred from its financial statement, by determining the net present value of all its future *Free Cash Flow*. Let us do this for Sothin and Sons.

Concept

The cash flow of a firm is the stream of cash that will be generated by the firm from its revenue less all the necessary cost, interest, and tax expenses. Cash flows, together with the income statement and balance sheet, provide information on a firm's liquidity and solvency. Improper management of cash flows is often the cause of the collapse of a company, more so than any other factor. The net present value of a firm's cash flow, a measure of the firm's overall money-making ability, can also be used to value the firm.

However, there are some complications in using the cash flow as it is conventionally noted. First, not all costs of the firm are expended directly. Many purchases are usually capitalized and then depreciated over time. This means that payments as recorded (not the same as what actually transpires) for purchases are divided into smaller portions and they are expensed annually over the specified depreciation period. Second, interest payments are a result of financing decisions made and so interest payments (less the tax deductible portion) and financing liabilities again confuse the cash flow.

Therefore, the so-called cash flow recorded in the accounting books, meant to satisfy accounting professional convention and tax authorities' requirements, does not correspond to reality. A new term, the *free cash flow* (FCF), has been introduced to help us understand the unadulterated movement of cash for the firm. Free cash flow is computed as follows: Start with the profit after-tax, add back depreciation, after-tax interest, and any non-cash decrease in net working capital.

Working

Using the standard financial statement pro forma, obtain or estimate the current values of the firm's line items. Project these values forward into the planning horizon (usually less than six years), by using estimated sales growth rates, tax rates, and ratios of the various line items relative to sales. From the computations, determine the after-tax profit for each of the years.

Set up another table with years as the row header and after-tax profit as the first data row below the header. Add other items below it that are needed to translate the after-tax profit into the free cash quantity for each of the years. This row of values would be the free cash flow. If the free cash flow is expected to be sustained into the future, then the sum of all future values beyond the planning horizon should be computed as the terminal value of the firm's free cash flow. One formula to estimate the terminal value is:

$$FCF_{last} * (1 + salesGrowthRate)/(WACC - salesGrowthRate) \text{ if } WACC > salesGrowthRate$$

$$\sum_{t=1}^{\infty} FCF_{last} * (1 + salesGrowthRate)^t/(1 + WACC)^t \text{ if otherwise.}$$

This value is then discounted into the current year, and summed with the other discounted free cash flow values to give the estimated value of the firm. How would you estimate the terminal FCF value for this firm?

A proper discounting rate (usually called *WACC*, the weighted average cost of capital), one relevant to the firm's level of investment risk, is used to compute the net present value of the free cash flow. The *WACC* is the weighted average of the *cost of equity* and the *cost of debt*. The weight factor for the *cost of equity* is the relative proportion of *equity* (E) to *debt* (D), that is $E/(E + D)$.

The complement applies to the cost of debt. *Cost of equity* is the return rate expected from owning the firm's stock, which can be computed from the firm's β; the *cost of debt* is the interest rate of the financing instrument multiplied by (1 – *Corporate tax rate*). The last term is to subtract any deductible interest from corporate income tax.

Usual net present value computations assume cash flows occur at the end of each period. It is however more logical to assume that they happen smoothly during each period. One way of approximating this is to assume the cash flows occur in the middle of the time period. The correction for this would be subtracting 0.5 from the powers in the discounting formulas.

From the results, examine how the firm's value may be increased or decreased by our actions to alter projected values in the pro forma model.

- Which factors would the firm's value be more sensitive to?
- How would the firm's value change with WACC?

BLACK–SCHOLES   Exercise 32

Challenge

The holder of a *call* option has acquired the right to buy an asset in the specified future at a pre-agreed exercise price. The holder of a *put* option has acquired the right to sell an asset in the specified future at a pre-agreed exercise price. You can buy or sell a call option and buy or sell a put option.

As derived by the two famous professors Fischer Black and Myron Scholes, the prices of these options can be computed as follows:

$$\text{Call Option} = S \times N\,(d_1) - X \cdot \exp(-r_f\,t\,) \times N\,(d_2)$$
$$\text{Put Option} = -S \times N\,(-d_1) + X \cdot \exp(-r_f\,t\,) \times N\,(-d_2)$$

where
S = Share price
X = Exercise price

$N\,(\ )$ is the cumulative standard *Normal* distribution
$\exp(\ )$ is the exponential function
r_f = Risk-free return rate

$d_1 = [\mathrm{Ln}\,(S\,/X\,) + (r_f + \sigma^2/2)\,t\,]/[\sigma\,\sqrt{t}\,]$
$d_2 = [\mathrm{Ln}\,(S\,/X\,) + (r_f - \sigma^2/2)\,t\,]/[\sigma\,\sqrt{t}\,]$
σ = Stock return volatility per year
t = Time to maturity (exercise date).

The formulas assume that share price changes in accordance to the *Lognormal* distribution as follows:

$$S(t) = S \times \exp[(r_f - \sigma^2/2)t + \omega \times \sigma \sqrt{t}]$$

where
ω = *Standard Brownian Motion* random variable value.

Concept

The formulas are already given, although they are rather hard to understand and difficult to enter into a spreadsheet, particularly without making errors along the way. This exercise explores how one would go about entering such formulas and learning the mathematical functions available in spreadsheets. It also highlights issues such as the following:

- How do you know that you have entered the formulas correctly?
- If the formulas themselves indeed represent reality, can the results of the Black–Scholes formulas be worked out in other ways, just as the financial functions can be replaced by simple spreadsheet calculations?
- What is the difference between having a right and having an obligation?

Working

Do not attempt to key in complex formulas all in one go, but rather break down the formulas into shorter subformulas, such as the formulas for d_1 and d_2. For each of these simpler formulas, key in small portions of them and hit **Enter** regularly to check that the answer generated thus far is correct. Of course, it is not possible to see if the formulas, as they are entered, are still correct each step of the way when there are no values in the referred input cells. So do try to fill the input cells with values first. It would be a good idea to have a trustworthy numerical example at hand and enter the input values of that example so that you can compare your result against the one given there.

As you construct the formulas, watch that you do not enter any numerical value directly into them. But rather keep all values in separate cells and have the formulas refer to them. There are however exceptions to that rule. What are the exceptions you can think of?

Try to extend your completed model to make it convenient for the user to change the input values.

- How would you present the option prices for various input values so that the user can see more of them at the same time?
- What kind of charts can you construct that allow the user to better understand how option prices would change with relative changes in the other variables?

• Can your worksheet be posted as a webpage? Is this webpage worksheet interactive?

Try out different values of the exercise price and determine what the buyer and seller of the various options would do.

BINOMIAL OPTION

Exercise 33

Challenge

Consider two fundamental assets: a stock and a bond. The price of the stock, currently at S, can go up or down in the next time period. The *call* option on the stock is the right to buy the stock at the specified exercise price X and the *put* option on the stock is the right to sell the stock at the specified exercise price, at the next time period. The formulas for the price of the one period *call* and *put* options are as follows:

Put option price = q_u Max$[S (1 + u) - X, 0] + q_d$ Max$[S (1 + d) - X, 0]$
Call option price = q_u Max$[X - S (1 + u), 0] + q_d$ Max$[X - S (1 + d), 0]$

where state prices

$q_u = (i - d)/[(1 + i) (u - d)]$
$q_d = (u - i)/[(1 + i) (u - d)]$

and i, u, and d are the one-period change rates for bond and stock price increase, and stock price decrease rates, respectively.

This is a very simple model which is quite easy to construct. Second only to the *Black–Scholes* model in its popularity as an option model, this model can be adapted to represent more complex option pricing problems. It can, for example, be extended to cover many periods, making it one of the most powerful ways for valuing securities.

Concept

To price the *call* option, using pricing by arbitrage, we find the combination of stock purchase and bond borrowing that will give the same return payoffs as the option. Let A be the proportion of the stock to buy and B the amount of bond to borrow. Then

(1) *Call* option price = $A * S - B$
(2) $S (1 + u) A + (1 + i) B = $ max$[S (1 + u) - X, 0] \equiv R_u$
(3) $S (1 + d) A + (1 + i) B = $ max$[S (1 + d) - X, 0] \equiv R_d$

Subtracting (3) from (2) gives

(4) $A = [R_u - R_d] / [S (u - d)]$.

Substituting (4) in (2) gives

(5) $B = [- (1 + d) R_u + (1 + u) R_d] / [(1 + i) (u - d)]$.

Working Construct binomial trees to show the transitions in the stock price with each period, according to the given increase and decrease rates. Bond value can only increase with each period at the bond return rate. Then, construct another set of trees to determine the net returns taking into account the exercise price. Compute also the state prices. Apply the state prices to the net returns to give the option prices. If there is another period, then the logic can continue to apply, taking the values to the next stage, working backwards and applying the state prices to the returns again.

Try to work out a way to compute beyond two periods. It is best not to have to use the trees as it will get too complicated with more periods.

Exercise 34 **FOREIGN INVESTMENT**

Challenge PXXE Corporation has decided to bid for a large build, operate, and transfer (BOT) infrastructure project in India. The financial management of the project will straddle a few currency denominations over a very long time period.

They cover the costs (denominated in USD) of construction, equipment purchases, labor, etc.; revenue (mostly in INR, the local currency); and profit repatriation to the headquarters (in SGD, the base currency of PXXE Corporation).

There will be a large outlay of about USD500 million net present value (NA) in the initial few years and a projected revenue of INR28,000 million NPV over the whole project duration of 10 years, after which the completed fully operational facilities are to be handed over to the municipal authorities.

PXXE may bid to be the operator of the facility after that, but that would be a decision they can make in 10 years' time. The main concern to PXXE right now, before bidding on the project, is how to protect itself in this project against fluctuation in the exchange rates.

Concept Currency risk can be mitigated by converting at the onset the investment amount from the base currency to the required currency. This way, any adverse change in the exchange rate between the base currency and the required currency will not affect the profitability of the project. However, if the exchange rate turns out to be favorable, the opportunistic gain is forgone. This is still a good strategy as investment in foreign currencies should be treated as a separate investment exercise and not be allowed to intermingle and affect the objective assessment of an investment prospect being evaluated.

Alternatively, a more flexible approach is to buy a call option on the required currency to contain the currency risk. The price of the option can be estimated based on your projection of the currency exchange rate volatility. If the offered option price is lower than what you have estimated based on your projection of the parameters, then it would be a cost-effective risk management measure.

Apply the approach used for computing the option price in the *Black–Scholes* exercise to get the price of the foreign currency option. Work through to understand what the option price means in this case and how it is exercised. How would having or not having the option affect the profitability of the project?

Working

GAME SCORING

Exercise 35

Challenge

Every game has its own unique culture, vocabulary, and scoring method. Some can be really difficult for the uninitiated to understand. Interesting games in this respect include golf, bowling, and tennis. In golf, for example, players are to complete 18 holes, using the least number of strokes to put the ball in the holes. Each hole is rated *Par 3*, *Par 4*, or *Par 5*. The points obtained by a player depend on the par of the hole and the number of strokes used. Interesting terms used by the golfing community include *handicap*, *bogey*, *birdie*, and *eagle*. By the way, golf was supposedly invented by shepherds, who hit the hardened sheep droppings as they moved along with their flock on the pasture. If you are a sports enthusiast, you may want to help the rest of us who are less sporty learn the finer points and share some spicy stories of your favorite sport.

Concept

Just as there are rules in games, there are also rules in business. The rules usually appear simple and may even be computed easily by hand. However, the complexities begin to surface when you try to explain the rules to others or get them into an automated computer system. It would be good to first learn how to capture sport and game rules in spreadsheets. This involves both spreadsheet skills as well as communication skills, particularly when you progress to more intriguing games of which you have no prior knowledge.

Working

First, know how the direct game scoring is done (e.g., number of strokes in golf or pin falls in bowling) and then understand how these scores convert into points. Take care of the simple, straightforward cases before you try to understand the exceptions and more complex ones.

Work through the following questions:

- What game did you model? Why do you think it is interesting to attempt modeling that game?
- How did you test your model to confirm that the scoring is correct?
- Which aspects did you find to be more difficult than initially thought? Why are they difficult?
- What appears to be simple for the human scorer to do but is hard to automate in a computer? Why?

Exercise 36   **SAILING**

Challenge

Sailing must be one of the oldest and most intriguing pursuits in life. Though classified as a physical sport, tremendous intellectual challenges are involved. These include the tasks in specifying the vessel design, and during execution, the effective employment of sailing strategies and tactics in response to the wind, current, and actions taken by other competing boats.

An attempt is made here to simulate sailing behavior and the basic characteristics of a sailboat. The modeling simplifying assumption made here is that the sail is made of rigid connected segments in two-dimensional space.

Concept

Complex problems may be simplified and divided into smaller subproblems, each represented by a row in the spreadsheet model. The simplification done here is to assume that the sail is two dimensional, taking the top view of the sailboat as a sufficient representation. The subproblem here is a short segment of a sail. The segments relate to each other, in that the ends of adjacent segments must meet. Using basic scientific principles from physics, we can examine how wind forces, whatever directions they may originate from, can be made to propel a sailboat forward.

To further evaluate the model, you may have to take into account the residue slip wind from each segment, to compute its effect on other segments further down its flow path.

Working

Review the *Explain* worksheet to understand the physics involved. If the mathematics is beyond you, accept the formula at face value. Now, understand how small segments can constitute the sail. The length of these segments can be made infinitesimally small with an infinite number of segments. This is of course carrying it to the extreme, which we will not bother doing.

Then, as usual, work out the formulas in a row for the first segment as if it is any segment and then apply the formula across all the other rows. The model is correctly set up if the resultant force is less than 1. The goal is to get the resultant force as close to 1 as possible, no matter which direction the wind is coming from.

> **MODELING TIPS**

Tip 21

Working in the vacuum

Before keying in a formula, ensure that all input cells relevant to your formula have values in them. If you do not yet know some of their values, just put in trial values. Leave a note to yourself, by changing the font color or adding a comment to it, so that you can revisit them later. Without input cell values, the formulas you key in may warn you of errors (#N/A, #DIV/0, etc.) You will soon develop a habit of ignoring them. This is not good. It is better to have values for your formula to work on as you key in, to help you check for true errors. When error messages appear in formula cells, you should not ignore them.

Tip 22

Entered before?

Data Validation is commonly used to restrict the data type or range of values permitted as valid inputs. There are situations where an otherwise valid input is not permitted if its value has been entered before. In this case, you can use the **Custom** option in **Data Validation** to put a formula that returns a TRUE or FALSE. If it is TRUE, then the data entry is permitted. The formula you can apply here uses **COUNTIF** to compare the current entry against all entries in the input column and count the frequency of its occurrence. If the count is more than 1, then it would be a duplicate entry and will be identified as a data validation error. Alternatively, you can use **Conditional Formatting**, using again **COUNTIF** to flag the duplicated inputs. You can use these two operations to check for other matters like missing entries and violation of capacity or budget limits.

Tip 23

Point and drag

When keying in a formula, it is advisable to point to cells rather than typing their cell references by hand. This way, you are surer that the correct cells are referenced. To double-check, put the cursor in the cell and move the mouse cursor to the formula in the formula bar. Cell references there will all be automatically colored and boxes of the corresponding line colors will appear around the referenced cells. With this, you can visually inspect if the formula is using the correct cells. If a cell reference is incorrect, you can change it by using the mouse to drag the color box to the correct location or resize it to cover the correct cell range. Pointing to cells is particularly useful when a formula takes values from other worksheets or even worksheets in other workbooks. This involves cell referencing syntax more complex than you and I care to learn by heart.

Right the first time

It is important to get the model right the first time than to have to go through the cells with a fine-tooth comb to find where you have gone wrong. One thing to remember about power of cell referencing is that all you have to do is get the first row (or sometimes column) of your table right and the whole table will still work when it is copied down (or across). You must master the skill to know when to use relative, absolute, or mixed cell references. This is one of the marvels of "programming" in spreadsheets. The "code template" is in this first set of key cells. As far as possible, avoid designing spreadsheet models where the formulas for other rows (or columns) are not derived from the first row (or column).

Break it up

When entering a long and complicated formula, it is best to break it up. Separate the formula into simpler sub-formulas, with each occupying a cell and the end result in the final cell connecting these cells. If you are a more seasoned spreadsheet modeler, you can enter the formula into one cell, but do it in stages. One way of doing this is to adopt the first approach and then transfer the sub-formulas (by **Copy** and **Paste** in the formula bar) from the other cells, one at a time to the final cell. Each time, check that the value in the final cell has not changed. On completion, the other cells holding the sub-formulas may be deleted. The compromise in this final step is that the formula in the final cell may not be that easy to upkeep.

Model documentation

Identify and document the minimal set of cells in your spreadsheet to make the model easier to read and maintain. These should be the input and key output cells above tables, and the cells in the first row (or column) of tables. The documentation should list in three columns the variable names, cells addresses, and their contents (whether an input or a formula). For each of the cells to be documented, select it and copy its formula from the formula bar, paste that into the relevant cell in the documentation with a blank prefix to display it as a text. Do check that all the cells referenced in the formulas are also included. Otherwise, your reviewer will not know what the formulas documented really mean. If an input cell is validated, mention that in the documentation against the cell as well. Similarly, document the use of DataTable, Goal Seek and Solver operations as well. See examples how they are done in exercises in this book that use them. We have written macros to automate most of the documentation work. You will find them in the *ModelingTools* and *UsefulMacros* workbooks.

FURTHER REFERENCES

- Benninga, 2008. *Financial Modeling, Third edition*, MIT Press.
- Day, 2002. *Mastering Financial Modeling*, FT Prentice Hall.
- Day, 2003. *Mastering Risk Modeling*, FT Prentice Hall.
- Jackson, 2001. *Advance Modeling in Finance*, Wiley.
- Leong, 2014. Spreadsheet Modeling Resources
    - http://isotope.unisim.edu.sg/users/tyleong/SpreadsheetModeling. htm#Finance
    - http://dl.dropboxusercontent.com/u/19228704/SpreadsheetModeling. htm#Finance
- Proctor, 2004. *Building Financial Models with Microsoft Excel: A Guide for Business Professionals*, Wiley.

- Keywords. Relevant topics to search in Google and Wikipedia
    - *Finance and Excel . Free spreadsheet . Time value of money . Option pricing*

PROBLEM SET 4

* Hard problems

Aunty May. Aunty May has taken a loan from the bank to start a new business. She expects a first year revenue of $50,000 and, thereafter, revenue growing at 8% per year. Her non-loan expenses are initially $30,000 per year and this grows at 4% per year. Her loan repayment is $25,000 per year for 5 years.

Qn 4.01

a. Construct a spreadsheet model to examine Aunty May's business financials.
b. Is the business viable within the first 8 years? When does it break even?
c. Do you think the loan amount is sufficient for overcoming cashflow concerns? How do you know?
d. What if the first-year revenue is $45,000, growing at 7%; first-year expense is $25,000, growing at 3%; and loan repayment is $20,000 per year for 5 years?

New startup. The company has $250,000 sales this month and this is expected to grow at a nominal 8% per year. Cost of goods sold (COGS) is currently at 45% of sales. Selling cost is at 20% of sales. Both proportions are expected to remain stable in the next 2 years. General and administrative cost (G&A), which includes technology and product development, is at $89,000. This overhead component should only grow at a slower 2% per year, and need not keep pace with sales.

Qn 4.02

a. Construct a spreadsheet model of the new startup's business financials.
b. When will the company hit their first (positive) profit? When will they break even? Breakeven takes longer since more months of positive profits are needed to cover all the losses made in earlier months.
c. Evaluate test cases with different growth rates and proportion values. In each case, determine its first profit and breakeven months.

Sales section. The section has 8 salespersons. Their base pays vary from $12,000 to $36,000 per annum, according to their seniority, and are given corresponding sales targets. In addition, they get 5% commission of all sales they bring in and an additional 1% point commission for every dollar they sell above their targets. Any salesperson who sells $1 million or more gets an additional bonus of $2,000. The salespersons are ranked according to the percentage they achieve above their targets. Only if the person exceeds target, the first and second top ranked each get an incentive trip to the annual sales convention and a five-day all expenses paid vacation there for four. This year, it is in Hawaii and the incentive package is worth $6,000.

Qn 4.03

a. Construct a spreadsheet model for this. Simulate 8 salesperson's data and compute the individual salesperson's commission, bonus, incentive, and total compensation.

b. For your data, what is the total compensation the company has to give out?
c. What percentage of the compensation is for base pay, commission, bonus, and incentive?
d. Would you recommend any changes in the pay structure? Why?

Qn 4.04

Replacement policy. The company buys their main operating equipment new, and retires and sells them after four years of use. This equipment can be bought for $90,000 each new and costs $15,000 per year to operate. Used equipment can be readily bought and sold in the market. Their prices can be approximated by depreciating the new equipment price at a compounding rate of 22% per year. That is, a one-year-old equipment costs ((1-0.22)× $90,000=) $70,200, a two-year-old equipment costs 0.78 of that at $54,756, and so on. Similarly, operating cost also increases at a compounding rate, with a rate value of 8% per year. They estimate that each replacement effort (in sell and buy as one episode) costs the company $5,000.

a. Construct a spreadsheet model to examine this problem. If the equipment is bought new, what is the best year to sell it?
b. Under what condition would the current policy of buying new and selling after four years be optimum?
c. What if they bought old equipment instead? What are the best years to buy and sell the equipment?

Qn 4.05

Mortgage plans. The bank wants to simplify how information is presented to their potential clients. Their most common product is consumer mortgage loan. Clients typically like to know the size of the monthly payments for their loan amount and duration.

a. Construct a spreadsheet model that presents the required information for any loan amount, duration, and interest rate. Test this for a 10-year loan of $500,000 at 5% interest rate.
b. Make three tables to show, for different combinations of loan rates and durations, what the size of each monthly payment, total payments, and total interests over the loan duration would be. Do this for loan interest rates from 3% to 8% per year and loan durations from 5 to 30 years.

Qn 4.06

New car. You have selected your dream car. Its retail price is $45,000 and down payment is 15% or $6,750. The dealer has four loan packages for you to choose from: Plan A, no price rebate, 2% per year rate; Plan B, $1,500 price rebate, 4% per year rate; Plan C, $3,000 price rebate, 6% per year rate; and Plan D, $4,500 price rebate, 8% per year rate. Loan duration is 4 years and repayments are to be made monthly.

a. Construct a spreadsheet model for the loan packages, showing their monthly payment amounts.

b. Compute also the net present value (NPV) for each package for your discount rate of 5%. Which plan should you take?

c. Recommend for other customers with different discount rates which plan is best for them. How do they relate to the loan rates?

New apartment. Billy and Carmen have been renting an apartment since their marriage four years ago. They have saved $200,000 and are now thinking of buying their own place. Their combined annual income this year is $150,000 and this is expected to grow at 3.5% annually. The return on investment of their savings is 4% per year. Income tax is at 20%. Current expenses is $2,300 per month and rent is $3,500 per month. Both expenses are increasing at an annual inflation rate of 2.5%. The condominium apartment they are eyeing is priced at $750,000. The maximum loan they are permitted to take is 75% of the apartment price. This means that they have barely enough cash to make the down payment. Loan rate is 6% and duration is 20 years. Buying a place would save them rental expenses, but they will have mortgage payment and property tax. Property tax for the apartment is estimated at $2,800 per year. Property value and tax are both expected to increase at the inflation rate. They are allowed to deduct property tax and loan interest payments from their income for income tax calculations. So there should be income tax reduction if they buy the apartment.

Qn 4.07*

a. Construct a spreadsheet model to support Billy and Carmen in the apartment purchase decision.

b. Should they buy the apartment or continue renting?

Investment project. A project proposal came to your office this morning. You are required to evaluate if this is a good investment for the company. The phased investment amounts at the start of project and for years 1 and 2 are $32,000, $37,000, and $50,000 respectively. Revenue would only flow in when operations start from year 3 onwards and it is expected to be $25,000 for year 3, $45,000 for year 4, $63,000 each year for years 5 to 7, and $78,000 each year for years 8 to 9. Operating expenses would be incurred each year from year 3 onwards. For year 3, it comprises $15,000 for raw material, $9,000 for maintenance, and $6,000 for labor. There is an expected 3.5% per year escalation in cost. The project terminates at the end of year 9 with an expected salvage value of $30,000. From preliminary risk analysis, an initial discounting rate of 9.5% is given for this investment project.

Qn 4.08*

a. Construct a spreadsheet model to evaluate the proposal. Provide the net present value for the project and track its cashflow for the whole duration. What is your decision on the project?

b. It is brought to your attention that the costs may escalate differently and the discounting rate may also change, as senior management may rate project risk differently. As a result, you decide to perform a sensitivity analysis of the impact of variations in cost escalation and discounting rates on the net present value of the project. Evaluate for discount rates of 7.5%, 8.0%, ..., 11.5% and cost escalation rates of 2.0%, 2.5%, ..., 5.0%.

Qn 4.09*   **Company acquisition**. An acquisition target is presented to you. This company is in your industry and has a good reputation for service and quality. The projected earnings for the company over the next 4 years are $6 million in year 1, $8 million in year 2, $10 million in year 3, and $11 million in year 4. You plan to sell the company for $45 million in year 5. Your corporate hurdle rate for acquiring this kind of company is 15%.

a. Construct a spreadsheet model to work on this acquisition. First, estimate the fair price to pay for this company.

b. The owner of the acquisition target saw your price and counters with a higher price of $55 million. He is however willing to be paid in four equal, interest-free amounts in years 1, 2, 3, and 4. Is this a good offer? What is the equivalent fair price given the payment schedule?

c. Your team further evaluated the project and revised the projected earnings of the target company to $6 million in year 1, $8 million in year 2, $10 million in year 3, $9 million in year 4, and selling price of $38 million in year 5. Is it still worthwhile to buy this company?

Qn 4.10*   **Project portfolio**. You are given 10 projects to consider. The funds in million dollars available to you to allocate over the next three years are year 1, 50; year 2, 55; and year 3, 65. The expenditure in million dollars for year 1, year 2, and year 3, and return net present value (NPV) for the projects are A, 6, 8, 8, 9.4; B, 6, 6, 8, 2.8; C, 9, 8, 10, 3.8; D, 7, 6, 7, 6.6; E, 9, 9, 7, 5.2; F, 9, 12, 15, 11; G, 5, 7, 7, 2.2; H, 6, 5, 6, 6; I, 7, 11, 15, 5.4; and J, 6, 5, 3, 3.8.

a. Construct a spreadsheet model for the project portfolio to determine which of the projects to approve. Ensure that the fund for each year is not exceeded. Compute for the three years the total funds used and amount still available.

b. Explain how you got the optimal project selection. What is the total NPV of the portfolio of selected projects?

5 Making Assumptions

LEARNING OUTCOMES

- Able to apply modeling to broader economic concerns
- Able to construct models for cases with more complex, realistic assumptions
- Able to discuss about problems with competitive or gaming responses

INTRODUCTION

In building any model, you make assumptions. Sometimes, assumptions are posed to you explicitly. Many times, however, they are implicitly suggested or not given. Knowing what to include requires intuition and a strong sense of discovery. You do this by interacting with the actual application environment, reading through business records and files, and finally interviewing key stakeholders. You need to determine what is important, available, or can be approximated.

Do not forget that there is a wealth of information in academic textbooks. If you know which industry or field of study the problem belongs to, you can refer to the relevant business domain textbook or consult your professors. These are usually more dependable sources of secondary information. The next step would be to search the Internet. There is a lot of information out there, and most of the time much more than you can handle. Another major problem with information on the Internet is that it is hard to tell if the information obtained is factual and truthful.

With the homework done, you can now think through what you found. Remember what you did not find can be as important as what you have found. If you are in a unique situation without precedence, you may want to consider looking for a parallel universe (a situation similar to the one you want to study) or an opposing universe (a situation diametrically opposite to the one you want

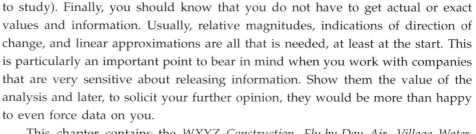

to study). Finally, you should know that you do not have to get actual or exact values and information. Usually, relative magnitudes, indications of direction of change, and linear approximations are all that is needed, at least at the start. This is particularly an important point to bear in mind when you work with companies that are very sensitive about releasing information. Show them the value of the analysis and later, to solicit your further opinion, they would be more than happy to even force data on you.

This chapter contains the *WXYZ Construction*, *Fly-by-Day Air*, *Village Water*, *Extreme Explorers*, *Walk Plans*, *Crazy Auction*, *Market Clearing Price*, and *Buy, Share, and Rent* exercises. They present a variety of different situations which require you to dig deeper to find out how their environments operate, what matters to the stakeholders, and how each stakeholder extracts maximum mileage out of the situation. *Make A Deal* and *Google Adwords* are given as games that you can play. You can learn how to build these games later after you have gone through Chapter 6. For Chapter 5, you will be asked to create new workbooks that help you play the games better, supporting your decision-making process to derive better outcomes for you.

The reminder again is to start simple, however incomplete the model may seem to you. Test the model and then extend it. The key idea is to understand the situation and support decision making, not necessarily to reproduce the situation as a spreadsheet model with detailed "photographic" precision.

DISCOVERY POINTS

Point 21

The key to an efficient economy is the market. This is where prices are set. How are they set? In a free market, they are broadly determined by the interaction of supply and demand forces. When the price of an item is low, its demand exceeds supply. Suppliers in their self-interest will want to find additional supply to sell, or increase the price to turn away customers less able to pay, or both. Price increase could be driven by greed to extract more value for the goods and it could also be justified by the fact that additional supply must come from more costly sources. In modeling, demand and supply to price behaviors may be approximated by linear or piecewise-linear "curves."

Market and auction

A market is usually bi-directional with many sellers and many buyers. There are other situations where one or a few people try to sell to many buyers, and correspondingly still other cases where one or a few people try to buy from many possible sellers. This can be done in auctions, as a different form of market. The many buyers make bids for the item offered for sale or to be purchased, one at a time. All transactions complete with willing buyers and willing sellers.

Auctions can be open or close, English or Dutch. An open auction is where participants announce, sometimes literally shout, what price they are willing to buy or sell at. To make it more orderly, biddings can be made incrementally upwards (from a minimum price, in an English auction) or incrementally downwards (from a high price, in a Dutch auction). Bidding ends when there is only one buyer or one seller left.

A close auction (or tender) invites bidders to submit their prices in secret, before a deadline. The auctioneer (or tenderer) then awards to the bidder with the lowest bid price in a buy auction and to the bidder with a highest bid price in a sell auction. There is tremendous pressure in an open auction because the bids are continually revised and everyone in the auction has information of who are bidding and at what prices. In contrast, all seems quiet and peaceful in a close auction. This is of course untrue, since bidders all have to act blindly, not knowing how others would bid and there is only one chance to bid. To coerce bidders not to game against each other and reveal their best prices, the auctioneer can choose to award instead at the second-best bid ("Vickrey") price, and not the successful bidder's bid price.

Point 22

Many modeling challenges are complex because they are inherently so. Complex problems, as explained in earlier discussions in this book, should be broken into simple components and each part individually analyzed. This is to be done with

Complexity and competition

good understanding of the parts, progressively pieced together to form the system, while working towards understanding the whole.

Now, some challenges may be simple but made complex by the existence of opponents or competitors. In the game of golf, the golfer tries to hole the ball in with as few strokes as possible and is scored against how he had been scoring in the past, as indicated by his handicap score. There are in this gentlemen's game no competitors, unlike the game of tennis where a player always tries to outwit his opponent. Both games are simple, but tennis is made complex by the presence of a competing opponent.

In the case of bidding for a project on tender, you as an interested bidder can compute what is the cost of doing the project, add the usual profit margin, and submit that as the bid price. Other competing bidders can be assumed to do the same. This is of course rather naïve as it leaves the success of bidding somewhat to chance and cost advantages of bidders. The smarter bidder has to anticipate how others will bid since only one bid, the lowest usually, will be successful. One can work hard at understanding who the individual competitors are and work out strategies against each one. Another simpler approach is to assume the competitors to be collectively probabilistic in their behavior and work out the distribution of competitive bids. You can then use this as the basis to determine your "best" bid price.

Point 23

Policy, not numbers

The main purpose of modeling complex challenges is about formulating policies and strategies, and not merely getting numbers. Using the example of project bidding, it is not enough to find out what is the best price to bid for a particular project. You should seek to identify all factors that influence the bid price for any project. Ask questions like how would your bid price be affected by the number of potential competitors. What if they are unlikely to bid? How would you know? To take out the guesswork, examine how much work they are doing now. Do they have enough resources, working capital, and people to take on more work?

Policies are more general in that they transcend changes in the environment. In many cases, they need only indicate direction of change rather than quantum of change. Similarly, strategies are more robust than tactics in an ever-changing environment. You should prefer broad directions under which you can apply your processes and adapt them along the way. For example, it is easy to figure out that bidding prices, and thus profit margins, become lower with more competitors participating. A policy could be to bid only when the expected number of bidders is small. A good strategy is to develop new capabilities that distinguish your company and let you take part where others cannot. Another is to find new markets with few players and shift some business volume there. From the tenderer's point of view, a concern is that bidders do not reveal their true lowest possible bid prices. The policy in this case is of course to apply Vickrey second-price mechanism to overcome the problem.

Point 24

Parametric analysis

We discussed earlier in *Point 2* that input numbers on their own are meaningless and they should be understood as values relative to other inputs. You can go further to apply this idea to output variables as well. In modeling to determine the best bid price, the solution sought should not be a bid price value but rather a ratio to other variable values. Specifically, the bid price can be given as expected bid price minus k times bid price standard deviation. A very useful ratio, coefficient of variation (CV), is defined as standard deviation divided by the mean. With this, the bid price becomes expected bid price $\times$ $(1 - k \times CV)$. The best bid price is found at optimal k, which in turn is a function of the number of competitors and probability of each competitor bidding. Alternatively, the bid price can be given as estimated project cost plus k times bid price (standard deviation). This different variable k incorporates the expected profit margin proportion.

The exploration started with finding the best bid price and now continues to find the relationship between best factor k and other input variables. A simple rule of thumb is to reduce the number of input and output dimensional variables, by replacing them with dimensionless variables. This takes the model away from being merely a "numbers-in, numbers-out" computing mechanism to become a tool for us to understand how the variables relate to each other.

EXERCISES

Exercise 37 **WXYZ CONSTRUCTION** **Worked Example**

Challenge

WXYZ Company is bidding on a construction project. A few known competitors are likely to bid as well. There will also be other unlikely firms or consortiums that will try their luck for a piece of the action. For all the bidders, most of the associated cost items for the project are obtainable from the same pool of suppliers and the rates they charge for their products and services are fairly common knowledge to the bidders. To clinch the project, you wonder if it is possible to evaluate how the company's bid should vary with its assessment of the competitive situation.

Concept

In setting its bid price, WXYZ has to consider a trade-off between bidding low which will generate only a small profit but a higher chance of bid success, and bidding higher, which will generate a larger profit but a lower chance of success. The two uncertainties associated with the chance of success are the number of bidders and the distribution of their bid prices. It is possible to present the competing bid prices as if they come from a probability distribution. The challenge would be what distribution function and parameter values to use.

Input variables for the model should be such that they can be easily applied without much modification to other situations. An excellent suggestion is to use ratio variables rather than magnitudes ones. For example, the coefficient of variation (CV) is the ratio of standard deviation to the mean. This value can be expected to be relatively stable in many situations against changes in the mean value. This is a helpful type of variable to use for this exercise.

Based on price considerations only, the successful bidder is always the one with the lowest bid. However, the awarded contract price for a project may not be the lowest bid price. Sometimes, it is given as the second lowest price. This supposedly is to help encourage truthful bidding. Try to see if this would make any difference to WXYZ's bidding strategy.

Working (Detailed)

The expected cost of the project may be any arbitrary value in the model. For convenience of discussion, let us set it as $300,000. The bid preparation cost is set at 1% of the project cost. A proportion parameter is preferred here as changing the project cost would automatically update the bid preparation cost. The number of potential bidders varies and the probability that they will bid can also be an input.

- Can these two variables be combined into a single "expected number of bidders" variable?
- Does this affect the nature of the results?

For each proposed bid price for WXYZ, simulate more than 35 replications. Compute the expected profit by averaging from the replications. From the results, evaluate the following:

- Is the number of replications sufficient? How do you know it is?
- What bid price for the project will maximize WXYZ's expected profit? What is its profit margin percentage?
- How would changes in the number of potential competitors affect the results?
- What if the contracted price is the second lowest bid price?

It is an industry practice in the construction sector to qualify companies by the type and scale of projects they can submit a bid for. Bigger companies with more capital and experience are usually permitted to bid for larger-scale projects, while smaller companies can only bid for the small projects. Thus, when a project is up for tender, the number of potential bidders and the probability of them bidding can be estimated.

a. Select the *Proto* worksheet.
b. The following initial assumptions are made in the model:
- Number of potential competitors (cell C4) is 12.
- Probability of each competitor submitting a bid (cell D4) is 0.9.
- Expected project cost (cell F4) is $300,000.
- Bid preparation cost to expected project cost (cell C7) is 1%.
- Expected profit margin (cell D7) is 25%.
- Coefficient of variation of bid (cell E7) is 0.05.
- Proposed bid price of WXYZ Company (cell H4) is $335,000.
c. Intermediate variables are computed as follows:
- Enter into cell F7 the formula =F4*C7 (i.e., *Bid preparation cost* = 1% of the *Project cost*).
- Enter into cell G7 the formula =F4*(1+D7) (i.e., *Mean bid price = Project cost + Margin*).
- Enter into cell H7 the formula =E7*G7 (i.e., *Standard deviation of bid price = Coefficient of variation * Mean bid price*).
- Enter in cell C10 the formula =C4*D4 (i.e., *Expected bidders = Competitors * Probability of bidding*).
d. To simulate the bids of competitors
- Given the number of competitors and probability of each bidding, the number of actual bidders can be assumed to follow the *Binomial* distribution, with parameter n = number of competitors and p = probability of bidding.

- The number of bidders is simulated using the "Inverse Binomial distribution function" CRITBINOM(trials, probability, *alpha*). Parameter alpha is the cumulative probability criterion value which will be randomly generated using the RAND function.
- Enter into cell D10 the formula =IF(D4=1, C4,CRITBINOM(C4,D4,RAND())) (i.e., actual number of bidders is the number of potential competitors when the probability of bidding is 1 and simulated by the "Inverse Binomial function" approach otherwise.)
- The number of bidders and their simulated bids are tabulated in cells F13:H25.
- Enter into cell G14 the formula =IF(F14<=D$10,"Yes","No")" to determine if it is a bidder.
- Fill the formula in cell G14 into cells G15:G25. If there are more than 12 competitors, you can easily extend the table to accommodate them.
- It is reasonable to assume that the bid price of other bidders follow the *Normal* distribution. With this, we can simulate the other bid prices using the Inverse Normal distribution function NORMINV(probability, mean, standard deviation).
- Enter into cell H14 the formula =IF(G14="Yes",NORMINV(RAND(), G$7,H$7),"").
- Fill the formula in cell H14 into cells H15:H25.
- Key **F9** several times to generate the different simulation results.

e.   To determine the winning bid and profit

The winning bidder is the one with the lowest bid. As prespecified in the project bidding rule, the awarded bid price is either the lowest bid price or the second lowest bid price.

   i.   Lowest bid approach

- Enter into cell E10 the formula =MIN(H14:H25) (i.e., Lowest of other bids = Smallest value in cells H14:H25).
- Enter in cell F10 the formula =IF(H4<E10,H4-F4,-F7) (i.e., if WXYZ's bid is lower than the lowest of other bids, WXYZ wins the tender with a profit of its bid price – project cost; otherwise, WXYZ's loss is its bid preparation cost. The project cost is assumed here to include all costs, including the bid preparation cost).

   ii.   Second lowest bid approach

- Enter into cell G10 the formula =SMALL(H14:H25,2) (i.e., Second lowest of other bids = Second smallest of all the generated bids in cells H14:H25).
- Enter into cell H10 the formula =IF(H4<E10,E10-F4,-F7) (i.e., if WXYZ's bid is lower than the lowest of other bids, WXYZ wins

the tender with a profit that equals the second lowest of all bids – project cost; otherwise, WXYZ's loss is its bid preparation cost). The second lowest of all bids equals the lowest bids of other bidders since WXYZ's bid is lower than the lowest bids of other bidders.

f. To simulate 150 replications

The simulation done thus far is one probabilistic occurrence or one replication for one setting of WXYZ bid price. To obtain the average profit, we must do many replications each, for different proposed WXYZ bid prices.

- Select the *Model* worksheet.
- The replication results are tabulated from columns L to S as a two-dimensional **DataTable**.
- The first variable of the DataTable (in cells L11:L160) is the number of replications. The number of replications should be large.
- The second variable of the DataTable (in cells M10:S10) is the proposed bid prices for WXYZ. Instead of static numbers, we compute the set of proposed WXYZ bid prices as a formula: *Project cost* + k*standard deviation of *Bid price*. By varying the value of k (in cells M9:S9) from 0 to 2.25, we get proposed bid prices that adapt to the other input variable values when they are changed.
- The output formula for the DataTable which resides in the table corner (cell L10) is =IF(L4,H10,G10) (i.e., if the second price check box in cell L4 is checked, the second lowest bid profit in cell H10 is used; otherwise, use the lowest bid profit in cell F10).
- To run the DataTable operation, select cells L10:S160 and select **Data/ What-if Analysis/Data Table**. Enter H4 as **Row Input Cell** and K4 as **Column Input Cell**. Note that the Column Input Cell here can in fact be any empty cell. The DataTable operation will "enter" the replication input value successively from L11:L160 to the empty Column Input Cell and each time causes the random values in the workbook to regenerate and thus generating a new replication each time.
- The average profit is computed in cell M6 for the case where $k = 0$ using the formula =AVERAGE(M11:M160) (i.e., the average of profits in the 150 replications). This formula is filled into cells N6:S6 for all the other k values. The largest of the average profit cells is highlighted using **Conditional Formatting**.
- The probability of winning is computed in cell M7 for the case where $k = 0$ using the formula =COUNTIF(M$11:M$160,">=0")/COUNT(M$11:M$160) (i.e., number of replicates with positive profit divided by the total number

of replications). This formula is filled into cells N7:S7 for all the other k values.

- The recommended bid price is the one giving the largest average profit and the profit margin.

- The maximum average profit is determined in cell R4 using the formula =MAX(M6:S6).

- The bid price that generates this maximum average profit is determined in cell Q4 using the formula =INDEX(M10:S10,MATCH(R4,M6:S6,0)) (i.e., show the bid price in cells M10:S10 that corresponds to the largest of the average profits in cells M6:S6).

- The profit margin is computed in cell S4 using the formula =IF(R4<0,"",R4/F4) (i.e., if the maximum profit is positive, then the margin = *Maximum profit/(Project cost)*.

- Key F9 to recompute the simulation to see different results. Notice that the maximum profit occurs most frequently between $k = 1.50$ and $k = 2.00$. You may want to change the k values to give a finer resolution of k values in this range. The more general result that WXYZ Company can take away from this simulation is the best k value, and not so much the best bid price. This approach can help WXYZ set their best bid price, with a good chance of winning and generating good profit, in all similar future projects.

Exercise 38   FLY-BY-DAY AIR

Challenge

Fly-by-Day Air operates a service route between Indianapolis and Detroit using a fleet of small planes. Tickets for the flight are nonrefundable and priced at $250 each. On average, some percentage of ticket holders would fail to show up for their flight and the airline gets to keep their ticket money. If more than a plane's capacity worth of people shows up for a flight, each customer who does not get a seat receives a refund plus penalty compensation.

Concept

The problem as usual needs to be clarified and defined. You have to ascertain what the pertinent aspects are and what specifically need to be examined. The important point is not to try to get everything and do it all, but simply to determine only the absolutely necessary assumptions to make. Data as in most cases are scanty and those provided may not even be relevant. Therefore, figure out the data that are actually needed and the values that you can first use while effort is organized to collect them. Setting up the table is also an important part of the modeling. It helps to clarify the structure of the problem. Try to organize the issues examined logically, working from the top-left to the bottom-right corner of your worksheet.

Work through with the following questions as a guide:

Working

- What are the data required?
- What does the airline need to determine?
- What is the best way to present the model?

For simplicity, we will assume a constant *no-show* percentage. Checking the airline's records can help you calculate the parameter value. It will take some effort to compute and therefore in the meantime you should first make a guess, making reference if necessary to other published reports on other airlines or similar situations. The parameter value may differ from flight to flight. This, however, does not mean that a flight-specific parameter is needed. Modeling requires some simplifying compromises to be made. Since the flight-specific *no-show* values are *a priori* unknown, it would then be a reasonable assumption to use a constant value in the basic model.

There should be ticket price, cost, and compensation values. Such data may not be obtainable because of their commercial-sensitive nature. However, you do not really need their specific values, only their relative ratios. For each total size of seat booking to accept, you can compute the expected *no-show* numbers and then correspondingly their revenue, cost, and profit. This suggests that the table in the model should comprise rows for the different total booking sizes and columns for no-show, revenue, cost, and profit. Some columns may be omitted if you believe that doing so does not make the model hard to understand.

VILLAGE WATER

Exercise 39

Challenge

The amount of rainfall in any region fluctuates seasonally during the year. In some places, there could be a few consecutive months of dry season without rain. This phenomenon poses tremendous difficulties for many rural communities, which depend on rain, directly or indirectly via rivers and wells, to provide water for drinking, cooking, bathing, washing, and agriculture.

Water supply for a village may be gravity-fed from springs or streams in the watershed hillsides to the village. Alternatively, it may be harvested from roofs, rock surfaces, or other open ground, and from wells, though the quality of water may be poorer. Without water treatment or boiling, water from such sources is the major cause of illnesses and diseases. Sometimes, due to serious shortages, all the collection methods are concurrently employed, with the better quality water conserved for drinking.

To be less subjected to the variability and uncertainty of weather, storage tanks may be constructed. The cost of these tanks, even using local materials and self-help labor to build, can be a financial burden to the villagers given their low income.

Concept

Water supply and demand can vary with time, weather, and other factors not easily characterized. Some of these variations are stochastic risks and others are generally predictable fluctuations. To be dogmatic, both kinds of circumstances need to be handled differently. Also, the cyclical changes for supply span a year while that of demand variations are over the hours of a day. As modeling shorthand, creative approaches should be devised to put all these together without making the model too complicated. In some cases, you may want to ignore the stochasticity completely.

Working

Consider these questions when developing the model:

- What value should be used for the village population? How would you cater for future growth?
- What is the essential difference in the analysis done for the village and individual families?
- What should the minimum size of the water catchment area be? What if the catchment is larger than this?
- Would enlarging the catchment area drastically affect the volume of water going down to feed the water table underground and thereby affect the wells?
- How to consider in combination the village and household storage capacities?
- Which pieces of data are not used? Do you need to extend the model using these?
- What if you account for risks in both supply and demand?
- How is the theoretical model different from the spreadsheet model? When would the theoretical model be more useful?
- What are the follow-up questions and actions?

Exercise 40

EXTREME EXPLORERS

Challenge

An expedition of four men went on foot to explore the great Sahara desert. In that expedition, with no resupply station along the way, each person carried enough food to last the journey to and fro. The team set off together and penetrated the desert as far as they could and then returned as a team.

As the corporate sponsor for Expedition 2, you suggest that not all four persons need to reach the extreme end of the expedition. They could combine resources to enable just one member to penetrate further into the desert, with others carrying the food in support. The team members will thus return one at a time.

Concept

One simplifying assumption that needs to be made is that regardless of the total depth of exploration, the pace is constant. With this, the total distance covered, including the return leg, would be double the distance the team is able to travel on foot into the desert. Food left is the total amount of food available at the start of the expedition less the amount taken by those turning back to the starting point.

Let us also assume that all team members are the same in terms of size and fitness, and carry the same equipment and total weight load. Such assumptions are acceptable in the planning stage of this model. In the actual execution, details concerning the specific tactics and who to carry what can be seen to.

Though these details often make or break the team and the expedition, the key objective in constructing this spreadsheet planning model is to get the main strategic design issues right first, before proceeding to the execution steps.

Working

Determine a suitable table layout that will capture all the required information. The important information to keep track in any day of the expedition would be the number of team members still moving forward, the total load of food available to the team, and the load per person to be carried.

The number of journey days that can still be made depend on the remaining team size and the total load available. The load per person cannot exceed what each person can carry. This should not be a problem if the team members only carry their own food. It becomes important when some of the food is transferred to the forward moving team. The onward explorers cannot carry more than they can bear and the returning members must have enough to last the walk back to the starting point.

Consider these questions when developing the model:

- How much further can the second expedition go?
- What if they take your new line of light food products which permits each man to carry more days of supply?
- What if the team includes more members?
- What if the team can be broken up along the way?
- What if the team includes some female team members? Compared to men, women can carry less food, but they also need less food and possibly have better endurance.

- What should be the best way to sequence the order of return for the team members?
- What other what-ifs can you think of?

WALK PLANS

Challenge

This workbook summarizes the key information that may be used for planning medium to long distance walks on the island of Singapore. The basic approach taken here is to build a schematic map of the island, from which a planner may devise numerous possible walks, depending on the length and desired interests of walk participants. You can adopt the same approach for your neighborhood walks as well.

Concept

The approach is to choose a higher level of abstraction and avoid getting into the details too soon. This makes it easier to see the big picture. There is a need to differentiate between a planning model and an execution model. The common habit is to plunge into operational specifics too quickly. The result is that the work becomes very tedious and no longer simple. You should start on this as a planning model. Later, you can develop it further to help work out more operational details.

The map is built by first identifying the nodes and then adding arcs between them to show feasible links. The first set of nodes represents main locations along the coast. New inland nodes are then added to show the points that must be traversed along paths connecting all possible pairs of coastal nodes.

The inland nodes are therefore governed by access tracks and roads, and major obstacles like restricted zones (such as airports and expressways) and water bodies (e.g., rivers and reservoirs). There is a preference to keep away from urban areas and heavy vehicular traffic, and hence the choice of locations as inland nodes generally covers public parks and major recreational features.

To plan a walk, choose a start node and the distance to be covered. From these, you can determine the end node, from among all the possible ones. Alternatively, you may choose the end node first and then settle on the start node. The specific start and end points may now be fixed from the general location of the start and end nodes. The particular path to walk can now be marked out, or you may just let the participants figure that out as they walk.

Working

Obtain a simple tourist map and superimpose grid lines on it. The grid lines should be to scale, say to mark out spacing of 1 km. Identify the key nodes and read off their (x, y) coordinates. Create a table to keep these coordinates. It may facilitate location of the nodes if the nodes are labeled N, S, E, and W according to the sector in which they reside. Put ready-made shapes from the spreadsheet on each node location and use connectors to link node pairs if there are possible routes between the nodes.

The distance between nodes is determined using the L_p norm: $d(i, j) = Const \times [|x_i - x_j|^p + |y_i - y_j|^p]^{1/p}$. The value of parameter p, usually ranging between 1 and 2, depends on the general topology of the road-path network. For a well-defined rectilinear network, $p = 1$ and in open country, $p = 2$. The factor $Const$ is for minor scaling correction.

The actual distance may be longer or shorter since the specific route may deviate from the overall general topology. That is, it is sometimes possible to move in a straight line and other times the route is more circuitous to follow the actual road network, or avoid large obstacles and restricted areas.

Organize other tables to list medium two-node routes and longer multi-node routes. Work out yet another table to keep the walk plans and contrast them against the actual walks taken.

CRAZY AUCTION

Exercise 42

Challenge

In a Tatarah™ auction, bidders pay $2 for each chance to bid for an auction item. The lowest unique bid is the successful bid. High bids will lose to low bids if the low bids are unique. Bidding lower increases the chances that your bid is the same as other bids, making it not unique. How would you bid?

Concept

Your bid value, assuming you want to get the item, should depend on how others bid. Conversely, others will be like you trying to outsmart the rest of the bidders. You will have to make assumptions about how the bids would be distributed and provide some estimation of values for the parameters of the distribution. The number of bidders other than yourself should matter. How should your bid value change in response to the estimated number of people bidding for the item?

Working

The first step would be to simulate the bid prices for an arbitrary number of bidders. You would then need to find the lowest unique bid price. This will require some effort. You would have made quite a few assumptions thus far and you eventually will have to justify them. The point about modeling right now is to develop a simple model as a first attempt. Vary the model with different input values and even the bid price distribution functional form.

- What conclusions can you draw from the bidder's point of view?
- Does it really make business sense for Tatarah?

- Given the estimated value of the auction item and the processing fee, can you deduce how many bidders Tatarah is expecting to bid for the item? This would be valuable information to help you improve your model.
- What other inferences can you draw?

There have been some recent changes in the way the auction is offered by Tatarah. Here are some further questions for consideration:

- What if the winner of the auction is now the highest unique bid?
- How does this change your model and analysis?
- Are there other ways to specify the auction winner? How do they make the auction more interesting and beneficial to bidders or more profitable to Tatarah?

Exercise 43

MARKET CLEARING PRICE

Challenge

In any market, there are buyers and sellers. Buyers specify the quantity and price of the traded item of interest at which they are willing to buy, and sellers do the same for what they are willing to sell. The function of the market is to determine a single price, known as the market clearing price, under which the bid and offer quantities match. This price should of course make successful buyers pay no more than what they bid for and successful sellers get no less than what they offer to sell.

It is possible that there is no single clearing price that satisfies these conditions. In some situations, no price exists at which the bid and offer quantities match, while in others the quantities match at more than one price. What additional specifications and changes would you suggest for the market clearing price to work?

Concept

This is the classic demand-meets-supply scenario in modern economic theory. Unlike pure theory, the reality is that supply and demand curves are not that smooth and therefore may not meet precisely to give a definite clearing price. The market maker would typically want to maximize the trading volume, here defined as clearing quantity multiplied by clearing price. When bid and offer quantities do not match, the smaller of the two applies. This means that some bid or offer orders can only be partially satisfied. A practical response defines the clearing price to be the average of bid and offer prices at which bid and offer quantities are closest to each other.

Working

First, reorganize the data in another table to allow the demand and supply curves of the market to be plotted. This would require the bid prices to be sorted in descending order and the offer prices to be sorted in ascending order. The values are then plotted against their cumulative order quantities. Do not use **Data Sort** to do the sorting as it, being not interactive, cannot respond to any changes in the data.

- What method would you use to sort the orders?
- How do you break the tie when prices are the same? Is your correction model to address this still interactive?

Devise and try different approaches for setting the clearing price. The simple guide is that it should be near the point where the supply and demand curves cross each other.

BUY, SHARE, AND RENT

Exercise 44

Challenge

Information goods such as books, journals, computer software, and audio-video media are often copied, shared, resold, or rented out by the buyer. There are various legal and illegal ways of doing this. The entities conducting this legitimately include libraries, video rentals, and used-book stores. Site licensing and application service provisioning are other schemes for managing the sharing of information goods.

When sharing is possible, content producers usually target to sell a smaller number of the goods at a higher price, believing this would bring in the most profit. Is this always the correct approach?

Concept

The firm's interests may not be aligned with the society's interests. The firm can realign itself with the society's interests by employing more innovative ways. The key is to take the difference between the society's value under the best scenario and its value under a prevailing scenario, and find a way to share the difference fairly among the stakeholders. For example, in this case, content producers can sell cheaply to rental stores, but recoup some additional returns by taking a cut of the rental stores' revenue. When properly executed, this may be what is best for consumers, rental stores, and producers.

Two models are proposed here for evaluation, though possibly many other models may be made. One model assumes that the firm can decide whether to sell the product to individual consumers or to organizations to rent out to their members. The second model assumes that buying, renting, and sharing (via illegal copying) can occur all at the same time. Examine the various scenarios to better understand when such a pricing policy may be advisable.

Working

This exercise is to be done in a very deliberate manner using the *Scratch* worksheet. It is not easy to form a model from the basic information given in Professor Varian's paper (which is referenced in the workbook). Try to identify all the variables and systematically form the *Influence* diagram. Follow through with a *Black-box* diagram and then start building the basic model's main tables. Adjust the basic model to evaluate the alternatives:

- What are the variables?
- What data are required? How can you find them?
- What are the different perspectives and possible objectives of the situation?
- What new management insights can you discover from your model?

  There are many media file-sharing platforms (e.g., *Napster*, *Kazoo*, and *BitTorrent*). Now, consider the following questions:

- How do they relate to the concepts examined in this exercise?
- Do they provide other perspectives that have not been covered in this exercise?
- How would you extend the model in this exercise or build a different spreadsheet model to evaluate them?

Exercise 45

Challenge

MAKE A DEAL

This game is based on a television series by Endemol, a Netherlands-based entertainment company. The player in each game is shown 26 briefcases, each containing cash prizes varying from $1 to $250,000.

The game starts with the player picking one briefcase. This briefcase remains sealed until the end of the game. The player must open the remaining 25 briefcases one at a time. At preselected intervals, the banker makes an offer price for the player's briefcase.

The player can either accept the deal or otherwise play on. With each briefcase opened, the odds of getting the higher value prizes fluctuate. The banker's offers may change quite unexpectedly too. Unless the player accepts a banker's offer, the game ends only when all the briefcases are opened. In this case, the player has to accept whatever his chosen briefcase contains.

What would you do if as a player an offer is made to you by the banker? Will you accept the deal?

Concept

This is a game of odds and getting the best outcome for the player depends on his luck and his ability to read the odds presented to him. This takes some understanding of the subject of probability. You can do so here by playing the game. At any point in time, with a number of briefcases opened, the probability distribution of the outcome is different from what it was before. Every time a briefcase with a large prize is opened, the expected value of the remaining unopened briefcases drops. You need to understand the relationship between the data before you and the choice you have to make when the offer is made to you by the banker.

You can develop a spreadsheet model to compute the relative value of staying in the game or accepting the banker's offer. It would be interesting also to second guess how much the banker would offer you. This way, you will get to understand some of the intricacies of the game and possibly glimpse what makes the game interesting.

Working

Play the game a few times to understand the basic operation and rules of the game. Think of strategies that will help you to win higher returns. Your project would be to construct a spreadsheet model that can be used to support the player in decision making. You can also try to understand the behavior of the banker.

- Taking into consideration the prizes that have not yet been revealed, how much will he offer to the player?
- How many more briefcases does the banker want the player to open next? What is this dependent upon?
- What other considerations and options can you think of?

In building your spreadsheet model, you always have to think of the following:

- What are the data and variables? What intermediate results should be given to the player?
- What is the best way to present your model?
- How do you know that your solution is the best or at least better than most?

FAST SODUKU

Exercise 46

Challenge

In this fascinating puzzle game, a 9 by 9 grid is given as partially filled with whole numbers taken from 1 to 9. The player is to fill remaining empty cells such that all numbers from 1 to 9 are present in each row, column, and (designated mutually exclusive) 3 by 3 subgrid. Equivalently, this means that no number is repeated in each row, column, and 3 by 3 subgrid.

What is your "algorithm" for completing the puzzle? What information could you extract from the partially filled grid to assist you? How would you produce your own Soduku puzzles?

Concept

Solving any puzzle requires a thorough understanding of its basic rules. This applies equally to business scenarios. The game structure here, being a puzzle, is relatively simple and transparent, unlike actual work situations. Instead of using paper and pencil, we can work on the puzzle in a spreadsheet. Using a spreadsheet to present this game allows more information to be displayed to assist the game player to faster determine the number to fill each cell or cells to fill any chosen number.

Making the Sodoku puzzle is as challenging if not more so than solving one. The puzzle cannot be formed by randomly filling the cells with numbers. Firstly, the numbers in each row have to be unique integers taken from 1 to 9. This means that in the attempt to create the puzzle you will have to sample without replacement from the set 1, 2, ..., 9. Secondly, the numbers also cannot repeat in each column, so doing each row independently of another is not correct. Thirdly, the numbers also cannot repeat in each subgrid. You will have to mask off the cells that you do not want the player to see before releasing the puzzle. The choice of the number and which cells you want the player to see at the onset can affect the level of difficulty of the puzzle.

Working

The generation of random numbers is discussed in the next chapter. In particular, review the *Lucky Draw* tool, which deals with random ordering and sampling without replacement.

Exercise 47

GOOGLE ADWORDS

Challenge

Your firm has been using Google™ as a platform to advertise your company's services on the Internet. Though some time had passed since this channel of distribution was introduced by your agency, you have not ascertained clearly how much additional business it had brought in and how best to use the channel to bring in even more business, or at least lower the cost of doing so. You wonder if you really understand *pay-per-click* (PPC) advertising and start to gather information to do some analysis and to create a good *Bid Manager* model. (Refer to the references given in the exercise workbook to learn more about PPC advertising.)

Concept

You will learn in this exercise more of what modeling is about. You need to ask the right questions and know what elements need to be captured in the model, while keeping it as simple as possible.

Any data that can be collected to show the relationships between bid price and rank position, click-through rate and rank position, conversion rate and rank position can be used to your advantage. You should use them to characterize the relationships, to get their functional forms and parameter values if possible. Even when such data are not available, you can make reasonable assumptions of how the variables should interact. Then, evaluate if the results are sensitive to the functional forms or parameter values.

You can use the developed model to evaluate the different approaches used by providers of the service and also the possible bidding strategies of advertisers.

Working

Introducing this exercise as a game makes it easier for us to appreciate the PPC advertising concept. This game can be played by a person against computer players or by real players pitted against each other. Your project is to do a spreadsheet *Bid Manager* model to support decision making in *Adword* bidding. Bidding is interesting and complex here because the per-click price is given by the price of the highest bid that is lower than your bid. If none is lower, the minimum price set by Google for the word applies.

An example of a learning point resulting from playing the game would be that it may not be a good idea to be first in rank position as it costs more and tends to have lower sales conversion rates. As such, you need to determine the best rank to target. In addition, in real life rank position is determined not only by your bid price relative to other bid prices; it is also affected by the number of bidders and their daily available bidding budgets. Some *pay-per-click* service providers may even adjust rank position on other criteria such as the number of clicks the *ad* is getting. With a limited budget, higher cost per click and a larger number of nonconvertible clicks, an *ad* may not appear all the time. This allows others to move up the ranks without necessarily paying more.

Here is another situation for consideration. If there is a close competitor who also advertises with the same key word in Google *Adwords*, you can be more cost-effective by bidding one cent less than them. The result is that your *ad* will rank only one position below them, possibly with slightly fewer clicks and marginally lower conversion rates. You have, however, forced him to pay your bid price which is almost equal to his while you only have to pay the price of the next in rank bid which generally is a lot less. You need to monitor the bids very carefully though, as your competitor and others can do the same to you.

Often, advertisers use more than one key word for each product. These key words may even be shared among many products. However, such an arrangement may cause the products to cannibalize each other's demand.

- How then can a model be developed to avoid or encompass this consideration?
- What about other issues? Can you list some and suggest how they may be incorporated into your *Bid Manager*?

Remember to start your *Bid Manager* model small and simple. Use the insights drawn from playing the game with others to test and enrich it.

Tip 27

Keep it simple

As a general rule, all models are wrong, but some models are useful. Therefore, do not expect your model to be perfect from the start or even in the end. Make some naïve assumptions and build a simple model first. Use very basic formulas to relate the variables. As a start, test it with simple cases. Do not worry about exceptions and difficult cases yet. After you get the base model to work, slowly add more realistic conditions to it. You should develop a good sense of knowing when to stop further extensions, as this can be an endless task. Sometimes, it may even be needful to make further simplifying assumptions that deviate from the problem specifications somewhat to make the model easier to understand or solvable. One guiding principle is that simplifications should make the model more conservative so as not to subject the client to undue risks.

Tip 28

Verify and validate

To verify a model is to test that all the formulas you wanted have been correctly entered and that their output values are the ones expected as you vary the input values. This only says that you have not erred with respect to constructing the model with the formulas you have devised. It does not mean that your model is right because your formulas may not accurately represent the problem in the first place. Validating a model, on the other hand, is to see if the model really solves the real problem as you have intended, giving you results that are appropriate for actual use. You compare the outcome of your model against what actually happens in the real world. Do check that you have entered the correct input values first, which must be the same as the actual situation being compared. This validation step is not the same as your spreadsheet's **Data Validation** or **Validity** feature, which only checks that input values satisfy conditions you specify for them. In short, model validation compares outputs with reality whereas data validation compares inputs against stated data conditions.

Tip 29

Test cases

Models should of course work for the sample data that you build them on. How do you know for sure that your model will work in general? It is therefore very important to test your spreadsheet model over a wide range of values for all the input variables. These so-called test cases are to ensure that the model works for all typical, extreme, and critical input values of each variable. They should cover values that straddle all the decision branching in your logical formulas. For example, if a formula in the model states that sales commission rate is to increase when the sales amount is over $10,000, then your test cases must include sales amounts that are slightly less than, slightly more than, and equal to $10,000. When the number of variables and possible values become too large, you may have to use Monte-Carlo simulation to automatically generate the values to probabilistically test it. Monte-Carlo simulation is explored in Chapter 6.

Back-testing | **Tip 30**

One way of validating your model to support decisions regarding the future is to apply your model to the past as if it had not happened yet. The process works like this. First, take a small subset of old data to develop your model and establish its parameter values. Then use your model to support decisions that are later in time than the data used in building the model. Since the "future" in this case is in the past, you can compare the performance of your model against actual outcome. Repeat this process moving slowly forward in time. Each time, you are only allowed to use data earlier in time than the decision point that you are trying to support. When there is no more data left, the model would have to contend with the real unknown future and we wait for the verdict. But since you have done the back-testing, as this process is called, you should be reasonably confident about how well or not your model should do thereafter. Anyway, you should not be overly concerned about whether your forecast is correct, as it will never be. Rather, seek to minimize the size of the error between your forecast and the actual result.

FURTHER REFERENCES

- Allen, Bennett, Carrillo, Goeller and Walker, 1992. "Quality in Policy Modeling," *Interfaces* 22(4): 70–85.
- Caulkins, 2001. "When Parametric Sensitivity Analysis Isn't Enough," *INFORMS Transactions on Education* 1(3).
  - http://archive.ite.journal.informs.org/Vol1No3/Caulkins/Caulkins.pdf
- De Haan, 2012. "Why Do Competitors Open Their Stores Next to One Another?" TED.
  - http://www.youtube.com/watch?v=jILgxeNBK_8
- Leong, 2014. Spreadsheet Modeling Resources
  - http://isotope.unisim.edu.sg/users/tyleong/SpreadsheetModeling. htm#Business
  - http://dl.dropboxusercontent.com/u/19228704/SpreadsheetModeling. htm#Business
- Lilien and Rangaswam, 1998. *Marketing Engineering*, Addison-Wesley.

- Varian, 2009. "Introduction to the Google Ad Auction," *Google*.
  - https://www.youtube.com/watch?v=a8qQXLby4PY
- Varian, 2000. "Buying, Sharing and Renting Information Goods," *Journal of Industrial Economics* 48(4): 473-488.

- Keywords. Relevant topics to search in Google and Wikipedia
  - *Auction market . Vickrey auction . Construction project bidding . Coefficient of Variation . Franchising . Pricing strategy . Information goods . Google adword . Online advertising . Marketing and spreadsheets*

PROBLEM SET 5

* Hard problems

New bus stops. A small community of 32 square km is planning to review its public transport infrastructure. Among the issues to evaluate are bus stops. Without resorting to actual counting, the project chief wants to know as a quick estimate how many bus stops there are now. It is a known fact that the bus stops are currently spaced quite evenly at about 600 m apart. He wants to improve access by reducing the average bus stop spacing to 400 m, with closer spacing at high population areas. He suggested that you divide the community into 1 km by 1 km squares and classify each square as low, medium, or high population density. You found 7 low, 16 medium, and 9 high population density zones.

Qn 5.01

    For each density zone type, you pick two squares, the ones with the lowest and the highest total lengths of road. Using a map, you measure the total road lengths in each of these six squares. The (lowest, highest) total km road lengths for low, medium, and high densities are (1.0, 2.6), (2.0, 4.0) and (1.4, 3.0) respectively. The total road lengths within each density zone type can be assumed to be uniformly distributed.

a. Construct a spreadsheet model to evaluate this issue for the project chief.
b. Summarize the data into a table by low, medium, and high-density zones.
c. Estimate the total number of current and proposed bus stops. Assume the bus stops in the low population areas are to be left unchanged, while in the medium and high-density zones, some bus stops will be relocated and new ones added.

Free subway rides. Massive congestion in the city mass rapid transit stations and trains during peak hours has been a grave concern for the local transport authority. They are considering making the transit train operating companies lower the off-peak fares to help shift the demand. Both operators and academic transport experts cite studies done by other cities to show that fare discounts have no impact on commuters' peak hour behavior. A radical idea of offering free rides during the early hours just before the morning peak was recently proposed. Will this work?

Qn 5.02

a. Construct a spreadsheet model to evaluate the impact of fare changes on train occupancy and fare revenue. Operating hours per day is now 16 hours, with peak duration of 2 hours, peak train occupancy of 120%, and off-peak occupancy of 11%. Using shorter trains and lower frequency, the capacity per hour during off-peak hours is only half that of the peak. Regardless of distance and time of travel, current ticket fare is $1. The proposal is to have different peak and off-peak fares.
b. Keeping peak fare at $1, reducing off-peak fare to 80 cents is estimated to change the peak duration to 2.5 hours, peak occupancy to 115%, and off-peak occupancy

to 12%. From fares of 80 to 50 cents, every 10 cents reduction increases peak duration by 0.5 hours, reduces peak occupancy by 5% points, and increases off-peak occupancy by 1% point. At off-peak fare of 50 cents, peak duration becomes 4 hours, peak train occupancy is 100%, and off-peak occupancy is 15%.

c. With $1.05 peak and free off-peak fares, the estimated peak duration is 4.5 hours, peak train occupancy is 95%, and off-peak occupancy is 16%.

d. Discuss possible practice concerns. Comment on how lower off-peak fares may be implemented as non-uniform fares over the hours with some free fare hours.

Qn 5.03 **Cheaper public housing.** There has been a lot of grumbling among citizens that public housing prices have risen above affordability ever since these prices have been allowed to keep pace with private housing prices. To make public housing apartments cheaper without affecting the purpose of letting citizens gain from property price increases, a suggestion has been to take the land value component out of public housing prices. The full price and thus also the property value proportion of the apartment, is made known at the point of purchase. When the apartment is later sold in the open market to eligible buyers after the minimum residency, the updated property value, obtained by multiplying the property proportion by the market-selling price, is returned to the public housing authority.

a. Construct a spreadsheet model to explain this suggestion. Assume property prices appreciate 7% per year and selling price of an apartment is approximately equal to the ratio of remaining lease to the original 99-year multiplied by the price of a new apartment.

b. For each year after purchase, determine the potential market price for an apartment that was bought new at $350,000.

c. The assessed property value of a new apartment is $200,000. What is the worth of the property in the subsequent years?

d. Comment on whether this suggestion is helpful. Can it be extended to apply to purchase of old apartments as well? What may be the possible consequences of this suggestion to the property market?

Qn 5.04 **Weather summary.** Temperature and weather conditions (sunny, cloudy, windy, rainy, or snowy) of the day are recorded by the geography club. They would like to summarize the data into key information bits for the rest of the school to see.

a. Construct a spreadsheet model to collate the weather data for a month.

b. Compute the average temperature of the month. Show also the lowest and highest temperatures and the days they occur. Use the latest if there are ties.

c. Compute the average temperature of each weather condition in the month. Show also their lowest and highest temperatures and the days they occur. Use the latest if there are ties.

d. Extend parts b and c to include second lowest and second highest temperatures and the days they occur. Second lowest temperature must be distinct from the lowest temperature; second highest temperature must be distinct from the highest temperature.

New magazine. The publisher of *New Magazine* is trying to determine the correct price for the new weekly publication. The variable cost of printing and distributing a copy of the magazine is $0.75. They are thinking of charging between $2.00 and $3.00 per copy. The estimated weekly sales of the magazine is 2.2 million copies if the price is $2.00, 1.3 million copies if the price is $2.50, and 0.9 million copies if the price is $3.00.

Qn 5.05

a. Construct a spreadsheet model to explore the new magazine's pricing strategy.
b. Chart the relationship between demand and price. Determine the approximate polynomial relationship between the two.
c. For any input price in the given range, determine the profit for the publisher. Rounding to the nearest 5 cents, what is the best price for the publisher to sell the magazine?
d. In addition to sales revenue, they want to charge advertisers $35 per thousand copies of the magazine sold. Again rounding to the nearest 5 cents, what is the best price for the magazine now? This price should be less than the earlier best price.
e. The optimal prices determined in parts c and d are not between $2 and $3, the price range for the demand-price relationship, and is therefore invalid. As correction, add a new demand estimate of 3 million copies sold per week for the magazine price of $1.60. Re-evaluate the best prices for parts c and d.

Photocopy. As a private tutor, you have been going to the neighborhood stationery shop every evening to photocopy the next day's exercise sheets and notes for your students. Each time, the number of copies made was about 100 to 200 of A4 sheets in black and white and 10 to 20 of A4 sheets in color. At a visit to the stationery shop, you noticed their price schedule and wondered if you could save money by copying more each time, going there weekly instead to copy enough materials for all five working days.

Qn 5.06

a. Construct a spreadsheet model to explore the situation. Work out, for different copies to be made, what the total charges are. Round them to the nearest 5 cents.
b. For a daily requirement of 100 black-and-white copies and 10 color copies of A4 sheets, what is the amount of money you save each week if copying is done weekly?
c. What if the daily requirement is 200 black-and-white copies and 20 color copies?

d. Class enrollment changes from week to week, with student additions and dropouts. As such for weekly copying, you need to make 10% to 20% more copies to avoid making extra trips to the shop when there are more students. With this considered, is it still worthwhile to copy only once a week?

Qn 5.07   **Towel production.** A factory produces towels from large rolls of toweling. Each machine moves the cloth forward and cuts towels of different sizes, according to settings made by the operator. The three towel sizes are A (1.28 m by 0.64 m), B (0.64m by 0.32 m), and C (0.32 m by 0.16 m). The 0.64 m wide roll is first cut horizontally to produce A's, each A can be cut horizontally into 4 to give B's, and each B can be cut vertically into 4 to give C's. Therefore, the machine setting decisions are how frequently to activate the second cut and the third cut. The factory has to balance the production of different towels to their demands. The profit per square meter is highest in C, followed by B.

a. Construct a spreadsheet model for managing the production of the towels.

b. Work out the optimal quantities of the towels to produce for the next period's demand of 100 A's, 350 B's, and 500 C's. Current inventory of the towels is zero.

c. A clever technician re-designed the machine to allow it to produce from the first horizontal cut either one A or one B. The second horizontal cut step is eliminated. The third vertical cut step remains as before. For this improved process, determine the optimal quantities of the towels to be produced for the next period.

d. Discuss what further changes can be made to the machines to make them more flexible to meet market demand.

Qn 5.08*   **Water bill.** The Water Utility Board is deliberating on changing its table of tariffs for water to encourage more conservation. The table of tariffs for water now is shown below:

Category	Consumption (per month)	Tariff (per m³)	Conservation Tax (of tariff)
Domestic	0 to 40 m³	$1.17	30%
	Above 40 m³	$1.40	45%
Non-Domestic	All units	$1.17	30%
Shipping	All units	$1.92	30%

One suggestion is to introduce three (low, medium, and high) tariff tiers and apply them to all categories. Currently, 65% of the users are domestic in the less than 40 m^3 category with average water consumption of 30 m^3 per month, 25% are domestic in the above 40 m^3 category with average consumption of 57 m^3, 7% are non-domestic with average consumption of 73 m^3, and 3% are shipping with average consumption of 90 m^3.

a. Construct a spreadsheet model to compute the revenue per user for the Board under the current tariff. Revenue for the Board comes from the water tariff and the conservation tax.

b. Suggest how you would design the three-tier approach, estimating the percentages of users in each tier and their average water consumption per month. Then compute what will be the revenue per user in the revised tariff.

c. Adjust the tariff and conservation tax rates for the tiers to make the new revenue per user the same as that of the current tariff. This revenue-neutral approach is politically desirable, as the goal of this tariff revision exercise is to encourage lower water usage and not raise more revenue.

Feedstock blending. Farmer Joe blends feedstock for his cattle from corn and soybean meal. The relative proportion of these two components is important to achieve the protein and fiber nutrition requirements. He also adds some limestone powder for its calcium. Overall, he must bear in mind the total cost of the blended feedstock.

Qn 5.09*

a. Construct a spreadsheet model to help Joe blend 50 kg of feedstock.

b. Corn costs 30.5 cents per kg, soybean meal is 90 cents per kg, and limestone powder is 10 cents per kg. Each kilogram of corn has 0.001 kg of calcium, 0.09 kg of protein, and 0.02 kg of fiber. Each kilogram of soybean meal has 0.002 kg of calcium, 0.5 kg of protein, and 0.08 kg of fiber. Limestone has 0.38 kg of calcium per kilogram.

c. A good feedstock has at least 0.22 kg per kg of protein, not more than 0.05 kg per kg of fiber, and between 0.008 and 0.012 kg per kg of calcium.

d. How much of each component should Joe use to blend his feedstock? What is the total cost of the mix? What is its cost per kg?

Investment trust. An investment bank started a new fund on large property development projects. In the fund, projects are divided into four types: A, B, C, and D. The fund manager identifies good projects in each type and chooses which ones to invest in. As time progresses, the fund sells the investments in the projects gradually and reinvests the money in other projects. The fund's capital is raised by

Qn 5.10*

selling unit trusts to smaller investors. These investors at the onset are individually given the flexibility to decide how their money is apportioned to the project types. Investment returns from the unit trust to each investor will be calculated based on their individual choices and actual returns from the projects.

a. Construct a spreadsheet model on the investment trust. Target capital of the fund is $30 million. The projects under consideration are project 1, type A, $6 million investment, $19 million net return; project 2, type A, $4 million investment, $11 million net return; project 3, type B, $8 million investment, $24 million net return; project 4, type B, $7 million investment, $20 million net return; project 5, type C, $5 million investment, $14 million net return; project 6, type C, $3 million investment, $8 million net return; and project 7, type B, $4 million investment, $10 million net return.

b. For the fund, determine which projects should be invested in. Projects have to be invested in full or none at all. Explain how this is done in the spreadsheet.

c. For the unit trust investor, determine what percentage of his unit trust should go to each of the project types. Explain how this is done in the spreadsheet.

d. Comment on observations made about the results and any real-world concerns.

Risks and Uncertainties

LEARNING OUTCOMES

- Understand the importance of using simulation to analyze business contexts with randomness
- Able to examine a situation with risks and uncertainties using Monte-Carlo simulation
- Able to compute basic statistics from a given data sample
- Able to generate a frequency table and histogram plot

INTRODUCTION

Risks are situations where the probabilities of events yet to happen can be characterized, whereas uncertainties refer to cases where the outcomes can be totally unforeseeable. There is yet a third kind of variability, which though not totally unknown, is also not under the control of the decision maker. For example, the demand for goods and services may vary with the seasons. In this sense, from past experience, you can tell which months of the year will see surges and plunges in demand and therefore you are able to take appropriate measures. The demand fluctuations are usually characterized by seasonal indices, which state the strength of each month's demand relative to that of the average monthly demand. Thus, multiplying the seasonal index by the projected average monthly demand gives a month's expected demand. This still carries some risks, as the seasonal index is a stochastic variable. The *Village Water* exercise in Chapter 5 is an example of a demand fluctuation situation. The stochastic variability is ignored there, as that is not relevant for its main objective in water storage sizing.

Different approaches can be taken to manage risks. Preventive measures are usually favored since it is much better to avoid than to have to correct. However, there may be too many things to guard against. In contrast, contingency measures are responsive actions that you can take when the feared risks are about to occur or have just occurred. The alert mechanisms selected may in fact cover a range of risks, thereby making them cost justifiable to set up. The challenges in many business situations would be the construction of such alert mechanisms and staging them, if possible, in a way that they will continue to adapt to new information, as and when they are revealed.

What-if analysis done in the earlier chapters discovers how the outcome varies with decision choices. Decisions are user-controllable inputs. However, risks and uncertainties appear in models as uncontrollable inputs, which may turn everything upside-down. You should do *Sensitivity* analyses to examine how results change with perturbations in each of these uncontrollable inputs, one at a time. When the number of such inputs is small and their changes cannot be characterized as probability distributions, you can use scenario analysis, for example, to evaluate base, worst, and best cases. Otherwise, a Monte-Carlo simulation (in which the uncontrollable variables are changed according to predetermined probability distributions) is a reasonable approach to evaluate sensitivity of the model. Do note that movements of stochastic variables may be correlated, positively or negatively. The number of replications needed in the simulation is usually large, so as to capture as much as possible combinations of input changes that may arise.

This chapter starts with the *Monty Hall* exercise, which is based on a popular television game show. You may wonder why such a simple game show can draw such tremendous audience attention and stay popular for so many years. The probabilistic behavior there is simple, but the analysis is more than meets the eye. Another simple but more difficult to model situation is the *Change Dispensing* exercise. How would you approximate what currency denominations people use to pay for their purchases? What strategies would you use to dispense the exact monetary change?

More complex distributions may be characterized as shown in the *Frequency Distribution* exercise, from which you can infer the possible theoretical distribution of your data. With a known distribution, the *Data Simulation* exercise shows how representative random values may be generated. The exercise also demonstrates through a series of examples how random values may be generated by resampling directly from given observed data. Other applications of Monte-Carlo simulations are demonstrated in *John Lim's Retirement*, *Portfolio Simulation*, and *Forecast Eyeball*. Finally, two general ways of managing risks are shown in the *Yankee Fruits* and *Wonder Cookies* exercises.

DISCOVERY POINTS

Point 25

Status quo and change

Examine every decision to see if there are areas that have remained unchanged. Not changing should be considered a choice, though a subtly implicit and convenient one. Make every choice a deliberate one. Adopt a zero-based analysis approach by taking nothing for granted, starting from scratch. Check every process that has always been done the same way and ask for a different way, a better way. The need to change may not be obvious since the current way has been perfected over time. Didn't they say, "Practice makes perfect?" Having been doing it the same way so long, should we now question its validity? If the process can be assumed to be best but the operator for the lack of skill unable to comply, then every chance to practice may lead to improvements, as errors are corrected.

However most of the time, practice does not make perfect, as commonly assumed. It is more accurate to say, "Practice makes permanent." So if the process is bad at the start, it may become permanently bad. Moreover, a process that is excellent at the start does not necessarily stay the best. Circumstances change with time and, with technology evolving, there is increasingly better access to previously unavailable and latest information. In the *Monty Hall* exercise, the common perception is that the probability of picking the prize door is 1 out of 3. It does not appear to make a difference if another door is opened. However, the fact that the door opened by the show host is by choice, being never the prize door, this means new information is gained. This should change the odds to favor the other unopened door not previously selected by the contestant. The contestant should therefore change his initial choice.

Point 26

Follow the contender

Game theory gives us many interesting strategies that may be applied in modeling. Examples include *follow the leader* and *brinkmanship*. In *follow the leader*, the critical idea is why spend effort innovating and finding the best way when there is already a clear winner who is doing the right thing, showing the way. All one has to do is to follow her and do everything she does and you can be as successful as her. The problem is that you may not have her scale of operations, for after all she is the leader and thus sizable. What works for the leader may not therefore work for others like you. The other issue is that leaders are generally not as innovative as we think. They carry with them the legacy of their successes and thus are reluctant to deviate from the "success formula."

Now as for the leaders, you may ask whom then do they follow? Here's a contrarian suggestion: *follow the follower*, or more correctly, *follow the contender*. The argument to support this goes like this: the contender, ambitious to become the next leader, tries harder. Relative to the contender at least, the incumbent leader is moderate and careful. She does not want to risk failure and fall from the place of honor by doing something stupid. The contender however knows that if he merely follows the leader, he can at best just keep pace with her. Being already behind the leader, he can never hope to overtake her. He must try something unusual at the right moment, to surprise and break ahead. Excellent contenders take risks where and when leaders cannot follow. Good leaders have to be wary of this and take steps to avert.

To illustrate, consider a sailing race in which competitors contest with yachts of the same design. Speed of a yacht is determined by wind and water conditions, the captain's choices, and the crew's ability to respond to orders issued. Yachts at the rear must watch front yachts to follow their best moves to stay in the race. With wind and water conditions common, doing the same thing by the teams means the race rankings stay unchanged. So good contenders know that they must do more than that, taking risks when necessary to speed ahead. The lead yacht must stay the course doing what they do best, but should keep a watchful eye on contenders. Who knows when one of their risky moves will translate to a fast break, changing the race outcome?

Point 27

Predictably irrational

The randomized strategy lets chance select a strategy from among a set of available. It does not appear that such an approach is sensible. After all, for any situation, you would want to work out the expected consequences of each strategy and make a stand on which is best for you. That is, unless the problem is so complex that you are unable to evaluate or that your analysis tells you that the candidate strategies are all equally viable and good. Are there situations where you can clearly evaluate the strategies, able to rank them for effectiveness, and it is still best to take a randomly chosen strategy? This is tantamount to saying that you should not trust yourself. Randomized strategies make sense, but only in certain situations. These situations are neither rare nor insignificant.

In the game of tennis, you evaluate the moves made by your opponent and decide on the response. If you are experienced and well-trained, you will quickly find a small set of possible responses. There is one among them that is best. However, your competitor possibly knows this set of possible responses and what you consider best. You already know that he has taken the time and effort to study all your past moves. He is now ready to take on your best response, and hit back with greater vengeance. Now, do you still consider making an unexpected though albeit non-optimal move to be not an enlightened one? Certainly not! The randomized strategy is the best strategy in many competitive situations, whether in sports or in business.

On a separate note, socially optimal strategies, the ones that are best for the society as a whole, do not always work out. People compete against each other. What's best for every one as a whole is not usually best for any single person. Every time a player makes a move to improve his situation, the opponents make theirs to improve their situation. This goes on until a point – known as the Nash equilibrium – where no player can improve his situation any more with further changes. In this and many other considerations, people are not necessarily rational. In fact, expect most people to be irrational. There is, as explained, logic to this madness.

Point 28

Flaw of averages

Imagine putting your left foot in a pail of liquid nitrogen at $-196°C$ and right foot in a pail of molten tin at $232°C$. The average of the two temperatures is $18°C$, a comfortable temperature for many people. Do you think you will be comfortable in the hypothetical situation? The answer is clearly no. Working with averages has this problem. You may not realize it, but the assumption made in most models is that input values are constants and this usually means they are averages. Thus, you have to review what you have done so far.

For example in working out the business plan of a project, we usually use expected values as inputs. The plan may show that the project is expected to be profitable. However, what is most critical in all projects is not its profitability but its cashflow. Profitability, though still important, comes second. It must have enough starting capital to ensure that on the average the project has enough to pay its bills. Secondly, there is usually an extra working capital buffer to cater to day-to-day fluctuations in receipts and payables timings and amounts, and also unforeseen expenses or unexpected increases in material input costs and wages.

EXERCISES

Exercise 48 **MONTY HALL**   Worked Example

Challenge XYZ Soap Company intends to sponsor the "Let's Make a Deal" Monty Hall game segment in the local television station's nightly variety show. The game will be played with three contestants each night. Booby prizes are worth $100 and the grand prize is $5,000.

Concept It is intuitively difficult to understand how the probabilities work in this situation and which strategy would work best.

- You should first understand how the game is played and why the game host chooses to play the game that way.
- What are the options available to contestants?
- What makes this game so successful?

The game helps us to understand that new information revealed is valuable and should be correctly used to influence our decisions, including those already made.

Working (Detailed) Consider these questions when modeling the problem:

- What are the possible strategies available to the contestants when they play?
- Can you think of more than two strategies? What are they?
- Can you explain without in-depth analysis why they are generally useful?
- How do you convince others that your strategy is the best? Why should others believe you?
- How much money is expected to be won by the contestants each night?
- How much should the company budget to give away in total if the game is played for 50 nights?

For the simulation, consider the following:

- How many trials are required in the simulation? How do you justify this?
- How would you collect more replications of the same model, without resorting to making more copies of it?

To understand the model, we must understand how the game is played.

i.   There are three doors (1, 2, and 3) and the $5,000 grand prize is placed randomly behind one of the doors (say door 1), and a $100 booby prize is placed behind each of the remaining two doors (doors 2 and 3).

ii. Contestant A is invited to select a door at random (say he selects door 2) and the game host will reveal one of the two doors not selected by Contestant A (in this case either door 1 or door 3). The door that is opened is not the door with the grand prize. At this point, only one door has been opened.

iii. Contestant A is then asked to make a decision between sticking to his choice (door 2) and changing his choice to the other closed door (door 1). Our model will attempt to compute the probability of winning the grand prize for the two decision choices.

iv. To illustrate that new information is valuable and should be correctly used to influence decision making, another contestant, B, can be invited at this point to make a choice between the two remaining closed doors (1 and 2). Here, it is clear that Contestant B has a 50% chance of winning the grand prize. Now, how should Contestant A use the information to gain a higher chance of winning the grand prize?

If we are able to determine the probability of winning for three contestants per night, we can estimate the expected budget for the prizes for each night and for 50 nights. Let us start to model the problem.

i. Select the *Proto* worksheet.

ii. The worksheet has three partitions, namely *Steps 1, 2*, and *3*.
   - *Step 1* simulates the grand prize door, Contestant A's selected door, and the revealed door.
   - *Step 2* simulates Contestant A's final selected door for the three cases: no change, change, and randomly choosing between changing and not changing.
   - *Step 3* computes the number of wins and probability of winning for the three different situations in Step 2.

iii. Enter into cells B10:B1009 the number of simulation trials from 1 to 1000. To obtain the average results, the larger the number of trials, the more accurate the solution will be. The total number of trials in cell B6 is computed to be 1,000.

iv. Enter into cell C10 the formula =RANDBETWEEN(1,3) (i.e., the prize door is randomly decided among the three doors). Fill the formula in cell C10 into cells C11:C1009.

v. Enter into cell D10 the formula =RANDBETWEEN(1,3) (i.e., Contestant A randomly selects from among the three doors). Fill the formula in cell D10 into cells D11:D1009.

vi. The game host is to decide which door to reveal. We need a matrix to help us determine which door will be revealed.

Revealed door		Selected door		
		1	**2**	**3**
Prize door	**1**	=RANDBETWEEN(2,3)	3	2
	2	3	=IF(RAND()>0.5, 1,3)	1
	3	2	1	=RANDBETWEEN(1,2)

From the matrix above,

- When prize door = 1 and selected door = 1, the game host can either reveal door 2 or 3. For this, we can use the formula =RANDBETWEEN(2,3) to make the random choice.
- When prize door = 1 and selected door = 2, the game host can only reveal door 3.
- When prize door = 1 and selected door = 3, the game host can only reveal door 2.
- When prize door = 2 and selected door = 1, the game host can only reveal door 3.
- When prize door = 2 and selected door = 2, the game host can either reveal door 1 or 3. For this, we can use the formula =IF(RAND()>0.5, 1,3) to make the random choice. Here, the RAND function generates a random number from interval [0,1) and compares against 0.5, and thus yield 1 and 3 with equal likelihood.
- When prize door = 2 and selected door = 3, the game host can only reveal door 1.
- When prize door = 3 and selected door = 1, the game host can only reveal door 2.
- When prize door = 3 and selected door = 2, the game host can only reveal door 1.
- When prize door = 3 and selected door = 3, the game host can either reveal door 1 or 2. For this, we can use the formula =RANDBETWEEN(1,2) to make the random choice.

Prepare the above matrix in cells F3:I6 and enter into cell E10 the formula =INDEX($G$4:$I$6,C10,D10) (i.e., the revealed door is selected from cells G4:I6 using the prize door and selected door values). Fill the formula in cell E10 into cells E11:E1009.

vii. Enter into cell G10 the formula =D10 (i.e., the same door is set equal to the selected door). Fill the formula in cell G10 into cells G11:G1009.

viii. We need to compute the door that Contestant A can change to if he so decides. The matrix that helps us see the door change possibilities is given below.

Changed door		Selected door		
		1	**2**	**3**
Revealed door	**1**		3	2
	2	3		1
	3	2	1	

From the matrix above,
- The cases where revealed door = selected door are not possible as the game will end if the host chooses to reveal the contestant's selected door.
- When revealed door = 1 and selected door = 2, Contestant A can only change to door 3.
- When revealed door = 1 and selected door = 3, Contestant A can only change to door 2.
- When revealed door = 2 and selected door = 1, Contestant A can only change to door 3.
- When revealed door = 2 and selected door = 3, Contestant A can only change to door 1.
- When revealed door = 3 and selected door = 1, Contestant A can only change to door 2.
- When revealed door = 3 and selected door = 2, Contestant A can only change to door 1.

Since the two matrices are similar except for the diagonal rows, we can reuse the matrix previously prepared in cells F3:I6, and enter into cell H10 the formula =INDEX($G$4:$I$6,E10,D10) (i.e., the change door is selected from cells G4:I6 using the revealed door and selected door values). Fill the formula in cell H10 into cells H11:H1009.

Alternatively, we can use a simple formula. Enter into cell H10 the formula =6-D10-E10 (i.e., the change door is = 6 – Revealed door – Selected door). This result is correct because the sum of the three doors is 6. Note that the revealed door and the selected door are never the same.

ix. Enter into cell I10 the formula =IF(RAND()<0.5,D10,H10) (i.e., Contestant A can randomly choose between changing and not changing his choice of door.). Fill the formula in cell I10 into cells I11:I1009.

x.   To compute the number of wins and probability of winning

- Enter into cell K10 the formula =(G10=$C10)*1 (i.e., if Contestant A's original choice of door = prize door, then return 1, otherwise return 0). Fill the formula in cell K10 into cells K11:K1009.
- Enter into cell L10 the formula =(H10=$C10)*1 (i.e., if Contestant A's new choice of door = prize door, then return 1, otherwise return 0). Fill the formula in cell L10 into cells L11:L1009.
- Enter into cell M10 the formula =(I10=$C10)*1 (i.e., if the random choice door = prize door, then return 1, otherwise return 0). Fill the formula in cell M10 into cells M11:M1009.
- By summing the number of 1's in each column, we can determine the number of wins for 1,000 trials to compute the probability of winning. Alternatively, we can enter into cell K6 the formula =AVERAGE(K10:K1009) or =SUM(K10:K1009)/COUNT(K10:K1009) to obtain the probability of winning for the first situation. Fill the formula in cell K6 into cells L6:M6 to get the probabilities of winning for the second and third situations.
- Key **F9** to view the simulated results. The results are
  - If Contestant A sticks to his original choice, the probability of winning is about 0.33.
  - If Contestant A changes his choice, the probability of winning is about 0.66.
  - The probability of randomly choosing between the above two choices is about 0.5.
  - This shows that switching choices is better than preserving the status quo. This is because, if the contestant sticks to his original choice of door, he retains the original 1/3 chance of winning. Changing his selection is equivalent to swapping his 1/3 chance of winning for a 2/3 chance of selecting the prize door (two doors give a 2/3 chance of winning). The 2/3 probability of winning has not been changed by the opening of one of the other two doors.

Exercise 49   CHANGE DISPENSING

Challenge   Vending machines, automated machines, and cash registers have to return the exact change when the money put in is more than the price of the purchase. These machines compute the change and, from the currency notes and coins available, release the relevant quantities of notes and coins.

It would be poor service performance if certain notes or coins run out so that the exact change cannot be provided even though the money in the machine is more than enough to cover the change. What would be a more robust way to dispense the change so that this does not happen too often?

Concept

This is an example of challenges which are not that simple to work out algebraically, even if you are quite gifted in mathematics. Monte-Carlo simulation is an appropriate tool to use to evaluate the different strategies and implementation algorithms.

A good principle to bear in mind is that the small change denominations are more critical than the larger ones since they allow more use. They should be dispensed sparingly.

Working

The table in the model should be compose of the purchase, offered, and change monetary amounts. You should also keep track of how much money is available in the machine at each transaction. A detailed breakdown of the total quantity of money of each denomination should be given. The spreadsheet model is therefore expected to be quite wide with many columns. Make these columns as narrow as possible so that there is enough room to accommodate all of them.

The purchase and offered amounts should be simulated. Think of how you would do this. It is likely that the purchase amount can be simulated as an aggregate total for each transaction, whereas the offered amounts have to be denominated.

Here are some questions to consider in your Monte-Carlo simulation:

- What is the desired objective of the simulation?
- How will you know that your simulation is appropriate?
- Can you think of a few strategies to dispense change? What are they?
- How will you know you have found a good strategy for dispensing the change? What are the quantifiable measures of success or robustness?
- Can you think of other situations where such a Monte-Carlo simulation may be similarly applied?

FREQUENCY DISTRIBUTION

Exercise 50

Challenge

This workbook demonstrates the various ways to compute the frequency distribution of a given sample data set and to produce its histogram.

In the process, you will learn about the **FREQUENCY** array function; other spreadsheet functions like **COUNTIF** and **CONCATENATE**; and the concatenation operator **&**.

Concept

There is usually more than one way to do anything in spreadsheets. You should learn all of them since the methods can be suitably applied in different situations. What is best for one problem context may not be for another. A point to note is that some methods are not dynamically "live" in that the worksheet would not update automatically with any changes in the data. The programs in **Analysis Toolpak** in particular are not interactive and should therefore be avoided.

Working

FREQUENCY is an array function. This function seems to work also as a simple function, though this aspect is not documented. Array functions and array formulas (which work on arrays of cells to give results in one or many cells) are very powerful concepts. To enter array functions and formulas, use **Shift + Ctrl + Enter** (hold down the first two keys before hitting the **Enter** key). The formula is differentiated by { } enclosing the whole formula inclusive of the equal sign.

The **COUNTIF** and **SUMIF** functions use a text string to specify the conditional criteria. The concatenation operator **&** may be used to link operators (<, <=, =, >, and >=) with cell references to give non-hard-coded criteria.

On a separate practical note, the data presented in the exercise are on wait times.

- What are the different service situations where customers have to wait?
- How would you collect wait time data in each of these?
- Are the data easy to collect? Are there better ways to collect them?

Exercise 51   **DATA SIMULATION**

Challenge

Random data may be simulated, without add-ins and macros, using only native spreadsheet features by employing one of these three methods: (1) resampling from frequency bins, (2) resampling from sample data, and (3) using inverse distribution functions.

Concept

Resampling is also referred to by others as *boot-strapping*. It allows us to generate additional data from a small set of real data to support our analysis. The data generated must of course be representative of the population from which the sample came. Other than resampling, random data may be simulated with add-ins and functions written in **Basic**, using the inverse distribution function method. Some inverse distribution functions are available in Excel and Calc. Additional ones may be indirectly derived from other available spreadsheet functions.

Worksheets *Example(1)* to *Example(5)* show the data simulation methods used. The last two worksheets in the workbook contain reference tables showing how random data may be generated for common continuous and discrete distributions using the inverse function method.

Go through the worksheets to learn how they work and do the practices.

- The situations presented for some of the examples are rather contorted. Why so?
- Can you think of other better situations to apply the resampling formulas?
- Without referring to the worksheets, do you know when each of the formulas may be used?

Working

JOHN LIM'S RETIREMENT

Exercise 52

Challenge

John Lim worked hard all his professional life. Hoping to have a comfortable retirement, he has accumulated a retirement fund of $500,000 comprising bank deposits, provident fund and life insurance endowment, bonds, and equity investments.

As his friend and financial advisor, John has asked you to compute how much money he can draw out to spend each year in retirement. John hopes the money he has set aside will last at least 20 years. He thinks his investment portfolio can yield an average of 10% return per annum.

Off-the-cuff, you believe the returns should fluctuate from year to year, possibly uniformly distributed between –5% and +25%. Financial experts are confident that a long-range average return of 10% is certain. Will the fluctuations make any difference?

Return rates are subject to market forces, which will affect the outcome quite differently. It is not advisable to model using an average return rate throughout the whole time horizon. Cases examined here depict the wide range of thinking with regard to retirement planning. One extreme case ignores any return from investment and year by year slowly spends the principal away. Another case saves an endowment for the next generation and hopes to live off the interest only. Yet another extreme case leaves nothing. Are there better ideas?

Concept

While working on the model, ponder these questions:

- Ignoring investment returns, how much can John spend each year?
- If John wants the principal to remain intact and spend only the investment returns, what will the answer be?

Working

- If John does not want to have any money left over, how much can he spend each year?

  Use Monte-Carlo simulation to examine the situation further:

- What impact does random variation in the annual return rate have on the retirement plan?
- What if return rates are not so free-changing but drift with small deviations from year to year?
- How would you change the way return rates are generated in the model?
- How does this change in assumption affect the results?

Exercise 53

PORTFOLIO SIMULATION

Challenge

Paul had been advised that it would be prudent to spread his investments over a variety of financial instruments so as to reduce risk and have some guarantee on overall return. The types of instruments he had been thinking about are treasury bills, treasury bonds, and common stocks. These are in increasing order of risk, but also of higher expected return: higher risks, higher returns!

Since the market is currently very volatile, he decided against using data from too far back to forecast the future. After taking some lessons on *Monte-Carlo* simulation, Paul decided to build a simulation model to resample the limited data and use them to help form a reasonable picture of interactions among the financial instruments.

- What proportion of his investments should he put in each of these three financial asset classes?
- What would the allocation proportions be if he wants to ensure that the return is guaranteed 95% of the time?

Concept

Prices of different financial assets do not move independently of one another. They are usually positively or negatively correlated. To model an investing situation involving more than one financial asset, you would have to use more sophisticated statistical approaches. Resampling can be applied to help simplify the modeling. The main idea behind resampling multivariate data is to treat the data as sets of values, rather than individual variable values. **Goal Seek** or **Solver** can be used to find the optimal portfolio. However, these tools cannot find their solutions if the resampling formulas keep changing the data values. It would therefore be a good idea to fix the resampled values as data first before running these operations.

The sample data collected are prices and not return rates. You will need to compute them into return rates for each period. As a quick check, apply the computation in reverse to see if the prices of the next period can be computed from return rates of the period and the prices of the previous period.

In the model, keep the return rates of the financial assets in rows as sets, one row for each set taken from a time period. The resampling therefore would be to choose from a random row of data. Such resampling, however, can only generate data values that are represented in the sample; there will be no values generated that will be in-between these values. You can resample with interpolation to get representative data points from in-between the sample's multivariate data points. Refer, in this chapter, to *Resampling* tool for more details. With the resampled data, analyze the case with the following questions:

- What do you want to optimize to get the best portfolio of financial assets?
- In allocating the available fund to the different assets, what criteria do you apply to determine which allocation is best?

FORECAST EYEBALL

This game explores the human ability to predict future demand. No fancy formulas or algorithm need to be used here. Just employ your "calibrated eyeball" and see how well you do.

While there are mathematical formulas to forecast the future, they tend to be difficult to understand. It will be interesting to see if the human eye, with a thinking brain behind it of course, can see patterns in plotted data to make good forecasts.

As a check, the standard deviation of forecast error, approximated by 1.25 times of the mean absolute deviation of the error, should be less than the demand standard deviation. Otherwise, you will do no worse to predict future demand to be equal to the average historical demand.

In the *Game* worksheet, select the *Demo* option and click repeatedly on the *Demand* button to see how demand fluctuates with time.

- What conclusions can you draw from your observations?

When you have fully appreciated the demand behavior, unselect *Demo* and follow the instructions for playing the game. Make your predictions and record the results.

Working

Exercise 54

Challenge

Concept

Working

- What logical process did you employ to predict future demand?
- How accurate was your forecast?
- What are the possible sources of errors?

Explore the game further as follows:

- Select the *ShowTrend* option, play another round of the game, and record your results.
- Select the *ShowForecast* option and play yet another round. Follow the suggested forecast as much as you want. Record your results.

Discuss the following:

- Did having a trendline help? By how much?
- What do you think of the forecast given by the model? Did you follow it?
- Was the forecast given by the model useful?
- What did you deduce is the logical reasoning behind the model's demand prediction?

Exercise 55

YANKEE FRUITS

Challenge

Paul, who runs Yankee Fruits Stall in the local market, wants to know how he can control his costs to make his business more profitable.

Paul throws away a lot of unsold honeydew melons, a high cost item, each week. The melons are delivered weekly by a supplier and those not sold by the next delivery would not be fresh enough to sell and, hence, he has to discard them.

Each week, Paul has to decide on the quantity of honeydew melons to buy from the supplier. He has presented you with data of the number of melons sold over the past 30 weeks. How should he proceed from here?

Concept

There are various ways to estimate the distribution behavior of any variable. The most common approach is to use a table of cumulative frequencies. Another is to adopt a standard function, such as the *Normal* distribution if it is valid, using parameter values estimated from the data sample. An easier and less prominent approach is to directly derive its empirical distribution. Linear interpolation between consecutive data points will yield a more accurate piece-wise linear representation. This last idea is exploited to help resample data, an approach demonstrated in the *Data Simulation* exercise.

Working

Start by sorting the past weekly demand values in ascending order. Do not use the **Data Sort** feature in spreadsheet as it will not update with changes in the data. From the first sorted value downwards, the cumulative relative frequency for each value is one divided by the order position value. That is where n is the sample size, and the cumulative relative frequency of the first value is $1/n$, the second is $2/n$, the third $3/n$, and so on. This result would constitute method 2 in the model. Plotting this ought to give a curve with staircase steps, but obviously it would require some effort to make it appear so in a spreadsheet.

The **FREQUENCY** array function used as a normal cell function will yield the cumulative frequency count. This can be applied to give the results for method 1. Method 3 is derived by finding the demand value for different percentiles. Method 4 assumes that the data fits the *Normal* distribution. The assumption is quite valid since the cumulative relative frequency from the earlier methods show that it is *S*-shaped. The mean and standard deviation parameters needed for the function can be estimated from the sample mean and sample standard deviation.

- How many honeydew melons should Paul take from his supplier each week?
- Which method gives the most appropriate answer?

WONDERCOOKIES **Exercise 56**

Challenge

WonderCookies distributes its freshly baked cookies in standard sealed packages from strategically located distribution centers (DC) to retail stores. Unlike other DCs, the small Bukit Terok (BT) DC supports only four stores: A, B, C, and D.

Physical distribution is done weekly, and each time, the existing stock is disposed of and new stock issued. Special trips have to be made from the DC whenever a store prematurely runs out of stock. For a 10% risk of stock-out, how many packages should stores A, B, C, and D each request?

To save cost, the company has decided to shut down Bukit Terok and have its stores supplied by Bukit Suku (BS), the next nearest DC. In addition, the stock-out risk for A, B, C, and D is now reduced to 5%. What should be the replenishment quantities for the stores now?

Alternatively, it is suggested that the stock-out risk for stores B, C, and D remains at 10% but store A's stock level be increased so that rush orders from B, C, or D can be serviced by those stores collecting from A. The stock-out risk for the district as a whole should be at a low 2%. How many packages should store A now request each week to ensure that it can serve this new role?

- Which solution is better?
- Are there even better solutions?

Concept

There can be more than one approach to the stocking structure and replenishment of a product to the retail outlets. Some alternatives are given below:

- How are they different from one another?
- What makes one more effective than another?
- For instance, pooling the inventory for a region can help reduce the amount of stock required to service a given service level. When would pooling work and when would it not?

Use the lessons learned to devise other alternative physical distribution approaches.

Working

The demand for cookies at each store can be treated as a single stochastic variable. Provided the expected demand does not change too drastically, the stock replenishment amount of each store for a given (no stock-out) service performance level in the recent weeks can be computed using the **PERCENTILE** function.

The region's demand can be totaled and that too is a single stochastic variable. Once again, we can apply the PERCENTILE function on the region's demand in the recent past weeks to determine the replenishment amount for the service performance level. Compare this value against that of the sum of the individual store's replenishment amount. Is it smaller? Can it ever be larger? Why?

Look at the *Analysis* worksheet to examine the scattergram of the demand between store A and the other stores.

- What does the data suggest?
- What can you deduce from this chart about the correlations between the demands of stores B and C, or any other pair of stores?

TOOLS

Statistical lies

Tool 5

In statistical reporting, information is often distorted (intentionally or otherwise) to influence what people think, and to affect their decisions and actions. This workbook illustrates some of the more obvious "lies." You may want to look out for them and others like them in your daily life.

Statistics review

Tool 6

This workbook helps you to revise some basic concepts in descriptive statistics and have a better understanding of the power of cumulative charts.

Probability functions

Tool 7

This workbook shows some common probability distribution functions, their properties, and application areas. Discrete functions deal with cases where variables can only take on discrete values, while continuous functions deal with cases where variables can only take on continuous values.

Understanding variable distribution is very helpful in modeling, even in situations where there are few or no data available. For example, if a variable is known to be fairly "bell-shaped" in distribution, you can, given its extreme values, estimate the distribution's mean by taking the average of the extreme values and standard deviation by dividing the difference of the extreme values by 6 (assuming a 3-sigma spread on both sides of the mean). With this, you can apply the *Normal* distribution.

Find out more about each function.

- What does its distribution shape look like?
- Where does it best apply?
- What if only limited data are available?

Resampling

Tool 8

This workbook demonstrates the resampling of univariate and multivariate continuous random data. Also introduced is the new concept of resampling with interpolation.

In the univariate case, resampling involves randomly picking a value from among all the values in the given data sample. To resample with interpolation, the **PERCENTILE** function is used. This function samples from the inverse empirical distribution, which it implicitly forms by piecewise-linear connection of consecutive ordered values in the data sample.

In the multivariate case, resampling involves randomly picking a sample data point in the multidimensional space. Resampling with interpolation is achieved by taking a convex combination of a randomly selected sample data point and its adjacent point. Adjacency of data points here is defined with respect to the sorted order of a preselected variable. For variance reduction, this should be the variable with the largest marginal standard deviation.

For the purpose of illustration, this workbook uses the historical annual return rates of T-bills, T-bonds, and stock as sample data. By visual inspection, the approaches presented here produce scattergrams and cumulative relative frequency plots that are very close to that of the original sample. The multivariate interpolated approach introduced here can be used even in situations where the original scattergrams (between any pair of variables) are noncompact and nonconvex.

Tool 9

Lucky draw

There are two ways to randomly select something. One is to do so with replacement and the other without replacement. Drawing with replacement means that every time a selection is made, the drawn item is placed back with the rest of the candidates to be drawn again. On the other hand, drawing without replacement means that the drawn item is permanently removed and cannot be drawn again. In either case, the order of draw is usually pertinent. For example, the draw may be to form the winning number of a lottery or to allocate the different prizes to be given away in a lucky draw. The case when all the items are drawn is the same as finding a randomized order of the items. This workbook lists some examples for you to study.

Tool 10

Card game

A simple game of chance is what you get when you play with a deck of cards. You can play it electronically too. Create your own spreadsheet card game.

Tool 11

Pick a number

Let us play a game. A whole number, within a specified range, has been picked by the game host. You are to guess what this target number is in as few tries as possible. After each try, the host would have to tell you if your number is larger or smaller than the target. To make it interesting, a prize may be given for correctly guessing the target, but each player must pay a small fixed fee for each attempt.

If you are to play this game, how would you use the clues? It would be natural to assume that the game host would pick a random number as target to initiate the game. Is this a correct assumption? What if he did not pick a random number? How else could he pick a number? Which of these ways would be best for the game host?

Bingo

Each Bingo card contains a 5-square by 5-square table. Other than the center, each square in the card is filled with a unique whole number taken from 1 to 75. Each player takes a card and mark out the numbers on the card, as they are progressively called out by the game master. The numbers called out are sampled (without replacement) one at a time using balls numbering 1 to 75. When the marked-out numbers on a card forms one of the pre-specified winning patterns, the player holding the card shouts "BINGO!" and registers completion of the required pattern with the game master. This marks the end of the round and the prize is awarded to the first player to complete a winning pattern.

There are other versions of this game with 80 or 90 balls, different types of cards and gaming patterns. To win in the 75-ball game, the card must have either a row, or a column or a diagonal marked out.

Can more than one person reach Bingo at a time? If so, who among them is the winner? How many unique Bingo cards are there for the 75-ball game? In a game where you are one of N players with a Bingo card each:

- What is the probability that you win?
- What is the average number of numbers called when the game round ends?
- What is the distribution of the number of numbers called when the game round ends?

Tip 31

Modeling versus models

Modeling is the art of developing a visible form to represent an actual situation. The visible form may be a physical structure in an analog system or a software program code in a digital system. In spreadsheets, we use a digital representation. Many ready-made spreadsheet templates are available to address various problem situations. Some effort may be required to update them to fit your particular case. This could be as simple as entering new input values. Most of these model templates, however, do not address the same problem as yours. More than just entering new inputs, you have to spend time understanding the use of the template and modeling details, before you can add new cells and revise their formulas.

It is also likely that your situation is rather unique and you have to model from scratch. Therefore, learn and do the modeling yourself, piecing together, often with other team members, the data, assumptions, variables, and relationships among the variables. The end product will be a jointly developed model, co-owned by the team. Few people we know of like to study and understand another person's spreadsheet model, particularly when it is not well formatted and documented. It is therefore important to work as a team, and also to dress and document your model well. This paves the way for easier implementation. The developed model is usually as a result simpler to maintain in the future even when circumstances are changed enough to require again more than mere adjustment of input values.

Tip 32

Types of models

There are various types of mathematical and computational models. One approach classifies them as descriptive, prescriptive, or predictive. A descriptive model emulates the behavior of the situation studied, a prescriptive model goes further to recommend a better or the best solution, and a predictive model projects into the future usually by extrapolating from the past. These models may be linear or nonlinear depending on how the variables functionally relate to one another. Models may also be either deterministic or stochastic. In a deterministic model, all values are either given or constants to be determined. In a stochastic model, one or more values are not only beyond your control, they also change probabilistically. Some models are of either a single or multiple periods, with either single or multiple actors, and if multiple actors, they are either noncompetitive or competitive in their interactions. Models can be pitched at the different decision levels of the organizational hierarchy, namely strategic, tactical, and operational. Spreadsheet models are best used as support tools for higher-level decision making and less as business operations systems. The key lesson to remember when you do the modeling is to try not to attempt too much in any single model, but to keep each model simple and devise ways of understanding the interactions between models.

Keeping it alive | **Tip 33**

Except for a few operations such as **Goal Seek** and **Data Sort**, spreadsheet models are generally "alive" in that every new entry in a cell will automatically trigger the whole workbook to be recalculated. Try to keep your models alive as far as possible. Therefore, instead of using Goal Seek, mathematically derive inverse functions, if that is feasible and easy, and use them instead. Also, while Data Sort is useful as an interactive data analysis operation, you should keep it away from your decision models. The better alternative is use the **SMALL** and **LARGE** functions plus a cell array of running serial numbers 1, 2, ... to sort values in any cell array in ascending and descending order, respectively. Methods from **Data Analysis Toolpak** in Excel should also be avoided where possible. Finally in many situations, macros and **Event Subs** may be needed to keep a model *alive*. A *live* spreadsheet model is wonderful as you can ask all those *What-if* questions and get immediate responses. If ever your model is not *alive*, a good practice would be to leave a prominent note in it to state so and specify the steps users must take to get all cells updated whenever relevant changes are introduced.

RAND in formulas | **Tip 34**

Each occurrence of **RAND** generates a different random value and its value changes with each recalculation of the worksheet. Therefore, a formula like =IF(RAND() < .., ..., RAND()* 2) is not likely to behave correctly since the test condition will be quite independent of the result it is supposed to return. It would be better in this and many other situations to hold the random value generating formula =RAND() in separate cells and have the evaluation formula make references to them. In such cases, it is as if the cells with the =RAND() formula are input cells with automatically generated inputs.

Still in other cases, you may even want these randomly generated values to be temporarily unchanging. For example, if your model uses **Solver** to find the optimal solution, having dynamically changing and randomly generated "input" values makes it extremely difficult for Solver to converge and terminate its computation. The remedy would be to have two sets of randomly generated values. The first (dynamic) set has the =RAND() formula in its cells and the second (static) set, with the same number of cells, holds data that are copied (as values) from the first set. Formulas in the spreadsheet model should make reference to the static set and a macro can be written to automate the transfer of the values from the dynamic set to the static set when another replication of the model is needed.

FURTHER REFERENCES

- Ariely, 2010. *Predictably Irrational*, Harper Perennial.
- Eckstein and Riedmueller, 2003. "YASAI (Yet Another Simulation Add-In)," *INFORMS Transactions on Education* 2(2).
  - http://archive.ite.journal.informs.org/Vol2No2/EcksteinRiedmueller/ EcksteinRiedmueller.pdf
  - http://www.yasai.rutgers.edu
- Evans, 2001. "Spreadsheets as a Tool for Teaching Simulation," *INFORMS Transactions on Education* 1(1).
  - http://archive.ite.journal.informs.org/Vol1No1/Evans/Evans.pdf
- Leong, 2014. Spreadsheet Modeling Resources
  - http://isotope.unisim.edu.sg/users/tyleong/SpreadsheetModeling. htm#Simulation
  - http://dl.dropboxusercontent.com/u/19228704/SpreadsheetModeling. htm#Simulation
- Leong, 2007. "Monte Carlo Spreadsheet Simulation using Resampling," *INFORMS Transactions on Education* 7(3): 188–200.
  - http://archive.ite.journal.informs.org/Vol7No3/Leong
- Leong and Lee, 2008. "Spreadsheet Data Resampling for Monte-Carlo Simulation," *Spreadsheet in Education* 3(1): 70-78.
  - http://epublications.bond.edu.au/cgi/viewcontent.cgi?article=1053& context=ejsie
- Savage, 2001. "Blitzogram – Interactive Histogram," *INFORMS Transactions on Education* 1(2).
  - http://archive.ite.journal.informs.org/Vol1No2/Savage/Savage.pdf
- Savage, Danziger, and Markowitz, 2012. *The Flaw of Averages: When We Underestimate Risk in the Face of Uncertainty*, Wiley.
- Taleb, 2001. *Fooled by Randomness*. Texere LLC, New York, and London.

- Keywords. Relevant topics to search in Google and Wikipedia
  - *Randomness . Risk uncertainty . Fluctuation . Monte-Carlo simulation . Monty Hall . Flaw of averages . Game theory and strategy . Gamesmanship . Brinkmanship . Don't just follow the leader*

PROBLEM SET 6

* Hard problems

Dice throws. A die is a small cube with six sides; each side is marked by dots to represent 1, 2, 3, 4, 5, and 6. Each throw of a die therefore produces a uniformly distributed integer between 1 and 6. More than one die can be thrown and their sums taken. Alternatively with one die, consecutive die throws in a round are summed. What is the probability distribution of the sum of two-dice throws? What about three-dice throws?

Qn 6.01

a. Construct a spreadsheet model to represent the sum of die throws.
b. Simulate 100 trials of two-dice throws and three-dice throws. Compute their averages and standard deviation.
c. Comment on what their distributions look like and how increasing the number of throws per round changes their statistics and shape of distribution.

Double or nothing. In the gambling game of heads or tails, a coin is tossed. You win if it is heads and lose if it is tails. A win means you keep the bet plus an additional bet amount given to you by the banker, and a loss means the banker takes your bet. In general, if the probability of winning is p, then the total returned amount when you win is the bet amount divided by p. In this case, p is ½ and therefore the total return (inclusive of the bet) to the winner is two times the bet. After a few rounds, your net balance or win is the amount you currently have minus the amount you initially have before the game started.

Qn 6.02

a. Construct a spreadsheet model to simulate the betting strategies in this coin toss game.
b. A simple strategy is to bet the same amount each time until money runs out or completing round 40, whichever comes first. Note the last bet, depending on what is available, may not be equal to the first bet amount. Using this strategy, with an initial fund of $1,000 and $10 bet size, what are the average and standard deviation of the last net balance? Do the same for $50 bets and $100 bets.
c. A "better" strategy, supposedly a sure win, goes like this: You first bet a fixed amount. If you lose, you double the bet and keep doing that until you win. Once you win, you quit the round and begin again from the start if there is still time. Again with an initial $1,000 and start bet sizes of $10, $50, or $100, evaluate the average and standard deviation of the last net balance. Can you really not lose following the *double or nothing* strategy?

Slot machine. The slot machine is a favorite among many patrons in casinos and private clubs. It has three identical reels, each reel with spots for 64 images. These

Qn 6.03

include cherry, plum, melon, ace, bar, bell, diamond, lemon, gold coins, orange, and seven. After inserting one or more dollar coins, the gambler pulls the handle and the reels spin. The machine displays three images, one from each reel, when the reels stop spinning. Depending on the counts of certain images displayed and the bet inserted, the machine gives in return nothing, some coins, or an overflowing payoff.

a. Construct a spreadsheet model to simulate the slot machine. Assume in each reel, there are 4 cherry, 4 plum, 4 melon, 5 ace, 5 bar, 7 bell, 7 diamond, 7 lemon, 7 gold coins, 7 orange and 7 seven images, all randomly arranged.

b. For every $1 inserted, the payoff for 1 cherry image is $2, 2 cherry images gives $5, and 3 cherry images gives $10; 2 plum images gives $20, 3 plum images gives $30; and 2 melon images gives $40 and 3 melon images gives $60. What is the net balance after 28 pulls when the initial is $100 and bets are all $1 each?

c. How do you handle more complex payoff conditions? For example, a set of 1 gold coins, 1 diamond and 1 melon images to pay out $150 per dollar bet.

Qn 6.04   **Car servicing**. A small gas station-based automobile service center has a list of customers, some regular and some not. They keep a record of the odometer readings of customers' cars at each servicing. From the record, they can see some service at approximately every 5,000 or 10,000 km intervals and some skipped or are irregular.

a. Construct a spreadsheet model that simulates the station's record of its customers' last four servicing. It should contain week numbers and odometer readings of each servicing.

b. For each customer on the list, project the next servicing week and odometer reading.

c. Assuming each servicing is charged at $250, estimate the revenue of the station for each week of the four-week horizon.

Qn 6.05   **Light bulbs**. The university maintenance section has been busy last year responding to urgent requests to change light bulbs when they failed. Currently, all bulbs are only changed when they fail. This meant each time a staff has to drop what he was doing to go within a short time to fix the lamp. They do this one lamp at a time, haphazardly across the campus. To make their work more predictable and less hectic, the department is exploring a few options. One idea is to change the light bulbs after a certain use time, systematically from room to room before they even have the chance to fail. Another would be to put two or three smaller bulbs in each lamp so that it still functions when at least one of the bulbs is working, though not as bright. These bulbs being smaller should be cheaper to procure and bulb change can be scheduled to be done in a more orderly fashion.

a. Construct a spreadsheet model to simulate this situation for 100 trials, assuming the bulbs' lifespan follows the Weibull distribution.

b. Each regular bulb A costs $3, with Weibull scale parameter a of 420 days and shape parameter b of 1.3. The smaller bulb B costs $2, with Weibull scale parameter of 350 days and shape parameter of 1.2. A random Weibull value can be simulated using formula = $b * (-LN(1-RAND()))^{\wedge}(1/a)$.

c. Compare the average or mean time to failure (MTTF) of the lamps for the scenarios: 1) bulb A, 2) bulb A with scheduled bulb change at 200 days, 3) bulb A with scheduled bulb change at 250 days, 4) 1 bulb B in each lamp, 5) 2 bulbs of B in each lamp, and 6) 3 bulbs of B in each lamp.

d. For each scenario, evaluate how often the maintenance department has to respond to ad hoc failed bulb-servicing requests.

Industrial engine. Sanjay's plant uses many industrial engines in its operations. As engines get older, they require more servicing and are more likely to break down, with some becoming non-repairable. While older engines still have resale value, a failed one is practically worthless. So, he thinks it may be more economical to better plan their replacement. While considering this decision, he realized the concern is equally applicable to other equipments. Thus, he is determined to analyze the issue thoroughly so that he can re-use the solution template.

Qn 6.06

a. Construct a spreadsheet simulation model to evaluate the replacement interval for the industrial engines. From historical data, an engine in year 1 fails with 0.04 probability during the year, costs $3,300 to maintain, and has a resale value of $9,500. Similar data for other years are year 2, 0.06 probability, $4,400 and $8,000; year 3, 0.08 probability, $5,500 and $6,400; year 4, 0.18 probability, $9,900 and $4,400; year 5, 0.24 probability, $12,000 and $3,000; and year 6, 0.32 probability, $13,200 and $1,100 respectively.

b. Assume current engine purchase price is $28,000, all prices are expected to change over time with an inflation rate of 3%, and all values are discounted to present values at 12% per annum.

c. Over a planning horizon of 25 years and for each possible replacement interval, determine the expected replacement interval and net present value per year.

d. Compute the results for at least 250 replications. What is the optimal replacement interval for the industrial engine?

Soft drinks vending machine. A soft drinks vending machine has two kinds of canned drinks: carbonated priced at $1.20 per can and non-carbonated priced at $1.00 per can. The machine can hold up to 200 cans and is replenished daily at 10 am. A quick survey was done of its sales pattern. For any 15-minute interval, the data shows that 0 cans were sold 20% of the time, 1 can sold 45% of the time, 2 cans sold 25% of the time, and 3 cans sold 10% of the time for carbonated drinks; and 0 cans were sold 40% of the time, 1 can sold 43% of the time, 2 cans sold 15% of the time, and 3 cans sold 2% of the time for non-carbonated drinks.

Qn 6.07*

a. Construct a spreadsheet model to simulate the vending machine sales operations.
b. For stocking level of 100 cans of carbonated drinks and 80 cans of non-carbonated drinks at replenishment, determine the average number of carbonated and non-carbonated drink sales, and average total sales per day.
c. For stocking level of 80 cans of carbonated drinks and 100 cans of non-carbonated drinks at replenishment, determine the average number of carbonated and non-carbonated drink sales, and average total sales per day.
d. What is the optimal stock level of carbonated and non-carbonated cans at replenishment?

Qn 6.08*

Intercity trucking. The truck rental company operates in cities A, B, and C. Past data shows that most of the trucks rented are returned to the same city. There is however a significant number of trucks used to move cargo between cities. The company is considering if they have positioned the trucks correctly at the cities. Trucks may need to be repositioned at their cost to cities where there are higher demands.

a. Construct a spreadsheet model for the company to understand the movement of trucks between the cities and the steady-state proportion of trucks at the cities.
b. For trucks rented at city A, 55% were returned at A, 15% were returned at B, and 30% were returned at C. For trucks rented at city B, 35% were returned at A, 45% were returned at B, and 20% were returned at C. For trucks rented at city C, 15% were returned at A, 15% were returned at B, and 70% were returned at C.
c. For trucks returned to the same city they were rented from, 50% of them were returned the next day, 30% were rented for 2 days, and 20% were rented for 3 days. For trucks returned to another city, 15% of them were returned the next day, 20% were rented for 2 days, 30% were rented for 3 days, 25% were rented for 4 days, and 10% were rented for 5 days.
d. In proportion to rental demands at start cities, the trucks were initially distributed with 50% at A, 30% at B, and 20% at C. Simulate for 200 consecutive rentals, where and when a truck will next be each time. Compute the stay duration for each city when the truck does not leave the city. What is the steady-state end city distribution of the trucks? What should the company do about the difference between start and end allocations?

Qn 6.09*

Spa package. A 45-minute massage and general skin treatment at a spa cost $100. The spa is very popular and getting a free slot for walk-in clients is difficult. Ad hoc clients can only make one-day advance appointments. 35% of the clients have signed up packages. These clients are given preference and can schedule multiple treatments a few weeks in advance. The price for a 10-visit contract at 15% discount is $850 and the package is valid for a year. Not all clients complete the 10 visits in their package.

a. Construct a spreadsheet model of the business for the proprietor.

b. For those without a contract, 15% do not come back at all, 20% come back for a second visit, 30% for a third visit, 25% for a fourth visit, and 10% for a fifth visit. For those with a contract, 50% complete the package, 30% came for 9 visits, 10% for 8 visits, 5% for 7 visits, 3% for 6 visits, and 2% for 5 or fewer visits.

c. Simulating 100 customers, determine percentage of total revenue, revenue per client, and revenue per visit of ad hoc clients. Do the same for contract clients.

d. The proprietor is considering offering a backdated contract to ad hoc clients who have completed two visits. They only need to pay the remaining $650 for the additional 8 visits, which amounts to a 19% discount. She hopes to get 40% of the clients offered the backdated contract to accept it.

e. Evaluate the revenue potential of the proposal, assuming the backdated contract clients are going to behave like the regular contract clients. Provide further improvement suggestions.

Telemarketing. Sally was introduced to a temporary telemarketing job opportunity. In this job, she has to call 500 prospects a day. After some inquiries, she discovered that an average prospect who does not buy anything needs 75 seconds to talk to and those who buy takes 350 seconds to complete the call. Not all prospects pick up the phone. Callers typically hang on for 10 seconds before aborting the call when no one responds. 16% of the prospects pick up the phone on the first call, 11% on the second call, 8% on the third call, 5% on the fourth call, and 60% on the fifth or more calls if they respond at all. Telemarketers typically make at most 3 call-tries per prospect. Of those reached, 82% do not buy anything, 9% take the $88 deal, 6% take the $188 deal, and 3% take the $288 deal. Commission to the telemarketer is 8% of sales.

| Qn 6.10* |

a. Construct a spreadsheet model to simulate this situation for the telemarketer.

b. Determine the number of calls made to unreachable prospects, prospects with no sales, and prospects with sales. Work out the time spent on each of the above.

c. How long does a telemarketer have to work per day? What is the expected commission per hour for Sally if she takes the job?

d. Suggest further extensions to your model.

Processes and Time

- Able to compute with time and data variables
- Able to simulate multi-server waiting lines
- Able to model real-time situations
- Able to record, edit, and write simple macros

INTRODUCTION

Date and time variables are not easy to deal with in a model as they do not follow the typical metric (base 10) standard and they have many other unusual characteristics. For example, if you try to compute the number of days from your date of birth to today, you will soon realize the immensity of the task. There is first, the unequal number of days in the months of the year and then there are extra days in leap years (and other corrections if you go far back enough) to contend with.

Excel has somewhat simplified the work by representing internally all dates as the number of days from 0 January 1900 and time in decimals as proportions of a whole day. Therefore, 12 noon of 15 January 1900 is 15.5 and, with 1900 being erroneously designated as a leap year by Excel, 6 pm of 20 January 1991 is 386.75. With these and other provisions such as the ability to screen out the weekends, you can, for instance, compute the number of working days between any two dates. It now takes only some formatting to change the numbers from decimals to dates or time, or both in combinations. The leap year error can be corrected by using the 1904 date system option. In this date system, 1 January 1904, instead of 0 January 1900, is day 0.

With such a representation scheme, you can now even simulate with some finest random time durations and work on queuing and other time-related processes. Spreadsheets also allows you to extract the date and time from your personal computer's operating system clock. You can, therefore, write spreadsheet

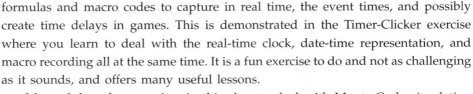

formulas and macro codes to capture in real time, the event times, and possibly create time delays in games. This is demonstrated in the Timer-Clicker exercise where you learn to deal with the real-time clock, date-time representation, and macro recording all at the same time. It is a fun exercise to do and not as challenging as it sounds, and offers many useful lessons.

Most of the other exercises in this chapter deal with Monte-Carlo simulation of queues: *XDB Bank, Call Center, Tandem Queues,* and *Emergency Services.* The breakthrough in simulation that allows these models to be constructed is a new parametric formulation we devised that simplifies the spreadsheet modeling of multi-server queues. *XDB Bank* is interesting in helping you to understand how to interpret data taken from a computer data log, extracting from it service durations and customer arrival process information. The queue inference engine there can be applied to infer in real time, the queues at the automated teller machines (ATM) or any other similar machines. The *Call Center* exercise shows the impact of different number of servers on service performance.

Sometimes, queue buffers have limited capacities and this in turn can constrict the flow of jobs from one production stage to the next. The *Tandem Queues* exercise illustrates the analysis of one such case. Another interesting example of queues in practice is the context where the server has to move around to service geographically dispersed service requests. This is examined in the *Emergency Services* exercise. The data required for all these models can be obtained in field observations quite easily using *Timer-Clicker.*

Finally, a different kind of time-related exercise in its own right is *Time and Tide.* This is neither a queue situation nor Monte-Carlo simulation, but rather an attempt to understand the periodic patterns of ocean tides.

DISCOVERY POINTS

Waiting is a common occurrence. No one can possibly claim they have never waited before. Even royalty and celebrities wait. Wait is of interest to many organizations because it is a measure of customer service performance. Let's say your project client is a bank and they want to study how long people wait in line at their tellers. How hard can it be to collect 30 to 50 data points for this analysis? If you work out the detail mechanics, you will know that it is hard. You need to track each person, know when she arrives and when the server starts serving her. If you follow one person at a time, you will have to suffer the whole wait time of each person and thus may not collect enough data in the time you have.

Waiting in line

Wait is actually the outcome of interactions between arrival and service times. It is thus an output of the system. Collecting output data of any system is useful for tracking its performance. However, they are rather worthless for improvement analysis. What does it say when the wait times are getting shorter or longer? Surely, you can only guess if it is because fewer or more customers are arriving or the server is working faster or slower. In this case, you might as well collect inter-arrival and service duration times and then use them to compute the wait times. You can then examine what strategies can be adopted to moderate and pace arrivals, and trim and adapt service times.

Wait times collected in fact are often flawed with errors. Imagine walking randomly into a bus stop and asking commuters there how long they have waited. These data collected are not truly wait times. To complete the data collection, you have to stay until the commuters board their respective buses. Moreover, the people you meet in the bus stop do not constitute a fair sample even though you randomly walked in. This is because the likelihood that your ad hoc appearance catching the commuters with short or no waiting is much less than those who wait longer. This random incidence problem can be better explained in another way. Suppose straws of different lengths are held in a hand with ends flushed for picking. Not being able to see the actual lengths of the straws, a simple pick from the bunch is a random draw. If the straws are instead scattered on the floor and after being blindfolded, you pick one straw from the floor. This straw is not a random pick because of how the straws lay on the floor. Longer straws have higher probabilities of being picked, more than shorter straws.

Event points do not happen instantaneously in real life. This is contrary to what theoretical models say. For example, Queuing Theory models conveniently assume the end of service for one customer is the start of service for the next person waiting

Power of observation

in line. Now go see if this is true in a fast-food restaurant. Isn't there a time lapse between end of one service and the start of the next? Given service durations are getting shorter, with more services emphasizing speed as a key service attribute, these time lapses can no longer be ignored. Also, observe that it is not always so simple to know who is being served and who is waiting. In particular, after taking orders from a customer at the head of a line, the server may ask this customer to step aside and proceed to take orders from the next customer. All this while the orders received are being fulfilled by the back kitchen staff. What kind of queuing system is this? How many servers are there in this single line? Isn't the kitchen also concurrently serving this line, and other waiting lines as well?

Personal care services are increasingly more sophisticated in managing customers' expectations and service satisfaction. They also deliberately blur the distinction between wait and service. If you go to a spa for your appointment, service can literally start the moment you arrive. They may not be working on your body with a massage, but you certainly get a cup of tea, a seat to recline on and soft music. The fact that you are actually waiting alludes many. Finding opportunities in modeling lie in making these keen observations. In fact if you are good with the theoretical models, it should be obvious from the difficulties encountered in data collection that practice is starkly different. Cultivate the habit of comparing theory with practice and from their differences get sharp insights.

Point 31

Single and multiple queues

Queuing systems are classified by three attributes: 1) how people arrive to the system, 2) how the arrivals queue in the system, and 3) how many servers are there in the system. Most service systems have multiple servers, and each server has a dedicated waiting line. The servers can be assumed to be identical. So there is no reason to choose one over another. On entering the service system, the natural thing is to join the line with the fewest people. Hence, the queue before each server automatically balances. Another queuing setting may have a counter with many servers and only one common queue that snakes up to a common exit point at the head of the queue. The person there goes to the first server who becomes available. There have been many debates as to which of the two systems is better or more efficient.

By the law of work conservation, neither approach is superior to the other. Since no extra work is created or destroyed, average wait-time and average queue-length of both approaches are the same. However, the impact on individuals is not the same. The multiple-server, single-queue system guarantees first-come, first-served. Not so for a multiple-server, multiple-queue system. A person may be unfortunate to be in a particular queue with people before him needing long service times. This person may decide that the line he is in is not moving and may *jockey* to another line with a shorter queue length. When queue lengths get to be too long, many times a new arrival may not even join the line and therefore is said to *balk* the system. Those already in line may have suffered enough and decide to leave, thinking it is not worthwhile to stay on. These people are said to have *reneged* from the system.

Point 32

Queue inference

Automation of many processes means data you need have already been collected by the system. This may be considered a case of *unknown knowns* (see *Point 34*) since the data logs of systems are often untapped information resources. One reason for not using more of these resources is that the data there may be incomplete. For example, most systems keep service-start and service-end times, but cannot record customer arrival times. Hence, the data cannot be used to study wait times and queue lengths of these systems. Data that cannot be collected however can be inferred. So the trick in getting better mileage for the latent data resource is to be better at making inferences.

The key ideas behind inference are to employ underlying assumptions known to be true and to apply well-founded theoretical results. One such assumption that can be made of the arrival pattern of people and jobs to a system is that they follow the Poisson process. This comes about because there are numerous interacting random processes that result in the probability of an arrival in any small time interval to be independent to that of another small time interval and they all have the same probability. That is, they are independent and identically distributed. We know from probability theory that Poisson arrivals have exponentially distributed inter-arrival times and for any fixed interval with some arrivals, these arrivals are also uniformly distributed over that interval.

EXERCISES

Exercise 57   **TIMER-CLICKER**   Worked Example

Challenge   This workbook provides a set of handy tools for project fieldwork: *Timer* and *Clicker*.

Timer is designed for queue system observation and analysis. It records arrival, service-start, and service-end times, and tabulates intermediate variables like inter-arrival, service, wait, and (service + wait =) system times.

Clicker, a slight adaptation of *Timer*, is designed for counting arrivals. It records arrival times of up to three types of customers and tabulates their frequency counts for given time intervals. In fact, both worksheets can be further adapted to collect other process-type field data.

Scratch is a blank worksheet for you to practice thinking about how to set up the template.

Proto is a blank template for you to practice creating the *Timer* (or *Clicker*) worksheet: fill in formulas, set formats, rehearse manual work steps, record macros, and assign macros to buttons. You can also customize your own data collection worksheet.

If needed, can you adapt and customize these sheets for your project work?

Concept   In many service situations, performance quality is determined by the length of waiting and size of queues. A long wait for customers is a sign of a shortage of servers. It would be good to periodically measure the wait time and queue length behavior, or at least know their average values.

- How would you go about collecting such information?
- Is it easy or hard to collect?

An alternative approach is to collect the inter-arrival and service duration times. These values can be verified to be typically exponentially distributed. These properties or the sample data (resampled) may be used in another model to work out the service performance.

Clicker is an attempt to provide a counting device, much like the physical clicking counter. However, the counting of arrivals typically has to be related to a time interval, such as counting the number of yellow-top taxis passing a junction in a 30-minute interval.

- What if the interval durations are too gross and needed to be finer?
- Would the data need to be taken again?

It is important to rehearse manually how the data are to be entered into the spreadsheet. The data capturing would eventually not be done by hand since this will not be responsive enough to the events as they rapidly appear. A macro can be recorded to do the work.

It is opportune to note that if the click times are also recorded rather than a count, it is not difficult to compute the frequency counts for any interval breakdowns. You can therefore construct *Clicker* by modifying *Timer*. Let us start working one tool at a time.

a. Time Recorder

This tool is designed for a single queue, first-come first-served, single server situation. It assumes that customers arrive one at a time and are served one at a time by the server. It also assumes that there are no balking and reneging in the queue system. That is, no arriving customers are turned away from joining a long waiting line and no one who has been waiting for a considerable amount of time leaves before getting any service. We will prepare the tool by recording three different macros to capture the time stamp for three events, namely arrival of a customer, service start, and service end. Upon obtaining the time data of these three events, we can do simple subtractions to obtain the customer inter-arrival interval, wait time, service time, and (wait + service =) system time.

  i. Select the *Proto* worksheet.

 ii. Enter into cell D3 the formula =NOW() (i.e., the current system clock time, which has to be refreshed whenever the latest time is needed). Right-click on cell D3 and customize its format to h:mm:ss.

iii. Key **F9** at a few spaced intervals to ensure that the clock is refreshed.

iv. Before we start to record the macros, prepare the worksheet with some initial data.

   • In cells C7:E7, enter the formula =$D$3. These three cells must be filled with some initial values so that the macro recordings with the **Ctrl + ↓** action can work properly.

   • Enter into cell F8 the formula =IF(OR(C7>C8,E8=""),"",C8-C7) (i.e., inter-arrival time is a blank if the previous arrival time is greater than the current arrival time and the service end time is not recorded. Otherwise, inter-arrival time equals the difference between the current and previous arrival times).

   • Enter into cell G8 the formula "=IF(E8="","",E8-D8) (i.e., *Service time = Service-end time − Service-start time*).

   • Enter into cell H8 the formula "=IF(E8="","",D8-C8)" (i.e., *Wait time = Service-start time − Arrival time*).

- Enter into cell I8 the formula "=IF(E8="","",E8-C8)" (i.e., *System time = Service-end time – Arrival time*).

v. To record the customer arrival time macro
  - Click **Developer/Record Macro**, enter the macro name (e.g., *Stamp_ Arrival*) and click **OK**.
  - Key **F9** to update the time in cell D3.
  - Select cell D3 and right-click to select **Copy**. This action will copy the current time.
  - Select cell C6. Key **Ctrl +** ↓ to set the last cell in the column with a value as the active cell.
  - Click **Developer/Use Relative References** to toggle it ON.
  - Key ↓ to move the active cell to the first available empty cell in the column.
  - Right-click and select **Paste Special** to bring up the **Paste Special** dialog. Select **Values and Number Formats**, and click **OK**.
  - Key **Esc** to clear the copy buffer, thus removing the dotted box around the selection.
  - Click **Developer/Use Relative References** to switch it OFF.
  - Click **Developer/Stop Recording** to end the macro recording.
  - To review the recorded macro, key **Alt + F11** and select the last module in the VB Editor.

```
Sub Stamp_Arrival()
  Calculate
  Range("D3").Select
  Selection.Copy
  Range("C6").Select
  Selection.End(xlDown).Select
  ActiveCell.Offset(1, 0).Range("A1").Select
  Selection.PasteSpecial Paste:=xlPasteValuesAnd
  NumberFormats,
  Operation:=xlNone, SkipBlanks:=False, Transpose:=False
  Application.CutCopyMode = False
End Sub
```

Let us look at the macro line by line.
  ○ `Calculate` activates the recalculation to refresh the clock time in cell D3.
  ○ `Range("D3").Select` selects cell D3 that holds the clock time.
  ○ `Selection.Copy` copies the value in cell D3.
  ○ `Range("C6").Select` selects cell D6, the header for the arrival time column.

- o `Selection.End(xlDown).Select` moves the active cell down to the last cell in the column that has a value.
- o `ActiveCell.Offset(1, 0).Range("A1").Select` makes active the cell one row below the last active cell. This new active cell is the first available empty cell in the column that will be used to keep the new time stamp. The first half of `Offset(r,c).Range("A1")` moves the active cell by r rows and c columns and the second denotes the size of the selected area. Here, "A1" means a range of one column and one row, whereas if it was "A1:F3", it would mean six columns and three rows. If relative reference mode is not activated in this part of the macro recording, the cell selected will be a fixed location. To understand relative reference in macro recording, refer to *Note 16* in Appendix B.
- o `Selection.PasteSpecial Paste:=xlPasteValuesAnd NumberFormats, Operation:=xlNone, SkipBlanks:=False, Transpose:=False` pastes the copied time value into the active blank cell.
- o `Application.CutCopyMode = False` removes the dotted selection box.

vi. To write the service-start and service-end macros
- Key **Alt + F11** to get to the VB Editor. Select the module with the *Stamp_Arrival* macro.
- Select all the lines of code in *Stamp_Arrival* and copy them. Then, paste them below the last line to create a new **Sub**.
- Revise *Stamp_Arrival* to *Stamp_Start* in this new subroutine (Sub).
- Replace `Range("C6").Select` with `Range("D6").Select`.
- Repeat the process above to create the *Stamp_End* subroutine. This time replace `Range("C6").Select` with `Range("E6").Select`.

vii. To assign macros to buttons
- Click **Developer/Insert/Form Controls/Button** to insert a button or **Developer/Insert/Shapes** to insert any shape. Resize your graphic object and move it to a suitable location in column C above the table header.
- Right-click on the object, select **Edit Text** and key the label as *Arrive*.
- Right-click on the object, select **Assign Macro** dialog and choose your recorded *Stamp_Arrival*. With it assigned, the macro will run whenever the object is clicked.
- Repeat the steps to make the buttons or the other two macros with captions *Start* and *End*, respectively.

b. Count Recorder

This tool is more flexible than a physical clicker counter, since the latter merely count and does not record the arrival times. Using *Timer* as the template, this tool can record the arrival times of three different types of customers. Additional columns and more copies of the subroutine can be made to record even more the count of more types of customers. With their arrival times recorded, we can compute and tabulate the arrival frequency of each customer type in the different time intervals.

i.   Select the *Clicker* worksheet.

ii.   Cell D3 records the current time with the formula =NOW().

iii. Cells C7:E7 are set to cell D3 with the formula =$D$3.

iv.   Time bins of different sizes for different time intervals of interest are defined in cells F8:F52. In the worksheet, for example, the time bins start from 8:00:00 to 17:30:00 with a time interval of 30 minutes.

v.   The frequency counts of each customer type in the time bins are to be computed in columns G, H, and I.

vi.   In cell G8, the formula =IF(F8="","",FREQUENCY(C$8:C$999,$F8)) computes the number of type A customers who arrive at or earlier than 8:00:00 (<= 8:00:00). The formula is filled down to cells G9:G52 to compute the number of type A customers who arrive in the other time bins (<= 8:30:00, <= 9:00:00, etc.).

vii. The formula in cell G8 is copied to cells H8:I52, to compute the frequency for types B and C customers accordingly.

viii. The buttons at the head of columns C, D, and E are still assigned to *Stamp_Arrival*, *Stamp_Start*, and *Stamp_End* macros, respectively. Their labels are correspondingly changed to *Count A*, *Count B*, and *Count C*.

Challenge

XDB Bank operates close to 800 automated teller machines (ATMs) in the city. The ATMs are in general well utilized. Mary, the VP of ATM operations, is particularly concerned about the machines in the business centers and major shopping complexes. Lately, there have been frequent complaints from customers about the long queues at some ATMs there.

Mary is considering hiring students from a local university during the coming summer vacation to observe and collect data for analysis. But the number of machines involved is large, and therefore the data collection work requires a large group of students. Her other concern is whether the data collected will be representative for the rest of the year.

She thinks that there must be a better way to monitor the service level of the ATMs (i.e., waiting time and queue length), preferably one that is automated for real-time feedback, without the need for physical observation. She has eliminated the use of video cameras to record the queue situation as the effort to review the tapes is too labor-intensive.

Mary consulted the bank's systems department and discovered that transaction time logs are kept for each ATM, which record the insertion times of users' bank card and the completion times of their transactions.

With this information in hand, Mary has asked you if you can help. She has given you a set of log data for a busy three-hour time-window of one ATM. Can you estimate the service performance of this ATM?

Concept

Data logs are rich sources of information. The information is, however, often ignored because nobody understands its potential beyond the immediate intended use. Looking at the time stamps in the data log is very much like listening to one side of a conversation. But with some smart guessing and interpretation, the data log can be used for getting the valuable service performance statistics. Can you think of other situations where similar data logs are kept that can also benefit from such analysis? Given a data log, can you infer the number of servers if that is not known?

Working

You can extract, from the data log, some basic statistics and distributional characteristics of the customer arrival and service duration processes.

*   What are the basic statistics you can compute?
*   What do you think are the distribution functional forms of the inter-arrival and service duration times?

After this brief data analysis segment, you may want to start thinking about how you would reconstruct the interplay between the arrival and service times. One approach to present the model would be to use the columns for the variables and a row each for the customers.

There are possibly two broad approaches to proceed from here:

- Reconstruct directly the situation as given by the data, or
- Simulate other similar situations and compute the statistics of key service performance indicators.

The simulated values can be resampled from a given sample data set or computed using an inverse distribution function.

Exercise 59   CALL CENTER

Challenge

The call center had been rapidly increasing in size in the last few years due to the fast growth of the company's business. It is beginning to seem like hiring, training, and setting up of the basic infrastructure for the operations may soon be outpaced by business growth. Before making further decisions as to what actions need to be taken (particularly about possible outsourcing), you decide to evaluate and understand how the business change can affect the demand for call center capacity.

Concept

While formulas for the service performance of a queue system exist, they are valid for the steady state case, including *Poisson* arrival process and *Exponential* service duration time distribution. Some of these formulas may not even be in closed-form and therefore need iterative computation to derive the results. Monte-Carlo simulation is an alternative approach. Doing it in a spreadsheet in particular allows the client to see the inner workings of the simulation, without dragging in too much technical detail. However, while it is easy to provide a single-server model, multiple-server models are more complex and need a separate worksheet each for the different number of servers. Some ingenuity is needed to overcome this problem to produce a parametric multiple-server model that only requires the user to change the number of server value.

Working

Use a row each to represent all the event points of each caller. Simulate all the required values for that caller: inter-arrival time and service duration time. Work out the single server case, making sure it provides all the necessary service performance statistics and a graph for easy review. The key point to note is the computation of the service-start time of the caller. As always, you should start by working on the first row (caller 1). However, you should have the mindset that the formula derived must be applicable to any caller. This way, when caller 1's row is copied and pasted down to other rows, they will still compute correctly. So the service-start time of caller 1 must be the larger of the arrival time of caller 1 and the service-end time of caller 0, assuming a first-come, first-served policy.

The multiple-server case can then be constructed by revising the service-start time formula to take into account that there are now c servers. Therefore, the service-start time would be the larger of the caller's arrival time and the service-end time of the cth largest service-end times of those who came before this caller. This is because with the departure of this caller, the system would have one server free.

TANDEM QUEUES

Challenge

This workbook simulates the behavior of queues in a system with multiple-server stations arranged in a series. There are limited buffer capacities between the stations, and the departure from an upstream station will be blocked if the downstream buffer is full. As a result, a server in a station cannot start serving the next job until the downstream buffer has free space to accommodate the job the server wants to release.

Concept

This is an extension of the multiple-server model in the *Call Center* exercise. The model is customized to the case of three multi-server stations in tandem. The number of servers for each station and the size of buffers between them can be parametrically changed, but not the number of stations. The model shows that we can build upon another model to modify or extend it to accommodate our current needs. Possible issues to consider include how best to allocate buffers among the servers and how to allocate the servers, if they are interchangeable, to the stations. This implicitly assumes that the servers are homogenous. What if they are heterogeneous?

Working

This may be a good exercise to practice from scratch. Alternatively, take the model in the *Call Center* exercise as the base and modify it, rearranging columns if necessary to create the columns for a station. Try to make the first station a general station so that its columns can be replicated for stations 2 and 3 without modification. This would mean there is a buffer before station 1. This buffer may be set with infinite capacity. Since the size of this first buffer may be set to be finite, the model is now more general than originally intended.

Try to understand the information given in the *Explain* worksheet which shows how the average number of people in the system may be approximated. This statistic is generally more useful than the average number of people in the queue. However, if the latter is required, how would you compute that?

| Exercise 61 | **EMERGENCY SERVICES** |

Challenge

Spatial queues take place when the servers are geographically distributed. Service requests may not be able to be immediately met because the server needs to complete what he is doing, and also serve the other requests that were made first. With each service completion, the server has to travel from the last location to the next. The traveling time adds to the wait. If there are more than one server, the wait can be reduced if the appropriate (usually nearest) server can be dispatched. However, the next available server may not be the nearest among all the servers. Emergency and utility services such as police, ambulance, fire rescue, water, power, and building elevator repair are examples of services that have to deal with such challenges on a daily basis.

Concept

Usually large-scale complex models are built to support the required decision making. We will try to construct a simple spreadsheet model, but limit our scope to analyzing the optimal service coverage area size and number of servers per service area. You can focus the peak service request time duration and work against service responsive performance targets as the design basis.

Working

Take the simple queue model from the *Call Center* exercise as the starting prototype. You can then add the new features like request and server locations and speed of travel. Work this as a design and planning model and not a model to support the actual operation. The planning model is easier to build and usually has a larger impact on the overall challenge. If you have the time and patience, you can continue further to work on the dispatch management and control operational model.

| Exercise 62 | **TIME AND TIDE** |

Challenge

The gravitational pull of the Moon as it revolves around the Earth causes the ocean water level to swell and subside to give us tide cycles. The Earth in turn rotates and revolves around the Sun, which further influences tidal movements. When the Earth, Moon, and Sun are aligned, the water level on the Earth's surface is pull further away from the Earth's center, and less so when they are not. Since the movements of these celestial bodies are cyclical, we can derive the timings of high and low tides from past cycles. At the same time, the timings for sunrise, sunset, moonrise, and moonset have corresponding cycles. The high and low tides, and rise and set timings would of course be location dependent. Do you know when it would be high or low tide each day for the next few weeks at the shoreline nearest you?

The cyclical patterns of the celestial body movements are regular and therefore can be quite predictable. The challenge is in using the simplest possible formulas to capture the patterns. There should be more than one formula, each embedding into the other. The first should give the outer envelope of the tidal movement, which will be the most extreme (lowest and highest) of the movement per day. This corresponds to a pattern that varies over a month. There are still the hour-by-hour changes within a 24-hour period.

Start with the pattern you can easily handle first. For some people, that would be to determine the hour-by-hour changes. The base function to use to capture the cyclical pattern is the **SIN** function. The time variable should be divided by the length of a full cycle and then multiplied by 2***PI**() to make the output of SIN cycle. A phase constant value should be added to shift the cycle so that the peaks and troughs would synchronize with the actual peaks and troughs of the location.

    The magnitude between the peak and trough should be given by the constant multiplier to the **SIN** function. Then another constant has to be added to shift the average height of the cycle higher. You can continue the model building like this. As you match your solution against the actual, observe the pattern of the deviation between the two and then think of new elements to add.

Concept

Working

Tool 13

Week schedule

This workbook contains planning worksheets laid out by the hours of the day and the days of the week for one week. It is useful for planning daily class and activity timetables for students.

Tool 14

Year planner – days and weeks

These workbooks contain planning worksheets laid out by the days and weeks for each year. The dates of holidays when listed in the input table will be automatically marked on the calendar so that you can better arrange your work and holiday plans for the year.

Tool 15

Week planner

This workbook contains the basic pages of a weekly planner: calendar, year planner by weeks, weekly timetable, and daily sheets to keep appointments.

Enter the key data and follow the instructions on the *Data* sheet. Then, select all worksheets less the *Home* sheet and print in booklet form (both sides) to produce your own management diary.

Tool 16

Investment journal

This workbook provides a handy tool for recording investment decisions, logging in date/time and actions. It illustrates how spreadsheets deal with time and date, and some of the more challenging macro programming features such as the calendar dialog. This is useful as a check (in addition to validation) against erroneous date input, in particular to avoid any problem arising from regional preferences: 10/4/2005 is 10 April 2005 in Singapore but will be 4 October, 2005 in the United States.

The dialog is a macro userform. You can also design your own forms and add codes to the buttons and features of these forms.

Just click on an empty date cell and a calendar dialog will appear to allow you to select a date. The default selected date will be today. When you click on a date cell that already has a date entry, the calendar dialog will use this date as the selected date.

Tool 17

Countdown

A major event is just around the corner. This may be the end of a project, completion of military service, start of a much anticipated overseas trip, Christmas, or New

Year. Add to the atmosphere by counting down the days, hours, minutes, and seconds to the event.

This workbook simulates a countdown clock. On the *CountDown* worksheet, the current time is recorded in the top-left corner. You will enter the name of the event (in this workbook, we are counting down the time left during a test), the duration to elapse, and the start time. The end time will be automatically computed by adding the duration to the start time.

There are three macros available – *Start*, *Pause*, and *Resume*. *Start* will begin the countdown process from the beginning; *Pause* will stop the countdown process; and *Resume* will continue the countdown process.

Tip 35

Invisible macro buttons

Buttons are provided by Excel in **Developer/Insert Controls** (or the **Forms** toolbar in Excel 2003 and **Form Control**s toolbar in Calc) to which you can assign macros. These buttons are good in that they will not show up in the printed copy of your worksheet. They are, however, available only in one color, namely grey. In its place, you can create a box from **Insert/Shapes** (or the **Drawing** toolbar in Excel 2003 and Calc) and use it as a macro button. This is a more versatile button. You can easily alter its displayed text, and the color and style of its text, line, and fill. You can even make the button invisible, with no text, no lines, and no fill. This transparent button is better still, since you can even vary its text, font, and fill color by simply making the macro change these properties of the cell beneath the button. This is easier than changing the characteristics of the shape itself. To make the button's existence more obvious to users, try to underline and italicize the button title. We would in addition apply a distinctive purple color font.

Tip 36

Snap to fit

Charts, drawings, and invisible macro buttons are objects that only hover above the worksheets, and are not per se part of them. It would make worksheets nicer to look at if these objects fit the gridlines or interlock each other neatly. To do this by hand requires excellent eyesight and very steady hands, even under large viewing magnification. A simple supportive technique actually exists. To fit the button exactly to a cell or set of cells, activate the **Snap to Grid** option in your spreadsheet application and drag the corners of the object you want to modify. See how it snaps to fit exactly the dimensions of the cells closest to it. In Excel, there is also the **Snap to Shape** option if you are trying to get a few objects to fit snugly into each other.

Tip 37

Less clutter

A cluttered worksheet is difficult to understand and use, and conveys lack of professionalism. To keep your spreadsheet model looking crisp and clean, reduce the number of colors used. Except in the few instances where you want to highlight and draw intense attention, use as little ink as possible. By this we mean use fewer and simple border lines and keep to lighter pastel shades and rounder shapes, no thick hard lines. Buttons should be invisible as much as possible and they should not be too large. Neither should they be so small that they cannot be easily clicked. Make a mental count of the number of vertical and horizontal lines formed in your spreadsheet model. They should be as few as possible: align the edges of tables, charts, and diagrams. Remove unnecessary borders and header shadings.

_____ **Six months later**

A good rule of thumb to apply to judge if your model is clear, simple, and user-friendly is whether you will be able to understand and use it after laying off it for a period of time, say six months from now. If you cannot wait that long, try showing your workbook to a total stranger or someone not familiar with spreadsheets and observe their responses. You may be surprised by what you find.

We have found some flaws when reviewing spreadsheets that we did not build or we built but have become unfamiliar with after a while. These are:

- Lack of model clarity and absence of user instructions.
- Cluttered, disorderly, and illogical layout of worksheets.
- Large number and poor ordering of worksheets.
- Presence of blank worksheets.
- Excessively long or cryptic variables and header labels.
- Hidden cells, rows, columns, and tables.
- Sheets in print preview mode.
- Unusually large or small viewing magnification.
- Excessive amount of up-down and left-right scrolling needed to view the model.
- Too many tables in each worksheet.
- Tables, when printed, need to be glued together using adhesive tape before they can be read.
- Tables and charts cannot be easily read when printed (or later photocopied) in black and white.

FURTHER REFERENCES

- Grossman, 1999. "Teachers' Forum: Spreadsheet Modeling and Simulation Improves Understanding of Queues," *Interfaces* 29(3): 88–103, May–June.
  - http://interface.highwire.org/cgi/content/abstract/29/3/88
- Ingolfsson and Grossman, 2002. "Graphical Spreadsheet Simulation of Queues," *INFORMS Transactions on Education* 2(2).
  - http://archive.ite.journal.informs.org/Vol2No2/IngolfssonGrossman/IngolfssonGrossman.pdf
- Leong, 2014. Spreadsheet Modeling Resources
  - http://isotope.unisim.edu.sg/users/tyleong/SpreadsheetModeling.htm#Learn
  - http://isotope.unisim.edu.sg/users/tyleong/SpreadsheetModeling.htm#Queues

- o http://isotope.unisim.edu.sg/users/tyleong/SpreadsheetModeling.htm#Operations
- o http://dl.dropboxusercontent.com/u/19228704/BusinessProcessModeling.htm#Learn
- o http://dl.dropboxusercontent.com/u/19228704/Operations.htm#Queues
- o http://dl.dropboxusercontent.com/u/19228704/SpreadsheetModeling.htm#Operations
- Leong, 2007. "Simpler Spreadsheet Simulation of Multi-server Queues," *INFORMS Transactions on Education* 7(2): 172–177.
  - o http://archive.ite.journal.informs.org/Vol7No2/Leong

- Keywords. Relevant topics to search in Google and Wikipedia
  - o *Queuing theory . Waiting line models . Queue inference . Automatic teller machine . Emergency services*

PROBLEM SET 7

* Hard problems

Forward dates. Look-ahead dates and deadlines are often set as some days or weeks   Qn 7.01
from today.
a. Construct a spreadsheet model that shows the dates for 7, 14, 21, 30, 50, and 100
    days from today.
b. Tabulate as well the forward dates for other start dates.

Age restricted. Movie theaters and nightclubs have age restrictions on patrons.   Qn 7.02
a. Construct a spreadsheet model that shows the age of patrons today given their
    birth dates.
b. Indicate for 10, 12, 16, 18, and 21 years age limits whether they are permitted to
    enter the restricted premises.

10,000 hours. Skill takes time to master. It has been said that to be an expert in   Qn 7.03
anything, the minimum hours of practice needed is 10,000 hours. Not everyone has
so much time to master all things of interest.
a. Construct a spreadsheet that shows for any start date and 1, 2, ..., 10 hours per
    day, what are the end dates to clock 10,000 hours. Do also for 1,000, 2,000, 3,000,
    4,000, and 5,000 hours.
b. Provide another table to show the required hours per day for different target end
    dates. Set these dates about one year apart for 10 years.
c. Explain why two different tables are needed here.

Daily information. Some calendars and diaries list, for each day, additional   Qn 7.04
information of interest to their users.
a. Construct a spreadsheet model that shows information relevant for today.
b. This should include today's date, number of days since 1 January of the same
    year, and number of days left until the end of the year.
a. Propose similar ideas of your own and add these to your model.

Project schedule. A project consists of a series of tasks, each with its planned start   Qn 7.05
and end dates. For various reasons, actual start and end dates may deviate from plan.
a. Construct a spreadsheet model to display the project's tasks schedule.
b. For each task, compute its project duration in number of weeks.

c. Use columns to represent weeks in the planning horizon. Set up formulas to automatically fill cells to form horizontal bars showing the planned and actual durations of the tasks.

d. Each bar should mark the start week, end week, and all weeks in between. If only one of the start and end dates is entered, it should still be marked on the schedule.

Qn 7.06   **Time schedule**. Vehicles arrive to and depart from a terminal facility according to a planned schedule. The terminal needs to track the number of arrivals, departures and durations of stay. There is a limit to the number of arrivals and departures during any hour and total number of vehicles cannot exceed the holding capacity of the terminal at all times.

a. Construct a spreadsheet model as a schedule for a terminal.

b. For each vehicle, compute its stay duration in number of hours.

c. Use columns to represent hours in the planning horizon. Set up formulas to automatically fill cells to form horizontal bars showing the planned and actual stay period of each vehicle.

d. Each bar should mark the arrival hour, departure hour, and all hours in between. If only one of the arrival and departure times is given, it should still be marked on the schedule.

Qn 7.07   **Same birthdays**. It is not unusual to find two or more people with the same birthday even in a small group. This is surprising considering there are 365 days in a year and the group size in comparison is relatively small. What is the chance of this happening? How does this change with the size of the group?

a. Construct a spreadsheet model for group sizes 15 to 45. Simulate the birthdays of the people in the group.

b. Let the first person on the list be the birthday boy. What is the probability that there is another person in his birthday party with the same birthday as him? Can there be more than one such person?

c. Can there be more than one common birthday? What is the probability of two or more people with the same birthday in this party? How is this probability different from the earlier one?

d. Think further on this and provide your analysis in the spreadsheet showing tables and charts.

Qn 7.08*   **Discount bond**. A long-term discount bond is an IOU that can be bought and sold in the financial market. Each such bond has a fixed face value, of say $5,000, $10,000, $20,000, or $50,000, and a maturity date. Durations of the bonds can be 5, 10, 15, or 20 years. When new discount bonds are issued by a government or commercial organization, they are sold at prices lower than their face value. The buyer of a bond can hold on to it until maturity and claim its face value from the issuer. The difference between the two values is the interest due to the buyer. A bond can be sold before its maturity date. Its price is determined, on a willing-buyer willing-seller basis, in a bond market. Bond price changes with prevailing interest rate and rates trend.

a. Construct a spreadsheet model that determines the price of a bond, given its face value, interest rate, and time to maturity; and correspondingly, the bond's interest rate, given its face value, current price, and time to maturity.

b. Work out for a person with some bonds, whether he should sell them and buy new ones listed in the market.

c. What other factors should one look out for in buying or selling bonds?

International projects. You are working on a portfolio of international projects. Information in the project proposals include, for example, project net present values given in foreign currencies, and non-working weekdays of each week, which differ by location need not be Saturdays or Sundays. This information needs to be reconditioned for the Singapore headquarters staff to evaluate and track the projects.

Qn 7.09*

a. Construct a spreadsheet model for managing your work. The projects' start and end dates and their present values in one or more foreign currencies are given. You have noted each project's local weekly full and half rest-days. For each project, you want to know its total days, workdays, and net present value (NPV) in Singapore dollars. One USD is equivalent to SGD 1.21, €0.78, or ¥117.

b. Try your model on these projects' data (NPV '000s, start-, end-dates, rest days):
   i. ¥30,000, 1 Aug 2011, 3 Aug 2011, Sun (full)
   ii. USD 1,200, €200, 10 Sep 2011, 18 Sep 2011, Sun (full), Sat (half)
   iii. USD 5,000, ¥10,000, 15 Sep 2011, 30 Oct 2011, Sun (full), Sat (full)
   iv. USD 15,000, €400, ¥35,000, 11 Oct 2011, 24 Nov 2012, Fri (full), Sat (half)
   v. USD 2,500, €8,000, ¥120,000, 22 Feb 2012, 31 Dec 2012, Fri (full), Sun (full)

Special days. Anniversaries, holidays, and other special days are often given as fixed dates. Sometimes, they are given as the first, second, third, or fourth Monday or Friday of particular months. It would be good to know for the horizon ahead what those days are and be ready for them.

Qn 7.10*

a. Construct a spreadsheet model to keep the data for selected special days with recurring order on the solar calendar. These should include Martin Luther King Jr. Day, 3rd Monday of January; President's Day, 3rd Monday of February; Saint Patrick's Day, 17th of March; April Fool's Day, 1st of April; Mother's Day, 2nd

Sunday of May; Father's Day, 3rd Sunday of June; UFO Day, 2nd of July; Friendship Day, 1st Sunday of August; Patriot Day, 11th of September; Columbus Day, 2nd Monday of October; Thanksgiving, 4th Thursday of November; Christmas, 25th of December.

b. For each special day, enter its date; or its month, day of week, and week of month—whichever is relevant.

c. Determine the number of days, and number of weeks, the holidays are from today.

8 Analyzing the Data

INTRODUCTION

When massive amount of data is available, it is prudent to be able to analyze and reorganize the data to discern the underlying behavior. The data can be either collected sample values or outputs of Monte-Carlo simulations. Statistical analysis methods like frequency tables and pie charts are handy. They help you to understand the shape of the distributions and suggest the appropriate functions that may better represent them. Fitting the data to standard distribution functions can help you estimate lost sales and the value of risk pooling. These are difficult to do mathematically. However, with some spreadsheet modeling, you will soon manage them well enough.

Simple descriptive statistical methods cannot handle multiple attribute data. For example, if you want to know how much sales each region has made over different quarters for each product category, the model to build would not be easy to construct on your own. The **PivotTable** operation is excellent for this task. This is not an intuitive process as most of us have not seen or done this before. Keep trying it even after you have learned it to fully internalize it. Filtering is another way to examine the data. It reduces the amount of data you need to see at any one time by showing only what you want to view. It would be advisable to try filtering first before applying **PivotTable** and **PivotChart**. Think of the different ways to use these methods. Others have used them to build decision-support systems.

The exercises included in this chapter to facilitate learning of the above are *Hotel Apex*, *Life Expectancy*, *Durex Global Sex Survey*, *My Hair Place*, *ABC Services*, *Offshore Development*, *Grand Grocery*, *Portfolio Analysis*, and *Portfolio Planning*. The exercises seek not to replicate the statistical data analysis that you can find in other textbooks but rather provide quite different points of view. In particular, the first three exercises attempt to extract interesting results from quite simple statistical data. *ABC Services* and *Offshore Development* are similar but cover different business contexts. They deal with interactive analysis of the data using **AutoFilter** and **AdvancedFilter**. *Portfolio Planning* extends *Portfolio Analysis* to provide the optimal allocation of available funds to the candidate stocks to form the investment portfolio.

DISCOVERY POINTS

Point 33

After collecting a large set of data for a variable, the first step to take is to compute the basic statistics. These are minimum, maximum, mean, and standard deviation. Three other statistics derived from these four are the range, mid-range, and coefficient of variation (CV). The range is the difference between the maximum and minimum values, and mid-range is the average of the two. The mean can be compared against the mid-range. If they are close to each other, then the distribution of the data is symmetrical and otherwise, skewed. The standard deviation divided by mean gives the CV. This value typically ranges from 0.05 to 0.25, with an average of about 0.15. A CV of 0.1 or less means the data have a small dispersion; between 0.1 and 0.2, average dispersion; and more than 0.2, large dispersion.

Practical data analysis

The range can be divided by the standard deviation to give factor k. This factor value ranges from 2.83 to 6. The smallest value corresponds to the case where all the data are either at minimum or maximum. Close to 3.64, the data is probably uniformly distributed, and near 6, they should be from the *Normal* distribution. To verify, you can plot their histograms to see their shapes and then apply the *Kolmogorov-Smirnov* (K-S) test for goodness of fit. This excellent test is applicable to both discrete and continuous variable cases, can work with very few data points, and is computationally simple. The K-S test uses only the maximum absolute difference between the empirical cumulative relative frequency and the theoretical cumulative distribution curves. If the K-S statistic is small (compared to the critical value), then the null hypothesis of the two curves being the same cannot be rejected.

Point 34

Black swans, very rare, are found only in Australia. Now before Australia was discovered, swans were always assumed to be white, except when they are young and grey, as told in the children story classic "The Ugly Duckling". If you were to study the whiteness of swan feathers, you can devise a whiteness scale from pure dazzling to dirty yellowish. In fact, you would be able to put up a *Normal* curve for the distribution of colors found among swans. Practically all the data points will fall within the mean plus/minus three times standard deviation (or $\mu \pm 3\sigma$) band of white. However unknown to you, lurking some 100 over σ away is the color black. The challenge in data analysis is that you only have the data you have and not the ones you don't have (such as "black swans"). This means that the standard deviation will be underestimated.

Black swans and data you don't have

In general, information can be classified into a two-by-two matrix: 1) *known knowns,* 2) *known unknowns,* 3) *unknown knowns,* and 4) *unknown unknowns.* At one extreme, *known knowns* are information that you already have and at the other extreme, *unknown unknowns* are *black swans*, things you do not know that you do not know. *Known unknowns* are information you don't yet have but clearly know exist. It could be that obtaining this information requires time and cost you are unwilling to spend or need expertise you do not have and cannot acquire. Therefore, you have to live with this situation. Though strange, the *black swan* concept is now much in vogue and many people are conscious of its impact. This originally *unknown unknown* is somewhat beginning to become a *known unknown*.

Lastly, with lower awareness, *unknown knowns* are information you already have but do not know you have. Like common sense, this latent resource is as if locked in a vault with its key missing. It is a potent untapped store of knowledge everyone can seek out with minimal effort but you must consciously start searching. A key intent of exploratory modeling introduced in this book is to discover *unknown knowns*.

Point 35

Inadequate and missing data

A common concern modeling is the lack of data and where they are found, incomplete with missing values. The challenge here is to discover powerful and interesting strategies to deal with this difficulty. One method is to anchor on a known datum and apply a multiplier. Say, sales data is known but costs are not. If you can assume that costs are about 60 to 80% of sales, then you have estimated the costs data.

Another example is to extract from past experience one or two "gut feel" anchor data. In the *ProbFunctions* workbook (refer to *Tool 7* in Chapter 6), we mention how the *Normal* distribution can be selected for use when the data is expected to be fairly symmetrical and "bell-shaped" in distribution. Its statistics can be estimated as *Mean* $\approx (Min + Max)/2$ and *standard deviation* $\approx (Max - Min)/6$. We can further generalize by using *standard deviation* $\approx (Max - Min)/k$, for k between $2\sqrt{2}$ and 6. With this, even without data, all the data you need can be generated by Monte-Carlo simulation. Missing data can also be interpolated or extrapolated from known data sets, assuming standard distribution functions or just simply linear relationship. If for example, the temperature of a particular day is missing, you can take the average of the temperatures of the days before and after as an approximation. *Point 30* in Chapter 7 shows how missing data can be inferred in a queue situation by assuming *Uniform* or *Poisson* distribution. Data resampling and inference are thus methods for *unknown knowns*.

Correlations and unintended effects

Many practical situations, decisions are made off-the-cuff. Data may be available, but the decision maker is either unwilling or unable to explicitly use them: 1) unwilling because he does not find them comprehensive or dependable and 2) unable because he does not know how to discern from the data what they mean and how to respond. An analytical way to find out how decisions are made in these situations is to regress the human decisions against the input data, and consequently, obtain the functional relationship between the decision variable and input data, and the weighted coefficients' values. Accuracy of the model can be tested by dividing the data into two halves, taking one half to build the prediction model and the second half to test the predictions made by the model against actual choices. Future data can be obtained to monitor if the model's functional form and coefficient values stay stable and to evaluate if prediction accuracy remains unchanged.

Together, data and decision inputs affect outputs. Intentional policy design has a set of outputs in mind. Thus, it is obvious to monitor how the inputs affect outputs. There are however, benefits, detriments, and policy resistance that were not originally intended. For example, the availability of piped water directly affects public health. Indirectly, it lessens the burden of labor on children and women, who used to fetch the water and do the washing. An unintended consequence is improvement in educational level, because mothers can now find time to borrow books from the library, read to the children, and attend schools and educational programs. A more recent phenomenon is the Internet. With it came many free services such as email, search engine, encyclopedia, news, and information sites. These services have sources of revenue that are indirectly related to their services. They are typically advertisements. The overall unintended consequence is the decline in revenue for producers of information goods such as newspapers, magazines, music, movies, and software. The financial future of writers, composers, musicians, singers, actors, and film producers is now in question. How are they going to make a living?

Analysis of such larger scope challenges deal not so much with data and decisions but the structural relationship among the variables. One variable affects another which in turn affects yet another. In fact, the relationships can cascade back to themselves and there are many interlocking cyclical relationships. Some cycles are reinforcing and thus can keep spiraling upwards or downwards. Others are balancing with negative feedback. A systems thinking approach is needed; there are no inputs and outputs in the system, only interdependencies. There can also be delays in responses between input-output variable pairs. Negative feedback cycles with delays generate oscillating responses and therefore are inherently unstable. There are many leverages that can be applied to influence the outcomes. The lowest leverages are in adjusting the parameter values. The highest leverages are in changing the system structure, goals, and aspirations.

EXERCISES

HOTEL APEX   Worked Example

Challenge
Your old friend Pablo, now general manager of Hotel Apex, asked if you could help him to analyze some data from his hotel. He showed you the data collected for the number of rooms sold on off-peak days in a season. Hotel Apex is planning to keep the business going as much as possible while carrying out a major room upgrading and refurbishment exercise during the next off-peak season. Pablo intends to use your analysis to better understand the hotel's demand to support his refurbishment plans.

Concept
Every study should begin with a proper analysis of the data. However, the data given may not be what they are supposed to be and may not even be relevant to the project. If no other data are available, then it will take some additional modeling effort to extract the needed information. If no specific questions have been posed, you will have to really understand the intention of your client to work out the relevant questions.

There may also be missing information, as in this case, the hotel's capacity, the room types, and the data for peak-days and other seasons. The information, if needed, may be obtained by further probing or inferred from what is already given.

Working (Detailed)
You can begin with the following analysis for the off-peak season:
- Determine the lowest, highest, average, and standard deviation of rooms sold.
- Fit the data against the *Normal* distribution.
    - What is the maximum absolute deviation between the data and *Normal* distribution?
    - Is this a good enough fit?
- What is the capacity of Hotel Apex? Can you determine this from the data?
- Determine how many rooms should be kept available to ensure that 70% of room requests could still be satisfied?
- How can you improve the revenue of the hotel?
- What if we have the room sales data by room type?

The 200 data points on the room sales per day during the off-peak season are given in the *Data* worksheet. Let us develop the spreadsheet model:

i.   Select the *Proto* worksheet.

ii. The same 200 data points are tabulated in ascending order in a single column in cells C14:C213. This way of organizing the data allows us to compute its cumulative relative frequency which will be used as the basis to fit a distribution using the *Kolmogorov-Smirnov* method.

iii. We can easily compute some statistics related to the data.
- Enter into cell C4 the formula =MIN(C14:C213) (i.e., minimum number of rooms sold).
- Enter into cell D4 the formula =MAX(C14:C213) (i.e., maximum number of rooms sold).
- Enter into cell E4 the formula =AVERAGE(C14:C213) (i.e., average number of rooms sold).
- Enter into cell F4 the formula =STDEV(C14:C213) (i.e., standard deviation of number of rooms sold).

iv. To fit the distribution for room sales
- Enter into cell C10 the formula =COUNT(C14:C213) (i.e., the number of data points).
- From the sorted data points in cells C14:C213, notice that room sales do not exceed 150 and there are many data points at 150. These evidences imply that the maximum capacity of the hotel should be 150. Enter into cell C7 the formula =MAX(C14:C213) to give the value 150 as the capacity of the hotel.
- Enter into cell D14 the formula =B14/C$10 (i.e., empirical cumulative relative frequency of the sorted data, CRF_{data}).
- Fill the formula in cell D14 into cells D15:D213 to obtain the CRF_{data} for all the data points.
- Next, we need to compute the cumulative relative frequency for each sales data point assuming the *Normal* distribution, CRF_{sales}.
- To do so, we need the mean and standard deviation values already computed in cells E4 and F4.
- Enter into cell E14 the formula =NORMDIST($C14,E$4,F$4,TRUE) (i.e., the estimated CRF_{sales} for the smallest sales data point).
- Fill the formula in cell E14 into cells E15:E213 to obtain the CRF_{sales} for all the data points. Notice that the CRF_{sales} for the last 46 data points remain constant at 0.8568. This is because we do not have the data for demand when it exceeds the hotel capacity of 150.
- Enter into cell F14 the formula =ABS($D14-E14) (i.e., absolute deviation between CRF_{data} and CRF_{sales} for the first data point).
- Fill the formula in cell F14 into cells F15:F213 to obtain the absolute deviation for all data points.
- Enter into cell F10 the formula =MAX(F14:F213) (i.e., the largest of the absolute deviations). Alternatively, we can compute this value in cell F10

using an array formula {=MAX(ABS($D14:$D213-E14:E213))}. The result in F10 is 0.1432. This means the difference between the CRF$_{data}$ and CRF$_{sales}$ is possibly more than 14%.

v. To fit the distribution for room demand

- To get a better fit, we will replicate cells in columns E and F to H and I. This time, we will enter values into the sales population average and standard deviation cells H4 and I4. The initial values of 116 and 32 are taken from cells E4 and F4, respectively. These values will be adjusted by **Solver** to minimize the maximum absolute deviation between the CRF$_{data}$ and CRF$_{demand}$.

- Check that cell H14 has the formula =NORMDIST($C14,H$4,I$4,TRUE) (i.e., the estimated CRF$_{demand}$ for the smallest sales data point).

- Check that cell I14 has the formula =ABS($D14-H14) (i.e., the absolute deviation between CRF$_{data}$ and CRF$_{sales}$ for the first data point).

- Fill the formula in cells H14:I14 into cells H15:I213 to obtain the absolute deviation for all data points.

- Enter into cell I10 the formula =MAX(I14:I168) or {=MAX(ABS($D14:$D168-H14:H168))}. Row 168 is the first row with the room sales data of 150. The rest of the rows are ignored because their values represent sales and not demand. Here, we assume that demand is the same as sales when it is less than the capacity and equals the capacity when it is exceeded, and that sales distribution follows the *Normal* distribution.

- To allow **Solver** to minimize the maximum absolute deviation by changing the mean and standard deviation of the *Normal* Distribution,

  o Click **Data/Solver** and the **Solver Parameters** dialog will appear.

  o Set **Target Cell** as I10.

  o Select **Equal To** as Min.

  o Set **By Changing Cells** as H4:I4.

  o Click **Solve** and the Solver will obtain the best fit mean of 121 and standard deviation of 39 for the *Normal* Distribution describing the room demand.

- To prepare the complete data for the demand curve, we need to enter into cells C214 and C215 the values 151 and 152, respectively. Then fill the cells C216:C313 from these two cells. Now, select cell H213 and fill cells H214:H313 with its value to provide the CRF$_{demand}$ for data values beyond 150.

- Let us plot the curves for the CRF$_{data}$, CRF$_{sales}$, and CRF$_{demand}$ against the number of rooms.

  o Click **Insert/Scatter/Scatter with Smooth Lines** and an empty chart box will appear.

  o Right-click in the chart box and click **Select Data** and the **Select Data Source** dialog will appear.

- o Click **Add** to add a new series.
- o Enter **Series name** as *Empirical* and select **Series X values** as C14:C213, and select **Series Y values** as D14:D213.
- o Click **OK** to complete the selection and the *Empirical* curve for the CRF$_{data}$ will appear in the chart box.
- o Click **Add** to add a second series.
- o Enter **Series name** as *Normal Sales* and select **Series X values** as C14:C213, and select **Series Y values** as E14:E213.
- o Click **Add** to add a second series.
- o Enter **Series name** as *Normal Demand* and select **Series X values** as C14:C313, and select **Series Y values** as H14:H313.
- o Click **OK** to complete the selection and the plotted curves will appear in the chart box.
- From the curve plotted in *Figure 8-1*, we can see that the *Normal Sales* curve (left-most, red curve) does not fit the *Empirical* curve (center, green curve) that well, especially near the 150-room point. After using Solver to tune the average and standard deviation statistics to minimize the maximum absolute deviation, the *Normal Demand* curve is skewed to fit the *Empirical* curve. The average and standard deviation values are larger after tuning because the missing data beyond 150 are now effectively included. The *Normal Demand* curve shows that there is significant demand beyond 150 up to about 200.
- Using *Normal Sales* to determine the number of rooms to keep open during the refurbishment period to satisfy 70% of demand, enter into cell E7 the formula =NORMINV(D7,E4,F4). The obtained value of 133 is an under-estimation because *Sales* mean and standard deviation are smaller than *Demand* mean and standard deviation. To use the *Normal Demand* for this, enter into cell I7 the formula =NORMINV(D7,H4,I4). The number of rooms calculated is 142.

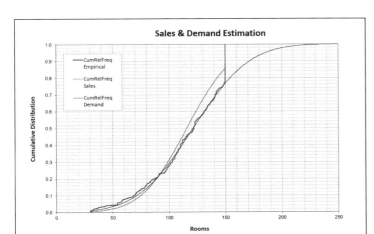

Figure 8-1

Sales and Demand Distribution Estimation Curves

Alternatively, enter into cell F7 the formula =PERCENTILE(C14:C213,D7) to get 141. This expedient approach is valid as long as the value it computes is less than 150, i.e., still in the data region where *Sales* and *Demand* are the same. Note that it makes no assumption about the *Demand* distribution functional form and thus is superior to the other approaches.

vi. To understand the difference between sales and demand

It is important to understand clearly the difference between sales and demand when there is limited capacity. By taking sales data as demand, the hotel is not properly accounting for lost sales. The powerful concept explored here involves extracting demand distribution from past sales data. With this, management will have a better understanding of lost sales and can use that information for hotel refurbishment as well as future expansion planning.

| Exercise 64 | **LIFE EXPECTANCY** |

Challenge

Francis, a financial planner you have been recently introduced to, is discussing with you the urgency of setting up a retirement plan. You are 40 years old now. Francis figures that, with a retirement age of 65 and life expectancy of 78 years for men in your country, you have about 25 years to save and invest for the 13 golden years of retirement before you. The numbers are elegantly simple to compute until you come across a book entitled *Fooled by Randomness* by Nassim Nicholas Taleb.

According to Taleb, this kind of calculation is wrong. To illustrate, if you are now 82 years old, it suggests that you should expect to live –4 years more! Should not having beaten the odds to live to a ripe old age count towards expecting an even longer life ahead? Moreover, life expectancy is just an average figure. You do want to save more to last beyond that because there is an approximately 50% chance that you would live beyond 78 years.

Concept

Not much information is given here. More can be extracted from the statistical reports. However, you may not even need to get the data if your intention is to get an insight into the matter rather than getting a specific numerical result. Modeling should not just be used for simplifying computations; it should be used for analysis to find the truth.

Learn to use the basic properties of functions and behaviors to estimate parameter values. From what you know, the oldest man who ever lived in your country survived 110 years and that in general the longest life span in modern human history has not increased much. In fact, the suspicion is that it might have decreased. Also, it has been claimed that life expectancy improvements have been due largely to a reduction in infant mortality.

- How do you include infant mortality into the analysis?
- What new insights can you find?

Make an assumption about the distribution of mortality age of people born in the same year. It would be reasonable to use the *Normal* or any bell-shaped distribution. The life expectancy given would be the population mean. Now, the standard deviation would have to be consistent with the longest life span recorded. How many deviations from the mean would the longest life span be? Since it is such an unlikely event, any factor of 3 or slightly more would be reasonable. Putting this value in as an input, infer the standard deviation of mortality age.

What would be the cumulative probability of survival at any given age? Create a table to keep the results, spanning 2 to 120 years. Can you then take these values to compute the mortality probability for age intervals? Verify that your computations are correct by recomputing from this second table, the average and standard deviation of mortality age.

Considering that you have lived thus far, the probabilities of mortality ages smaller than your age should no longer be of any value. Taking only the probabilities of mortality ages greater or equal to your age, deduce the conditional probabilities of mortality ages for years beyond your current age.

DUREX GLOBAL SEX SURVEY

Someone was curious to know if there is statistical significance between the frequency of sex and sexual satisfaction. Three columns were extracted from the survey data, which only reported the average value for each country. Therefore, conclusions cannot be drawn for each country, but they can be reached across the countries surveyed. This would mean that we would have to take the results with a big pinch of salt or possibly a whole mountain's worth of it because the cultural complications across nations are enormous.

In spite of the nature of the topic, the 2005 survey results reported by the sponsor in a table format do not give an interesting story. A chart with some statistical correlation analysis and function relationship fitting would probably draw more readers' attention instead.

Working Try plotting the results on your own, using a line chart and x-y chart.

- Which would be the right one to use?
- What statistical method would you use to draw conclusions?

Correlation between sexual satisfaction (as depicted by responses to the two selected questions) and frequency of sex is not high. However in social studies, *R-squared* of 0.3 would be considered good enough.

- Can the *R-squared* be improved? Try removing the outliers. Is this permitted?
- What about using a nonlinear relationship between the variables?
- What conclusions can you draw?

Exercise 66 **MY HAIR PLACE**

Challenge Basic information about the hair salon's customers extracted from customer profile cards can be stored in this workbook. The data can be used for business review, analysis, and customer support. To review, revise, or add customer data, click on *S/N* in the header of the *DataBase* sheet. A form will pop up to assist you.

Concept Data can be stored in a spreadsheet as a **Data List**. Each row represents a customer with the row header specifying the various data fields in the columns. You can either enter data into the data list directly or use a form. The Excel spreadsheet has a standard pop-up window form for data lists. Alternatively, you can use a worksheet as a form. This however requires some additional work and possibly some minor macros.

Though you may want to make the worksheet form look like a paper form, the data elements of that form can be linked to a row so that the row may be copied to the data list in one go. This is left as a task for you to explore and learn. Also, the data are more meaningful when displayed graphically. Think of the various information that your client would want to see and the ways you can show that information to her.

Working The data elements should be ordered with the most important and more pervasive data on the left and then moving progressively to the right. Shade the headers with colors to group the data elements so that they do not look like an endless set. The data list should be tested before the first real data are even entered. You can do so by making up your own data. This is particularly important for preparing the various summary tables and charts for management review.

Challenge

ABC Services has a long list of loyal customers (more than 300), many of whom have long-term contracts with the company. The contracts span one to ten years. From time to time, contracts can run into difficulties: customers request change of terms or threaten to terminate patronage prematurely. To keep on top of the situation, the company has an elaborate series of activities to keep the customers engaged, especially towards the end of the contract when getting it renewed becomes a paramount concern. These activities are preludes to the final rounds of negotiation that should seal the contract for yet another time duration.

Given the limited manpower in the department, the VP (Commercial) requested you to help provide a way to monitor the status of each customer contract and the progress of the company's engagement activities.

The tracking method must be simple and user-friendly for the executives' daily customer follow-up and for departmental discussions. ABC's senior management does not want to be surprised by past-due expired contracts or last-minute customer walk-outs.

Concept

Data are useful when they are exhaustive and comprehensive. However, a massive amount of data makes it difficult to select records that should be highlighted. We therefore need the ability to temporarily hide unwanted data, filtering out the pertinent few for the user to zoom in on. The user may also want the data to speak on their own, drawing attention to themselves when specified conditions arise. **Filtering** and **Conditional Formatting** can do these, but some more work is required if the workbook is to be friendly to users who may not be so conversant with spreadsheets.

Working

Apply **AutoFilter** to the table by activating it with the cursor first placed inside the table.

- What happens to the missing data which have been filtered away?
- How would you know what filtering has been applied?
- How can you improve the tracking?
- How do you highlight what had been changed since the last update?

Try out **Advanced Filter**. Be careful not to include too many rows in the criteria range. The additional blank rows will be interpreted as universal "wild cards"; filtering will therefore show all the records as if no filtering has been done.

- How would the **COUNT**, **SUM**, **MAX**, and **MIN** functions operate in a filtered table? What about **SUBTOTAL**?
- Do the results computed include data in the hidden rows?

Exercise 68   **OFFSHORE DEVELOPMENT**

Challenge   SAA is a national airline with numerous IT projects outsourced to offshore vendors. At any one time, SAA's IT department has to monitor about 50 outsourced projects, and for each project, the several major milestones towards completion. From time to time, these outsourced projects do run into difficulties because of changes in end-users' requirements and technical implementation problems.

To keep on top of the situation, the company needs a more systematic way to keep tabs on the projects' progress and, where necessary, activate suitable actions to nip any potential problem in the bud before the situation worsens.

Given the limited manpower in the department, the VP requested you to help provide a way to effect closer monitoring of the projects' status against the predetermined milestones. This mechanism for a start should at least raise alerts when the major milestones are not completed on time.

The tracking method must be simple and user-friendly. The senior management does not want to be surprised by the inability of the IT department to deliver on-time solutions to the end-users.

Concept   Decision making is not always about getting the right answers. Sometimes it is about knowing what is happening. This workbook is a simple spreadsheet-based information system that provides the needed status tracking information. It therefore introduces to you yet another possible application of spreadsheets. Monitoring alone is powerful, but with the information collected, some trend and statistical analysis can also be done.

Working   Using the *Proto* worksheet, you can practice using **AutoFilter** and **Advanced Filter**. Try also to improve *Proto* to make it more interactive and user-friendly.

Compare what you have done with the solution in the *Model* worksheet. To drill down, select from **CustomViews**. In there, select *Neat* and later *Raw*.

- What would you want to filter data for?
- What if no such features are available?
- What information request can you support using **Advanced Filter** that you cannot do with **AutoFilter**? What about the other way around?
- Do you think your users can handle an **AutoFilter** activated model on their own?
- Are there areas in your work where you can use a model like this?

GRAND GROCERY

Challenge

Historical sales data had been downloaded from your company's database. You want to be able to organize the data into a format that is easier to understand, which at the same time would permit you to examine the company's sales performance on the fly from different perspectives: overall, by quarters, by category, and by products.

You now stare at the data and wonder how to begin to do what is required. This seems like a lot of work and maybe you should call off tonight's date. You have consulted a senior colleague who suggests that you try using a **PivotTable**.

Concept

Data available from company records, for example sales record and inventory movement record, can be quite raw. A lot of effort is required to extract the answers to simple questions. The data given in each row overlaps that of another row by quite a bit and are therefore somewhat repetitive. This is because the data are given in a single dimensional form, with many of the columns being merely descriptors of the data, rather than the actual data. Putting the descriptors into row and column headers, and organizing the data into the table proper would make the data more readable.

Working

Apply the **PivotTable** operation to the given data. Do not be afraid to try various possible layouts. The layout can always be rearranged later.

- Suppose someone gives you a PivotTable and you need the original data for another analysis. How are you going to extract the original data?
- Can you recognize the type of data organization that can best be used here? Provide some suggestions.

PORTFOLIO ANALYSIS

Challenge

Paul plans to invest his money. As a start, he began to collect data of financial assets that he may invest in and started analyzing the historical performance of their trading price movements.

- What would be the relevant information to get?
- What should be analyzed in the price movements of these assets?
- How should the large dimensional structure of the data be dealt with?

Concept

Two workbooks are prepared for this exercise. The simpler workbook involves only two stocks while the other workbook has six stocks and a market index. Obviously, it would be better to start learning from the simpler one before proceeding to the larger problem context. While analyzing price movements may be interesting, what really matters is the movement of return rates of the stocks. The return rate for each period of a stock can be computed by comparing the stock prices of the current and the immediate past period. There are two possible approaches; one assumes simple compounding and the other continuous. The relevant statistics to compute include the return rate average, standard deviation, variance, and covariance. Other characteristics of the stocks to compute are the intercept and slope values (also known as the *alpha* and *beta*, respectively) of the plot of the stock return rate versus market index return rate.

A portfolio would comprise a mixture of the stocks. The return rate of a portfolio is determined by taking the weighted average of the stock return rates. Again, the basic statistics can be computed for the portfolio. How would the different possible portfolios perform? If there are only two stocks in the portfolio, what should be the criterion for choosing the two stocks to form the portfolio? How would you exploit the negative correlation in their price movement in trading them on the market?

Working

First, convert the stock prices into return rates and then compute their average and standard deviations. Then, work out the variance-covariance matrix. Compute the portfolio statistics, which should generally be a form of the weighted sum of the component stocks' statistics. If you are familiar with financial investments, test your understanding against the model.

Exercise 71   PORTFOLIO PLANNING

Challenge

Paul is ready to build up his portfolio of financial assets. The challenge, as he begins to discover, is working through the complex mathematics. Maybe it is easier with spreadsheets. What if Paul already has a portfolio and wants to adjust it to achieve better results? He may want to change only a restricted monetary amount of each asset class or percentage points from his current allocation at each time period. How would these considerations change his model?

- How would you recommend him to adjust it to achieve better returns?
- Should he sell some stocks and use the money together with some that he has saved to buy other more worthy stocks?
- Which are the stocks to sell or buy, and how much of each?

Concept

This exercise continues from the *Portfolio Analysis* exercise. The two workbooks prepared extend from the earlier exercise. In the previous exercise, you are left to explore on your own how the portfolios are obtained by different weightings of stock performance. Here, you can be more systematic in the analysis.

Among the many questions to ask are the following:

- What combinations of the stocks would dominate other combinations?
- What would be the lowest risk combination for each targeted expected return rate?
- What range of return rates is possible from investing in these stocks?
- How would adding a risk-free asset to the portfolio help?
- What if you are allowed to short sell (i.e., selling what you do not have)?

Working

> **TOOLS**

Tool 18

Special statistics

Data sets given may contain "outliers." For example, some extremely poor countries have a few very rich millionaires. Including them in computing statistics will over-inflate their values and give other people an incorrect impression of the country. Trim mean can help eliminate the impact of the extreme values on the computed mean.

What are the other situations you know of that need special statistics? What other special statistics do you know of?

Tool 19

Data fit

This workbook shows how a nonnegative data set may be fitted to common continuous statistical distributions. Distribution functions are defined by up to four parameters, the values of which may be optimized using **Solver** to better fit the data set. The steps for doing this can be recorded as a macro to make them easy to repeat.

The maximum absolute deviation (MAD), defined as the largest gap between the cumulative relative frequency of a given data set and that of its fitted distribution, is a measure of goodness-of-fit (referred to as the *Kolmogorov–Smirnov* test). The distribution function (and associated parameter values) with the smallest MAD, unless this MAD is too large, may be selected to be the required distribution. Further analysis may be performed (as in the *Goodness of Fit* tool) to give formal statistical interpretation of the fit.

The empirical distribution of the sample data may be plotted by first sorting the data values in ascending order and then ascribing to each value in the kth order the cumulative relative frequency of k/n, where n is the total number of data points in the sample. The cumulative probability of each of these data points can be found for the distribution functions to be evaluated. The function's input parameters can be estimated from the sample statistics. These parameters may be further tuned, using **Solver**, to minimize the maximum absolute deviation for the empirical distribution from the theoretical distribution being evaluated. The choice of distribution functions to evaluate can be narrowed down to those that have similar cumulative relative frequency shapes. (See *Data Fit(A)*, the second workbook in the *Data Fit* tool for a larger set of distribution functions.)

Goodness of fit

The maximum absolute deviation (MAD) is the largest gap between the cumulative relative frequency of a given data set and that of its fitted statistical distribution, as used in the *Kolmogorov–Smirnov* test.

The MAD of a sample data set assumed to be from a distribution should be no larger than the MADs of data generated using that distribution's function. Hence, using MADs generated from simulated data sets, we can derive the critical MAD values or goodness-of-fit thresholds for each level of statistical significance.

Tip 39

Modeling analysis and data

There are many types of data. Simple data we have encountered are numbers and texts. You have also learned how to deal with date and time, which are just numbers formatted according to a set of conversion rules. Rules encapsulated in formulas and model structures are data too. Other forms of data are increasingly important. These include sounds, graphics, pictures, and videos. As they say, a picture paints a thousand words. How much more would it say if it moves and gives out quadraphonic sound? Take for instance Google™ Earth, Google Maps, and Geographic Information Systems. The physical location and feature descriptions when interacted with our human minds are powerful.

Our eyes can easily pick up efficient paths between points without any deliberate computation. They are even more powerful when the collective knowledge and wisdom of other users in the community are collated on the common platform. Users of Google Earth can share what they know of a place by marking its location and providing a short description. A satellite photo annotated with *place marks* is a valid model, and reviewing it should still count as analysis, just as looking at a well laid-out set of data is analysis. The presentation forms of data count as models, and they do not have to be tables of values only. While a *decision matrix* as a table of data and relationship is a model, other forms of models include street maps, *decision trees*, *treemaps*, and *mind maps*. Therefore, modeling is not just about numbers, and analysis is not restricted to computing optimal or even good answers.

Tip 40

Real client

As analysts, we often think we know what the problem is in the business context we are studying. In fact, we are often wrong. Having a real client exposes us to actual and new concerns that we are not aware of. Much of what we now know thus far is shaped by what we have learned in school and from textbooks. The problems examined there are usually stylized to fit pedagogical constraints. Real-world problems do not really fit these standard molds. Data obtained from actual situations are noisy and often incomplete. For the data to be useful, we must instead learn to abstract the core problems from the source, which are usually less well-defined situations, and then frame them in ways that others can validate. This is a highly valuable set of skills that is much sought after in the business world. Working with real clients and real problems is the only way to acquire them.

Work with the client

Giving a completed model to a client who had not been much involved in building it can lead to quite unpleasant outcomes. First, the client will find the whole model too overwhelming to assimilate quickly, having not gone through earlier previews. Second, the client has no sense of ownership, a result of not having participated in the development of the model. Finally, the client will certainly request changes, usually in matters that he will assert are trivial to include. In particular, he often wants you to evaluate the studied problem on peculiar sets of data he has in mind, independent of whether the data are really applicable or generally robust. The remodeling and modifications involved are usually not that simple and can be rather drastic when they are requested almost at the end of the modeling project. This puts to waste a lot of the hard work expended earlier. So overall, it is much better to keep interacting and checking with your client no matter how tedious this may seem to you.

Spontaneity and planning

It has been said that nobody plans to fail but they often fail to plan. With our world getting wirelessly connected, and mobile devices getting ever more portable and comprehensive in function, the tendency is not to plan but to move along with the flow. Some even assert that the conventional "ready, aim, and fire" action sequence is being superseded by the more progressive "ready, fire, and aim."

In supply chain management, this means to ("ready") set up the production, and then ("fire") produce and ship out without having received firm customer orders. The goods produced are being moved generally towards the consuming markets in rough relative portions. As actual orders are progressively received, ("aim") the goods are tagged in transit, and diverted when necessary, to effect the final delivery. From the customer's point of view, he is ordering from the factory but the response is as if from stock out of the warehouse next door, with much shorter lead-time.

Having the preparation and plan done, and actions set into motion, aiming does the final adjustments to direct the activated action. This is particularly so when the whole action takes much time and effort. This does not mean planning is out of fashion. Modeling and analysis is still essential to ensure that the preliminary actions are activated appropriately. In this contention between strategy and execution, strategic thinking anticipates, avoids, and activates resources in the right directions, and execution completes the job. Just as luck favors the prepared, good strategies and plans put you in situations from where you can better maneuver forward. The "fire" step is therefore not arbitrary but with great thought, infrastructure development, and planning. Without good planning, the high-speed reactions you have may not be fast enough to get you back on track to move forward and, in the worst case, may even send you around in circles.

Tip 43

Enterprise resource

Spreadsheet models are often used incorrectly and are usually developed without the same stringent controls as regular software. As a result, a very high proportion, possibly over 90%, of mission-critical business spreadsheets audited have been found to contain serious errors. The major root causes are:

- Spreadsheet users tend to be inappropriately overconfident of their ability to model, and
- Spreadsheet models are treated as disposable software, rather than enterprise resources.

Spreadsheet model development and maintenance, whether it is just data updating or model assumption changes, are not well managed. As a consequence, many a time new ad hoc spreadsheet models are developed when suitable useful ones already exist. It would have been wiser to better manage and keep improving what is already there than to reinvent the wheel each time. Some useful practices can be adapted from software engineering and information systems management to apply to spreadsheet model construction, maintenance, and operational deployment. These include a formal process for managing change request and version control, and proper authorization and training in the use of released models.

FURTHER REFERENCES

- Bell, 2001. "Teaching Business Statistics with Microsoft Excel," *INFORMS Transactions on Education* 1(1).
  - http://archive.ite.journal.informs.org/Vol1No1/Bell/Bell.pdf
- Erkut and Ingolfsson, 2001. "Let's Put the Squares in Least Squares," *INFORMS Transactions on Education* 1(1).
  - http://archive.ite.journal.informs.org/Vol1No1/ErkutIngolfsson/ErkutIngolfsson.pdf
- Leong, 2014. Spreadsheet Modeling Resources
  - http://isotope.unisim.edu.sg/users/tyleong/SpreadsheetModeling.htm#Stats
  - http://isotope.unisim.edu.sg/users/tyleong/SpreadsheetModeling.htm#RealWorld
  - http://isotope.unisim.edu.sg/users/tyleong/SystemDynamicsModeling.htm

- o http://dl.dropboxusercontent.com/u/19228704/PracticalAnalytics.htm#Stats
  - o http://dl.dropboxusercontent.com/u/19228704/SpreadsheetModeling.htm#RealWorld
  - o http://dl.dropboxusercontent.com/u/19228704/SystemDynamicsModeling.htm
- Leong and Cheong, 2009. "Spreadsheet Modeling of Hotel Room Sales and Demand Distributions Estimation," *Decision Sciences Journal of Innovative Education* 7(1): 89–97.
- Meadows, 1999. "Leverage Points: Places to Intervene in a System," Sustainability Institute.
- Ragsdale, 2001. "Teaching Management Science with Spreadsheets," *INFORMS Transactions on Education* 1(2).
  - o http://archive.ite.journal.informs.org/Vol1No2/Ragsdale/Ragsdale.pdf
- Rosling, 2011. "Magic Washing Machine," *TED*.
  - o http://www.youtube.com/watch?v=BZoKfap4g4w
- Rosling, 2010. "200 Countries, 200 Years in 4 Minutes," *BBC*.
  - o http://www.youtube.com/watch?v=jbkSRLYSojo
- Rosling, 2010. "No More Boring Data," *TED*.
  - o http://www.youtube.com/watch?v=VWQnQRsxGn0
  - o http://www.youtube.com/watch?v=DQQkDks-q4E
- Sterman, 2006. "Learning from Evidence in a Complex World," *American Journal of Public Health* 96(3): 505–514

- Keywords. Relevant topics to search in Google and Wikipedia
  - o *Data sort filter . Pivot table . Goodness of fit . Kolmogorov-Smirnov . Statistics and spreadsheets . Revenue management*

PROBLEM SET 8

* Hard problems

Qn 8.01

Melons. Five randomly picked assorted samples of melons were taken from trucks delivered from a supplier. Each kind of melon is graded and thus should not deviate too much in quality and size. The samples are first weighed and then given to five inspection agencies to give their independent evaluations.

a. Construct a spreadsheet model to estimate the weight of each kind of melon.

b. The first sample with 1 watermelon, 2 honeydews, and 3 cantaloupes weigh 13 kg; the second sample with 2 watermelons, 3 honeydews, and 4 cantaloupes weigh 20.6 kg; the third sample with 3 watermelons, 4 honeydews, and 1 cantaloupe weigh 21.9 kg, the fourth sample with 4 watermelons, 2 honeydews, and 3 cantaloupes weigh 22.4 kg; and the fifth sample with 3 watermelons, 2 honeydews, and 2 cantaloupes weigh 18.2 kg.

c. What are the weight averages and standard deviations of each kind of melons? Explain how the results were obtained.

d. Will having more samples improve the accuracy of the results? Can the results be improved without getting more samples?

Qn 8.02

Change. Marina bought $2.70 of candies. She offered a $5 bill for payment.

a. Construct a spreadsheet model to show the change from the cashier.

b. Relevant currency denominations used by the store are $2 and $1 notes, and 50 cents, 20 cents, and 10 cents coins.

c. List the ways she could get her change using no more than 10 items (notes or coins). How many ways are there? Which way uses the least number of items?

d. What ways use the least number of coins?

e. Simulate how the change may be randomly taken from the possible ways in part c.

Qn 8.03

Distance Matrix. Given a local region, the travel distances between any two points may be measured using a map. The straight-line distance between the two points is of course less accurate than the distance measured along the shortest or most convenient route between them. Shortest distance and route suggestions are now available in many Internet services for free. They facilitate the deployment of resources such as delivery vehicles and support operational scheduling. However, it is still tedious to do the planning for large numbers of delivery points using such services. A more suitable approach for planning is to be able to generate the travel distances between any pair of locations quickly, though not necessarily accurately.

For any two points with location coordinates $(x1, y1)$ and $(x2, y2)$, the Lp distance between them is given by $Dp = (|x1 - x2|^p + |y1 - y2|^p)^{(1/p)}$, where

$0 < p \le 2$. By calibrating the value of parameter p, you can estimate distance across general situations. Where $p = 1$, the distance norm is the *rectangular* norm. This norm is suitable for estimating distances in city streets. Where $p = 2$, the distance norm is the *Euclidean* or *straight-line* norm. This norm is suitable for estimating distances in unrestricted open spaces. Also, a scaling factor is multiplied and a constant is added to correct for local conditions such as twisting and turning of the roads to follow rivers and crossing bridges, and one-way streets.

a. Construct a spreadsheet model to evaluate the application of the Lp norm.
b. Pick 30 well-scattered points in your district or city map and note their (x, y) coordinates. From them, randomly form 15 point-pairs. For each pair, find their distances using any of the Internet services available.
c. Determine the estimated distances using p values of 1 and 2. Evaluate the average absolute relative errors of distances estimated using them. The absolute relative error is defined as $(actual - estimate)/actual$.
d. Determine the best p value for your map. How can this value be accurately found?
e. Suggest further extensions to the formula that will reduce the absolute relative error.

Checked-in baggage. Airport baggage check-in for an airline now permits three bags and 25 kg total weight. With automation and for better customer service, the airline is giving a higher weight allowance of 32 kg but will limit the number of bags to two, to make it a common standard across all routes.

Qn 8.04

a. Construct a spreadsheet model to evaluate the new requirements situation.
b. Weights of the bags for a sample of 20 passengers are given below:

Pax	Bag 1	Bag 2	Bag 3	Pax	Bag 1	Bag 2	Bag 3
1	18.1	6.9		11	3.8		
2	6.8	3.4	3.4	12	11.0	7.5	
3	5.0			13	17.3	2.1	
4	16.3	8.5		14	13.2	7.2	4.6
5	2.1	1.1		15	9.9	9.9	5.2
6	8.6	5.9		16	13.0	9.2	2.8
7	17.8	2.6		17	20.2	3.8	
8	12.7	8.1	3.7	18	15.7	9.3	
9	19.1	5.9		19	10.8	9.6	
10	14.4	6.7		20	8.6	4.3	

c. Estimate how bags' weights will change with the new requirements for each passenger on the sample list.

d. Compute the number of bags, total weight, and average, standard deviation and maximum statistics.

e. Comment on the impact of the new requirements on the check-in counter and behind-the-counter terminal baggage handling.

Qn 8.05   **Medical triage.** Medical emergency cases had been divided into three categories: 1) those who are likely to live, regardless of what care they receive, 2) those who are likely to die, regardless of what care they receive, and 3) those for whom immediate care might make a positive difference in outcome. Hence, the term triage is used to classify patients' priority in getting treatment, though no longer always three categories. The triage scale currently used in Australia classifies as level 1 resuscitation cases needing immediate attention, level 2 emergency cases to be served within 10 minutes, level 3 urgent cases to be served within 30 minutes, level 4 semi-urgent cases to be served within 60 minutes, and level 5 non-urgent cases to be served within 120 minutes.

a. Construct a spreadsheet model to examine what the service level of a small Australian emergency response center will be with only one doctor.

b. Patient arrival times, service durations, and triage priority levels are given below:

Case	1	2	3	4	5	6	7	8	9	10
Arrival	8:00	8:48	8:59	9:30	9:58	10:03	10:31	10:53	11:03	11:36
Service	0:06	0:46	0:16	0:06	0:04	0:07	0:26	0:06	0:20	0:30
Priority	2	3	4	2	2	2	5	2	1	3

Case	11	12	13	14	15	16	17	18	19	20
Arrival	13:31	13:31	13:36	13:40	13:45	14:56	15:07	16:03	16:36	17:19
Service	0:03	0:35	0:04	0:30	0:19	0:20	0:14	0:28	0:37	0:51
Priority	3	3	4	2	1	4	3	2	3	4

c. Using the data directly, evaluate the wait time for each patient as if there is no triage level classification. Highlight the wait time violation cases.

d. Make a duplicate of the model in part c and then manually adjust the service start times of the same set of 20 patients with triage pre-screening. Triage priority level 1 patients are immediately served upon arrival. Other patients being

served would have to "restart" their service when the doctor becomes available again. Higher priority patients move ahead if upon arrival there are only lower priority patients waiting in line. Highlight the wait time violation cases.
e. Compare the average waiting times between the no-triage and triage cases.

Supermarkets. Prices of selected items are collected from three supermarkets. Some of the item prices are lowest at supermarket A while others are lowest at supermarket B or C. The consumer association wants to know which supermarket should be recommended to their members based on their prices.

> **Qn 8.06**

a. Construct a spreadsheet model to compare the item prices from the supermarkets.
b. Prices of 12 items at supermarkets A, B, and C respectively are item 1, 6.50, 6.60, and 6.35; item 2, 3.10, 3.00, and 3.05; item 3, 1.70, 1.80, and 1.90; item 4, 7.30, 7.50, and 7.25; item 5, 4.95, 4.70, and 4.90; item 6, 1.80, 1.90, and 1.95; item 7, 5.35, 5.40, and 5.30; item 8, 1.75, 1.80, and 1.85; item 9, 3.75, 3.65, and 3.70; item 10, 7.10, 7.15, and 7.05; item 11, 3.30, 3.05, and 3.10; and item 12, 2.70, 2.80, and 2.95.
c. What are your recommendations of where to shop?

Green shoes. The shoe store is trying to determine how many large, medium, and small pairs of its popular green shoes to order ahead of the coming St Patrick's Day holiday. It costs $35 to order a pair of shoes, and each pair sells for $75. After this special holiday, the store can sell leftover shoes at a steeply discounted price of $15 a pair. Estimated from past years' sales, expected demand of large, medium, and small green shoes sizes are projected to be 150, 285, and 200, with standard deviations of 35, 75, and 50, respectively. Demand is approximately Normal distributed. The store has allocated space to hold up to 500 pairs of green shoes.

> **Qn 8.07***

a. Construct a spreadsheet model to evaluate the green shoe stock situation for the store. Simulate for 100 trials.
b. If the store orders 500 green shoes in proportion to expected demand of the sizes, what are the order quantities of large, medium, and small green shoes? What is the sales revenue?
c. If the store optimizes its orders of the three shoe sizes, what are the order quantities? What is the sales revenue now?
d. Explain how you get the optimal results in part c and comment on the differences in results of parts b and c.

New build cost. Container ships are the main type of ships carrying general cargo. Its advantages lie in the speedier and safer cargo handling. These ships are getting larger, keeping in step with increases in trade volume. The main driver for the increasing sizes of new container vessels is that larger vessels have lower cost per unit capacity. This can be deduced from the published data on new build costs.

> **Qn 8.08***

Twenty-foot equivalent unit (TEU) capacity of a container vessel is the number of containers it can carry if all containers are twenty-foot units.

a. Construct a spreadsheet model to fit current cost and capacity data to a function, and to use this to estimate cost of future larger capacity vessels.

b. A new 500 TEU ship costs USD10 million to build, a 1,000 TEU ship costs USD17.5 million, a 1,250 TEU ship costs USD20 million, a 1,500 TEU ship costs USD25 million, a 1,750 TEU ship costs USD27 million, a 2,000 TEU ship costs USD30 million, a 2,500 TEU ship costs USD35 million, a 3,000 TEU ship costs USD40 million, a 3,500 TEU ship costs USD42.5 million, a 4,000 TEU ship costs USD45 million, a 5,000 TEU ship costs USD55 million, a 6,000 TEU ship costs USD60 million, a 7,000 TEU ship costs USD65 million, a 8,000 TEU ship costs USD70 million, a 9,000 TEU ship costs USD75 million, and a 10,000 TEU ship costs USD80 million.

c. Using only the data from 500 to 5,000 TEU ships, find a function to fit the cost to carrying capacity relationship that minimizes the average absolute relative error. Absolute relative error of fit is defined as ABS (*estimate −actual*)/*actual*.

d. Estimate the build cost for 6,000 to 10,000 TEU ships. Compare the estimated against the actual. Compute the average absolute relative forecast error.

e. What is the estimated cost of a 20,000 TEU ship? Upper and lower limits?

Qn 8.09* **Job interview**. The company uses three mid-level managers to interview and select their job applicants. Subject to positions available, candidates with at least two "Yes" votes from this panel are given job offers. The company recently engaged the services of a human resource consulting company in a one-time exercise to evaluate the effectiveness of the interview panel. For this, the expert consultants independently interviewed shortlisted applicants and rated them for quality and suitability. This way, the company can compare the ratings of those they offer jobs to and those not offered.

a. Construct a spreadsheet model to evaluate the abilities of the three interviewers.

b. The consultant ratings and the decisions of managers A, B, and C are shown below.

Applicant	Rating	A	B	C
1	3.9	N	Y	N
2	2.9	Y	Y	Y
3	2.5	N	N	N
4	4.1	N	Y	N
5	3.3	Y	N	N

Applicant	Rating	A	B	C
6	2.7	Y	N	Y
7	2.1	N	Y	Y
8	1.5	Y	N	N
9	4.5	Y	Y	N
10	3.7	N	N	Y
11	2.3	N	N	N
12	1.3	N	N	Y
13	1.9	Y	N	Y
14	1.7	N	Y	Y
15	1.1	Y	N	N
16	3.1	Y	N	N
17	3.5	Y	Y	N
18	4.9	Y	Y	N
19	4.7	Y	Y	N
20	4.3	N	N	Y

In the 5-point rating used by the consultants, 5 is best and 1 is worst. The managers' votes are recorded as Y for *Yes* and N for *No*.

c. Which manager is best at identifying the high rating candidates? Who is worst?
d. Suppose the interview panel is reduced to two persons, still needing two "Yes" votes to approve the candidate. How do the two-persons panel perform?
e. What are your recommendations for the company for their future interviews?

Project screening. The company is doing a review of major projects completed in the past five years. Evaluators A, B, C, and D, based on the average of their ratings, approved these projects. Each evaluator's prior rating, with values from 0 to 5, is an aggregate score obtained after completing a 10-page questionnaire using projected data. Projects with 3 or more points are considered good while those with less than 3 points are bad. Post-hoc reviews are done using the same questionnaire, but this time more objectively with actual data and the ratings are rounded to nearest whole numbers for presenting to the board. The company wants to seize this opportunity to assess the evaluators and review the evaluation process.

Qn 8.10*

a. Construct a spreadsheet model to examine the performance of the evaluators and the evaluation process.

b. Post-hoc project ratings and prior ratings from each evaluator are given in the table below. The projects and evaluators have been sorted in descending order of quality.

Post		Prior Ratings			
Project	Rating	A	B	C	D
1	5	5.0	5.0	2.9	1.0
2	5	4.9	1.7	5.0	4.1
3	5	4.9	5.0	5.0	3.8
4	5	5.0	4.4	5.0	4.2
5	4	4.7	5.0	3.0	3.6
6	4	5.0	5.0	5.0	3.3
7	4	5.0	3.9	0.9	2.9
8	4	3.8	5.0	5.0	0.8
9	3	4.3	1.4	0.1	2.8
10	3	4.2	3.4	1.0	1.6
11	3	2.2	4.0	0.8	0.3
12	2	1.3	1.9	1.1	0.1
13	2	3.1	0.9	4.1	1.2
14	1	1.6	4.2	2.5	0.1
15	1	1.8	0.2	2.1	0.1

c. Compute the average prior ratings for each project as the evaluation committee's ratings. Determine the critical threshold they could have used to approve the projects that will minimize type I (rejecting good projects) and type II (accepting bad projects) errors.

d. Evaluate the situation where the projects are reviewed sequentially in A-B-C-D order and another in D-C-B-A order. Projects rejected by an evaluator will not be reviewed by the evaluator next in the sequence. This will reduce the amount of review work by the evaluators but may result in degraded project selection ability. What are the critical thresholds now for each evaluator? Which of the three approaches is best?

CHAPTER

9 Modeling Projects

LEARNING OUTCOMES	• Able to define and work on new spreadsheet projects
	• Able to build spreadsheet tools to support future project work
	• Able to provide simple and complete documentation for projects

INTRODUCTION

If you have persevered with us thus far, we congratulate you. We are sure you have learned quite a bit of spreadsheet modeling by now. Particularly to those of you who have worked through the book on your own, we take our hats off to you. We know this is a tough book to learn from because it requires you to do a lot of thinking on your own. However, this is the only way, we believe, you can improve your spreadsheet modeling ability.

A few thousand projects have been completed by students taking spreadsheet modeling courses taught by us and our colleagues, of which this book is the required text. The projects are for real companies and organizations. They were kind enough to provide business challenges for our students to work on and most have reaped substantial benefits from their participation. We therefore salute and thank our business and public community for their gracious and continued support as project sponsors.

This chapter mainly showcases student projects. The spreadsheet workbooks of a few are also included in the accompanying *Online Learning Center*. Actual names and project settings in the workbooks have been changed for privacy and commercial sensitivity reasons. Covering a variety of issues and scale of operations, the selected project examples presented in this chapter are:

- *B. Tankee, Volunteer Management, Family Services Center*,
- *New Car Purchase, The Better Bookshop, Cake Legacy, Animal Exchange, Suzie Ice Rink*,
- *Metro Get-Away, Freelance Dancers, Love-In-The-Air*, and
- *Family Clinic, LL Legal, CAT-TV*.

Of these projects, the only one that has received extensive sprucing by us is *B. Tankee*. You can use it as an exercise too, as we also wrote up its challenge, concept, and working comments, as has been done for all the exercises presented in the other chapters. The other project examples' workbooks are generally left as much as possible in their original submitted form.

As you will see from the spreadsheet workbooks, not all our students followed our tips on spreadsheet work and modeling. One reason is that most of the selected project examples were done by earlier batches of students at which time we had not formalized the ideas we now present explicitly in this book. Another reason is that students being young are fond of adopting different styles and putting their creativity to good effect. Our approach is generally plainer, but noticeably efficient and effective. The contrast in styles and approaches is good and will help train you to see, without compromising effectiveness, which are simple and which are not.

As with the exercises, there was a tendency among weaker students in the class to just watch and learn from their professor, whom they look upon as the "master"; they seldom attempted as pre-class preparation to do the modeling themselves unless they were coerced. To help you start learning deeper by doing, we have extracted the essence of many projects our students have done, plus some that they have been doing, and present them in this chapter. Their spreadsheet workbooks are not included in the accompanying *Online Learning Center* because we really want you to do the modeling on your own. Moreover, there are too many projects in our collection for us to review and desensitize. The scenario descriptions of these projects, where sensible, are directly lifted from student project reports (with minor editing from us). They should provide you with enough ideas of what the challenges are. You can also draw inspirations from them to propose projects for any of your courses, internships, or even consulting work.

Over and above the 101 exercises and tools in the other chapters, there are another 101 projects in this chapter. Other than the first 14 project examples, the others are organized for easy reference into eight categories: 1) Community and Individual, 2) Business and Services, 3) New Venture, 4) Finance and Administration,

5) Transportation and Supply Chain, 6) Manufacturing and Operations, 7) Information Technology and Communications, and 8) Global and Environmental.

Finally, to further assist you, we provide *New Exercise*, *New Project*, *Modeling Tools*, *Learn*, *Useful Macros*, *Limited Trial*, and a few other workbooks to serve as tools (and examples) for your project work. The four *New Exercise* and *New Project* workbooks are skeleton workbooks from which you can start your modeling work. These, plus *Modeling Tools* and *Learn*, make it easier for you to organize, format, and document your work. *Useful Macros* demonstrates how macros can be applied. The *Limited Trial* tool allows you to release your project to others for limited time evaluation. After the time limit, the worksheets in the workbook become inaccessible.

Do not wait until you have reviewed all the exercises and tools in the earlier chapters before turning your attention to this chapter. Visit this chapter every now and then, and review it as you learn from the other chapters and *Notes* in the Appendices. It will serve you well. For example after you have learned Excel's DataTable or Calc's Multiple Operations, you may want to examine the TableSolve tool. This tool imitates and extends the said native spreadsheet feature to allow it to work with any number of input and output variables, across sheets, and run macros with each change of input data. It is a tremendous aid to us in our own academic research.

DISCOVERY POINTS

Point 37

Community and individual

This is a popular theme students like to do their projects on. They are easy to identify and revolve around day-to-day life. Individual projects cover personal hygiene and health issues, such as grooming, nutrition and weight management, and personal wealth issues, such as charity giving, financial stability, and retirement planning. Community issues are broader, involving groups of people, clubs, and societies, and municipal and voluntary welfare organizations. Many of such groups depend on volunteers to run their services and donors to fund them. So, volunteer and donor management features are very high on the agenda. Key goals are to keep volunteers motivated and ensure the flow of contributions continues to come in. Event management is another big concern since the people working on them are not always the same and they have not worked with each other on a regular basis. The scale of these events can range from very small to mega sized. Different skill sets are required for different events and the various roles in each event. The challenge is in ensuring there are enough people and a right mix of people covering the skill sets and operating levels. All in all, the work has to be simplified and made fun to keep people coming back for more.

Point 38

Business and services

The second most convenient area to explore as a project is local retail outlets, cafes, and personal services such as hair salons and spas. Their business models are common knowledge to most, and everyone assumes that he or she knows how the business is operated. This is of course far from true. Every business has its secrets and services that maintain their market share and sales growth by continuously improving the way they operate and adding innovative products. Another service area students like to pursue for their projects are the internal administrative services of their schools and colleges. Common processes encountered included queue management at receptions and registrations, service provisioning, payment processing, and aftersales servicing. Businesses are concerned about working out bottlenecks and identifying cost control measures. These include better manpower scheduling and inventory control.

A really fun but challenging area is to examine how a new business may be started or a new product developed and launched. Existing businesses may want to look at local or regional expansion. Expansion can be horizontal by starting or acquiring businesses of the same kind, or vertically integrated by starting or acquiring businesses upstream or downstream from their current business. For example, a manufacturing company may decide to produce its own input materials to reduce dependency on a supplier, or by setting up retail shops to sell directly to consumers. To get more capital and managerial talents without acquiring them directly, many successful businesses expand very quickly by offering franchise licenses. These include fast-food restaurants, shoe retailers, convenience shops, fitness gyms, kindergartens, and hotels. On the flip side, others without much experience and expertise who are starting to go into business for the first time may want to look at these available franchising opportunities.

> **New venture**

Financial management deals with two main issues: 1) how to make the most of the current available financial resources and 2) how best to get additional funding to support further activities of the firm. Financial resources include cash and current assets, fixed assets, amounts borrowed and owed, and equity contributions from business co-owners. Some of these resources are easily convertible to cash and other assets while others are more difficult to redeploy. The various sources of funding also come with different costs. Conversely, financial assets of the firm can be used directly to generate income for the firm, although rightly the company's main earnings should come from its business operations. To execute these operations, money is needed in advance for purchasing fixed assets, capital equipment, and raw materials, with which it produces goods and services that it sells to generate its operating revenue.

> **Finance and administration**

The firm's sustainability and growth depend on its ability to generate profit – the difference between revenue and cost of its business. While profit in the long run makes the firm, the dynamic shortage of funds in the short-run breaks it.

It therefore must manage its cashflow diligently to ensure that at all times there are sufficient funds to meet its obligations to suppliers and creditors, while waiting for customers to purchase its products and effect their consequent payments. This area is considered very mundane. Accounting rules can be tedious to follow and clinical financial analyses leave very little room for innovative discovery. This perception can be proved wrong if you dig down. A starting point is to take a standard financial and accounting analytical framework or scenario, and seek to discover its weaknesses or rigidities. Explore how liabilities can be turned into opportunities and inflexibility into resilience.

The administration area, usually co-located with finance in many corporate headquarters, covers human resource, strategic development, corporate development, corporate communications, company secretariat, and legal counsel. There are many interesting topics for exploration. Again to the untrained eye, most things in administration seem dull and routine. You start by looking at how to make the work easier to do and more efficient. Next, pursue how to get more advantage and value for the organization. Look also for interesting issues that you did not know existed in the corporate headquarters and general administration office. New topics in administration include business process outsourcing, telecommuting, flexible work arrangements, work-life balance, continuing education, gender balance and racial diversity, and corporate social responsibility.

Point 41

Transportation and supply chain

Supply chain is the whole process of acquiring raw materials, converting them to sub-assemblies and final products, and distributing them to final consumers. Each player in the chain usually plays a small role, and it is the collective effort of all involved that makes everything happen. The orchestration of individual efforts is generally provided by the mechanisms of supply, demand, and market prices. However understandably, the detailed operations are far more complex. In the various stages of the field's historical development, it has taken on different emphases. In the early years, management's main concern was in getting manufactured goods to the retailers and consumers. It was then more known as physical distribution and channel management, both as areas of the marketing function in the firm. The primary interest shifted to that of improving competitive advantage by lowering costs in inventory and transportation management with better consolidation and integration. This brings the field into the operations domain.

Supply chain management subsequently blossomed and became strategic, driven by three mega trends: globalization, outsourcing, and infocomm technology. Firms first moved beyond their national boundaries to seek new markets and lower cost manufacturing locations. Getting better economies of specialization, tax, and exchange rates and trading advantages, they involved increasingly more offshore subsidiaries and also external outsourced manufacturers, third- and fourth-party transportation and distribution service providers. The challenge of managing such large global multinational coordination is only possible with sophisticated and reliable information and communications technologies. This is not the end; the field is still evolving. The next frontier likely lies in linking in new product design with customization and sophisticated demand management.

Point 42

Manufacturing and operations

Operations is the heart of any organization, where it produces the goods or services that it offers to people it seeks to serve. Whether private or public, for-profit or not-for-profit, an organization's operations defines the role it plays in society. Here, it interacts with the community, serves it, and in return, gets its patronage. Operations has to be staffed and financed, its inputs sourced and suppliers managed, and its products marketed to beneficiaries. These support activities, namely human resource, finance, procurement, and marketing are themselves on their own also "operations." The principles of operations also apply in each of these cases though their direct "client" is the organization's "core" operations. The focus of all internal stakeholders should of course be on final actual customers, as they are the real paymasters.

In simple terms, operations uses raw materials and services offered by suppliers and operates its facilities and equipment to generate products, whether goods or services. Goods can be produced ahead of time and held in stock before being readied to ship to customers according to their orders. This is more expedient to customers. Alternatively, when a product is non-standard or needs extra specifications, it can only be produced after customer orders have been received. More particular, services require the customer's presence or needs to be done in a customer-specified location. The challenges of operations are therefore which factors of production to employ; what, how much, and when to produce; and how the products may be transported and distributed to where they are required. In addition, the quality of the products needs to be assured and productive capacity – which takes time to be expanded – is acquired in a timely fashion.

Point 43

Information technology and communications

Technology is the application of scientific knowledge to practice. The scope is wide and the limited focus adopted here is on its use in Operations and Supply Chain Management. Technology must first be managed as it is ever changing. Its appropriate selection, application development, and timely deployment make all the difference. The critical factors lie in understanding the nature of the business while keeping a keen eye on the evolving technologies experiments in the research centers and laboratories.

The Internet offers a ripe playing field. Many interesting ideas now come in bite sizes. The firm can choose to incorporate them in their software development effort or, as is increasingly a better option, buy the relevant modules and plug in. Technology should not be seen in piece-meal but as well-integrated systems. The systems not only have to work well within all the functional areas in the company but also out of the firm, integrating and communicating with partners and customers.

Point 44

Global and environmental

The concern of the greatest scale but also the most difficult is about making the world a better place. Just too many issues are of interest here. To name a few: energy, climate, food, water, sustainability, disease control, and poverty reduction. The issues are about development as well as avoiding irreversible change, urgent aid, and sustained persistent effort. They are also overlapping, with energy concerns affecting agriculture and climate, for example. There are also too many stakeholders, and at various levels, from individual to community, province, nation, regional, and continental. Where do you start? Start with one issue at a time, one level at a time, working from what you understand and doing what you can to change and influence.

Point 45

Phase out skeuomorphs

There are many potential challenges to explore. *Discovery Points 37* to *44* introduce broad areas that you can work on. Pick one topic at a time and dive deeply into it. Read up and talk to people close to the chosen topic. Most of the key concerns are not new and as such, people with experience in the fields tend to look with "old eyes." They seek out convenient solutions, those that make work lighter and easier for the operators and executives, such as how to: 1) reduce manual data entry and 2) better collate information to show patterns and trends. Going beyond, you with "fresh eyes" should seek to contribute on how to transform and innovate, leveraging on better technology and new insights, and adding more value to the work. Consider a project in a sales office. Do not just automate the manual processes with electronic forms. While they are better than manual ones, there is much more you can do. For example, can the data once entered be automatically retrieved for the same user every time he uses the system? The user in fact never needs to see the forms. Based on his past usage pattern, the system should actually preempt the workflow for him and seek his concurrences only.

Many transitional applications of technology uses skeuomorphs, a derived object that keeps design cues from the original it replaces. For example, motorcars (formerly short for motorized carriages) started out as horse carriages pulled by steam engines, and the calendar on your computer looks like the paper ones you used to have. The trend had been to make computer objects and their ensuing processes mimic those being phased out. While a good idea to smooth transitional difficulties and alleviate psychological barriers, it limits the potential of what you can do with the technology. To illustrate, imagine asking for directions to go to town from the countryside. The villager you meet tells you to walk east to the river, follow its banks northerly to a bridge, cross it, turn right on the next three junctions, then take a left and follow the south-easterly windy road. With this input from your local "expert," do you start up your helicopter and fly following the zigzag path specified, or do you quickly sketch out a map, take a compass bearing, and head straight into town? Certainly, you must not let your recommendations and solution design be limited by the mindset and technology of the past. As some have said, "don't fight the next war with the strategies and weapons of previous wars."

Point 46

Design thinking and social change

You can change your community and its immediate environment, and after that go further afield to influence others and change the world. To effect change, we must first understand how behaviors are shaped and motivated. Psychologists tell us that people are motivated by rules, money, emotions, and environment. We do not litter because there are laws against it, with enforcing policing and penalty fines. Fines are monetary disincentives. Career prospects and bigger paychecks are positive inducements to work harder in school to complete your education. Some people work hard though they are already rich because they want to live up to the expectations of others. Others negatively influenced by their environment waste their time on destructive habits, for after all they have enough money stashed to last many lifetimes. Behaviors become habits, which in short, are just actions not guided by clear thought.

To change a habitual behavior of an individual and later transform society as a whole, you must identify the underlying habit and ask what contributed to it. Then, seek out to disrupt the triggers and redirect the people to a different, better habit. Here are some interesting examples.

- Schiphol airport authority found male travelers to be always in a hurry and not using the urinals in toilets properly, thus leaving the floor wet with spilled urine. To disrupt that undesirable behavior, they introduced a fly icon in the urinals. This tempted those peeing to aim and shoot at. Incidents of spillage as a result were drastically reduced.

- Project H Design founder Emily Pilloton was asked to help redesign an elementary school in rural Bertie County, USA. This is a poor neighborhood and the school there has a dismal record. She brought the classroom outdoors into the playground. Using chalk to mark numbers on half-buried rubber wheels in the sand pit, these wheels are "rocking horses" for the kids to ride. The pupils get to mount them if they can solve the addition or multiplication problems shouted out by the teacher and find the correct answers marked on the wheels. This motivated the boys who are the ones not doing particularly well in class and easily distracted to focus and compete to win in the playground game and learn arithmetic at the same time.

- Jamie Oliver's Better Food Foundation works with schools to help young students learn how to sow and grow their own food. It also teaches them basic nutritional knowledge and cooking skills to combat overeating and obesity. They learn to eat better and be healthier. He also takes in 15 disengaged young people to work as apprentices in his restaurants for 12 months, to make them more disciplined and better people in their community. This program gives them lifelong employment skills that they can use to raise their quality of life, and get out of poverty and unproductive life-styles.

- The Philippines has many rural poor. To help reduce poverty, the Davao city government, working with donors and the national department of agriculture, started a goat dispersal program. Each community support group sets up a collective demonstration farm with material and labor contributions from the community. Participating farmers learn on the job working on the collective farm and contribute feeding pastures. The farm is given 10 does and two bucks as starting stock. Goats are fast breeders. A kid becomes mature in about a year and can start breeding. It can give birth to one or two young of its own after a short gestation period of only five months. This way, the 12 goats quickly multiply. Qualified farmers progressively receive goats from this program to raise on their own. The farmers have to return a kid for every goat dispersed to them, after which they receive the certificate of ownership for their goat.

Experience is not relevant unless you can examine and extract principles to apply. Some people spend their whole life in an organization and have not progressed much beyond what they learned in their first two years. Now if you let experience help you understand the underlying currents of your situation, you can apply that knowledge to find interesting ways to turn things around. The first step is in discovering what is wrong and the second step is to design a way to put it right. Keep doing this, in every big and small way, and soon you will be changing the world.

PROJECTS

B. TANKEE	Reworked Example

Home appliance and electronic goods retailers provide free home delivery service for items such as refrigerators, washing machines, ovens/stoves, televisions, and audio-visual equipment. These items are either too large or numerous to be considered cash-and-carry purchases. The success of a sale often depends on how quickly the delivery appointment can be set up, how the appointment can best accommodate customers' convenience, and how soon the delivery date is. In addition, customers do not like to have to take time off from work to wait at home only to find the delivery cannot be made at the appointed time.

B. Tankee operates its own fleet of vehicles of various load-carrying capacities for the delivery runs. They divide each large city where they have stores into five approximately equal-sized geographical zones (north, south, east, west, and central), adjusting slightly to fit historical demand patterns. Each day is divided into two time slots: morning (AM) and afternoon (PM). This yields a total of 10 zone slots a day, i.e., north-AM, north-PM, south-AM, south-PM, etc. Typically up to three deliveries can be made by a vehicle within a time slot, the constraint being not travel time but loading, unloading, and customer service time.

A simple static plan would assign a vehicle to each zone such that its daily work plan for a week would be to visit the assigned zone in the morning and afternoon if there are deliveries there. Under this plan, drivers can become conditioned to want to work in their dedicated zones only and the size variety of vehicles cannot be better leveraged to help support the dynamic delivery demand changes. A more sophisticated plan, still static, would be to assign vehicles to zone slots according to the relative delivery demands for a longer planning horizon of, say, three months. Some zone slots may be visited by multiple vehicles, but as a consequence, other zone slots may only be visited every two weeks. Delivery service to those zone slots being relatively poorer may in turn lead to fewer purchases from customers in these zones.

Static plans are less efficient than dynamic plans as they do not attempt to rebalance and match workloads among the vehicles with different carrying capacities. A clear symptom of this would be that some vehicles are underutilized while others are overutilized, with the overall effect of delaying customer deliveries unnecessarily. A better approach is a delivery schedule that adapts to booking requests as they are being made. However, this plan must still be simple enough for schedulers to create and easy for all the drivers to understand.

This elaborate and comprehensive workbook covers basic modeling and analysis to understand the business context to provide simple rules to support the operation. This is in the first set of worksheets. The second set of worksheets makes operational the solution for decision support. In constructing this business operations system, a host of practical day-to-day difficulties surfaced. It is not likely that the workbook can be completely reviewed, much less constructed, during an hour or two in class. You should look at this workbook as a benchmark to judge your spreadsheet projects, comparing it against what you have done or plan to do. The workbook is accompanied by presentation and document files to yield the complete project package.

Concept

You should start with the business modeling and analysis first. Only when you have an understanding of the nature of the problem and structure of the solution, do you then complete the analysis to determine the strategy and tactics for actual implementation. The implementation may be better suited to a proper operations and scheduling system. However in many instances, a spreadsheet will do fine. Try working out the problem with a skeleton prototype operational worksheet and apply it repeatedly in actual use. Follow through by taking feedback on how to improve the spreadsheet "system" both in minimizing data entry, information reference, and decision support. Finally, make the system robust by adding worksheet protection to avoid mishaps and putting in macros to automate and simplify its use.

Working

Analyze the spreadsheet workbook and deduce the conclusions that should be brought to the management's attention. Select the relevant tables and charts, and individually paste them into the presentation and document files. It is extremely important that these are pasted as pictures and not spreadsheet objects to the other files. The reason for this is that you can unknowingly pass confidential information to parties not privy to it since spreadsheet objects pasted into other files bring along with them the rest of the workbook. In short, it is not just the chosen tables or charts that have been pasted, but the whole "lock, stock, and barrel."

You can test this out. Just double-click on the spreadsheet object that you have pasted into either the presentation or document file and see how the whole working workbook pops out. It is tempting to keep it like this as you can use it to evaluate alternative input values and work with your audience interactively instead of needing to separately open the spreadsheet file. Once again, for reason of showing only the carefully selected material and that visible to your audience alone, do not copy them over as objects. Also, this will retain your existing workbook as the one and only official copy that you can use to interact with the audience and store the latest consequent outcomes.

Project 2   VOLUNTEERS MANAGEMENT   Example

Voluntary Welfare Organizations (VWOs) need the support of kind-hearted individuals to provide many of their services. The management of volunteers at times is even done by the volunteers themselves. Such VWOs have to actively seek out and engage their volunteers, encouraging them as well as monitoring how they have been participating, and where and when they can be better deployed to carry out the VWO's activities. Well-established VWOs even train their volunteers to take on wider and more critical roles and responsibilities.

Project 3   FAMILY SERVICES CENTER   Example

The Family Services Center of the community runs many events. Given its limited funds, all obtained from public generosity, it has to be very careful in planning activities and allocating the financial resources. The events have to satisfy the mission of the organization and achieve a balance between short-, medium-, and long-term goals. Other than finances, the center is also constrained by manpower and volunteer availability and skills. For fund-raising and volunteer activation, they are keeping data in various forms which do not allow for easy tracking and engagement support.

Project 4   NEW CAR PURCHASE   Example

Cars rank as the second most valuable asset that an average person can own (homes are the most valuable). Relatively high tax, duties, and car prices increase the financial significance of buying a car in crowded cities such as Hong Kong and Singapore. Purchasing a new car requires the average resident there to consider carefully the specifications of the vehicle as well as his ability to finance it. The host of international car manufacturers, each with its own stable of car models and makes, poses a decision problem for genuine new car buyers. They have to sift through racks of car magazines, visit countless websites, and talk to numerous car dealers to obtain relevant data. Car buyers are often daunted by this mountain of information and are confused as to how to process them.

Project 5   THE BETTER BOOKSTORE   Example

Every year, parents and students form long lines at the elementary school in the week preceding the opening of the school year to purchase the required textbooks and stationery. The books a student has to buy depend on his/her grade level, choice of second language, and subject specializations. Some of the reference materials like dictionaries and atlases, may be carried over from the previous year, if the student had already bought them. The bookstore is therefore a very busy place and it needs some help to simplify and speed up its operations so that this year will not see a repeat of past years' incidents where there were many angry parents and very tired bookstore staff.

Example	CAKE LEGACY

Project 6

Chew Boon is migrating overseas with his family and is looking for an interested party to take over Cake Legacy, the neighborhood confectionery shop he started five years ago. While the business has been doing well, he does not really know what the numbers are as he has been busy running the operations. To persuade prospective buyers about its value, Chew Boon has asked a few of his friends to help collect data and analyze his business. The tasks involved should include assessing the demand for his confectioneries and constraints on sales volume, and working out the financials.

Example	ANIMAL EXCHANGE

Project 7

The Singapore Zoo, considered to be one of the most beautiful in the Asia-Pacific region and well acclaimed for its open concept where animals live in spacious natural environment, enjoys an average of 1.2 million visitors per year. It occupies some 28 hectares of space and at present, houses 3,200 animals covering 322 species, 20% of which are listed as threatened animals. As the zoo's primary attraction, it is very important that the animal inventory is well maintained.

   Like most zoos, it keeps a list of animals that they have in surplus as well as a list of animals they wish to add, as they continually renew interest in the zoo to boost visitor numbers. Currently, for the zoo to seek out animals to exchange with other zoos, whether selling, buying, or bartering, they must request for and go through each of their partners' lists. This entails long hours of searching and checking. Many zoos have their data spread over several files and stacks of papers, which makes the task even harder.

Example	SUZIE ICE RINK

Project 8

Good skating experience is determined by the quality of the ice surface. This is kept up by periodic resurfacing. The resurfacing schedule now in use is based on past human traffic pattern and has since become no longer relevant. The human traffic data have to be recollected and maintained. The rink usage varies greatly between weekdays and weekends, and between normal and promotion days.

The ice rink has a small management team of four, each covering operations, accounting, marketing, and the skating school. The executive in charge of the skating school has many duties under her care – mainly coordinating the school's daily schedule, answering parents' inquiries, and organizing special events.

The school's daily schedule coordination, the most tedious of the work, comprises the following activities:

1. A parent or student signs up for lessons at the information counter.
2. The applicant fills out the application form to choose the coach and time slots.
3. The applicant pays the fees to confirm the booking.
4. The school executive transfers the data into a spreadsheet to update each coach's schedule and files the booking form away.
5. The coaches constantly go to the information counter to inquire about the latest situation in their individual schedules and hence consuming a lot of the executive's time.

Project 9	METRO GET-AWAY	Example

Metro Get-Away is a small guesthouse in eastern Europe, wholly owned by the current operator. The guesthouse does not have any formal account and management system, keeping poor records of their customers and financial situation. Given that the owner has plans for expansion, it is important to first improve the current system. Better records will also give the owner more data to substantiate and justify the need for physical expansion and additional staff.

Currently, room bookings and equipment rentals require the staff to flip through pages of the order book to determine their availability. The duty staff has to spend a lot of time double-checking the thick room reservation book with each arriving group of customers before they can check in. Operational costs are not adequately recorded by the management at Metro. Instead paper invoices are filed and have to be constantly dug up for review when financial decisions have to be made.

At the owner's request, the project must establish a simple computerized room and sports rental equipment management system to more speedily serve the guests. Also needed is a better way to keep track of the accounts and information to assist him in making business expansion decisions.

Example	FREELANCE DANCERS	Project 10

Alpha D Arts is an established private school that offers a wide variety of music and dance classes. It has often been called upon to provide artistes for corporate events and dance performances. Every month, about 20 to 30 dancers would approach Alpha D seeking freelance work. However, Alpha D does not always have suitable performance opportunities for them. Conversely, when dance and events companies request Alpha D for assistance in sourcing for professional dancers on short notice, they are not able to respond adequately. Currently, most of the contact information is provided through individual dance instructors, by word of mouth, and friends in the performing dance community. This is highly inefficient and laborious. The typical situation is such that some dancers are tired from having too many engagements while others are literally starving to death waiting for a chance to perform.

Example	LOVE-IN-THE-AIR	Project 11

Love-In-The-Air Matchmaking Agency is a service business that assists clients in finding their significant other. A venture capitalist has expressed an interest in injecting new capital into the company. Your consulting team has been engaged to provide an independent assessment of the agency's financial strength and expert opinions for improving their matchmaking process.

Matching clients with suitable potential partners is a difficult process because of the massive amount of information involved. It is very time consuming and inefficiency often results in lost sales when clients lose patience waiting to be served. Improving the way of matching clients with potential partners can drastically improve the business revenue.

Future demand for Love-In-The-Air's services should first be projected based on historical data and then moderated according to how much improvement can be made to the service processes. From this, a multi-year projection of their income statement can be prepared. The VC needs to know if the investment should go ahead.

Example	FAMILY CLINIC	Project 12

The daily operations of the family clinic cover three main areas: patient data, medication inventory, and financial accounts. The main problem hindering work flow at the clinic is their use of manual patient records. Patients' particulars and medical records are written down on paper cards which are filed in alphabetical order into metal cabinets. The current approach is cumbersome and human-error prone, as the cards are easily misplaced or mixed up. Valuable patient data may be lost or wrongly recorded when patients have similar names. It is also very hard to keep track of medicine and equipment inventory; in particular, managing the availability of essential drugs with short shelf-life has been challenging. Manual stock taking can at best be done weekly. The order amount and frequency of ordering the drugs have to take into account consumption rates, expiration dates, and special discount rates offered by pharmaceutical companies. The clinic also has to manage their finances and watch their cash flows.

Project 13	LL LEGAL	Example

LL Company is a legal service provider that deals primarily with litigation contracts, debt collection, and accident cases. Established in 2002, the firm currently employs two lawyers and four paralegals. The lawyers have acquired experience over a wide range of civil law work, and the paralegals have been cross-trained to perform various duties. This allows LL to flexibly deploy their staff to the cases as they arise, and the lawyers can seamlessly cover for each other and clock billing hours for the firm when some of them become too busy. Under the country's legal system, each firm can only bill the client by simple hourly rates, independent of the experience, reputation, and stature of the lawyer or lawyers they deploy on the case and so the sharing of cases among lawyers is a common and accepted practice.

LL currently faces two main problems. Firstly, as a small firm, there is a tendency for LL to overstretch itself in accepting new cases. This was an issue that a judge had recently raised in chambers and over which a law firm had been taken to task. Secondly, LL does not have a well-structured quotation process for estimating their effort and cost for each new case. Most of their quotations are made off the top of their head. As each new case seems to come with unique characteristics and work demands, LL has previously decided but procrastinated on developing a quotation system to make more accurate and speed up this important initial interaction with their clients.

Project 14	CAT-TV	Example

CAT-TV is an established local TV channel with a wide audience and astounding ratings. For growth, they are beginning to explore new regional ventures. They have come across an opportunity to start a new broadcasting channel in an undisclosed country in Southeast Asia. As most of their income comes from advertising and the size of audience relevant to advertisers is affected by what is shown on the channel, it is imperative for CAT-TV to find better TV programs and schedules, and correctly price their advertising packages. A study is thus been proposed to review how CAT-TV allocate time slots for their programs and advertisements, and recommend suggested improvements.

Community and Individual

AUTO CHALLENGE

Project 15

A Japanese automobile maker publicizes its presence in the local community by sponsoring a much attended contest. In this contest, shortlisted participants put their hands at designated locations on a few latest model cars. Other than the 5-minute rest for every hour, the contestants must keep their hands on the cars to stay in the contest.

The event can span three to four days and the last person remaining in the competition is declared the winner and takes home a car. With increasing popularity, more cars are used in the competition to accommodate more contestants. The contest has also been divided into man, woman, and team categories. The contest specifications and number of shortlisted entrants are changed each year to add variety.

The winning time has been improving each year with contestants lasting longer. Mr. Mikimoto is wondering if the event will break into an additional day this year since they have to pay for the use of the public plaza where the contest has been taking place since its inauguration.

FREE BUS STOPS

Project 16

It costs a lot of money to build a bus stop to provide the needed shelter from sun and rain. The costs can be estimated by examining the proposal put up by contractors bidding for these jobs and the number of bus stops specified in the tender. There is, however, a recent concept that the bus stops construction contract be awarded to marketing companies. These companies, in fact, are willing to construct and maintain the bus stops for nothing and yet pay annual dues to the city government. Assess how much it would cost your community to rebuild all the bus stops. Make a reasonable estimate of the returns you would expect if the project is awarded to a marketing company for the next five years.

ALUMNI GIVING

Every year, the university works out programs and activities to solicit financial support from its alumni. Newly graduated students are not expected to do much until their careers take off and they become more settled in life. The planning office wants to estimate the amount of donations that they can expect from the alumni through the university's annual giving plan. It must select what segment of the alumni to work on and how much to expect in monetary contributions from each segment.

VWO FINANCIAL RESERVES

Voluntary Welfare Organizations (VWOs) raise funds through voluntary donations, fund-raising events and direct solicitations for special projects. The financial needs of a VWO may change from year to year and the level of support from the community can wax and wane depending on the economic well-being of the supporters. To ensure that the organization does not fail to meet its obligations, some have put forward the suggestion that the VWOs keep a certain amount of reserves. A VWO with too large a reserve would discourage people from giving more, but having not enough in reserve tends to push the VWO into difficult situations where it has to cut back on vital services while emergency funds are being raised. Analyze the reserves of an existing VWO and compare this against the level and type of its activities. Suggest reasonable guidelines on how to judge what would be an appropriate level of reserve.

Z-LINK

Z-Link is a nonprofit organization that aims to reach out to the disabled and assist them in gaining independence and dignity, and facilitate their integration into mainstream society through both open and sheltered employment. The yearly sale of Christmas and Chinese New Year cards designed by disabled artists is one of Z-Link's main fund-raising activities. It also doubles as a way of generating income and creating job opportunities for disabled artists.

A challenge Z-Link currently faces is that their data of more than five years are in separate nonintegrated spreadsheets. This hinders the company from making full use of the information they have to identify regular and lost customers and observe sales trends. A critical consequence is that additional time-consuming effort is required for their telemarketers to promote sales.

Their current customers can be divided into three categories, namely companies that purchase 1) Christmas cards only, 2) Chinese New Year cards only, and 3) both seasonal cards. Knowing the difference allows Z-Link to better solicit orders from the almost 300 companies in their records, and minimize overprints. They would also like to know which companies are supporting them more and give them extra attention. B-Link has lost some customers over the years and they would like to identify those who have stopped buying and find out how they may regain their support. Finally, there are also companies that have never been contacted before and therefore are not supporting B-Link yet. B-Link likes to know how to prioritize these companies and then take systematic steps to attract their patronage.

COMMUNITY MAPPING   Project 20

Public participatory community mapping seeks to unify and strengthen communities by offering individuals, nonprofit organizations, and educational institutions information and tools to help manage a community's interests. Simple process charts and geographical maps empower grassroot stakeholders and foster participatory planning, community education, and cooperative organization. The community through them can take integrated approaches to community health, environmental conservation, open-space and historic preservation, water resources and community assets management, neighborhood revitalization, and economic development.

The first steps usually involve registering the households and members in the community. In many rural communities, the people have no official birth and identity registration papers and thus do not know how to spell their names or tell what their exact ages are. Sometimes, there are no house numbers or street names to provide any form of street address. Taking GPS coordinates of the households and key resources (e.g., water sources and wells, transmission and distribution pipes, storage tanks, community standpipes and pumps, access paths and bridges, and wood collection, food gathering, and hunting areas) allow for better understanding of the community's geographical span, distribution, and needs.

Where there are no doctors, volunteer medical teams can travel with the community health facilitators and trainers to screen the people and keep health records. The state of their living conditions and livelihood can be indirectly surveyed, and traditional community leaders can be persuaded to participate in collective problem solving and decision making. The community as a whole can then better pool their resources, and request technical equipment and expertise, and financial resources from government agencies and nongovernmental organizations to support their projects. They can learn from the experiences of other communities and also share their successes, failures, and lessons learned with others.

Project 21   **STUDENT SOCIETY**

Students Society of Economic Research is a student organization established in the W School of Economics in mid-2002. Its mission is to extend the knowledge of its distinguished members in research fields such as economics, finance, and politics. This is accomplished through sharing of information and discussion in weekly meetings and working on projects. With its growing popularity, the organization is confronted with the challenge of managing the extensive amount of data arising from increased membership and more new projects.

They are now spending more time than before enrolling new members, allocating projects to members, and managing the membership and project information for reporting. The data now kept include:

- Personal information of members
- Information for project management
- Information for discussing oncoming events at meetings

Project 22   **WATERWAYS WATCH**

The Waterways Watch Society (WWS) is an independent volunteer group led by its own committee of volunteers. Their duties largely include the monitoring, restoration, and protection of the aesthetics of the city's waterways. The means to this end include weekly boat patrols along the rivers, and also designing and running bi-annual children's camps to educate the community about keeping the environment clean.

Your client, as chairman of the society, desires a system which will enable him to, accurately and quickly, send weekly mass emails to the scheduled volunteers on the duty roster. He wants to drastically reduce the amount of manual work and human error involved working out the weekly manpower and activity plan and activating the duty roster.

The volunteers, now numbering a hundred, have different availability time windows. The manpower plan covers a 4-month work schedule, which is done three times in the year. Volunteers are not always able to keep their assigned duties as the schedules are based on promises made so far ahead and weekly reminders must be sent to prompt those rostered to turn up for their assigned duties. It is also currently hard to review how many hours each volunteer has contributed to date and who the dependable ones are.

ATTAINING THE 5Cs | Project 23

In the course of one's life, a person may dream of having the 5Cs, namely cash, career, credit card, condominium, and car. Attaining them is not impossible given time. However, this is dependent on multiple factors such as the amount of income earned and general costs of living and taxes. Accomplishing the goal is similar to running a business project as it takes into consideration various financial issues such as treating one's savings as a form of personal investment. On the whole, although people wish to obtain these 5Cs, they have no inkling of the length of time needed to achieve them. Recognizing this problem, your project team wants to come up with a personal financial planning tool for people under various scenarios. Your model is to help analyze how long it takes for different people (single, attached, married with a spouse not earning an income, and married with a spouse earning an income) to achieve their dream of attaining the 5Cs.

CPF LIFE | Project 24

In the beginning of year 2008, the Singapore government announced a new Central Provident Fund (or CPF) scheme. The intent of this *CPF Life* scheme is to provide citizens with a lifelong income from a lump sum they leave for that purpose after they withdraw all their money at the retirement age from their compulsory CPF individual retirement savings account. The current *Minimum Sum* scheme will only provide a monthly payout that will cease after 20 years. Should the CPF member die earlier, the residue amount will be given to the designated beneficiary. However, if the member lives longer, there will not be any monthly payout for subsequent months. With the new *CPF Life* scheme, an insurance component is added so that the plan will continue to provide monthly payouts until the death of the member.

The Singapore CPF board has highlighted a total of 12 plans to choose from. However, with scarce information and only basic example calculations given by the board, the average person cannot really understand the full intricacies of the

CPF Life scheme, which will come into full effect in year 2013. The potential cause for concern for the general population is how this would affect their life savings. Another concern is making the right choice. Governments of other countries would also want to understand how the scheme works and evaluate if this is applicable for their implementation. How does this scheme compare and contrast against other schemes that you are familiar with?

Project 25   BUY OR RENT PROPERTY

Rent or buy? This is a question commonly asked by those who are setting out in life after graduation. Everyone would want to own their home at some stage of their lives. Few actually consider renting as a long-term option. Perhaps, it has something to do with our culture. Our desire is to have a roof that is ours over our head. To achieve this goal, most couples living together work their whole life to service mortgage payments on their home. As a result, many in their old age have little cash savings and investments for their retirement. This "asset-rich, cash-poor" phenomenon is now fairly widespread among city dwellers.

Those people living in rented accommodations could be doing so due to their lack of financial resources rather than a deliberate life-style choice. Others may be just waiting for the right time to buy a property, the right time being when their savings are enough for the first down-payment or the trough of a down-cycle when property prices are at their lowest. However, you may wonder whether the return on your property investment will be higher or lower than the renting alternative. Perhaps, you can do better using the money otherwise locked in a property as your investment capital. You may be able to get better returns on other investments to retire more comfortably and never ever own a property. Imagine all the apartments and houses you can enjoy and the wonderful variety of places in the world you can see, not being tied down in one place. If owning your own home is that important, perhaps it can be a very modest one where you can keep your memorabilia and use as a tiny homing point. You can still move around and rent another place to stay for work or play.

Project 26   CALORIES AND NUTRITION

People these days are generally more conscious of what goes into their stomachs; they are more aware of their body weight and concerned about their health. With obesity and over-eating becoming major health threats, there is a need to better educate people on: 1) how much they can eat, 2) what they should eat, and 3) what they can do about their current weight situation.

The individual must first know his current health and life-style status. From that, he can determine the optimal caloric and nutritional needs, and contrast that with the typical amount and type of food consumed each day. Any excess calorie intake or nonideal body weight can be addressed by changing food habits and doing different kinds of exercises.

Business and Services

CAFE STOP

Project 27

Cafe Stop is a local chain of cafes selling an array of food and beverages, with a strong product focus on gourmet coffee and innovative thirst quenchers. They have outlets in the major downtown shopping areas, airport, and educational institutions. Business is booming and their outlets are fully packed, with barely any standing room and seats all taken up even during off-peak hours. The local newspapers have reported on this and noted the trend of students overstaying at coffee joints. The most recent incident took place at the airport outlet where the police had to be called in to resolve the issue.

The students who are also their main customers will stay at the cafe for up to nine hours, usually making only one to two orders per person. By the length of their stay, they reduce the turnover of the outlets and prevent other patrons from enjoying their coffee. Matt Latte, an outlet manager of Cafe Stop, complains that this issue is a big headache for him, particularly during peak periods when it seriously affects business volume. How is he going to meet his monthly revenue target and maximize profit for his outlet?

KJC RESTAURANTS

Project 28

KJC Group has 12 restaurants all over the country. It has in recent years experienced surges in demand which is clearly evident at most of their branches, principally the conveniently located downtown restaurant. There is a shortage of tables when the restaurant is swamped with customers. Hence, KJC has adopted a queuing system during peak hours. Each arriving customer group is given a queue number which would be flashed on the electronic display when a table of the appropriate size is available.

This does not however solve the customer waiting problem, as lines still form outside the restaurant with people packed onto the narrow walkways waiting for their numbers to be displayed. KJC understands that customer waits and long lines can potentially translate into lost sales since they will affect customer satisfaction and may deter them from coming back. Some may even renege midway in the line and go to the competition instead. In fact on seeing the crowd formed, many potential customers may balk at dining at the restaurant. Other than process improvements at the current restaurant, KJC is considering renting the adjacent shop space when the current tenant, whose shop front is continually blocked by KJC's waiting customers, moves out at the end of its lease. If KJC takes over the shop, it will evaluate whether it should change its table mix when it renovates for the expansion, putting in more small rectangular tables instead of the current mostly 10-seat round tables.

Project 29 | ## SOUND EQUIPMENT

A sound equipment rental company has a wide variety and huge amount of equipment. The company needs an organized way to keep track of their equipment and customers to better cope with pricing, order taking, rental servicing, equipment collection, maintenance, and storage. The customer and equipment records are currently kept on cards. Equipment records in particular are filed by brands and models. The process of taking orders from customers, checking availability of the requested model, and presenting the budget-differentiated options to the customers is often tedious. This would inevitably affect the efficiency and customer perception of the service. Servicing customers who are in a hurry for immediate confirmation is particularly challenging.

Project 30 | ## VIDEO RENTAL

Video U is a franchise that specializes in renting out DVDs and VCDs, covering a wide range of English and Korean movie titles. The company also sells video and audio disks. Demand for the rental disks is difficult to gauge as interest in a movie title cannot be sustained and tends to taper off with time. The franchise main office recommends the number of disks to purchase for each new movie released. To maximize turnover, the franchisee has to correctly moderate this. Since disk purchases are one of the main cost drivers for each shop, it has to achieve a good match between demand and supply over the long term to be profitable.

Demand is managed by varying the number of days a movie can be rented out as well as the rental charge. The rental duration for new releases is one day because of the high demand for them. As demand for a movie wanes, the rental period can be increased. Longer durations are also granted to old movies and to customers who rent multiple disks. A fixed per day fine is imposed if the customer returns a disk late.

KARAOKE
Project 31

QU KTV has approached you for help. Recently, their popularity has gone down and hence the drop in profits. This is basically due to rival company VBOX opening a lounge in the area nearby. VBOX has taken away a large share of their customers and if this continues QU KTV might have to face closure. You are to do an analysis of their current problems and suggest solutions. They have already decided to review their hourly rates as well as the price of beer, the most popular drink in the pub. You are to estimate how their profits might be affected with the proposed changes. Other recommendations can also be made. For example, they have been wondering about adding auxiliary facilities such as pool tables.

QU KTV has enjoyed geographical monopoly advantage as the only KTV in the neighborhood from the time it opened 10 years ago until recently. Naturally with the opening of another lounge in the vicinity, profits will be hard hit. Your team has discovered that QU KTV is slow, as compared to VBOX, in bringing in the latest hit songs. QU KTV does not believe that this is necessarily a problem. You have serious doubt about this assumption and hope to quantitatively prove it one way or another.

BLACKJACK
Project 32

From Las Vegas to Monte Carlo, blackjack is among the world's most popular card games. The game's relative simplicity makes it appealing to casual gamblers, while its deceptive odds ensure a constant stream of revenue for casino operators. The objective of the game is to accumulate cards with a total points as close to but not over 21. Face cards (Jack, Queen, and King) are worth 10 points. An ace can be 1 or 11, whichever gives the best outcome to the card holder. Other cards are represented by their numeral values.

Before any card is dealt, each player must place his wager. Then, the players are dealt two cards each, with both cards facing up. The dealer gets one face up and another face down. After that, the first player gets to decide if he or she wishes to "hit" (to draw another card) or "stand" (not draw another card). This will be followed in sequence by other players until all players have their turns. Then, it is the dealer's turn to similarly decide. To win, a player needs to have more points than the dealer without going "bust." The player busts when his cards total more than 21 and loses automatically. If the player ties with the dealer, it is a "push" and neither wins nor loses.

Blackjack dealers in casinos around the world abide by a simple house rule – they must "stand at 17." This means that the dealer must draw when his points are 16 or lower; on 17 points or higher, the dealer can no longer draw a card. It is interesting to note that this rule is not enforced by any regulatory body, but is followed by virtually every casino. Casinos are allowed to vary their house rules within limits, as long as they are effectively communicated to the patrons.

Project 33	**NEWSPAPER READERSHIP**

XQ Holdings Limited is a local company engaged in publishing, printing, and distributing newspapers, magazines, and multimedia content and services. The company's core business is in newspapers and magazines. It publishes 20 newspaper titles in all the major languages in the country. Although the company knows its circulation volume, it wants to know the readership size. The two numbers are not exactly the same since many people can share or have access to the same copy of a newspaper at home or in the office. Readership, more than circulation, should determine how much the company can charge advertisers. As with all mass circulation publications, advertising revenue is the major contributor to the company's profit.

XQ has engaged MN Media Research to determine the readership size of its major English newspaper. MN, as a reputable and trusted information provider, seeks to find a more cost-effective way to derive the readership estimate and possibly further value add with future readership projections. As a market research analyst with MN, you think that the answers may be extracted from published household and national demographic statistics, and XQ's subscription-based circulation and their limited subscribers' personal data. XQ has indicated that MN should carefully evaluate the impact of free newspapers as they are gathering more readership and new ones are being approved by the government authority each year. MN's management thinks that the approach for estimating readership can be applied to other printed mass publications and wants to do a good job with this project to entice XQ to give them more work to research the readership for their other newspapers and also the magazines.

KINDERGARTEN

H Community Foundation is a nonprofit organization that manages over 300 kindergartens in the city. It is a leading provider of preschool education, catering to the low- to middle-income families in all the housing estates. Their Q branch has approached you for assistance. They are currently using the traditional manual process in managing the school and find it increasingly difficult to consolidate and access their information. Your help is needed to streamline and simplify the student particulars records, attendance records, fees collection, test results, and class time-tables. You will want to provide operational analyses and help design summary tables and charts for their monthly reporting to the supervisory board.

UNIVERSITY LIBRARY

A university's library is its central repository of knowledge. Some will claim that it, depending on how efficient and well run and stocked, can make or break a university's reputation. Your local university recognizes these requirements and has embarked on a drive to expand and modernize the capabilities of its library. It is difficult to build a world-class library with a large physical collection overnight, so it has chosen to try and provide students and faculty members access to as many databases, leased books, and digital libraries as possible. Your project is to support the automation of the library's resource acquisition process, to work towards achieving the goal of providing a wide selection of material to the user community while working within benchmarking and budgetary constraints.

INTERNATIONAL CONFERENCE

The International Monetary Fund (IMF) Conference will be held in the city this coming September. Over 3,500 international delegates will be arriving via various flights at different times throughout a single day. To deal with such a large number of *Very, Very Important Persons* (VVIPs) with a seemingly random schedule, planning a glitchless flow through the airport processes for the delegates is of paramount importance. The client, the International Monetary Fund Airport Work Group (IMF-AWG), asked for a tool to troubleshoot for possible problems in manpower allocation in the VVIP welcoming team. The goal is to provide a smooth airport walk-through upon arrival for each and every VVIP, minimizing wait for the VVIPs and providing excellent personable service. The tool is to provide computer simulations to significantly reduce the costs and need for repeated real-life simulations of the events. Your simulation model should allow the user to tweak the parameters as a preview of possible scenarios, taking into account various contingencies that may happen.

New Venture

Project 37

FRANCHISE

You are on a look-out for a franchise business to invest in. This will be a lower risk way of getting into business and working for yourself, provided you pick the right franchiser to work with. With the increased prosperity of the country, you believe the future is a service-based economy. So, the service sector may be a good place to start. The key cost and revenue drivers would be people and the hours they serve the customers. Typical service franchises include education and tuition centers, and domestic help sourcing, and cleaning agencies. The brand of the franchise and their operational expertise are important elements that you will be buying from the franchiser. The evaluation analysis should be based on your projected cash flow and profitability of the business. Decisions to be made are:

- Which franchise is the best option for you?
- What agreement terms do you need to be careful of to assure cash flow, profitability, and sustainability of the business?

Project 38

MULTI-LEVEL MARKETING

E-Marketing (EM), an eastern European enterprise, started business selling a foam-based, nonrinsing detergent that was perfected by their company founder. Over the years, more innovative household products have been introduced. EM embraces the direct-selling multi-level marketing (MLM) concept as a means to help individuals operate their own independent businesses and through them grow EM.

The company and its products are well received in eastern European countries such as Bulgaria, Georgia, and Armenia. As part of its globalization effort, EM has targeted Singapore as the gateway into the Asian market. EM's executives have met with representatives from the Direct Selling Association of Singapore (DSAS) and are positive about complying with the latter's requirements. EM understands that Singaporeans are receptive to direct selling but wants to know the sustainability of its model in view of Singapore's small population.

BRIDAL SALON

Project 39

Choosing and fitting the bridal suit and gown are considered by many to be the most crucial aspects of the wedding preparation. Bridal shops provide service for the creation and fitting of bridal gowns by taking the customer through the process. While other activities such as photo-shoot of the wedding couple and the wedding party are also offered, the main service component revolves around the fitting of the bridal costumes. The overall process is time-consuming: choosing the best suited bridal package, deciding between rented or customized bridal suits and gowns, fixing appointments for fitting sessions, and finalizing photographing and video-shooting plans for the wedding event itself.

Your client is a group of lady friends considering starting a bridal shop in a new shopping mall. The first subchallenge they want you to focus on is to ensure service quality. The major elements would be in clearly defining the process, sizing the service area, and determining the number of fitting rooms. The next subchallenge is to promote the store and generate sales. Before exploring the problems further, you may need to interview employees of an existing bridal salon or salons to gain better insights on the day-to-day operations of the business.

DIFFERENT CUTS

Project 40

You are evaluating the feasibility of setting up a hair salon on the university's new city campus. The intent is to provide an exciting array of high-quality hair and nail services at affordable student rates. The campus is near other commercial private schools, general trade and bank offices, hotels, shopping centers, movie cinemas, theaters, and museums. Other than undergraduates, there may be many vibrant youths and working professionals that will frequent the campus to enjoy the campus green and patronize the food court. Moreover, a new subway line will pass through the campus with a station right under it to be opened in about a year's time.

LINGERIE XY

Project 41

The client is a businessman who is parallel importing internationally sought-after lingerie from France and Germany. The two lingerie brands, X and Y, the client imports to the city are very popular and at the high-end range of lingerie in the European market. Fortunately or unfortunately, they are still not very established in the local market. Although brand X has been in the market for a while now, its sales volume in the city is still very low. The only outlets that bring in products from X are the two largest department stores and a boutique chain with only two branches. They are all selling X lingerie at really exorbitant prices. Brand Y, on the other hand, has not yet been introduced into the city by the other players. However, brand Y undergarments have been surveyed to be well liked by the locals due to its no-frills and highly comfortable attributes.

At present, your client has a private clientele base of slightly more than 50 people. He has been making steady profits and is also looking into expanding the business into new geographical frontiers. He has already discussed this with interested parties from neighboring cities but has yet to make any decision. The client has been working from home, with the help of his wife and daughters. He has no fixed cost and is paying 10% commission to freelance sales personnel, who have been promoting and selling the intimate apparel.

Though the sales have been making profits for the client since start-up, he hopes to set up a shop in the city center to increase revenue and profit, and use that as a stepping stone for future expansion beyond this city. Opening a shop would boost the branding and marketability of X and Y, since the brands are not well established enough in the region. You begin to survey several locations in town and list the possible location targets. The client requests that you analyze and present the various consideration factors for setting up a new shop and work on the business feasibility analysis.

Project 42   VEGGIE MANIA

Veggie Mania is the name of a vegetarian mini-mart your client intends to set up in a local housing estate. This is to support the healthy life-style that many residents there are fast adopting. Studies have reported that vegetarians are 40% less likely to die from cancer when compared to nonvegetarians living similar life-styles. They also suggest that vegetarians are less prone to heart diseases, cancer, and diabetes. Bird flu and mad cow disease just spur more individuals to go green in their diet. A wide variety of vegetarian produce will be made available in the mini-mart to cater to the different needs and tastes of consumers. They may be frozen, fresh, packet, and canned, as well as organic products.

Project 43   FRIED TOFU

The client is contemplating setting up a small retail food outlet to bring to consumers easy-to-eat fried *tofu* that comes with a wide selection of sauces to satisfy different palates. You are to assist him in establishing the short-term cash flow viability, longer-term profitability, and sustainability of the business. The basic fundamentals of running an outlet like this must first be understood: how turnover affects staffing, inventory policies, and other core business variables. The main objective of the study is to assess the feasibility of setting up the outlet. The critical market concern is whether there is demand.

GRAB-FOOD EXPRESS   Project 44

In the present society, time is a precious commodity. For the busy single executive, a lot of that is spent, in this Asian cosmopolitan city, standing in line to buy the breakfast or dinner meal. Every morning and evening, commuters rushing to and from work can choose to go with an empty stomach or spend 30 minutes or more queuing for food near the subway or bus station. Cooking at home is usually not an option. Though food centers are conveniently located near most residences, there are still some areas where food is not so readily available. Getting food near their transport pick-up and drop-off points may be the only alternative.

Your client is deciding whether to start a business catering to such individuals. The aim is to provide freshly cooked and hot food to commuters with minimum queuing. The client's key concept is to set up a chain of outlets near subway stations, serving as ordering, collection, and eating points. In the morning, the commuter can place his food order and make payment at the outlet at his origin subway station near the residential area. The order will then be relayed to the specified destination outlet, usually at a Central Business District (CBD) station. During the journey, the food is being prepared and readied for his collection just in time when he disembarks. The process is reversed in the evening when the commuter travels from the CBD to home.

The food packages would be boldly labeled and neatly lined up at the collection point. All that the customer has to do is to swap the package with the matching label given to him at the ordering outlet and go. After collecting the food, he can either eat it piping hot with disposable utensils at the standing area provided or consume it at his office or home. Orders can also be made on the spot but collection would be a while later.

To test the feasibility of this Grab-Food Express service, you need to collect the data and subsequently do the process flow and financial analyses. You need to observe the commuter traffic at the various targeted subway stations and also check out food options available there. The starting scale of the operations has to be right. You wonder if three residential outlets and three Central Business District outlets would not be too large to handle.

Project 45   ## SINGAPORE FLYER

The Singapore Flyer officially opened on 1 March 2008. Larger than the London Eye, it is one of the tallest observation Ferris wheel in the world, with a diameter of 150 meters and a height of 165 meters. Located at the Marina Bay, the wheel holds 28 observation capsules, each is capable of holding 28 passengers. The premises include three floors of retail space, with an adjacent open-air Greek theater along the waterfront for live performances as well as a 210-meter-long waterfront dining promenade. The Singapore Flyer is easily accessible, with half-hourly free shuttle bus services to and from the City Hall MRT (Mass Rapid Transit) station, a covered multi-story car park for 300 vehicles, and even a jetty.

The project costs S$240 million, the largest single foreign investment in the Singapore entertainment industry at that time. Given the Singapore Flyer's recent tie-ups with high-profile developments in Singapore, such as the Marina Bay Sands Integrated Resort and the Formula One Grand Prix, it is interesting to find out whether it will enjoy a similar degree of success as its European predecessor. The structure was erected with an intention to create a new landmark in the region as well as to establish a profitable business.

In addition to the initial development cost, the Singapore Flyer would be challenged with heavy fixed and variable operating costs, such as maintenance, advertising, management, labor, site lease payments, and taxes. On top of that, there are macroeconomic factors such as inflation and wage increases over the years. On the other hand, there are limited revenue sources. Most of the revenue (about 80%) is expected to come from admissions and the rest from rental income on commercial space. Currently, they charge different ticket rates for adults, children, senior citizens, and corporate clients. Given the high contribution from ticket sales, any incremental increase in visitors to Singapore is expected to translate into higher revenues. The major start-up concern for investors is how long it will take to break even.

Project 46   ## GRASS SKIING

Four good friends have recently been retrenched. After much thinking, they decided to pool their resources and make the best use of this opportunity to bring a new sport and tourist attraction to Singapore. Grass skiing is a young sport originally used to train skiers when there is no snow. It has become a fast-growing leisure sport for all seasons and for people from all walks of life.

Grass skiing would be mainly targeted at tourists in Singapore as well as ski enthusiasts and skating related sports people. Sentosa has been identified as the most ideal location based on a survey conducted and detailed research done on a few other alternative locations. It will reach the target audience and get good admission sales. Facilities have to be built from scratch and all grass skiing equipment is to be newly purchased. Being the first of its kind, there is no immediate direct competitor, but tourists do have many options in Singapore. The decision to start up a new and major venture involves a huge investment.

BIKE TOUR

Project 47

Cycling as a form of recreation is visibly popular in Singapore. During weekends, public and school holidays, many cyclists can be seen along East Coast Park, Pasir Ris Park, and even Pulau Ubin. The annual *Nite-Bike* event organized by the Singapore Management University's *Xtremists* sports club is always a sell-out. There is definitely a market for alternative cycling activities. However, land-scarce Singapore does not allow alternative cycling routes beyond the public parks and reservoirs' fringes.

To tap this promising market, your client is considering setting up a bike tour service to design routes for cyclists and organize group tours with a companion guide to introduce places of interests on the island of Singapore and possibly beyond. This can be modeled after the successful "Mike's Bike Tour" of Munich, Germany, which has since established franchises in Barcelona and Paris.

Finance and Administration

NBA PLAYER SALARY

Project 48

Every NBA team's aim is to get a position in the playoffs and ultimately win the championship. But the basic responsibility of each NBA team manager remains focused on making the most profit for its owner. So, there is a fine balance to achieve between revenue and cost, to better understand how to enlarge the box office collection but with the right level of total cost, the bulk of which is the team's salary. Generally speaking, there should be a direct relationship between performance and potential of NBA players and the salary they earn, especially for the superstars already at the peak of their careers.

However in recent years, some NBA teams have encountered difficulties in managing their players' salary expectations. In the games, a player's performance is determined by his ability to shoot, rebound, defend, and other factors. Each factor can be clearly measured, for example in defensive ability by the statistics on blocking, stealing, and fouling. The operational data of the players are well recorded and publicly reported. The historical data themselves can be used in future performance projections, as benchmarks and targets, and for setting players compensation in the next contract review.

Project 49 — SALARY INCREMENT BUDGETING

Anthony is the Managing Director of a manufacturing plant in Cirebon, West Java, Indonesia. The company currently employs around 1,000 staff in their operations. Anthony wants to increase the staff head count to further expand the business operation, but is constrained by the payroll budget approved by the company headquarters in Europe. He noticed that the total annual payroll costs have been steadily rising over the years, and there are resentments among lower level staff over the increasing gap in salary between employees in the same job grade.

To move ahead, Anthony wants you to help him plan and forecast the payroll budget for the next year. He suggests that you look at using the *Compa-Ratio* to benchmark employee pay and propose a new way to better define pay increments for staff, particularly those not promoted out of their current job grades. This is to give management more precision in the payroll budgeting work, help them reduce manpower turnover, and improve employee morale.

Project 50 — RATIO ANALYSIS

The *balance sheet* and *income statement* are essential financial documents for the successful management of any firm, but their existence is only the start. Applying *ratio analysis* to them for better understanding of the success or failure, and progress of the business is critically important. Ratio analysis enables business managers to spot trends in their individual businesses, comparing their performance and operating conditions against the average performance of similar businesses in the same industry. The ratios can be watched over time for starts of unfavorable behaviors to provide the all-important early warnings that top management can act on to resolve the problems and not be taken by surprise.

Liquidity ratios provide information about a firm's ability to meet its short-term financial obligations. Short-term creditors prefer high liquidity ratios since they indicate lower risk for them. Liquidity ratios include the *current*, *quick*, and *cash* ratios.

Asset turnover ratios indicate how efficiently the firm utilizes its assets. They are sometimes referred to as efficiency, asset utilization, or asset management ratios. *Inventory turnover*, *asset turnover*, and *asset-to-equity* ratios are in this category.

Market ratios can be used to evaluate the firm's stock performance and growth potential. These ratios are particularly for investors, who watch them closely to make important investment decisions. *Price-to-cash flow (P/CF)* and *price-to-earnings (P/E)* are two important examples.

Financial leverage ratios provide indications of long-term solvency of the firm. Unlike the short-term focused liquidity ratios, financial leverage ratios measure the extent to which the firm is using long-term debt. *Debt*, *interest coverage*, and *debt-to-equity* ratios are common examples.

Profitability ratios offer several different measures of the success of a firm at generating profit. These ratios can examine the firm's ability to maximize profit and minimize various costs. *Return on equity (ROE)*, *return on asset (ROA)*, *profit margin*, and *earnings per share (EPS)* are the ones most often used.

Each set of ratios focuses on a single specific aspect of a firm. How they work together is reflected in the *DuPont Analysis* framework. This framework aids management in understanding how different approaches can be applied to improve their *ROE*, the usual ultimate goal for any company. Your consultancy company makes financial and operational recommendations to clients. You need a simple, professional tool to support your consultants in serving clients. The tool should calculate the financial ratios and apply the *DuPont Analysis*.

INTERNAL CREDIT RATING   Project 51

Corporations around the world often seek a public credit rating before issuing a bond or raising debt. Sometimes, they may even do it just to create a profile for the company in the financial market. However, prior to engaging a rating service, the company may want to estimate on their own what the company's credit rating may be and take the necessary remedial actions to improve their potential rating first. A credit rating exercise is costly and time-consuming. It would be a waste of valuable resources if the company is not able to attain their desired rating when it is publicly announced.

Credit rating can be estimated by comparing the company's financial ratios against its rated peers in the industry. In the process, you can also evaluate how much additional debt the company can raise before their credit rating deteriorates and affects their cost of new debt. This puts the company in a better position when they seek funds for capital expenditure.

Project 52

LOAN DELINQUENCIES

Institutions giving loans carry a portfolio of loans of different status. The status of a loan can be classified as *customer at current*, *past due 30 days*, *past due 60 days*, *past due 90 days*, and *past due 120 days* (or *write-off*). The overall portfolio performance can improve or worsen over time. There is a need to watch over it closely, particularly in a difficult economic environment, so that timely decisions and actions can be taken to mitigate losses. The data can be used to project into the future to anticipate potential problems. They can tell the business for example whether they should tighten the approval rate, review customer segmentation, or adjust collection strategy.

Project 53

UNSECURED LOAN

After the year 2007–2009 financial crisis, both financial lenders and borrowers became more conservative. To keep the default rate under control, M Finance placed *Everyday Credit*, their short-term unsecured loan product, under tighter risk management. As a result, more than half of their applications were rejected while the lending capital allocated for product stays grossly underutilized.

The internal product team has found it hard to comprehend and control the overall risk of offering the product as the current credit rating model evaluates the loan applications individually, all at their points of application. As such, product sales executives take the most conservative approach, favoring low-risk customers with good credit rating and low default probability. The firm is therefore losing potential profit from higher-return loans to higher-risk customers. They need a portfolio approach to manage their basket of loans so that there can be a dynamic balance between risk and return for this product.

Project 54

INTERNET VALUATION

The number of Internet users has exponentially increased in the last 10 years. With better Internet connectivity and pervasive use of mobile devices, the growth will certainly continue to be explosive. There is of course the corresponding proliferation of new "website" companies, all vying to lay claim and capture a piece of the very lucrative online advertising market. These companies are often start-ups with founder and "angel" investor funding. At some point, they will need to either solicit bank loans or sell equity to support their business expansion. The companies would then need to be valued. However, many such companies are relatively new and with an insufficient financial track record. It will be difficult to value the companies using only financial data.

This has triggered various responses from experts in online business financing, marketing, and information technology management. An important input variable to the modified valuation methods include website visitor ("eyeball") traffic volume. This indirectly affects revenue and expense. The three main revenue sources are banner advertisements, clicks, and click-generated sales. Expenses include advertising, hosting, Internet access, merchant, and bank expenses. The valuation should also account for the two-phase growth pattern of Internet website traffic: usually strong growth for the initial five years and then a stable growth rate after that.

FIRM VALUATION

Project 55

It is always challenging to analyze and evaluate a firm, not to mention one with negative earnings. The difficulty lies in estimating the future, which becomes more challenging when historical revenue growth rate and earnings are negative. As such, conventional valuation methods that do simple forecasts of earnings and cash flows, and discounting them to determine the firm's value cannot be applied. The root causes (both transient and long-term) of the negative earnings have first to be identified before the analysis can proceed.

If the causes are temporal or cyclical, the firm's earnings should be normalized. On the other hand, if the causes are structural, leverage, or long-term operational, the firm has to be valued using a more detailed cash-flow forecast, starting with current revenues and costs, and estimating the reduction and elimination of problems over time. Industry averages or other data on larger and more stable firms within the sector can be used as reference bases.

The firm's *free cash flow* can be computed using either the *free cash flow to firm (FCFF)* or *free cash flow to equity (FCFE)* approaches. The *FCFF* valuation approach is used for firms with high but progressively declining leverage and firms with partial leverage information or volatile leverages. The aim here is in valuing the firm rather than its equity. In contrast, the *FCFE* valuation approach is used for firms with stable leverage, which focuses on the valuation to manage the controlling interest of the firm and how cash may be redeployed as investment elsewhere.

PROPERTY VALUATION

Your city, like many others in the world, is witnessing a phenomenal boom. Property prices have been increasing very fast in recent years. Apartments are now being sold at prices near historic highs. Given the numerous factors that can affect the prices of properties, the valuation process is too complicated for home seekers who are eager to find a suitable unit at an appropriate price. Home sellers similarly find it hard to get a firm estimate of their properties' value.

Professional valuers are generally inclined to rely simply on the latest transaction prices of similarly sized units and from these prices, moderate in other factors that may significantly influence them. These factors include:

- Proximity to the city and major amenities
- Proximity to public transportation, especially mass rapid transit railway stations
- Age of the apartment
- Remaining tenure of the property
- Location height of the apartment in the building

As you are planning to buy an apartment in the near future, you would like to better understand the valuation process and accuracy, and hope to estimate future prices so that you can better time the purchase of the apartment.

HEALTH INSURANCE PREMIUM

Health and medical insurance is an important part of our lives, especially with today's rising health care costs. Consumers buy health insurance to protect themselves financially against accidents or major illnesses. Companies get health insurance to better manage the medical expenditures of their employees. In the current dynamic business environment, insurance companies need to price their premiums competitively in order to operate effectively, sustain profitability, and stay relevant.

Your task is to analyze the factors that affect the profitability and sustainability of a typical health insurance plan in your country. You need to cover:

- Assessment of subscriber's risk
- Calculation of optimal premiums for the insurer
- Expected compensation payout
- Investment of insurance premiums in equities and bonds

This would entail an overview of the cash flows of the health insurance plan for multiple years and assessing its sustainability. It should only be a simplified simulation of the actuarial process and serve as a preliminary tool to aid full insurance product development.

RELATIVE-VALUE EQUITY TRADING

Project 58

Relative-value trading is based on a mixture of fundamental analysis and technical analysis, with more emphasis on the latter. It is more commonly applied in fixed income securities and foreign exchange markets. This is because these securities exhibit stronger relationships to macroeconomic variables and thus are more predictable. The strategy consists of matching assets with similar behavior, such as high price correlation, and trade when the behavior starts to diverge. You want to apply the strategy to the equity market.

To do this, you can for example shortlist a set of stocks with strong fundamentals and from it, form pairs of stocks with 0.7 positive price correlation or higher. The price ratio for each stock-pair is monitored and projected using simple moving averages of two periodic durations. The short-period moving average is more sensitive to changes while the longer one is more stable. A trade opportunity arises when the two moving averages cross over each other.

You want to determine if relative value trading can beat the market and if so, by what magnitude. There are still a few important details you have to work out, such as the length of the two periodicities and what specific actions to take at each trading opportunity. You may want to first back-test your strategy against historical data before you participate in the market for real.

If the strategy works, you can then further consider the following questions:

- Is there a trading strategy based on high negative price correlation stock-pairs?
- Can you think of any other similar strategies?
- Can you devise a general approach to deal with the strategy variations?

FIXED INCOME ARBITRAGE

Project 59

Fixed income arbitrage is a broad set of market-neutral investment strategies intended to exploit valuation differences among various fixed income securities or contracts. During the hedge fund crisis of year 1998, market participants were given a revealing glimpse into the proprietary trading strategies used by a number of large hedgers. Virtually every major investment banking firm on Wall Street reported losses directly related to their positions in fixed income arbitrage during the crisis. However, despite these losses, fixed income arbitrage has since become one of the most popular and rapidly growing sectors within the hedge fund industry.

This mixed history raises a number of important issues about the fundamental nature of fixed income arbitrage. Is fixed income arbitrage truly arbitraging? Were the large fixed income arbitrage losses during the hedge fund crisis simply due to excessive leverage, or were there deeper reasons arising from the inherent nature of these strategies?

You want to illustrate the optimality of relative-value trading strategies for isolating and exploiting arbitrage opportunities arising in the short-, intermediate-, and long-term maturity of debt markets. Your purpose is to identify mispricing opportunities of overvalued and undervalued bonds by comparing the affine model and market spot rates and compute the expected maximum profits using short and long arbitrage strategies.

Transportation and Supply Chain

Project 60 — SHUTTLE BUS SERVICE

A small business park is home to a cluster of a few hundred companies that work closely together. The companies have petitioned their business park management firm to provide a shuttle service in and around the park to permit their staff to travel to and from the major transportation hub nearest the business park and also from the various pickup points near the sprawling parking spaces provided for those who drive to work. Other than such morning and evening traffic, there is also a steady flow of people moving between the offices of the various companies as they attend meetings to conduct business with each other. Before attempting to examine the financial viability of such a proposal, you seek first to understand roughly how such a bus service can be operated and how well the capacity of the buses plying the shuttle service routes would be utilized.

Project 61 — COMMUTER PLUS

Commuter Plus Pte. Ltd. is seeking lucrative investments to improve its financial performance and grow the business. As part of their business development unit, you have been assigned the task of selecting an appropriate residential area where current public transportation is inadequate and planning a new bus service for it.

You must establish the profitability of the project and draw up a proposed bus schedule.

RENT-A-CAR | **Project 62**

C Rent-A-Car is one of the largest car rental companies in the region. They have over 600 vehicles of more than 65 makes and models, ranging from small 1,300 cc engine capacity Japanese cars to luxury European sports cars and continental limousines, to suit the specific needs of customers. C offers two main services: self- and chauffeur-driven car services. Their chauffeur-driven car operations are presently sited at two locations, a five-star hotel and an office complex, where the services can be booked and provided to hotel guests and corporate clients, respectively.

Bookings for the chauffeur-driven cars can be "at hirer's disposal" (AHD) or "point-to-point" (P2P). In the AHD arrangement, the company provides a car with a driver to stay with the client for the contracted time duration. The chauffeur is ready to drive him wherever he desires, while in the P2P arrangement, the client is picked up and dropped off at customer-specified times and places. For instance, a P2P service can be to fetch the client from home to a shopping center or office block and vice-versa, or even a one-way pickup to or from the airport.

The company currently has many ad hoc "systems" to track its drivers and vehicle fleet records. They have no way to share driver and vehicle availability information across the two sites other than calling each other on the phone and taking up valuable time of the operators and potential clients. It is important for C to meet customers' demand promptly and efficiently to stay competitive.

The cumbersome process has also in the past led to misunderstandings when, because of poor monitoring and information transmission, customers were offered services with resources from the other site when they were really not available. The cooperation between the two sites is as a result affected and this does not let the company synergize easily the overall deployment of resources. Other than improving internal operations, the company would also like to better organize their clients' data and be more proactive and responsive to their future needs.

CHARTERED BUS | **Project 63**

Your client, S3 Federated Transport Company, offers chartered bus services to schools, tourists, companies, and organizations. Its fleet of buses varies in capacities ranging from 10- to 40-seaters. Service is typically divided into fixed contract and ad hoc assignments. As highlighted by the owner, the demand for their bus services is rather cyclical and erratic. For example, demand would be high during school terms and low during the holidays. The erratic part of the business is from ad hoc assignments that can come at any time of the year.

The fluctuations and uncertainties make it challenging for them to organize the deployment of the company's resources. For the longer term, the owner has to decide how many buses to keep in his fleet, what the right mix of buses to have, and the number of drivers to employ to meet future demand. He would like to grow the business but he does not really know how demand is growing and where the potential markets and pitfalls are. He would also like to better manage his driver pool and the mileage they clock on the buses daily. This would let him know whether the buses and people are well utilized.

Project 64 | ## SS SUPERMART

SS Supermart Pte. Ltd. is a key player in the retail market. Since its incorporation in 1986, it has managed to garner a loyal following by offering products priced lower than other supermarkets in the state. Over the years, the company has expanded very quickly with many branches and has captured a sizeable market share. The company is constantly looking for ways to improve its competitiveness by lowering its costs and fine-tuning its operations.

The supermarket chain now has 11 branches and 15 delivery trucks mainly to distribute perishable products and groceries from its central warehouse to its supermarkets. Charlie Frebar, manager of the Transport Division, wants you to look specifically into the daily delivery of vegetables and fruits. You are to disregard the present transportation network and formulate a "whole new best" minimum cost approach. The study can ignore one branch as it does not currently offer vegetables and fruits to its customers.

Project 65 | ## SUBWAY SCHEDULE

The use of electronic tokens and entry/exit turnstiles at mass transit railway train stations permits easy counting of commuters entering and leaving each station. The needed information about commuter behavior is a little bit more complex. To determine how best to provide their services at the least possible cost, subway operators also want to know how many passengers travel between any origin-destination station-pair. From this information, they can allocate passenger carriages to the trains and plan train headways (i.e., inter-arrival times) over the span of the day for each of their many service routes.

Though possible to directly measure origin-destination passenger traffic, given more sophisticated tokens and computerized ticketing systems, the local transport authority and train operators, in keeping the operating costs as low as possible, generally adopt simpler systems. This means that origin-destination passenger traffic information has to be measured by sample surveys, or alternatively inferred from whatever data that currently are electronically captured. The latter approach is favored since it can be done automatically around-the-clock, all year long.

SUBWAY FARE   **Project 66**

For the last financial year, the revenue of the subway operating company declined by 3% from the previous year. According to their analyst, this is due to the absorption of the 1% increase in Goods and Services Tax (GST) and decrease in subway fare revenue arising from lower average fare. With no fare change that year, this could only mean that the commuters were taking shorter distances on the trains. If revenue continues to drop, it will certainly affect profit and thus tempt service quality compromises. The operator has decided to make a thorough review of their operations and pricing strategy so as to remain competitive in the industry.

The current fare is a standard distance-based one. The cost and quality of service are however higher per hour during the peak hours with high frequency of trains arriving. This suggests that the fare prices should be increased during peak hours. The counterargument is that train occupancy during the peak hours is higher, which translates to lower cost per commuter per distance traveled. Even though the trains are arriving less frequently during off-peak hours, they are really not well filled. The cost per commuter per distance traveled then is thus higher. Some would counter that the fares during off-peak should be raised instead to ensure that they are adequately covering operating costs and need not be cross-subsidised by peak-hour commuter fares.

Passengers using the train service during peak hours may also complain that comfort is compromised due to higher occupancy during these hours. This may be used as a reason to justify train passengers paying relatively lower rates during peak hours. Alternatively, a higher fare during peak hours can be used to dissuade commuters from creating the congestion in the first place. All in all, you would have to take into consideration the willingness of commuters to pay for their subway rides. A thorough investigation needs to be carried out to fully understand all the pro- and counterarguments. You also need to relate these to the profitability of the subway operator. Finally, do examine if time differentiated fares for peak and off-peak hours really make sense at all.

| Project 67 | **CRUISE ITINERARY DESIGN** |

Given the start/end base port and total duration, the cruise itinerary design problem is to determine the choice of places to visit, visit order sequence, and stay durations at these places. It can be assumed (up to a certain point, of course) that the longer the cruise ship stays at a place, the more attractive that place becomes to the tourists. However, this increase in attractiveness will be marginally decreasing. Similarly, slowing down the cruise ship will let passengers better appreciate the scenery and marine life along the journey, increasing the value of the cruise vacation to them. But the additional time spent is at the expense of including more stops or spending more time at the stops. How would you go about designing an itinerary for a cruise ship? How do you know that your solution is satisfactory, good, or even best for the constraints given?

| Project 68 | **CRUISE TERMINAL DESIGN** |

A large cruise center in the city provides passenger terminal operations for international cruise ships and very large ferries. A full cruise ship has a capacity of about 1,000 to 4,000 passengers, much larger than that of the largest commercial air flights. So, the surge in passengers coming in for a departure check-in or disembarking from an arriving cruise ship is a major concern to the terminal operator that manages the functional processes, namely passenger check-in, baggage check-in, baggage claim, CIQP (Customs, Immigration, Quarantine, and Police) checks and security. This is compounded by the fact that the cruise center also doubles as a ferry terminal and provides services to many large ferries, with capacity of 50 to 200 passengers, berthing and unberthing at much higher frequencies than cruise vessels.

Increasingly, for reasons of security, sporadic unplanned delays, and workload surges at terminals, passengers are, by choice or requirement, arriving earlier for their cruise and ferry departure trips. This smoothens the peaks in passenger arrivals to the terminal and relieves stresses on the functional processes. But it also lengthens the time passengers spend in the terminal, a large portion of which is discretionary "slack" time. Given the smaller size of this terminal relative to international airport terminals, the common boarding lounges for departing trips may need to be revamped to function both as a departure cum boarding lounge.

The quality of the stay in the terminal for passengers will be upgraded if people unrelated to the waterborne trips are not allowed to inter-mix with passengers once inside the terminal and more and better retail outlets are placed in the departure lounge to cater to passengers. Further, the cruise passengers may be totally separated from ferry commuters. However, such a consideration will block out a large portion of space for the cruise operations which would be unutilized most of the time.

A yet unresolved challenge is the huge congestion at baggage claim at the end of each cruise as passengers disembark unceasingly from the arriving cruise vessel. The operator management is increasingly concerned about the ability of the terminal to cope with the changes in traffic pattern and volume, and the need to quickly come out with plans to refurnish and better position the terminal for the next two to three years. Classical queuing theory models they previously employed cannot deal with the heterogeneous and nonstationary passenger arrivals and service operations characteristics. A consultant to the cruise center proposed that they use the deterministic discrete-time fluid approximation (DTFA) approach instead to examine passenger dwell time in their departure lounge and queue conditions at the functional processes. The baggage claim process also deserves closer analysis possibly using the stochastic discrete-event fluid approximation (DEFA) approach.

AIR FLEET EXPANSION

Project 69

Inam works in the planning department of the Singapore-based M Airline (MaMa Air). The carrier has just changed to a low-cost carrier (LCC) business model. Passenger volume has gone up as a result and the current fleet is no longer sufficient to cope with the growing demand. The management board has recently approved the budget for new aircraft purchases. Inam's challenge is to determine the number and type of aircrafts to acquire, and how they might be deployed to service MaMa's expansion plans. Each aircraft type has a different flight range, seat capacity, fuel consumption rate, and price. The airline currently flies direct-return services to 14 destinations: Cairo, Hong Kong, Istanbul, London, Los Angeles, New York, Manila, Moscow, Paris, Rome, San Francisco, Shanghai, Sydney, and Tokyo.

SERVICE FACILITY LOCATION

Project 70

The choice of where to locate a facility to serve a region depends on many factors. These include the shape of the region and location of key travel constraints like water bodies and bridges, and customer dispersion. You can assume in this business context that customers come to the facility if they need the service, and not service personnel from the facility going to customers' locations upon request. There may be a set of possible locations to site the facility. How would you compare the candidate locations to determine which is the best choice? What if there can be more than one facility in this region? How would you determine the best number of facilities, where each facility should be sited, and how the service subregions' boundaries should be drawn?

Project 71   **TRAFFIC GROWTH**

The traffic flow volume (V_{ij}) between any origin–destination node-pair ij is a function of the total traffic volume (V_i) leaving origin i, total traffic volume (V_j) entering destination j, and the degree of interaction (ρ_{ij}) between the nodes in the pair. The traffic volume of node-pairs changes with time when one or more of these variables change. If the traffic flows are independent, the proportion of overall flow $(P_{ij} = V_{ij}/V)$ that goes through pair ij can be found by multiplying the proportion of overall flow leaving the origin $(P_i = V_i/V)$ with the proportion of overall flow entering the destination $(P_j = V_j/V)$, with V being the sum of all node-pair volumes. That is, $P_{ij} = P_i \times P_j$.

In general, $P_{ij} = \rho_{ij} \times P_i \times P_j$, with the additional ρ_{ij} factor. Variable $\rho_{ij} = 1$ when the flows are independent, $\rho_{ij} > 1$ when the flow between node-pair ij is more than its fair share of the flows to and from the two nodes, and $\rho_{ij} < 1$ when the flow between ij is less than its fair share. The ρ_{ij} values themselves are expected to change over time. Given past origin–destination volumes and projected inbound and outbound traffic volumes of every node, future origin–destination volumes may be estimated by projecting these future ρ_{ij} values.

This model may be used to estimate port-to-port traffic flow in global ocean freight and city-to-city package delivery demand for air express services.

Manufacturing and Operations

Project 72   **TECHNOLOGY CHOICE**

Manufacturers of products are increasingly faced with dynamic changes in demand and short product lifecycle. A way to deal with this is to have flexible capacity. There is a choice between having dedicated production with large volume and lower unit cost, and flexible capacity with higher unit cost but larger product variety to better adapt to market competition. What would be a better choice? Is there a hybrid solution?

FLEXIBLE CAPACITY

Project 73

The actual manufacturing of many products is increasingly not done by the brand owners but outsourced to contract manufacturing firms. These vendors can have greater economy of scale since they specialize in certain production capabilities and provide their services to many other companies. Given a large stable volume, such vendors can produce at a lower cost than the firms could have done themselves. However giving all the volume for a product to a single contract manufacturer is unwise as there is a risk that they may not deliver on time the required quantity or quality. A solution is to use a second source. How should the requirement volume be split among the two or more contract manufacturers?

CAR DEMAND

Project 74

A car manufacturer with a presence in many countries worldwide is considering further expansion. There are a few countries that are potentially profitable and can help drive the growth of the firm. The business development division is doing an analysis to estimate how the demand for cars in each segment may grow over time. The chief analyst is postulating that the car demand in any market should be dependent on population size, per capita income, and human development index. One would wonder if the approach can be applied to any product that their parent conglomerate is producing and whether it may even be relevant to their power and other utility businesses. Can the demand growth of another product be used as a leading indicator?

INSPECTION SAMPLING

Project 75

The quality of incoming material is assessed by taking a random sample from the arrived lot. The items in the sample are inspected and tested according to the specifications laid out in the agreed supply contract. The decision to accept or reject the lot delivered depends on the sample results.

An immense amount of work is required if every single item in the lot is inspected. Complete inspection may not be as effective as it seems even if it can be done since the monotony and tedium of the inspection will lead to inspection errors. The advantage of taking only a small sample is that the items can be more thoroughly and leisurely inspected. The difficulty is in understanding what assurance of quality of the whole lot can be made from the result of the sample inspection. This of course is a function of the size of the sample.

A sampling plan needs first to be set out. This spells out the size of the random sample, and the acceptable number of defectives or defects in the sample. A defective is defined as an item with one or more defects, and a defect is the failure to meet a specified criteria.

Project 76

ECONOMIC ORDER QUANTITY

The project is to devise a game to explore the issue of how much to order each time a stock-keeping unit (SKU) is replenished and therefore also indirectly how often to order new stock for this SKU. Having a large order quantity means that ordering is done less frequently but on the average holding a higher level of stock. The number of orders per year equals annual demand/order quantity. The average stock level (not including the safety stock that mitigates against uncertainty in order lead-time demand) equals half the order quantity. The best solution is a trade-off between ordering and holding costs.

Project 77

NEWS VENDOR PROBLEM

The project is to create a game that explores the classical problem of determining how much of a product to order when there are uncertain demand and overage and underage costs. The problem derives its name from the case of a newspaper vendor deciding how many copies of the daily paper to order from the publisher. The news vendor is assumed to have to pay for every copy of newspaper he orders (though this may no longer be the case in our modern context). Now, if he is unable to sell all of the papers ordered, he would bear the losses arising from leftover copies, since yesterday's paper is worth significantly less. If he tries to be prudent and orders insufficient copies, he would miss the opportunity to earn more.

Of course, this problem structure is equally applicable to other seasonal goods (like Christmas trees and fashion wear) and perishable goods (e.g., dairy and medical products). In the manufacturing and logistics settings, over-ordering would result in leftover stock and therefore incur extra holding cost. If the demand exceeds the quantity stocked, there would be service penalty and back ordering costs. The concept is therefore applicable for determining the level of inventory safety stock.

INVENTORY ABC

The long list of inventory items carried in the warehouse can be grouped into *A*, *B*, and *C* types. Doing this allows the user to provide different levels of attention to the stock-keeping units (SKUs), each according to its demand value and special requirements.

Commonly, the top 20% of SKUs (out of the total number of SKUs) cover 65% or more of the stocks' demand value (defined as Demand volume x Unit cost). These items are called *A* items. Giving them more attention (closer monitoring and more frequent replenishment) goes a long way in managing the overall inventory costs, without compromising service performance.

The next 30% of SKUs normally constitute the *B* items and these cover about 25% or less of the demand value. The last 50% of the SKUs (called the *C* items) cover the remaining 10% or less of the demand value.

Where there are special requirements, like high unit cost, short shelf-life, high demand volatility, and specialized storage or handling, the item types of SKUs involved may be upgraded. The revised types can be labeled *AA*, *BB*, and *CC* correspondingly.

MULTIPLE-PERIOD INVENTORY SYSTEMS

There are generally two main policies for multiple time-period inventory management: *continuous* review and *periodic* review.

The *Q* system takes a continuous review approach. Here, the inventory position of a stock-keeping unit (SKU) is marked against a predetermined reorder level (*R*). In practice, "continuous" means daily review or at least whenever stock is added or removed. If the inventory position after a review is at or below *R*, a new order for a fixed *Q* quantity is placed. Typically, the economic order quantity (EOQ) may be used as *Q*. *R* should be large enough to cover the demand during the delivery lead time.

The *P* system takes the periodic review approach. Here, the inventory position of a SKU is reviewed at predetermined fixed time intervals. This time interval, usually a day, week, fortnight, month, or quarter, may be assigned on completing the inventory ABC analysis. For SKUs on daily review, the inventory position is usually reviewed at about the same time each day and the same goes for the other review interval lengths. After each review, new stock is usually ordered to bring the inventory position up to a desired level (*M*). *M* should be large enough to cover the demand during the review interval plus delivery lead time.

Inventory position is more accurately defined as the sum of *stock on hand* and *stock on order*. This stock on order portion is particularly applicable when the delivery lead time is longer than the review interval. Demand per day and delivery lead times may be probabilitistic.

PRODUCTION SEQUENCE

Alectronics, a large contract manufacturer, produces a line of computer products for a major computer company. The customer recently called for a review of the coordination of production plans between them and Alectronics.

Some of the requirements coming out of that discussion are as follows:

- Change from a nine-month planning horizon to six-weeks.
- Change from one-month committed build orders ("frozen" period) to one week.
- Orders to be revisable within the week before end of week shipment.
- No more production to stock; finished goods inventory (FGI) to be zero.

As a senior manager in Alectronics, you have been appointed project leader to study how this may be implemented. The company has engaged a SCM consultant to advise you. The consultant had asked that you collect as much historical data as possible for analysis and so you dug up all the past production forecasts for discussion.

BUCKET BRIGADE

Typically, work on assembling a product with many components or picking out an order with many items can be subdivided into roughly equal work portions. The portions may be unequal because of lumpiness in the work elements. There should be as many work portions as there are workers, and the workers are arranged in a "line" (usually straight or U) with each worker doing one work portion in turn. This so-called production line process can work at a faster rate than having the same number of people with each person doing the whole work by himself. The advantage comes from job specialization with each person learning to do a subset of the work faster and better. The number of work tools that each person must have is also reduced, thus saving costs for the company.

The production line's disadvantages are work stress and fatigue arising from the explicit or implicit forced work pace and dehumanization of labor as no single person actually makes a whole product. The output rate of the production line is dictated by the slowest workstation, which may be because of the disproportionately larger work portion given to that station or the worker there is relatively slower that the rest, whether for a day or every workday. This means that finding the right dynamic work-balance to accommodate product and workers' characteristics is very important to overall productivity.

The *Bucket Brigade* is an alternative way of organizing workers that self-balances work in a production line. It can also be used for managing order-picking in warehouses. The method has been implemented in companies such as The Gap, Subway, and Mitsubishi Consumer Electronics America. The basic concept here is to make the boundary between each work portion more flexible. The worker upstream in the line does as much as he can until the worker downstream has finished his work and is ready to receive work from upstream. At this point, the work is handed over to the downstream worker. So, each worker sometimes does more than an average work portion and sometimes less, as he adapts to the work pace of other workers. The *Bucket Brigade* is supposedly able to give a higher output rate and better accommodate the state of the workers during the workday.

BEER GAME SOLITAIRE

Project 82

This beer game is adapted for the spreadsheet, from the famous game played in Massachusetts Institute of Technology (MIT) classrooms. In this "Solitaire" version, the distribution network structure is the same as that played in MIT: a serial system with one player at each stage of the supply chain.

However, what is unique about this version is that a person by himself (if he so desires) can play all the roles. He can work through the roles one time period at a time or set up ordering rules for each stage and for all the time periods in one go. This is as opposed to a group gaming situation where we need a group of people to play, with each player responding to requests one stage downstream and one time-period at a time.

The spreadsheet also makes it easier for the user to analyze his inventory management tactics and do multiple simulation "game" runs for the various possible customer demand scenarios. The game controller can set up the initial scenario and the demands (hidden from the player) for the whole time horizon. Players are to evaluate various inventory management approaches (ordering and shipping rules) and report their results.

They are then asked to make their inventory management tactics more robust. When they are ready, the instructor would release, one at a time, the other scenarios to see whether the students' models perform as they expected.

Project 83

XOS TIRES

XOS Tyres is an international distributor of a complete range of quality tires, wheels, and supporting services. The company has a dominant retail chain in the country and also provides fleet tire maintenance, management services, and rethreading to large vehicle fleet owners in the construction, mining, logging, transportation and port operations sections. Their MegaMart branch vends the products carried by the company and also provides other services such as basic vehicle servicing and maintenance repair of punctured tires and wheel alignments. There are now five service bays in this branch, three are single-purpose and two are multi-purpose bays. The two main activities carried out on the service bays are wheels changing and vehicle servicing with oil change. Due to space constraints, the branch has been unable to meet their turnaround time target for both services during the daily peak hours.

The company has already acquired a vacant land plot beside the branch. The branch manager needs to decide how the vacant plot should be utilized to improve service performance. He is considering three possible alternatives: 1) four additional lots for customers to park their cars and wait for their turns; 2) the fourth single-purpose service bay for tire changing; 3) the third multi-purpose service bay for tire change or vehicle servicing and oil change. With the space expansion, the branch manager is also considering the hiring of more temporary helpers.

Information Technology and Communications

Project 84

SOFTWARE DEVELOPMENT PLANNING

The Software Development Unit (SDU) recently studied their project management workflow and identified three key shortfalls: lack of consistency in approach, over-budgeting of project cost and effort, and not being able to learn from past mistakes and best practices. From the past two years' data, they discovered that 85% of projects were over-budgeted, with an average 34.35% difference between actual cost and approved budget. The unit has thus been tasked by management to quickly improve their performance.

Currently, SDU has 25 project managers (PMs) working at any one time on over 50 development projects. These PMs had each adopted their own peculiar method in planning and tracking projects. All three section managers have found it hard to monitor the projects they supervised because of inconsistencies and diversities of approaches. With this, they have not been able to pool past project data to obtain meaningful reference and planning norms to effectively and efficiently plan new projects.

SOFTWARE PROJECTS PORTFOLIO

COPQ Bank's program management office (PMO) runs about 200 projects yearly. These project requests come from various departments. Each year, substantial effort is spent prioritizing project proposals for selection and then planning and tracking the approved projects. There is currently no single view of the bank's projects portfolio, both current and future, overall projects health, and how the projects measure against the bank's strategy. As such, the PMO needs some help to better organize its information to help the bank select, plan, and track projects.

The projects should be tracked using a standardized matrix of cost and schedule targets, and monitored consistently across the organization on their alignment to the bank's overall strategy map. From their ratings against the key factors, the priority of proposed projects can then be established according to their weighted scores. The management must be able to consider possible alternatives in their projects portfolio make-up and decide on actionable choices when new circumstances arise as the projects are being planned and later tracked in execution.

SOFTWARE DEVELOPMENT VENDOR MANAGEMENT

The senior management of a bank expects more progressive visibility of return on investment, and wants to see new technology help achieve business goals and organizational targets. However, getting a standardized project report is often a challenge. Different project managers use different formats to manage and communicate project schedule and costs. Senior managers should not need to waste a lot of time trying to digest these differently formatted reports.

In managing external software development vendors, management would like to have information on the track record of the vendors' past project performances. This would likely be based on projects they have done for the company and if available, from external sources as well. The company should be able to draw from consolidated data the most suitable vendors to recommend for any new project and shortlist them for "Request for Proposals" (RFP). The vendors upon selection should also be tracked during project execution to ensure that they work in accordance with the planned schedule and cost budget. The project manager responsible can take timely corrective actions if necessary when he reviews the tracking reports.

Project 87

IT OUTSOURCING

BDE is a traditional private bank based in Europe, with offices all over the world. It provides wealth management, financial investment, and securities and foreign exchange trading services to some of the world's richest private and institutional clients. Last year, the IT Solutions group of the Operations Division of the bank was asked to drastically reduce cost and increase operations effectiveness for the current financial year. The CEO dictated that they outsource their IT operations, a noncore operation of the private bank. An outsourcing partner was found and the transfer of operational roles and responsibilities is now in progress. Your team is to support this transfer process, track the before and after IT operations cost and effectiveness, and report the extent of success of this outsourcing exercise in clear performance measures.

Project 88

ONLINE TRADING

H69ven Securities has 200,000 clients accessing its trading system. Trading volume is usually high and increasing at an alarming rate year after year. As trading volume increases, there is a need for more system servers to cater to the growing customer demand. The company's IT systems administrators need to constantly monitor the volume and respond accordingly. One of the challenges they face is knowing when any server has reached its capacity. They have gathered some data and are studying the trading volume trends and hope to be able to forecast when each server has reached its capacity.

In the past, IT administrators performed tests to thoroughly stress the trading system and through trial and error, determine the servers' capacities. The process entails estimating the expected transaction volumes that may push the servers to their limits. The maximum capacity is found when the service thresholds are reached. Setting up and maintaining the test environment is expensive and resource-intensive. Moreover, such testing does not really replicate the real-world production situation. Methods to quantify, without the need for actual testing, a server's capacity from its transaction and performance response data are highly desirable.

Project 89

TRADE PROCESSING

Documents submitted by customers for a trade transaction are received at the Singapore office of a bank, every working day from 9:00 a.m. to 6:00 p.m. Singapore time. Transactions that need minimal processing can be completed on the spot. For most transactions however, the bank has to scan the submitted documents and forward them electronically to a processing center in India, where they will complete the transactions in the bank's central computer system. The Indian processing center operates from 8:30 a.m. to 5:30 p.m. local time (i.e., 11:00 a.m. to 8:00 p.m. Singapore time). The processing time at the center for each transaction is found to vary from one to 30 hours. Management is dissatisfied with the current transaction turnaround time as 15% of the transactions take longer than the 24-hour limit specified in their Service Level Agreement (SLA). The bank is seeking ways to improve the situation but is cautious about any increase in cost.

The bank utilizes a tracking system to record the critical time points in each transaction:

- Start of registration (customer makes request at the Singapore office)
- Scanned documents sent (to the Indian processing center)
- Transaction processing completed (in the bank's computer system)

A log file containing a few days' worth of data is taken from this system. The data is sanitized (with irrelevant fields removed and customer names made anonymous). Other than this, no additional information is available of the processing operations in India:

- Number of processing agents
- Work practices, such as shift patterns and, if any, request prioritization and deferment

INCIDENTS MANAGEMENT

Project 90

Incidents management seeks to minimize the impact of business disruptions by restoring IT operations to agreed levels as quickly as possible. The client wants to know whether the solution measures taken have any positive effects and if the problems are fully resolved. They would also like to infer what proactive steps can be taken to prevent future recurrence and further improve system performance.

For these reasons, incident logs are kept for problem recording and resolution tracking, covering:

- Incident
- Problem
- System

- Severity
- Solution
- Outcome

Detailed follow-up analysis should be done on the logs. The analyses are to investigate the underlying causes of incidents, and aim to prevent similar incidents from recurring. By removing root causes, which often require changes to people, process, and technology, the number of incidents can be reduced over time. The analysis should not be done by technical staff alone. The data have to be organized in a form that is accessible to different levels of the organization and to people from different business functional areas. This interface must be intuitive and new data easily updated. There must also be intelligent and user-friendly features for executives to self-serve in their problem analyses and solutions brainstorming.

Project 91   **BANDWIDTH PLANNING**

Recently, there has been a lot of complaints that the network on the university campus is responding exceedingly slowly. Natalie, the infrastructure analyst, discussed this with the professor teaching the network design course over at the School of Information Systems and reviewed the basic concepts with him. Now, referring to a standard textbook and a network design manual, she sits down to systematically list all the necessary variables and collate the parameter values. She hopes to put up a rigorous review of the current situation and propose a plan for continued monitoring and expansion of the campus communications infrastructure to ensure that it is adequately provided all the time at the lowest possible cost.

Project 92   **WIRELESS NETWORK DESIGN**

To deploy a wireless local area network (WLAN), the following has to be decided: 1) number of base stations and their placement locations and 2) assignment of available frequency channels to the base stations. The objective is to use the least number of base stations to provide total signal coverage over the required area of interest, with little or no co- and adjacent-channel interferences. Analytical methods to solve this problem can be devised but such approaches requiring a large number of data (to be taken from field measurements) may not be suitable for practical use.

Global and Environmental

GLOBAL OIL PRODUCTION

A key question that came up during the unprecedented large oil price changes from year 2000 to 2010 is what the correct level of global oil production should be. This depends of course on who wants to know. Oil producers and producing countries would have perspectives that are different from consumers and environmentalists. Can a reasonable compromise be found?

RENEWABLE ENERGY

Renewable energy can be generated from sunlight, wind, river, rain, tides, and geothermal heat. About 18% of global final energy consumption comes from renewables, with 13% coming from traditional biomass (mainly for heating) and 3% from hydroelectricity. The new renewables (namely, small hydro, modern biomass, wind, solar, geothermal, and biofuels) make up the remaining 2.4%, but this percentage is rapidly growing with further technological research and development. In electricity generation, renewables are already contributing around 18% of the total, of which 80% comes from hydroelectricity.

Wind power though still small is growing at a rate of 30% annually. It is widely used in European countries and the United States. Other technology being explored are photovoltaics, solar thermal and geothermal power generation, all mainly in the West. Brazil, with one of the largest renewable energy programs in the world, is producing ethanol fuel from sugar cane, and ethanol now fuels 18% of the country's automotive needs. Other than these large-scale operations, renewable technologies are also suited to small off-grid applications, particularly in rural and remote areas where energy is often crucial in human development.

Renewable energy technologies have been criticized for being intermittent or unsightly. Climate change concerns, coupled with sporadic high oil prices and increasing government support, are driving more renewable energy legislation, incentives, and commercialization. Nuclear energy though not really a renewable energy is increasingly put on the agenda as a clean energy to combat energy shortage and global warming. Another twist to the overall argument is that bio-diesel may not be that clean after all as it diverts agricultural land and forces more forest to be cultivated for energy purposes.

Project 95   **SAVE THE FORESTS**

Many trees have fallen to make way for urban development and commercial cultivation. Human population growth and the ever-changing patterns of their consumption can cause catastrophic effect on the environment. How fast should we allow the remaining trees to be harvested or forest cleared, and how many trees should be replanted to restore and keep the system in healthy balance?

Project 96   **AGROFORESTRY**

There is an increasing mandate for forest expansion through afforestation of arable and degraded land. An attitudinal study found that local landowner groups are resistant to the planting of land with trees, which is partly attributed to the long-driven agrarian character of these areas. To some landowners, forestry is envisaged as antagonistic, rather than synergetic to agriculture and thus not socially acceptable. However, there are many benefits that come with planting crops and trees side by side. It has been a goal for many farmers and governments to find a suitable trade-off, aiming to achieve maximum economic return of planting trees alongside agriculture farmland.

Agroforestry is the collective name for land use systems and practices in which woody perennials are deliberately integrated with crops, animals, or both on the same land unit. The integration can be in a spatial mixture or temporal sequence. There are normally both ecological and economic interactions between woody and nonwoody components in agroforestry. The various agroforestry practices include windbreaks, silvopasture, forest farming, and alley cropping.

For example, alley cropping, also called the "sun system," is an intercropping strategy. In this practice, crops are planted in strips in the alleys between rows of trees or shrubs. The trees provide shade in hot, dry environments (thus reducing water loss from evaporation), retain soil moisture, increase structural diversity, and provide some wildlife habitat. The woody perennials in this system can produce fruit, fuel-wood, fodder, or trimmings to be made into mulch.

Your goal is to assist landowners to evaluate the feasibility and efficient operation of agroforestry. This could go down to the specific details such as efficient spacing of trees and appropriate choice of crop and tree combinations. The two key questions that need to be answered at the end are:

- Is agroforestry economically viable?
- How best to arrange crops and trees to maximize the profit?

You know you need to be forward-looking and flexible in your analysis, to accommodate current experimentation, future technology breakthroughs, and unanticipated potential socio-political changes.

FISHING STOCK

Fish and shellfish are the only wildlife food resources that humans are consuming on a large scale. All other livestock and crops have gone into cultivated agricultural modes. River and marine ecosystems are, however, in danger due to pollution and over-fishing.

Fishing has been in the historic past done by small isolated groups of people. With fishing gone commercial and the use of powered vessels and modern fishing equipment, more fishes are caught in many places than the rivers and ocean fisheries can replenish. Fishermen, for sport, subsistence and commercial, are complaining that the catches are getting leaner with each passing year.

If the over-fishing goes unchecked, fish and other marine life will eventually collapse. Most fisheries in the world today are being fished close to or above their maximum sustainable yield. Examples of over-fishing tragedies can be seen in the California sardine fishery, the Newfoundland cod fishery, and the king crab fisheries of the Bering Sea.

In particular, since nobody owns the ocean's resources, everyone and anyone tries to exploit it for profit. International laws and regulations are not adequate or are powerless to police human and business abuse of the oceans. Where governments can exercise controls, more regulation and licensing controls may be needed. Some may argue that fishing in the wild may be a thing of the past. The future lies in fish farming and commercially controlled fishing stocks.

POTABLE WATER

Potable water is water of sufficient quality that can be used without risk of immediate or long-term harm. Most developed countries supply water to households, commerce, and industry that can be directly drunk, though only a very small proportion is actually consumed or used in food preparation.

Elsewhere in large parts of the world, people have inadequate access to potable water. UNICEF reports that over 884 million people still use unsafe drinking water sources. Their most immediate water supply is contaminated with disease vectors, pathogens, or unacceptable levels of dissolved chemicals or suspended solids. Such water continues to spread acute and chronic illnesses and is a major cause of high infant mortality and adult deaths in many countries.

The key issue is not lack of water, with water covering most surfaces on the planet, but the lack of access to clean water. Water is not clean because it is not properly collected and stored. Rivers which traditionally carry fresh water from the sources in the hills and mountains have been contaminated. A lot of women and children in the third world countries spend a great part of their time manually transporting the limited water they can find to their homes.

The fortunate ones live near wells or have wells dug in their front yard. Increasingly, underground water sources too are tainted by over-population and industrial pollution. In fact, water tables are falling from over-drawing of water. The current technology to filter or desalinate water is still energy intensive and relatively expensive. The promise of low-cost micro filters is beginning to be realized. One wonders how much longer we have to wait.

Project 99	**SUSTAINABLE PLANET**

Sustainability is a wide-ranging term applied to almost every facet of life on Earth, from local to a global scale and over various time periods. Long-lived and healthy wetlands and forests are examples of sustainable biological systems. Invisible chemical cycles redistribute water, oxygen, nitrogen, and carbon through the world's living and nonliving systems, and have sustained life for millions of years. With the rapid increase in human population, natural ecosystems are stretched and have caused changes in the natural cycle balances with detrimental impact on both humans and other living systems.

Is the current human life-style sustainable? If not, can human use of natural resources be brought to sustainable limits, and how fast can it be done? Will scientific research lead to development of new technologies that will resolve all our projected concerns and allow us to continue our life-style and further abuse our planet? What is the foreseeable sustainable maximum size of human population? Will there be enough biodiversity for the earth to survive any unpredictable shocks in climate and biohazard challenges.

Project 100	**PANDEMIC CONTROL**

The World Health Organization (WHO) collects and publishes data on reported confirmed cases and deaths for deadly influenzas (e.g., H5N1 and H1N1) and other contagious diseases that are threatening to reach pandemic scale. The data are given by country and time period. The National Health Agency of your country wants to analyze this data to infer, among many other purposes, the minimum required quantity of medical drugs and material (such as vaccines, antibiotics, surgical masks, and protective supplies) that need to be readied as contingency for general public use. They are also trying to understand and infer what factors would govern the extent and rate of disease spread. Among the considerations evaluated are level of economic development, population size and density, people mobility within the country and across borders, disease transmission mode (aerial water droplets, physical contact, oral, bodily fluids, or vector borne), and rate of mutation and reproduction of the viruses.

MALARIA

Project 101

The world continues to be plagued by a disease that is arguably as old as mankind itself. Not as well publicized as the killer influenzas, the global spread of malaria has been and continues to be the primary health and economic concern for a third of human population. It is estimated that 1.5 to 2.7 million people worldwide die from malaria yearly, 70–90% of which are children under the age of five. There are still many more falling victim to malaria and, though surviving, are suffering painfully from the debilitating nature of the disease and have lower life expectancies.

The malaria parasite is now in practically every country: 52 of 58 countries in Africa, 11 of 18 in southwest Asia, all Oceania, and 9 of 24 in south-central and southeast Asia. The parasite is spread by the Anopheles mosquito, and their breeding and movement are determined by social and climatological conditions. Tropical countries, as predominantly poor nations, lack resources to fight against their spread. Many of them exacerbate the problem by their residents' living and livelihood habits. Choked irrigation canals and unmonitored housing construction pits encourage the growth of Anopheles populations. Nomadic pastoral culture helps transport the parasite from infected individuals into uninfected areas.

With little commercial return, the malaria problem cannot be solved by market-driven efforts alone. After almost 40 years of silence, malaria eradication returns to the global health agenda following the Gates Malaria Forum in October 2007. Key organizations are debating the pros and cons of redefining eradication as an explicit goal of malaria control. With 60 years of fighting the disease behind them, the World Health Organization (WHO) asks itself what has been achieved and learned from the past. The world now knows so much more about the biology, transmission dynamics, social, economic, and cultural implications at household, community, and national levels, and the demands on health systems in endemic countries. We still need to better synthesize and integrate this knowledge to achieve malaria elimination in different settings.

Tool 21

New exercise

A short introduction on the problem context should be provided here. No specific information is required. The problem description must be clear enough to help start the modeling process, but yet open-ended and unstructured so that there is room for discovery.

The exercise's main intent must be to help the novice modeler understand more of the business context and learn the effective use of the spreadsheet as a modeling and analysis tool.

Additional questions should be provided to challenge the modeler beyond the simple initial model that he may develop. This is to further stretch the applicability of the model to a broader setting as well as establish its practicality in implementation.

There are two workbook versions of this tool, one without macros and the other with macros. The macros facilitate the hiding and unhiding of documentation and other worksheets, and the protection and unprotection of all the sheets.

Tool 22

New project

A short introduction on the problem context and the approach adopted to manage the situation should be provided here. The description must be clear enough for the user to know the key essence of what is being addressed and how the workbook is to be used.

Beyond this introductory worksheet, separate worksheets may be created to give detailed user instructions, and notes on the proper use and maintenance of the workbook. If this workbook is part of a series of workbooks, it would also be helpful to note their existence and how they work together.

Care must be taken to ensure that this workbook once it is started as an actual project file is not released to unauthorized parties. In some cases, a user may be authorized for a limited use of a workbook, or be notified of the existence of only a subset of the workbooks.

There are two workbook once it is started as an actual project file versions of this tool, one without macros and the other with macros. The macros facilitate the hiding and unhiding of documentation and other worksheets, and the protection and unprotection of all the sheets.

Tool 23

Modeling tools

This workbook provides the selected function and procedure subroutines that you can use in your spreadsheet modeling projects. Copy the relevant modules to your project and apply them as in the worksheets here.

Learn

This workbook contains master copies of all the *Learn* notes, which are scattered as applicable among the other workbooks distributed with the associated book. Having them all here in one place makes it easier for your learning reference. You can also copy the relevant worksheets to your exercise and project files as instructions for your users.

Useful macros

This workbook contains samples of useful **BASIC** macro codes. Demos are provided in the following worksheets, covering their use in a cell range, worksheet, chart, workbook, dialog box, and events. You can copy and paste whole subroutines or portions of the codes to your workbook and modify them for use in your projects. To view the codes, go to the **Basic/Macro Editor** of your spreadsheet application and select the relevant **Modules** that contain them.

Spin wheel

This workbook emulates a spin wheel that will rotate when you click the *Spin* button. The text on the spin wheel (fictitious names of students in this example) is visually designed to have different text sizes, such that the text in the middle is the largest. The spinning effect appears real as the wheel will slow down to a stop. The spin wheel receives its input text from the *Data* worksheet.

We use this tool in class to randomly select a student to perform a certain task, such as giving a presentation. Have fun with this tool.

Limited trial

A workbook may be released to the client for trial evaluation. To deny unauthorized extended use, you can "lock out" the workbook after the evaluation deadline. This is demonstrated here using a subroutine procedure.

Examine to see if this approach is effective and elegant enough. What else would you do to make it even more effective and user-friendly?

When applying this approach to an actual release trial workbook, the password should not be made known and the space required to display the warning and termination messages should be cleared for use.

Text data import and export

This workbook demonstrates how data in (*dat* or *txt*) flat files can be imported into a worksheet and conversely how data in a worksheet can be exported to flat files. The values from each line of text file will be imported into a row and each subsequent line will be placed in the next row. Each data element is separated from the next in the text file by a separation character. This is typically a comma or semi-colon. The data elements imported are placed in different columns in the worksheet.

These subroutines are useful when data are given in flat files or when dealing with inherited macro codes. This approach is more efficient than opening the flat files as spreadsheet workbooks and using macros to convert text to columns. Comma-separated text file with *csv* extensions can be directly opened as an Excel or Calc *csv* file, which can be later saved as a *xls, xlsx, or ods* file.

To test the subroutines in this workbook, download the latest *dat* files from your local stock exchange and then import them into the *Import* worksheet. Copy these data over to the *Export* worksheet and then try exporting them to another file. If no file name is provided in the *Import* worksheet, the file name is *Import.dat* and the folder path is the current workbook folder path. Similarly, if no file name is provided in the *Export* worksheet, the file name is *Export.dat* and the folder path is again the current workbook folder path.

Tool 29

Rename files

Files created in digital cameras, videocam, and other devices need to be filed into your data storage.

These files are often incongruously named as *img_0001.jpg, img_0002.jpg*, etc. You may like to rename them to make each name more intelligible. However, there are just too many to do this manually.

The project is to create a workbook to extract and list the names of all the files in any specified folder. You can then use spreadsheet formulas to create new names for each file and then apply a macro to automatically rename the files.

Tool 30

TableSolve

DataTable (or **Multiple Operations** in Calc) is a wonderful tool for automatically tabulating for a model the outputs for corresponding input values. This can be used for sensitivity analyses, and also for Monte-Carlo simulation replications. A limitation of the DataTable operation is that it does not permit macros to run in the model. To address this, two subroutine procedures are presented here. They retain much of the original structure used in DataTable, but in addition allow a special subroutine, e.g., one involving **Solver**, to run with each input change. These can thus be considered as enhanced versions of DataTable.

TableSolve extends the operation of 1-D and 2-D DataTables

- Set up as in a DataTable, with row and column input cell addresses as input arguments to the subroutine to accept values for one or two input variables.
- An additional optional argument specifies the name of the special subroutine.

TableSolveMV is a multivariable extension of the vertical 1-D DataTable

- Set up as in a vertical 1-D DataTable, with input cell addresses placed in cells one row below their corresponding headers to allow more than one input variable, an approach different from DataTable.
- Tabulates the results of many output variables, with links to the cell location of the results placed in cells one row below their headers, an approach no different from DataTable.
- The only optional argument specifies the name of the special subroutine.
- Input cell can be a cell in another worksheet of the same workbook, for example, Sheet5!B7.

Tip 44

Excellent spreadsheet projects

The best spreadsheet projects are simple, appropriate, and innovative. They are neither examples taken out of subject matter textbooks nor ideas straight out of students' imagination. Real problems provide the most challenge and yield the best returns. It is more exciting if the class votes on a common theme to pursue. The selected theme should not be on a business functional area or of narrow interest and scope. We find single industry sector and current interest themes work very well. From the selected theme, they can choose whatever functional area or focus they want to work on and seek out the common grounds with their clients.

To approve a project when each project team proposes it, we ask:

* Does your project fit the theme selected?
* Who is the client (real user who cares about the result)?
* Is spreadsheet the right tool to use? Do you think it is under-powered or over-powered for the task?
* What value does your project add?
* Can you get good closure?
* Can you make it not a "one-off" project?
  In grading the projects, we look for the following:
* Problem originality, model elegance, and innovativeness
* Ability to reveal problem structure and apply analysis
* Appropriate use of techniques and tools
* Clarity, completeness, and accuracy of the report
* Good report writing skills

We require our students to be responsive to their collaborating organizations and complete the work even if it takes more time after the course to do so. We respect our sponsors and appreciate the effort they put in to help our students expand their learning. Thank your sponsors. Since the project is based on the client's selected problem and with his/her benefit in mind, if you have done a good job, he/she should, in fact, thank you instead. Most clients have benefited from the interaction and have asked that more projects be done for them. Some of our students have been such invaluable help that they have received letters of appreciation and even awarded corporate gifts and small favors.

Not system development

Many students get easily carried away when applying interesting and powerful spreadsheet features and usually try to "show off" what they have learned. There is a tendency, for example, to put in their spreadsheet project user login and sophisticated data management components. The unnecessary use of macros and codes obfuscate the effort, alienating the client in the process. The project is diverted from its main goal of discovering the nature of the business challenge, finding the key drivers of change, and providing workable solutions for the client. We therefore warn our students that they are not graded on the level of difficulty of the spreadsheet features they use, but rather their appropriateness. No employer cares about your fancy spreadsheet ability; they want to know how you can solve their business concerns and do it as simply and effectively as possible.

The end result should not be just a working business operations system but one that contains rich insights for better decision making. This is not to discount the fact that a well-developed spreadsheet model can serve as a cheap and good prototype operations system. There are however severe scale and security limitations. The spreadsheet project should only serve to provide an interim solution until the organization finds the time and budget to translate the prototype into a proper system. The project should extend well beyond just building the prototype system; it should add further value by deciphering the business environment and analyzing the data and system use outcomes.

Not a one-off effort

Modeling is very hard work, especially when it involves actual problems and real clients. The work would only pay off if the modeling and analysis effort is for a very large project or if the developed model can be used repeatedly over a longer period of time and by many more people. Try to treat your current client not as your only client but your first of many clients, and the problem to solve as only an instance of problems of the same type. The other clients if not yet identified can be role played by you and other modelers, anticipating other issues to incorporate. The aim in having more clients and modeling inputs is, surprisingly, to help make the model simpler, not more complex. This is because single clients tend to overspecify problems to fit their unique situations; commonality surfaces from the analysis of inputs from many clients, to help separate exceptions from the typical. The additional guidance sieves out the critical elements and helps generate better alternative solution approaches.

Tip 47

Confidentiality constraint

Projects often cannot take off because the client deems his data too sensitive to be released to others for analysis. The two broad intentions of doing a spreadsheet project are to understand the situation and to provide a working analytical tool for the client. It need not be the analysis of a specific set of data and deriving conclusions for that individual setting alone; it is definitely not about numbers-in and numbers-out. There is really no need for confidential data if the client does not want to release them. What is most important to get the project going is to be able to gather insights into the business challenge: interactions between relevant variables and structure of the solution policy. You may need to ask for the type of data and range of their values, and gain access to organization and industry knowledge and general information.

With these, you can simulate your own realistic data and make whatever exploration, assumptions, and analysis. Your main deliverable should be a spreadsheet tool that the client can use to understand his business scenario in general and, after entering the confidential data at his own private convenience, also draw specific conclusions and action responses.

Tip 48

Data security concerns

In building the spreadsheet analytical tool for your client, you would need to understand what the user roles are and how they interact with each other and with the workbook tool or set of tools. Each potential user may have more than one role and each role may have different levels of access to confidential information. There is also concern for information privacy. You can color code, separate, and add security features (such as **Protect Sheet**, **Hide Sheet**, and **Very Hide Sheet**) to protect information and privacy. Also, do set up the necessary training for users and explain to management how the security features work.

Spreadsheets cannot rightly serve as depositories of data. There are severe limits as to how effective the security measures are in spreadsheets. The project owners, to whom you transfer the project workbooks, have to be advised on how they should organize the maintenance of the integrity and further enhancement of the workbook tools and the management of security concerns. Data backups and archiving should be independently worked out by their internal security team. The client remains fully responsible for fulfilling his corporate reporting, fiduciary, and regulatory requirements.

Short names

Excruciatingly long names, whether they are project titles, macro subroutine and function names, file names, sheet names, header labels, variable labels, and named cell names, are a common feature of spreadsheet projects. They should be as short as possible. As a guide, keep them less than nine characters long. It would also help to remove blank spaces and capitalize the first letter of each word if there are multiple words in the name. For example, a worksheet that contains the data of volunteers can be just called *Data*, if it is already obvious from the project title and file name that it is about volunteers. Or, it may be appropriate to name it as *Volunteer*. It should not read *Volunteer Database* or, worse still, *Information on volunteers extracted from submitted forms*. Also in the table of volunteers, it will suffice for the column with names of volunteers to use *Name* as its header label. Labels such as *List of Volunteer Names*, *Name of Volunteers*, *Volunteer Names* or even *Names* are actually longer than necessary. Do also remember to break the data elements up so that they can be better analyzed. For example, you should have a separate column header on postal code and not have it included as part of the street address.

Project files

Our habit is to have three files for each project: a spreadsheet workbook, a management report, and a management presentation file. If the project's short name is *Joe'sBakery*, then the files are *Joe'sBakery.xlsm*, *Joe'sBakery.docx*, and *Joe'sBakery.pptx*, respectively. The latter two files are management focused. User instructions should be incorporated into the workbook and user training done directly using the workbook. There is usually no need for a user manual document or user-training presentation file. There may be more than one workbook if the project requires, for various reasons, that the model be split into more than one spreadsheet file.

You should have been doing most of the thinking and modeling work in spreadsheets and kept technical and user-directed notes there. The project presentation file can be made by extracting relevant tables and charts and pasting them into slides. Similarly, you can paste these into a document file and complete the management report. The presentation and document files usually have an audience that is different from that of the workbook and thus should be correctly positioned. Specifically, these two files are usually intended for management, and their focus should be on the outcome rather than the construction or use of the model.

If for some reasons you are unwilling to release the files as they are, you can use their *pdf* versions instead. In this case, for the example above, the files will be named as *Joe'sBakery.pdf*, *Joe'sBakery.xlsm.pdf*, and *Joe'sBakery.pptx.pdf*. It should be clear which is the source of the files using this naming convention.

Tip 51

Learning from others

Take a set of spreadsheet project workbooks (from your friends, course instructor, company, or the Internet). Study them and pick out common structural types, preparing *Influence*, *Black-box*, or more advanced (such as UML's *Use Case*, *Class*, *Activity*, and *Sequence*) diagrams. For example, ask if the project can be posted as interactive webpages or as spreadsheets on the Internet. Make use of spreadsheet features and macros to set up toolbars and menus and to consolidate files, etc.

Evaluate each project's technical and business modeling strengths and weaknesses. Record and improve upon the good features. Devise remedial solutions for weak and missing features. Write documentation, add copyright and liability protection, and include common corporate branding features. Make new and better projects out of them, acquire the experience in modeling and hone your spreadsheets skills along the way. This is an endless journey. Get started on it.

FURTHER REFERENCES

* Duhigg, 2012. *The Power of Habit: Why We Do What We Do in Life and Business*, Random House.
* Frye, 2005. *Excel Annoyances*. O'Reilly.
* Grossman, 2006. "The Spreadsheet Analytic Value Chain," *OR/MS Today*, August.
* Leong, 2013. Spreadsheet Resource websites
  o http://isotope.unisim.edu.sg/users/tyleong/SpreadsheetModeling. htm#Topics
  o http://isotope.unisim.edu.sg/users/tyleong/FinanceManagement.htm
  o http://isotope.unisim.edu.sg/users/tyleong/Operations.htm
  o http://isotope.unisim.edu.sg/users/tyleong/SupplyChain.htm
  o http://isotope.unisim.edu.sg/users/tyleong/Technology.htm
  o http://dl.dropboxusercontent.com/u/19228704/SpreadsheetModeling. htm#Topics
  o http://dl.dropboxusercontent.com/u/19228704/FinanceManagement.htm
  o http://dl.dropboxusercontent.com/u/19228704/Operations.htm
  o http://dl.dropboxusercontent.com/u/19228704/SupplyChain.htm
  o http://dl.dropboxusercontent.com/u/19228704/Technology.htm

- Leong and Chu, 2007. "Wireless Network Design: a Space-filling Curve Approach," *International Journal of Mobile Network Design and Innovation* 2(3–4): 180–189.
- Leong and Ladany, 2001. "Optimal Cruise Itinerary Design Development," *International Journal of Services Technology and Management* 2(1/2): 130–141.
- Leong and Lau, 2007. "Generating Job Schedules for Vessel Operations in a Container Terminal," *2nd Multidisciplinary International Conference on Scheduling: Theory and Applications* (MISTA), August, Paris, France.
- Thaler and Sunstein, 2009. *Nudges: Improving Decisions about Health, Wealth, and Happiness*, Penguin Books.
- *Unified Modeling Language* (UML)
  - http://www.sparxsystems.com.au/UML_Tutorial.htm
- Pilloton, 2008. *Design Revolution: 100 Products That Empower People*, Metropolis Books.
  - http://www.youtube.com/watch?v=16ec3ItVAhM
  - http://www.youtube.com/watch?v=AAp_rZh3bw4
- Shea, 2012. *Designing for Social Change: Strategies for Community-Based Graphic Design (Design Briefs)*, Princeton Architectural Press.
  - http://www.youtube.com/watch?v=d45Y5eFHdjE
- Varian, 1997. "How to Build an Economic Model in Your Spare Time," *Passion and Craft: Economists at Work*, University of Michigan Press.

- Keywords. Relevant topics to search in Google and Wikipedia
  - *Social change design . Unified modeling language . Project H design*

PROBLEM SET 9

*Hard problems

Qn 9.01*   **River width.** Select a good sized river near you. It should be wide enough that you cannot shoot an arrow across and narrow enough for you to clearly sight a large object such as a tree on the far bank. Think about how you can estimate the width of this river without having to cross it. If needed, search the Internet and ask others for ideas.

a. Construct a spreadsheet model that demonstrates two or three methods you consider simplest to use in practice.

b. Prepare a handy aid that may be carried in the pocket of an army scout out on a reconnaissance mission to collect the river width data.

Qn 9.02*   **Animal lifespan.** Some insects last only a few days while the larger reptiles and mammals can live to be 100 years old. A common perception therefore is that large creatures generally live longer. This however may not be true.

a. Construct a spreadsheet model to collate the data for a random selection of 100 animals. The data elements should include animal name, species family, average and maximum lifespan, average and maximum overall length, and average and maximum body mass.

b. What does your data tell you? In longevity, does size really matter?

Qn 9.03*   **Saga seeds.** You are picking red seeds from the Saga tree for your wife's handicraft project. The seeds naturally fall around the large tree. The explosive effect of the seedpods scatters the seeds randomly onto a donut-shaped ring area on the grass-covered ground. This is because pods are found mostly near the ends of branches, away from the central tree trunk. Divide a sufficiently large area around the tree into 6 by 6 squares. Simulate the number of seeds in each square according to its location relative to the tree trunk.

a. Construct a spreadsheet model to work out the most efficient visit sequence of squares. Start the search for seeds from the first square in your sequence and move to the adjacent square. Continue from each square to its adjacent. If the visited square has been visited before, the move still has to be counted.

b. What is the minimum number of moves to pick 75, 100, or 125 seeds?

Qn 9.04*   **Rescue search.** A person is lost at sea. His last known location coordinates (x,y) two hours ago is noted. The sea current has a northeasterly drift of about 5 kilometers per hour (kmph). The drift direction and speed are of course changing with time. The probable current location of this missing person therefore fans out like a trumpet. The search pattern for rescue helicopters is to zig-zag this possible zone from the search start point, after the initial flight from the helicopter base. Rescue helicopters can travel at maximum speed of 230 kmph. From a flight height of 200 meters, visibility is only 600 meters and thus gives a maximum search sweep width of 1.2 km. In bad weather with low visibility, these helicopters have to take narrower sweeps. Search travel speed can also be slower to help increase the probability of detection. Sweep width and helicopter travel speed affect the forward speed of the sweep. For the lost person to be found, this forward speed has to be significantly larger than the lost person's drift. There is also only enough fuel for 4.8 hours of flight. The endurance range is 2.4 hours, as the helicopter has to return for refueling. Therefore, more helicopters may be needed.

a. Construct a spreadsheet model for this issue, considering for a start only some of the factors.
b. Examine what is the minimum number of helicopters needed for this search. Does this change with time when the lost person is still not found?
c. Discuss the trade-off between drift speed and detection, and make the needed recommendations to the search approach.

Random points. A server moves from one location to another to respond to a service request. Assuming the requests are addressed in a first-call first-serve basis, the distance to travel from one location to the next is the same as the distance between two randomly selected points in the service region.

Qn 9.05*

a. Construct a spreadsheet model to examine this problem for a (1×1) unit square region. Estimate the average distance to service the random call requests when call requests are assigned to the server practically at the end of his current service.
b. Explain how the results may apply to a region that is elongated or has more complex shapes. What if the service requests are not uniformly distributed over the whole region?
c. In practice, there are often slack time between completion of current service and new service requests. The server now has the choice to wait for the next service request either at the completed service location or at a more central location, to be potentially nearer to the next service location. The new service request may arrive en route to the central location. When that happens, the server breaks journey to move directly to the new service location. Discuss how this extension may be accommodated in your model.

Tour distance. Sometimes, the needed result in tour planning is not the tour sequence or route but rather an estimation of the tour length. This value is to support tactical

Qn 9.06*

planning and deployment decisions in local distribution. Decisions thereafter on specific operational details of the trip may be taken by the drivers, and possibly assisted by in-vehicle GPS systems. The distance of a traveling salesman tour under any routing algorithm can be approximated by the simple formula $\alpha\sqrt{(nA)}$, where $n \geq 2$ is the number of locations to visit, A is the area of the region, and α is a parameter to be calibrated. Assuming that the locations to be visited are distributed over the region according to a probability (usually uniform) distribution, can be estimated by Monte-Carlo simulation.

a. Construct a spreadsheet model for this and use it to estimate the value of α for your region of interest. Do this for n values from 2 to 5. For small n, the optimal tour and its distance can be found by complete enumeration. Lower and upper bounds for larger n are 0.7078 $(\sqrt{n} + 0.551)\sqrt{A}$ and 1.015 $(\sqrt{(n/2)} + 0.72)\sqrt{A}$. The factor $\sqrt{A}$ corrects the results that were based on a unit square instead of a square of area A. These results can be used to evaluate the effectiveness of any chosen routing algorithm.

b. Comment on whether the bounds given are tight.

Qn 9.07* **Computer art.** Graphic art is a combination of lines, colors, and shapes. Animals like chimpanzees and elephants have demonstrated their ability to put brush to paper to produce "random" art, sometimes pretty good ones! Can a computer produce art that may be pleasing to the eye or at least serves as inspiration to budding artists?

a. Construct a spreadsheet model that produces random lines and curves on a graph.

b. Provide options for users to adjust various art elements, such as color and degree of dynamic changes in the lines, to customize the outcomes to their preference.

Qn 9.08* **Game of life.** Cambridge mathematician John Conway invented the *Game of Life* in the 1960s. This zero-player game takes place in an infinite two-dimensional grid. For practical purposes, it may be played in a finite (say 20 by 20) grid. Except for cells at the edges, each cell has eight neighbors, with four touching its sides and four touching its corners. A cell in the grid is either dead or alive. The game board can be made pseudo-infinite by "bending" over itself such that bottom-most cells continue to the top, left-most cells continue to the right most, and vice versa.

A live cell in a time period will survive in the next time period if it has two or three live neighbors. It will die of overcrowding if it has four or more live neighbors and die of exposure if it has zero or one live neighbor. A dead cell in this time period will generally remain dead in the next time period. However if it has exactly three live neighbors, a new birth is generated in its place and it will become alive in the next time period. These rules apply to all cells simultaneously as they move from one generation to another with each time period.

a. Construct a spreadsheet model for this game. The user specifies which cells are alive in the first time period. The subsequent generations are sequentially determined by the rules established by Conway.

b. Try out different initial cell colony configurations and find a few examples of cell colonies or patterns of colonies that:

   i. die out

   ii. stay the same

   iii. grow large and stay alive

   iv. live and keep expanding

Qn 9.09*

Time bomb. In the quintessential bomb disposal scene in an action movie, the hero reaches the ticking bomb moments before it is about to go off. On the bomb is a digital display, counting down the last 20 seconds before it finally blows up. Connecting the time mechanism to the explosive material are these mysterious colored wires. The hero has to cut the wires, but only in the precise sequence. Any mistake will lead to a premature massive damage and fireworks. Now, is it red before black, or blue then yellow?

a. Construct a spreadsheet model to demonstrate how this works. The first row in the main table has five cells: the first four for the colored wires, each set initially with value 1 and the last cell is the bomb state. This should be 0 at the start and becomes 1 when it explodes. Explosion is triggered when the wires are cut in the wrong sequence.

b. Assume as a start, the correct sequence is the wire layout sequence: 1, Red; 2, Black; 3, Green; and 4, Yellow. Use (1, 1, 1, 1) to denote the initial state where all the wires are not cut; this is the initial safe state. The next safe state is (0, 1, 1, 1), followed by (0, 0, 1, 1), (0, 0, 0, 1) and finally (0, 0, 0, 0). Work out the logical formula that permits only these states.

c. Randomize the correct disarming sequence to generate a new set of safe states. Provide another row of cells to deal with the disarming of a bomb with a randomized correct sequence. Again, the bomb state cell should show 0 when the correct sequence is done and 1 if a wrong sequence is used.

Qn 9.10*

Tic-Tac-Toe. This is a simple children's game of putting X's and O's in a 3 by 3 matrix. The first person to complete a straight of three of his marker wins. Some people say that if both players are intelligent and play with care, it would always be a draw. Is it possible to find sure-win strategies? Does the person who starts first have the advantage? Can this game be automated so that a person can play against the computer?

a. Construct a spreadsheet model that examines the game. Show in a diagram the possible interaction of moves between two players. Record the possible game board states and show how it changes from one move to another.

b. Work out which next move is best for every game board state presented. If there is more than one possible "best" response move, pick one randomly. Illustrate how symmetry can be used to reduce the complexity of the diagram.

c. For automation, each game state is best recorded as a single number and not a diagram. Demonstrate how the game board's nine squares with the players' O or X marks entered can be seen as a 9-digit ternary base-3 number. This number can of course be converted to a more convenient decimal base-10 number.

d. Explain how legitimate moves change the game board from one state number to another with an additional (next player's) mark added.

Excel 2010–2013 Features and Functions

INTRODUCTION

The main features and functions of Excel 2010 and Excel 2013 are introduced here. Since they share the same features and functions, all mentions of Excel 2010 are also applicable to Excel 2013. Go through this appendix to start learning the simple technical material. To effectively and instinctively apply them, you have to practice modeling. The notes and exercises in the main text of this book are specifically provided for that purpose. As you do the modeling, remember to periodically review the list below and identify items you should know but are still unclear. Be sure to check out **Help/Contents** in Excel and **Help** in the **VB Editor**. They contain more information than most Excel and **VBA Macro** reference books.

<u>Elementary</u>
Files
    Default directory and some file management, Properties
    New, Open/Close
    Save, Save as, *.xlsx, *.xlsm, *.xltx, *.xltm, *.xlam; *.xls, *.xlt, *.xla, *.csv, *.htm, *.pdf
Rows, Columns, and Sheets
    Insert/Move/Hide row/Column/Sheet, Change column width, Change row height
    Rename Sheets (Tab name, color)
    Cells and Ranges, Comments
    Formulas (+-*/^, calculation order of $A1 + 2*B1/C1^2$)
    Editing formulas, Formula auditing
    Number formats (general, fixed, scientific (E), $, and %) Date/Time formats
    Font (size, type, color), Alignment, Border, Patterns, Protection (locked, hidden)
    Buttons (bold, italic, underline, 0.00, $, and %)
    Character strings and string arithmetic ("=A"&B6&"B")
Commands
    Cut/Copy/Paste,
    Absolute/Relative/Mixed referencing (A1, $A$1, $A1, and A$1)
    PasteSpecial (Formats, Values, Transpose, Operations), Fill, Undo

Options File (password) protection, Macro Security
Page layout: Gridlines, Row and Column Headers, Formulas, Page Break
Drawing: Draw, Group, Order, Rotate/Flip, Auto-shapes, Arrows, Shadow, 3-D

Intermediate
Functions: Function wizard, SUM, COUNT, AVERAGE, MAX, MIN
Functions: IF, SUMIF, SUMIFS, COUNTIF, COUNTIFS, SUMPRODUCT
Data: Goal Seek, Scenarios, DataTable
Charts: Types (Bar, Line, XY), Formats, Series (add, delete), Legends, Axis, Titles
View: Windows, Menus, Toolbars, New (Multiple) windows, Freeze pane, Split, Custom
       views
Customization: File/ExcelOptions
Page layout: Set/Clear Print Area, Print Preview, Header/Footer, Fit to Page
Options: Formula calculation (Automatic, Manual, Iteration)

Advance
Data: Sort, Validation, Form, Filter, PivotTable
Functions: LOOKUP, VLOOKUP, HLOOKUP, MATCH, INDEX, INDIRECT, CHOOSE,
       OFFSET, ADDRESS
Functions: NORMDIST, NORMSDIST, NORMINV, NORMSINV, EXP, LN, BINOMDIST,
       CRITBINOM, LINEST
Functions: Array function and formula, FREQUENCY, RAND, RANDBETWEEN
Functions: DSUM, DCOUNT, DAVERAGE, DMAX, DMIN

Add-ins: Analysis Toolpak, Solver
Form: Button, Group, Option, Check, Spinner, Slider, Control
Macros: Sub and Function procedures, User-defined functions (CellFormula, ShowFormula)
Protection: Worksheet, Workbook, File Sharing, VBA Project
Developer: Visual Basic Editor (Alt+F11), VB Help, Object Browser, Project Reference

FURTHER REFERENCES

- Banfield and Walkenbach, 2010. *Excel 2010 for Dummies: Quick Reference*, Wiley.
- Microsoft Office Developer site
  - http://msdn.microsoft.com/en-us/office

- Leong, 2014. Excel Web Resources
  - http://isotope.unisim.edu.sg/users/tyleong/SpreadsheetModeling.htm#Excel
  - http://dl.dropboxusercontent.com/u/19228704/SpreadsheetModeling.htm#Excel
- Winston, 2011. *Microsoft Excel 2010: Data Analysis and Business Modeling*, Microsoft Press.
- Winston, 2014. *Microsoft Excel 2013: Data Analysis and Business Modeling*, Microsoft Press.

EXCEL 2010–2013 PRIMER

Knowing the basic features and functions of the spreadsheet well is paramount before you can ever be competent in spreadsheet modeling. A short review is done in this appendix to help first-time users learn it faster, and experienced users learn it better. This cannot replace the many excellent books in the market that deal directly with Excel 2010 and Excel 2013, which you may want to refer to after you are through with Appendix A. *Note 1* through *Note 4* are essentially for first-time users. If you have used Excel for some time now, you may skip these notes and proceed straight to *Note 5*. Users of spreadsheet applications other than Excel will find similar features in their applications and should be able to draw parallel inferences.

NOTES

Note 1: SPREADSHEET WINDOW | The Excel spreadsheet file is designed to be like a book and is thus referred to as a **Workbook**. In any workbook, there are several pages, each denoted as a **Worksheet**. By default, a new workbook contains three worksheets (aptly named *Sheet1*, *Sheet2*, and *Sheet3*). You can easily insert or delete worksheets, which is similar to adding pages to or deleting pages from an exercise book. These worksheets can also be renamed and their tabs colored by you. Right-click on the worksheet tab. You will see, in the side menu, the options to do this and more.

There are rectangular spaces on each worksheet, each referred to as a **Cell**, into which you can enter values or formulas. These values can be texts, numbers, or logical values (i.e., TRUE or FALSE). The mathematical formulas that you write into the cells are used to compute any desired results. This is the most formidable part of spreadsheets since their formulas can be made to link data and values from all other cells.

Cells, arranged in a grid, are identified by their row and column positions. There are two alternative ways to identify a cell: the default **A1** or the **R1C1** reference styles. For example, D2 refers to the cell in row 2 of column D and equivalently R2C4 refers to the same since column D is the 4th column. Alphabet column labels go from A to Z, then AA to AZ, BA to BZ, and so on to XFD. These correspond to columns 1 through 16,384.

> Trivia Fact
>
> Q: How many rows and columns are there in an Excel worksheet?
>
> A: Like Excel 2007, each Excel 2010 worksheet has 1,048,576 rows and 16,384 columns. Excel 2003 and older versions have significantly fewer with 65,536 rows and 256 columns. The numbers look rather odd because they are numbers expressed in powers of 2. There are actually few situations where these limits are ever reached and the workbook would usually work rather slowly when the spreadsheets get to be so large.

To enter a formula into a cell, begin with the = sign. For example, to compute 1 + 2, just type =1+2. Once you hit the return key, the result will immediately appear in the cell as the value 3. Note that Excel does not by default show the formula expression in the cell itself, but rather the result of the formula. You can view in the **Formula bar** the formula for the cell where the cursor resides. Alternatively, you can change the worksheet option to view formulas (instead of values) in all the cells of the sheet. This can be done by keying **Ctrl** + ` (typically located just left of the **1** key in the upper-left corner of your keyboard). To switch back to the default option, key Ctrl + ` again. If this does not work, change your keyboard settings and restart Excel and/or Windows.

Quick Tip 1

The usual mathematical operators, namely multiply (*), divide (/), add (+), subtract (−), and power of (^), are applicable in Excel. Do note that symbols used in Excel for multiplication and division are not × and ÷. The order of calculation still follows the usual mathematical BODMAS (bracket, of, divide, multiply, add, subtract) convention. Only round brackets ( ) can be used to group and alter the calculation order. Other types of brackets are not permitted in Excel. Also, brackets do not automatically indicate multiplication and so the multiply (*) operator has to be inserted between brackets where applicable.

Of course, Excel's computing ability is more than just adding two numbers. It has a large set of functions, and together with its (absolute, relative, and mixed) cell referencing system, you can construct complex mathematical and other kinds of formulations in a small collection of cells and massively replicate them with little effort to other cells to complete your model. In fact, you should only be working with **Cell References**, and not data values, in formulas. This will be further illustrated and discussed in *Note 2* and *Note 3*.

Note 2: COMPUTATION   Let us try to compute the average, maximum, and minimum of stock prices for company XYZ for all the months in a year, as given in *Figure A-1*.

Figure A-1

Stock Prices for Company XYZ

	Month	XYZ
1		
2		
3	Month	XYZ
4	1	4.53
5	2	5.62
6	3	3.42
7	4	7.89
8	5	5.78
9	6	6.43
10	7	5.88
11	8	4.67
12	9	3.55
13	10	3.89
14	11	4.12
15	12	6.57
16	Average	5.20
17	Maximum	7.89
18	Minimum	3.42

We will compute the average stock price in cell C16. You would have learned in high school that the average stock price is equal to the sum of all the 12 months' stock prices divided by 12. If you still remember this, your Math teacher will certainly be proud of you. To make it easier for you, Excel provides the **AVERAGE** function to do the same arithmetic calculations. Now, enter into cell C16 the formula =AVERAGE(C4:C15) and key Enter. The result is exactly what we want!

Quick Tip 1
_____

While entering the formula, you can select cell C4, hold down the mouse's left button and drag it to cell C15 instead of typing the cell reference C4:C15 in the formula. This is quicker and less prone to error. Indeed! Excel has such a useful function! Yes, and it has about 250 more. To view the other functions, you can either go to Excel **Help**, or simply click on the *fx* button in the **Formula** bar.

_____

Now, continue to compute the maximum and minimum stock prices in cells C17 and C18, respectively. What Excel functions should you use? You have guessed it, the **MAX** and **MIN** functions. Enter into cells C17 and C18, the formulas =MAX(C4:C15) and =MIN(C4:C15) to obtain the results.

Let us imagine that we want to analyze the average, maximum, and minimum prices for five different stocks, as shown in *Figure A-2*. We do not need to type the same functions five times. Instead, we can perform a **Fill** operation. To begin, we can just select the three cells with formulas, namely C16 to C18, as a group, bring the cursor to the lower-right corner of the group, and drag it to the next four columns (i.e., to column G). Magically, the average, maximum, and minimum stock prices for the next four stocks will be computed.

A	B	C	D	E	F	G
1						
2				Stock Prices		
3	Month	XYZ	Stock 2	Stock 3	Stock 4	Stock 5
4	1	4.53	6.65	4.33	3.11	8.97
5	2	5.62	7.56	4.21	3.22	9.01
6	3	3.42	5.34	3.99	3.45	9.12
7	4	7.89	5.46	3.89	3.67	8.99
8	5	5.78	6.98	4.34	3.57	8.76
9	6	6.43	5.89	4.65	3.45	9.15
10	7	5.88	6.33	4.58	3.37	9.24
11	8	4.67	6.21	4.66	3.21	9.06
12	9	3.55	5.99	3.98	3.09	8.95
13	10	3.89	6.23	4.12	2.99	8.88
14	11	4.12	6.34	4.23	3.12	9.17
15	12	6.57	6.01	4.55	3.45	8.94
16	Average	5.20	6.25	4.29	3.31	9.02
17	Maximum	7.89	7.56	4.66	3.67	9.24
18	Minimum	3.42	5.34	3.89	2.99	8.76

Figure A-2

Stock Prices for Five Stock Counters

Fill, performing **Copy** and **Paste** operations, will automatically duplicate the formulas. It will copy the first set of selected cells and paste them over cells in other locations. In our example above, the formulas in the destination cells take their inputs not from the first set of stock prices, but the stock prices of cells directly above them. This phenomenon is known as **Relative Referencing**. The Fill operation can also be performed on cells that contain data values instead of formulas like what we have demonstrated so far. This will be discussed later.

Quick Tip 2 _____

Dragging the selection one column to the right will cause an increment in the column letters in the formulas by one letter. Similarly, dragging the selection one row down will increment the row numbers in the formulas by one.

_____

What if you do not wish the column letters or row numbers to be changed when performing a Fill operation or Copy and Paste operations? Well, you can switch off the relative referencing to use **Absolute Referencing** or **Mixed Referencing** instead (see next section). **Cell Referencing** is one of the most, if not the most, useful features in electronic spreadsheets. It is also one of the most difficult to understand. Most people find it confusing when they are first introduced to it. However, you will benefit tremendously from it if you put in an effort to understand it. Once you have learned it, you will never go back to the old way. Let us move on to *Note 3*.

| **Note 3: CELL REFERENCING** | Cell referencing, that does not permit column or row, or both, to change when the cell formulas are copied elsewhere, is done using the $ sign. To disallow column change, just prefix $ to the column letter in the cell reference; to disallow row change, do the same to the row number in the cell reference. You can also do both concurrently. That is, =$A$1 will stay as =$A$1 when the cell formula is copied to any other cell in the worksheet. A cell with =$A1 will only have its row number changed in the destination cell formula when copied to another cell in a different row; a cell with =A$1 will have its column changed in the destination cell formula when copied to another cell in a different column. Let us try to understand this concept further by working through the following example. Prepare a multiplication table as shown in *Figure A-3*. How can we apply the Fill operation to compute the results effectively?

Figure A-3

_____

Multiplication
Table for the
Number 3

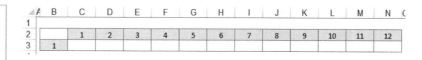

⁊A	B	C	D	E	F	G	H	I	J	K	L	M	N	O
1														
2		1	2	3	4	5	6	7	8	9	10	11	12	
3	1													

In cell C3, type the formula =B3*C2. If you simply drag this cell selection to the cell to the right of C3, the results will be incorrect. This is because B3 will be changed to C3 in the formula in cell D3, to D3 in cell E3, and so on. To keep B3 as it is, modify the formula to =$B3*C2. Now, drag this cell selection to the right again. You will see that $B3 remains as $B3 in all cells. The **$** before B indicates that column letter B must not be changed in a Fill operation.

Quick Tip 1 _____

$A$1 refers to **absolute referencing** where the same value in cell A1 will be applied after a Fill operation, regardless of dragging across rows or across columns, because the **$** sign preceding column letter A restricts increments in the column letter, while the **$** sign preceding row number 1 restricts increments in the row number.

$A1 refers to **mixed referencing**, where only the column letter is restricted from increments. A$1 is the other mixed referencing where only the row number is restricted from increments.

The **F4** key in the top row on your computer keyboard is a toggle key to facilitate changing the cell reference to the different forms (A1, $A$1, A$1, $A1). Just hit the key after you have typed a cell reference to cycle through the set of cell reference forms.

_____

As a further challenge, let us prepare a bigger multiplication table in *Figure A-4*. Can you figure out where the $ signs should be added in the formula?

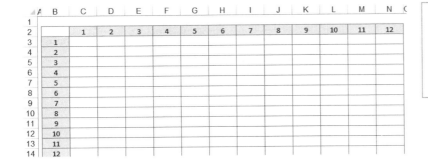

Figure A-4

Multiplication Table for 1 to 12

In this multiplication table, enter into cell C3 the formula =$B3*C$2. The $ sign preceding column letter B ensures that the reference to column B remains static, while the $ sign preceding the row number 2 ensures that the reference to row 2 remains static. Try it out. If it works, expand the multiplication table to 50 by 50 or even 200 by 200 to see if it is still okay.

Quick Tip 2

All cell formulas should only contain cell references, operators, and functions. There should not be any numerical, text, or logical value in them. Formulas therefore show the relationships between cells, which in turn can contain values or formulas. This makes updating the input data values explicit and clearer to the user.

To see a visual representation of the cell relationships, click on the cell of interest and then click the cell formula in the **Formula** bar. The cell references in it will then become color-coded and boxes whose colors match those used in the spreadsheet will frame the corresponding cells referenced in the formula. You can even modify the cell formula by dragging or changing the shape of these boxes.

An alternative approach is to use **Formula auditing**. This is found in the **Formulas** tab. Click **Trace Precedents** or **Trace Dependents** to visually show arrows linking the cells. Also try **Show Formulas**. This works the same as **Ctrl + '**.

Hopefully, examples used in this note have helped to illustrate the usefulness of cell referencing and clarified its correct use. We are now ready to learn more advanced features of Excel. As you model and analyze more complex problems, you will need to learn these additional spreadsheet features to be proficient and effective. In the following few notes, we will cover some of the more useful advanced features.

Note 4: FORMATTING   The appearance of a cell can be altered by changing its row height or column width. Rows or columns can be moved, deleted, or inserted to alter the arrangement of cells in any spreadsheet model. The cell references in the affected formula will automatically change without altering the underlying logic in the cell formulas. Most of the formatting actions can be done intuitively using the options available in the **Home** tab as shown in *Figure A-5a*. The options available include changing the font type, style, size, alignment, cell shading, and borders.

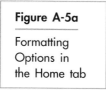

Figure A-5a

Formatting Options in the Home tab

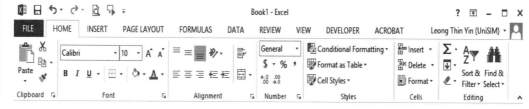

The value in a cell is automatically formatted according to the way you entered it. If you enter 0.3501, then it would appear as such with the same number of decimal places. If the intended entry is 35.01%, it may be better to enter as such. The decimal value entered can of course be formatted to be a percentage by clicking the % icon in the menu. Other icons allow you to change the number of decimal places displayed, add commas, or add a currency prefix. You can also right-click on a cell and then select **Format Cells** to open the dialog.

No matter how a value is reformatted, the value stored in the cell remains unchanged. In particular, a cell with the value 35.01% displayed is actually stored as 0.3501 and will be computed as 0.3501 and not 35.01 in formulas. There is therefore no need to divide by 100 to get the proportion value. You should, however, exercise caution when reducing the number of decimal places displayed as it may lead to calculations being misinterpreted. As a convention, it would be good to keep the number of decimal places the same for all values of the same variable and possibly across similar variables in the whole spreadsheet.

The format of a cell may be changed conditionally. The condition may be the state of value in the cell to be formatted or based on a logical formula. The logical formulas topic is discussed in *Note 10*. Simple **Conditional Formatting**, in the form of **Data bars**, **Color scales**, and **Icon sets** (e.g., traffic lights and directional arrows, shown in *Figure A-5b*), are available to make it easier to sense cells values, picking up the relevant ones especially when they are among many in large tables.

Figure A-5b

Simple Conditional Formatting

More complex Conditional Formatting will require the use of logical formulas. In the Excel **Home** tab, select **Conditional Formatting/New Rule**. Select **Format only cells that contain** to change the format based on the cell values or select **Use a formula to determine which cells to format** to specify the desired logical formula, as shown in *Figure A-6*. In Excel 2010, the maximum number of rules is 64 and you can specify whether the checking should stop or continue if the rule is TRUE.

Figure A-6

Complex
Conditional
Formatting

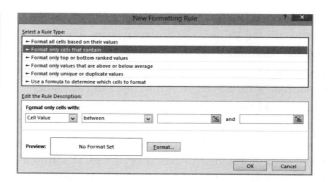

Note 5: DATA VALIDATION AND LOOKUP

Data Validation

Whereas cells with formulas may be protected, input cells need to be available for users to enter the required values. These cells can therefore be subject to entry mistakes. To offer some assurance that the input cells are correctly used, you can apply **Data Validation** to check the inputs as they are entered. Data validation checks the variable type and value range for applied cells.

To set the validation for a cell, select the cell and then select **Data/Data Tools/Data Validation**. In the dialog as shown in *Figure A-7*, select the variable type in **Allow**, and then the conditions in **Data**. Enter also the lower and upper limits of the values, where applicable.

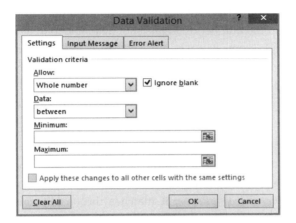

Figure A-7

Data Validation

Ever think of allowing users to enter inputs by letting them choose from a list of permitted values? Excel's Data Validation also allows you to prepare a list of given values to be assigned to a cell. Once assigned, a drop-down list will appear to allow the user to make the selection. This helps to minimize mistakes in data entry.

Let us construct a drop-down list to allow a user to select *gender* (*female* or *male*).

1. Select the cell where the drop-down list is to appear.
2. From the **Data** menu, select **Validation**.
3. In the **Settings** panel, in the **Allow** drop-down list, select **List**.
4. In the **Settings** panel, in the **Source** input area, enter *Female, Male*.

Quick Tip 1

For more flexibility, you can put the source input values as a group in a separate vertical or horizontal cell range, and in step (4) above, set the cell range reference or make the selection instead of entering the values.

For more complex data validation, you can use the **Custom** option in **Allow** of the Data Validation dialog to set logical formulas to govern the cell's data validation. For example, you may want to validate that a particular data value in a column of a table has not been entered in the rows preceding. To be able to do this, you must first learn logical formulas and the **COUNTIF** function. These topics are covered in *Note 10*.

Table Lookup

One of the most useful features of Excel is its ability to find the corresponding result for a lookup value in a table. For example, at a game stall, if you have shot three or less targets, you win yourself a bronze medal, and if you have shot four to seven targets, you win a silver medal, and finally, if you have shot eight to 10 targets, you win a gold medal. The stall owner needs to look up the number of targets shot in a table to determine what kind of medal to award. This example seems trivial because there are only three categories of results. Imagine having to manage a large number of categories, with dynamically changing lookup values. The values in the table themselves may even be dynamically changing. The table lookup feature will prove to be extremely helpful then. Here are some lookup functions:

LOOKUP(*lookupValue*, *lookupRange*, [*valueRange*])

- Returns the value in *valueRange* that has the same relative position that *lookupValue* has in *lookupRange*. The values in *lookupRange* must be in ascending order. If LOOKUP cannot find *lookupValue* in *lookupRange*, it matches the largest value in *lookupRange* that is less than *lookupValue*.
- For example, LOOKUP(6, A1:A6, B5:B10) with (3, 5, 7, 9, 11, 12) in A1:A6 and (2, 4, 6, 8, 10, 12) in B5:B10 would return the value of 4, as the value 5 in A1:A6, the largest value less than or equal to 6, is in the second position, and the second value in B5:B10 is 4.
- LOOKUP(RAND(), *lookupRange*, *mid-binValueRange*) returns a random value, according to the distribution of the values listed in the table defined by the mid-bin value and lookup ranges. This is one of the ways you can generate random values from a given distribution frequency table. Refer to *Note 6* for comments on the **RAND** function and other ways to generate random values.
- LOOKUP is best applied when the *lookupRange* and *valueRange* are not residing in the same table or are not of the same (row or column) orientation.

VLOOKUP(*lookupValue*, *tableArray*, *columnIndexNum*, [*rangeLookup*])

- Searches for *lookupValue* in the left-most column of *tableArray*, and returns the value in the same relative row position in the column identified by *columnIndexNum*. The *columnIndexNum* is a positive integer and *rangeLookup* is a logical value. The square brackets around *rangeLookup* indicate that it is an optional input. This square bracket convention applies to all other functions as well.

- When *rangeLookup* is TRUE (or omitted), the function will look for an approximate match for *lookupValue* in the left-most column, similar to the way the LOOKUP function works. For approximate match lookup, the values in the left-most column of *tableArray* must be in ascending order.

- However, when the *rangeLookup* is FALSE, an exact match for *lookupValue* in the left-most column is searched, and returns #N/A if none is found. The first matched position is returned if there are multiple possible matches.
- VLOOKUP is best applied when the *lookupValue* is compared with values in the left-most (i.e., first) column of *tableArray*.

MATCH(*lookupValue*, *lookupRange*, [*matchType*])

- Returns the relative position that the *lookupValue* is in *lookupRange*.
- If *matchType* is 0, MATCH looks for an exact value of *lookupValue* in *lookupRange* and returns #N/A if none is found. The first matched position is returned if there are multiple possible matches.
- If *matchType* is 1 or omitted, MATCH looks for the largest value less than or equal to the *lookupValue*. The *lookupArray* must first be in ascending order: ...–1, 0, 1, ..., A–Z, FALSE, TRUE.
- If *matchType* is –1, MATCH looks for the smallest value greater than or equal to the *lookupValue*. The *lookupArray* must first be in descending order. Only MATCH can deal with the approximate matches of a descending sorted *lookupRange*.

INDEX(*tableArray*, *rowIndex*, [*columnIndex*])

- Returns the value found in the relative *rowIndex* and *columnIndex* positions in *tableArray*.
- When *tableArray* is a single column of values, then *columnIndex* is not needed.
- However, when *tableArray* is a multiple-row and multiple-column matrix, then both *rowIndex* and *columnIndex* are needed to identify the value.

Quick Tip 2
_____

The clever use of MATCH within INDEX allows us to identify values using dynamically changing *rowIndex* and *columnIndex*, where the *rowIndex* and *columnIndex* are results obtained from using MATCH twice.

Note 6: RANDOM NUMBERS AND RESAMPLING

Random Numbers

Random numbers are useful, especially in Monte-Carlo simulations, where variations of input values are needed. Two functions are available in Excel to generate random numbers, one for continuous values and the other for discrete values.

RAND( ) returns with equal probability a random value in [0, 1), i.e., between 0 and 1, inclusive of 0 but not of 1. The brackets, with nothing inside, are needed when you enter the function into a cell. This function can be used in formulas to generate random values of other probability distributions and interval values. For example, to generate a random real value uniformly distributed between 5 and 9, we can use =5+RAND()*(9–5). So when RAND is 0, it returns 5; when RAND is almost 1, it returns a number that is almost 9 and when RAND is a value between 0 and 1, it generates the interpolated value between 5 and 9 with uniform probability density.

RANDBETWEEN(*loNum, hiNum*) returns with equal probability a random integer in {*loNum, loNum* + 1, …, *hiNum*}, i.e., integers between *loNum* and *hiNum, loNum* < *hiNum* being integers. For example, RANDBETWEEN(1, 6) can be used to simulate the toss of a die. This function is only available when **Analysis ToolPak** (a standard **Add-in** in Excel) has been activated. You do this by selecting **File/Options/Add-ins/Excel Add-ins/Go**. Alternatively, without invoking Analysis ToolPak, formula =INT(RAND()*(*hiNum – loNum* + 1)) + *loNum* would also give the same result. That is, you can also simulate the toss of a die using INT(RAND()*6) + 1.

Quick Tip 1
_____

Calculation Options is found in the **Formulas** tab. When the Calculation option is (by default) set to **Automatic**, any recomputation or data entry into the worksheet will cause the random function to generate a new random number. To restrict this, especially when it is rather disruptive during model construction, set the Calculation option to **Manual**, and key **F9** whenever you wish to regenerate a new random value.

Resampling Data

Data resampling is important when we want to generate random data points from a handful of sample data points. Excel has some useful functions that can be used to perform data resampling. (Refer to the *Data Simulation* exercise and the *Resampling* tool in Chapter 6 for more details.)

SMALL(*valueRange, k*)
- Returns the *k*th smallest value, with *k* being an integer, in the data set specified by *valueRange*.
- For example, SMALL(A1:A20,1) returns the smallest value in A1:A20 (same result as MIN(A1:A20)), SMALL(A1:A20,2) returns the second smallest value, SMALL(A1:A20,3) returns the third smallest value, and so on. When used against a column of running serial numbers 1, 2, 3, …, it can be used to sort a set of numbers in ascending order.

- SMALL(*valueRange*, RANDBETWEEN(1, *n*)) resamples with equal probability the *n* sample data values stored in *valueRange*.

LARGE(*valueRange*, *k*)

- Returns the *k*th largest value, with *k* being an integer, in the data set specified by *valueRange*.
- For example, LARGE(A1:A20,1) returns the largest value in A1:A20 (same result as MAX(A1:A20)), LARGE(A1:A20,2) returns the second largest value, LARGE (A1:A20,3) returns the third largest value, and so on. When used against a column of running serial numbers 1, 2, 3, …, it can be used to sort a set of numbers in descending order.
- LARGE(*valueRange*, RANDBETWEEN(1, *n*)) also resamples with equal probability the *n* sample data values stored in *valueRange*.

PERCENTILE(*valueRange*, *k*)

- Returns the *k*th fractile, with *k* being a real number between 0 and 1, from among the data in *valueRange*.
- For example, PERCENTILE(A1:A5,0.5) with (91, 33, 52, 45, 67) in cell range A1:A5 returns the 50th percentile value of 52. PERCENTILE(*valueRange*, RAND()) works like SMALL(*valueRange*, RANDBETWEEN(1, *n*)), except now PERCENTILE also interpolates when the fractile required does not coincide with one of the given sample data points and it returns a continuous value.
- By using PERCENTILE to resample data points, you may end up having a resulting data point which is not one of the given sample data points, due to interpolation. When used with the **INT** function, it is even applicable for resampling discrete data.

| **Note 7: AUTOMATIC TABULATION** | **DataTable** is an Excel feature that auto-matically generates a table of results of a spreadsheet model by replacing up to two of its variables with many given sets of input values for them. This can be done for a single input variable (in 1-dimensional DataTable) with one or more output variables, or for two input variables (in 2-dimensional DataTable) with only one output variable. This operation is particularly useful when the model comprises more than just a formula in a single cell.

We will illustrate, as shown in *Figure A-8*, the construction of a 1-dimensional DataTable to compute the values of two output variables Y and Z using different values of input variable X. We arbitrarily define Y = 2X and Z = 3X + 2.

1. Prepare a column containing the candidate values 3, 6, ..., 30 for input variable X in cells B5:B14.

2. Enter output formula Y = 2X into the cell C4 as =2*B2. Note that the formula for output variables must reside in the row just above the first candidate input value for X, with the first output variable taking the first column to the right of the input value column, the second output variable in the second column, and so on. In addition, these output formulas must refer as input variable X a cell outside of the table. In this example, this cell is B2.

3. Enter the second formula Z = 3X + 2 into the cell D4 as =3*B2+2. This second formula resides to the right of the first formula. Repeat the step for additional formulas (if any).

4. Select the whole table in B4:D14 and then activate the computation by selecting **Data/Data Tools/What-If Analysis/Data Table**.

5. A dialog will prompt you to enter the **Row Input Cell** and **Column Input Cell**. Since this is a 1-dimensional DataTable constructed with input X values in a column, you can ignore the Row Input Cell and enter B2 as the Column Input Cell.

6. Results for the output variables will be computed automatically and placed into the table.

Figure A-8

One-dimensional DataTable

A	B	C	D
1			
2	2		
3			
4		=2*B2	=3*B2 + 2
5	3		
6	6		
7	9		
8	12		
9	15		
10	18		
11	21		
12	24		
13	27		
14	30		

The set-up of a 2-dimensional DataTable that computes the values of output variable W = X1 * X2 for given values of two input variables X1 and X2, as shown in *Figure A-9*, is illustrated as follows:

1. Prepare a column containing the candidate values 3, 6, ..., 30 for the first input variable X1 in cells C6:C15.

2. Prepare a row containing the candidate values 2, 4, ..., 10 for the second variable X2 in cells D5:H5.

3. Enter output formula W = X1 * X2 into the cell C5 as =C2*C3. Note that for a 2-dimensional DataTable, only one output variable can be computed. Its formula should reside at the upper left-hand corner, where the candidate values of X1 and X2 intersect. As in the 1-dimensional DataTable, this formula must refer to two cells outside of the table as X1 and X2. In this example, the two cells for X1 and X2 are C2 and C3, respectively.

4. Select the whole table in C5:H15 and activate the computation by selecting **Data/Data Tools/What-If Analysis/Data Table** from the main menu.

5. In the dialog, you will be prompted to enter the Row Input Cell and Column Input Cell. Enter C2 as the Column Input Cell and C3 as the Row Input Cell; both refer to variables X1 and X2, respectively in the formula.

6. Results for output variable W will be computed automatically and placed in the corresponding positions in the table.

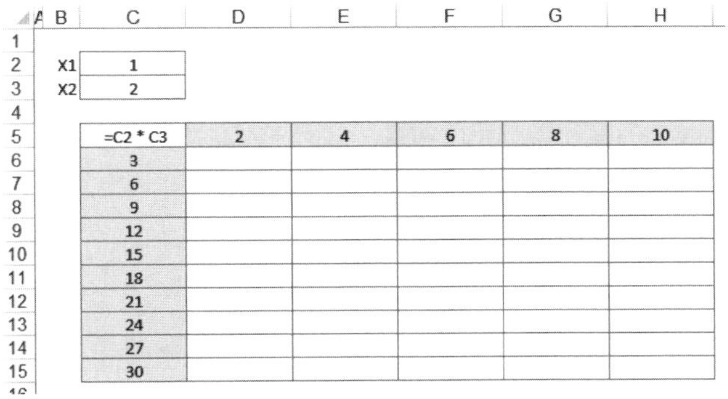

Figure A-9

Two-dimensional DataTable

Quick Tip 1

DataTable can be used to collect replication results in *Monte-Carlo* simulations. To do this, simply use the row (and column) input value (or values in combination) as the replication counter and use any arbitrary empty cell(s) to be the input cell(s).

Tool 30 (*TableSolve*) in Chapter 9 provides macros that emulate DataTable operations and extend upon them. They allow you to do multiple operation computations that concurrently involve more than two input variables and more than one output variable. Also, the TableSolve subroutines can be set to call any subroutine of your choice with every change in data values in its operations. This is particularly useful when the computation involves any form of search or optimization.

Note 8: CHART   Charts are visual representations of data points that can in most cases display results more effectively than tables. Some of the commonly used charts in spreadsheet include bar chart, pie chart, and XY scatter plot. Excel provides a series of corresponding icon buttons in the **Insert** tab for you to select from. Let us construct a column chart for a stock investment portfolio given in *Figure A-10*.

Figure A-10

Stock Investment
Portfolio Data

	A	B	C
1			
2		Type	Percentage Investment
3		Stock 1	20%
4		Stock 2	25%
5		Stock 3	10%
6		Stock 4	5%
7		Stock 5	40%

Figure A-11

Charts in Excel

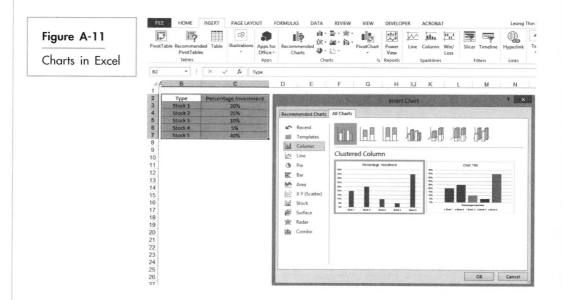

Select the data to plot (inclusive of table headers if any) and then click on the **Insert** tab to access the **Charts** group and work from there, as shown in *Figure A-11*. If you are plotting all the data in the table, you can simply put your cursor anywhere in the table. The whole table will be automatically selected as you (following the steps above) select the chart type. Once constructed, you can modify your chart using the tools available in the additional **Design** and **Layout** tabs, which only appear after a chart is selected.

In **Scatter** charts, you can right-click on the data markers or plotted line to **Add Trendline**. In the dialog for this, there are various options available, including setting the trend type, forecast, equation, R-square and format. A new feature added in Excel 2010 is **Sparklines**. It allows you to add tiny charts into cells next to tables. Find out more about how to do it in **Excel Help**.

Note 9: DATE, TIME, AND TEXT

Date and Time

There are two date systems in Excel, namely the default 1900 date system and the 1904 date system. In the default date system, 1 January 1900 is day 1, and 2 January 1900 is day 2, and so on. To change to the alternative date system for a workbook, go to **File/ Options/Advanced/When calculating this workbook.**

Now, why does Excel need to have an alternative date system? There is an error in the 1900 date system because Excel erroneously assumes 29 February 1900 exists but 1900, unlike other years that are divisible by 4, is not a leap year! Therefore, all dates after 29 February 1900 are in fact assigned an integer one larger than they should be. Calculations using dates that straddle 29 February 1900 will be off by a day. If you will not be doing computations involving dates before 1 March 1900, this mistake will not affect you. The 1904 date system corrects for this mistake by starting instead with 1 January 1904 as day 0. This system is however not applicable when you use dates before 1 January 1904.

There are several functions in Excel that allow us to manage dates and days:

- **TODAY**() returns the current date.
- **YEAR**(*serialNumber*) returns the year corresponding to the *serialNumber*
  - Wrong: YEAR(14-Jan-05)
  - OK: YEAR("14-Jan-05")
  - OK: YEAR(B15) where B15 has the value 14-Jan-05
  - OK: YEAR(39014) = 2006
- **MONTH**(*serialNumber*) returns the month and **DAY**(*serialNumber*) returns the day corresponding to the serial number.
  - MONTH(39014) = 10, DAY(39014) = 24 since 39014 is 24 October 2006 in Excel.
- **DATE**(*year, month, day*) returns the serial number.

QuickTip 1
_____

When dealing with subtraction of dates, the minus sign is easily mistaken as the dash used in dates. So, please take note of the correct and wrong ways to denote dates subtraction.

- WRONG: 14-Jan-05 – 23-Sep-04
- OK: "14-Jan-05" – "23-Sep-04" = 113
- OK: DATE(2005,1,14) – DATE(2004,9,23) = 113

Time is also managed in a serial number format, except time is stored as the fractional part of the serial number, that is, the digits to the right of the decimal point. A 24-hour day will make up a whole number 1, so part of a day, say 12 hours, will be 0.5. Let us look at some of the functions that can help us manage time.

- **NOW**() returns the current date and time.
- For example, if now is 8:00AM 25 December 2005, then the value of NOW() is 38711.3333333 where
  o 38711 is the day, which is 25 December 2005, and
  o .3333333 is the time of the day, which is 1/3 of the day.
- So, 8:00AM 26 Dec 2005 is 38712.3333333.
- **TIME**(*hour, minute, second*) returns the serial number to the right of the decimal point in the 0.####### format.
- **HOUR**(*serialNumber*), **MINUTE**(*serialNumber*), and **SECOND**(*serialNumber*) return respectively the hour, minute, and second of *serialNumber*.
  o HOUR(39461.847) = 20
  o MINUTE(39461.847) = 19
  o SECOND(39461.847) = 41

Text Management

Other than values and formulas, Excel can also manage texts (or commonly known as strings, denoting in short a string of characters). Important text functions include **CONCATENATE, LEN, FIND, LEFT,** and **RIGHT**.

CONCATENATE(*string1, string2, …*)

- Combines end-to-end text strings *string1, string2,* and others. The alternative approach is to use the concatenation operator **&**.
- Therefore, "ABC" & "DEF" will yield "ABCDEF". This can be done to text or cells with values. For example, ">" & E20 yields ">5" when cell E20 contains the value 5. In this context, Excel implicitly converts number into text before completing the concatenation.
- This operation is helpful for specifying the criteria in functions such as **COUNTIF, COUNTIFS, SUMIF** and **SUMIFS**. These functions are discussed in the last section of *Note 10*.

LEN(*string*)

- LEN returns the number of characters in text *string*.

FIND(*findString, string,* [*startNumChar*])

- FIND searches for text *findString* in text *string*, starting from the *startNumChar* position in *string*. Integer *startNumChar* is assumed to be 1 if it is not specified. If successful, it returns the position of the first character of *findString* in text *string*, counting from the left. If there are multiple occurrences of *findString* in *string*, then the first occurrence will be the one found.
- For example, FIND("o", "Flower shop") returns 3 and FIND("er", "Flower shop") returns 5.

LEFT(*string,* [*numChar*])

- LEFT returns the left-most *numChar* characters in text *string*. Integer *numChar* is assumed to be 1 if it is not specified.

RIGHT(*string,* [*numChar*])

- RIGHT returns the right-most *numChar* characters in text *string*. Integer *numChar* is assumed to be 1 if it is not specified.

All these text functions can be creatively applied to do many interesting things in your spreadsheets. It can for example split a full name into first name and last name, or extract postal codes from full addresses.

Note 10: LOGICAL FORMULA AND FUNCTION | A logical formula is one that returns a TRUE or FALSE value. For example, a cell with formula =(B4=C5) will return a TRUE when the result contained in cell B4 is the same as that of C5 and a FALSE otherwise. In logical formulas, several operators other than the equal operator (=) can be used. These include:

- < less than
- <= less than or equal to
- > greater than
- >= greater than or equal to
- < > not equal to

There are also logical functions such as **AND, OR, NOT**, and **IF**. AND and OR can combine the results of more than one logical test to depict more complex evaluations. AND returns a TRUE if and only if all logical tests within it are TRUE; OR returns a TRUE when at least one logical test it evaluates is TRUE; NOT transforms a FALSE to a TRUE, and a TRUE to a FALSE. The results of evaluation using AND, OR, and NOT with two arguments can be summarized as follows:

Function	Result
AND(TRUE, TRUE)	TRUE
AND(FALSE, TRUE)	FALSE
AND(TRUE, FALSE)	FALSE
AND(FALSE, TRUE)	FALSE

Function	Result
OR(TRUE, TRUE)	TRUE
OR(TRUE, FALSE)	TRUE
OR(FALSE, TRUE)	TRUE
OR(FALSE, FALSE)	FALSE

Function	Result
NOT(TRUE)	FALSE
NOT(FALSE)	TRUE

Logical formulas can be used in conjunction with arithmetic computations. In such cases, TRUE will be evaluated as a 1 and FALSE as a 0. Therefore, formula =(B4=C5)*1 will return a 1 when the result contained in cell B4 is the same as that of C5 and a 0 otherwise. Also, the multiplication of two logical tests would be equivalent to an AND operation. That is, =(B4=C5)*(D5>F2) would give the same conclusion as AND(B4=C5, D5>F2), except that the former will return a 0,1 result and the latter a TRUE, FALSE result.

IF(*logicalTest*, *resultIfTrue*, *resultIfFalse*)

The IF function is designed to evaluate a *logicalTest* condition, that should return a TRUE or FALSE. If *logicalTest* is TRUE, then *resultIfTrue* will be displayed; if FALSE, then *resultIfFalse* will be displayed. The *logicalTest* condition would be as in a logical formula, except without the = sign prefix. Both *resultIfTrue* and *resultIfFalse* can be values, cell references, or formulas. For example, to test if the age of a person who is above 18 to enter a club is IF(age > 18, "Welcome", "You are underage!").

Quick Tip 1

An IF function with another IF function as its *resultIfTrue* or *resultIfFalse* is known as a nested IF function. Excel 2007 and later versions allows up to 64 levels of nesting.

A more complex example would be a club that requires female members to be above 18 years of age while male members to be above 21. The IF function for this will be IF(OR(AND(age>18,gender="Female"),AND(age>21,gender="Male")),"Welcome",   "You are underage!").

Quick Tip 2

MAX(*value*, 0) and **MIN**(*value*, 0) are shorter and more elegant substitutes to IF(*value* > 0, *value*, 0) and IF(*value* < 0, *value*, 0), respectively. So indirectly, MAX and MIN, though classified by Excel as statistical functions, are also logical functions.

IFERROR(*value, valueIfError*)

Function IFERROR checks value against the error types #N/A, #VALUE!, #REF!, #DIV/0!, #NUM!, #NAME?, or #NULL!. If *value* is not in error, then *value* is returned. Otherwise, *valueIfError* is returned. It functions as an error trap to correct equations such as X/Y when Y can be 0. This function is not available in Excel 2003 and older versions. So do not use it if your workbook is to be shared with users of older versions.

Logical Count and Sum

The **COUNT** function counts the number of cells in the specified cell range that contains numerical values, while **COUNTA** counts the number of cells that contains numerical or text values. When you need to count the number of cells that satisfies a certain evaluation criterion or a set of criteria, use respectively the **COUNTIF** and **COUNTIFS** functions. Similarly, there are **SUM**, **SUMIF**, and also **SUMIFS** functions. The **SUMIFS** and **COUNTIFS** functions are not available in Excel 2003 and older versions.

COUNTIF(*range, criteria*)

- Counts the number of values in the specified cell range that satisfies the criteria.
- The criteria is a simple logical expression expressed (in quotes) as a text. For example, COUNTIF(A1:A20, ">5") counts the number of values that is greater than 5 in cells A1 through A20.
- Now using the & concatenation operator and setting the value in cell E20 to 5, COUNTIF(A1:A20, ">"&E20) becomes equivalent to COUNTIF(A1:A20, ">5"). The advantage of the latter is that the value in cell E20 can be arbitrarily changed to suit your purpose. Excel 2007 and newer versions have the **COUNTIFS**(*range1, criteria1, range2, criteria2,…*) function, which is even more powerful.

SUMIF(*criteriaRange, criteria, [sumRange]*)

- Sums the number of values in *sumRange* for all corresponding values in *criteriaRange* that satisfy the criteria. *sumRange* may be omitted if it is the same as the *criteriaRange*.
- The criteria is a simple logical expression expressed (in quotes) as a text. For example, SUMIF(A1:A20, ">5") sums the number of values that is greater than 5 in cells A1 through A20.
- Now using the & concatenation operator and setting the value in cell E20 to 5, SUMIF(A1:A20, ">"&E20, B1:B20) becomes equivalent to SUMIF(A1:A20, ">5", B1:B20). The advantage of the latter is that the value in cell E20 can be arbitrarily changed to suit your purpose. Excel 2007 and later versions have the more powerful **SUMIFS**(*sumRange, criteriaRange1, criteria1, criteriaRange2, criteria2, …*) function.

Also introduced from Excel 2007 onwards are the **AVERAGEIF** and **AVERAGEIFS** functions. Their structure and use are similar to those in COUNTIF and COUNTIFS.

Note 11: DATA MANAGEMENT

Data List

A **data list** is a list of records, with each record occupying a row and its attributes distributed over the columns. Each column corresponds to a data field, which is a variable in a record. *Figure A-12* shows an example of a data list of club membership information.

Figure A-12

Example of a Data List

Membership Number	Name	Address	Gender	Age	Date Joined
M00001	John Chew	56 Maryland Street	Male	35	1 Jan 2005
M00002	Mary Green	89 Futon Street	Female	33	25 Mar 2005
M00003	Michelle Pipe	90 Kronnen Street	Female	29	5 May 2005

Excel 2003 has provided a quick way for users to enter and edit data in a data list. This **Data Form** feature is also available in Excel 2010 but you have to customize it into your menu Ribbon to use it. To do the customization, click the **File/Options/Customize Ribbon** sequence of steps to reveal the dialog as shown in *Figure A-13a*. Select **Commands Not in the Ribbon** in **Choose commands from** and then scroll down the left selection panel to find **Form**. Select **Data** on the right selection panel and click **New Group**. A new group will be added below the last group in the **Data** tab list. Click **Rename** to change the name of this new group to *Form*. Click the **Add** button to include the **Form** icon to the **Data** tab. Click **OK** to close the customization dialog.

Figure A-13a

Customizing the Ribbon

Follow the steps below to create the table in *Figure A-12*.

1. Enter the field labels as table headers into cells B2:G2.
2. Select the field labels in cells B2:G2. An entry form dialog will appear, as shown in *Figure A-13b*.
3. Select from the menu **Data/Form** and an entry form dialog will appear.
4. To add a new record
   a. Click **New** to clear all current data in the input boxes.
   b. Enter your information into the form.
   c. Click **New** again to append your input to the data list, and continue with more new records, or click **Close** to append the data and end.
5. To edit an existing record
   a. Locate the record using **Find Next** and **Find Previous**.
   b. Edit the information and click **Close** to update.

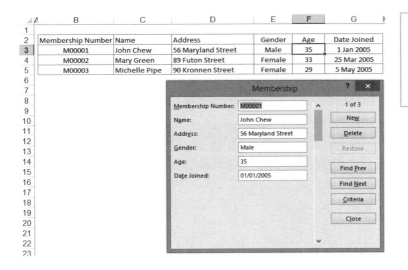

Figure A-13b

Data Form for
Club Membership
Information

After experimenting with Data Form, you may notice its several limitations. Here are some we have found:

- No option for adding a drop-down selection list to simplify data entry. This would be particularly useful for fields like *Gender*.
- Does not validate input values. The *Age* field requires an integer input and so a quick check to ensure only valid values within a reasonable range will help ensure data integrity.
- Fixed input box width. A field like *Address* needs a longer input box, whereas *Postal Code* should have a shorter one.

Sort

To sort values in ascending order in a **data List**, put your cursor in a cell in the column of interest inside the table and click the $\frac{A}{Z}\downarrow$ icon. Similarly, you can click on $\frac{Z}{A}\downarrow$ to sort in descending order. A quick way to properly sort a table with data entry that has ties in values in the fields is to move your cursor to the relevant columns to sort and each time click on the sort ascending or sort descending icon. The order in which the columns are sorted is important. You should start with the least significant column, then move progressively to the most significant one.

Alternatively, select all the data you want to sort and click on the icon to the right of the $\frac{A}{Z}\downarrow$ and $\frac{Z}{A}\downarrow$ icons to call up the Sort dialog and work from there. If you have instead put your cursor anywhere in the data list before you do so, the whole cell range that contains the data will be also automatically selected and a dialog will appear, as shown in *Figure A-14*. If you indicate that your data list has a header row, the **Sort by** selections will be made according to the header labels. Otherwise, the worksheet column labels will be used instead. Again, you can choose whether to sort each attribute in ascending or descending order. Unlike Excel 2003 where sorting can be performed by cell values only, Excel 2007 and newer versions in addition allow sorting to be done on cell color, font color and cell icon.

Figure A-14

Data Sort

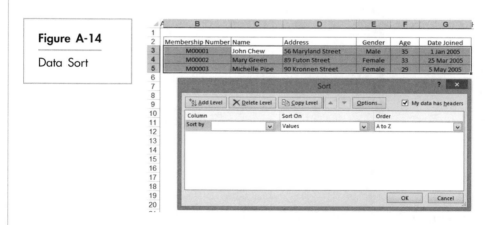

AutoFilter

AutoFilter allows us to filter a large number of records in a data list for simple user-selected criteria. This feature is particularly useful when the number of records has grown so much that it is no longer possible to view all records at the same time without excessive scrolling. For example, a club with 2,000 members wants to organize a ladies' event and therefore needs to view the data of female members within an age range to work out a reasonable invitation list.

To set up the AutoFilter for *Figure A-12*, follow the steps below:

- Select any cell within the data list.
- Select Data/Filter/AutoFilter to activate it. With this, drop-down tabs will be added to the field labels in the data list header for you to select the various filtering operations for each data field.

It will be a good idea to increase the height of the header row and format the cells there with the text alignment set to top so that the drop-down arrows provided by AutoFilter will not hide the field names in the header. The filtering operations available are:

- **Sort ascending** – sorts the records so that the data in the selected field are in ascending order.
- **Sort descending** – sorts the records so that the data in the selected field are in descending order.
- **Sort by Color** – sorts by colors.
- **Number Filters or Text Filters–** sorts by various rules, **Top 10** (see *Figure A-15*), **Above Average, Below Average,** and **Custom Filter. Top 10** is not provided in **Text Filters**.

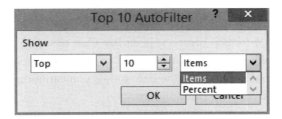

Figure A-15

Top 10 AutoFilter

Custom AutoFilter

- Allows you to create a customized filter with up to two criteria, which can be combined by either an **AND** or **OR** logical operator (see *Figure A-16*).
- The criteria include:

o Equals	o Begins with
o Does not equal	o Does not begin with
o Is greater than	o Ends with
o Is greater than or equal to	o Does not end with
o Is less than	o Contains
o Is less than or equal to	o Does not contain

- Allows you to use wildcards such as **?** and ***** to represent any single character or a string of characters, respectively.
- For example, we may want to filter for members whose ages ranged between 30 and 39. You can set the filter for criteria as "**Is greater than or equal to**" 30 **AND** "**Is less than**" 40.

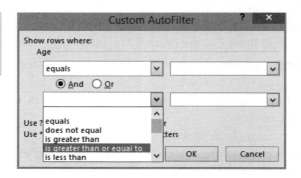

Figure A-16

Custom AutoFilter

Advanced Filter

Consider now that the club would like to remind its members who have joined for at least one year to collect a special gift. The filtering criteria to set up could be to compare their *Date Joined* with a date that is one year ago from today. If their *Date Joined* is less than or equal to this date (which means it is earlier than or equal to this date), then the member would have joined for at least one year. As this threshold date (one year ago from today) is a value that depends on the date today, you cannot use **Custom Autofilter**. You will have to use **Advanced Filter**.

In this example as shown in *Figure A-17*, you can set up the spreadsheet model as follows:

1. The criteria range is defined in rows 4 and 5, where row 4 contains the selected field labels as a header and row 5 contains the criteria values for the corresponding fields. The field label to use in the filtering is *Date Joined*, and the criteria value is set up as a formula in cell G5 as ="<=" & TEXT(G2,"d MMM yyyy"), where cell G2 contains the date for one year ago from today.
2. When the advanced filter is activated, by selecting **Data/Filter/Advanced Filter**, the dialog prompts for:
   - **List Range** – the data list range, here defined in B8:G20.
   - **Criteria Range** – the criteria range, here defined in B4:G5.
   - **Action** – the user has the choice to filter the list in its original place by hiding records that do not match the filtering criteria, or to copy the filtered results to another location.

- o **Copy to** – the destination location, if the user selects to copy the filtered results to another location.
- o **Unique records only** – the user checks this check box to hide duplicate records.

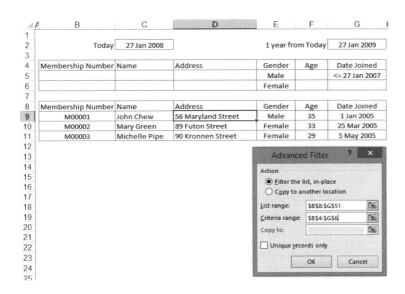

Figure A-17

Advanced Filter

Here are some rules to follow when using Advanced Filter:

1. There must be at least one empty row separating the criteria range and data list range.
2. There must be at least one field header in the criteria range that matches a field header in the data list range.
3. Criteria field labels can be arranged in any order in their header and they need not be directly above the corresponding field label in the data list header.
4. An empty criteria field value implies no match restriction for the field.
5. All field entries in the criteria range are combined within a row by the **AND** operator, and criteria of multiple rows are combined across rows by the **OR** operator. For example, in the criteria table in cells B4:G6 in *Figure A-17*, we have two filtering criteria rows, where the first criterion row of male *Gender* member AND *Date Joined* earlier than or at 27 January 2007 is OR to the second criterion of any member who is of the female *Gender*. All records that match the second set of criteria will be appended to records that match the first set of criteria.
6. Do not include an empty criteria row unless your intent is for Advanced Filter to show all records in the data list.

Database Functions

Filtering data in a **data list** hides some of the data. When you use functions such as **COUNT**, **SUM**, **AVERAGE**, and **STDEV**, the statistics they provide include all the values, including those that have been filtered out.

Like **COUNTIF** and **SUMIF** types of functions, there are also **DAVERAGE**, **DMAX** and other database functions that allow you to compute the results of the data under the specified field (i.e., the header label or equivalent, the column position in the table) that complies with the criteria you give, as is done in **Advanced Filter**. In all these functions, the data in the table are all visible to the user. To filter and then compute the results for the filtered data, you have to use the **SUBTOTAL** function.

SUBTOTAL(*functionNum, range1, range2, ...*)

Depending on the value you specify for *functionNum*, SUBTOTAL returns a statistics of the values in cells *range1, range2*, etc. These ranges have to be columns and you can have up to 254 ranges. If the cells are in a data list where the data may be filtered, the statistics you collect can be made to either include or ignore the hidden values as given by *functionNum*. *functionNum* constants ranging from number 1 to 11 will include hidden values and from 101 to 111 will ignore hidden values, as follows:

Function Number (includes hidden values)	Function Number (ignores hidden values)	Function
1	101	AVERAGE
2	102	COUNT
3	103	COUNTA
4	104	MAX
5	105	MIN
6	106	PRODUCT
7	107	STDEV
8	108	STDEVP
9	109	SUM
10	110	VAR
11	111	VARP

Rows or columns you hide using the **Row Hide** or **Column Hide** format commands are not considered by SUBTOTAL as hidden.

Pivot Table

PivotTable and **PivotChart** help us to create table and chart reports with automatic computation of certain results of interest, such as sum and average, and organize the results according to different attributes. The attributes can be in rows, columns, or pages. Consider the sales performance of a small flower shop for three months as shown in *Figure A-18*. There, sales figure for different product and customer types are given for the months of January to March. This information would be better organized if January, February, and March are themselves headers. This argument extends to using the individual product types as headers and customer types as headers. The only data entries in the example are really the sales figures. This would be a 3-dimensional table. PivotTable can take the given data to automatically create a table such as the one shown in *Figure A-20*.

	A	B	C	D	E
1					
2		Month	Product Type	Customer Type	Sales
3		January	Flowers	Walk-in	$1,000
4		January	Flowers	Corporate	$2,000
5		January	Gifts	Walk-in	$800
6		January	Gifts	Corporate	$500
7		February	Flowers	Walk-in	$1,500
8		February	Flowers	Corporate	$3,000
9		February	Gifts	Walk-in	$1,000
10		February	Gifts	Corporate	$900
11		March	Flowers	Walk-in	$1,200
12		March	Flowers	Corporate	$2,300
13		March	Gifts	Walk-in	$2,000
14		March	Gifts	Corporate	$1,100

Figure A-18

Data for PivotTable

To create a PivotTable in Excel 2010, put your cursor anywhere in the data list and then select **Insert/PivotTable** or **Insert/PivotChart**:

1. Select **PivotTable** from the drop-down list.
2. Select **Table/Range** in the dialog as shown in *Figure A-19a* and enter the cell reference for the data. If your cursor is in the data list before you proceed with step 1, then it will be automatically selected. You can alternatively choose an external data source and then specify the connection details.
3. A layout template will then be shown, according to your selection, on either the worksheet or a new worksheet with the **PivotTable Field List** on the extreme right, as shown in *Figure A-19b*.

- ○ The field labels from the data source are listed as buttons on the top of the field list.
- ○ Drag these labels, one at a time, into the **Report Filter**, **Row**, **Column**, or **Values** areas according to your preference. In the example shown in *Figure A-19c*, we put *Month* in Report Filter, *Product* in Row, *Customer* in Column, and *Sales* in Values.
- ○ Excel by default selects **Sum of Sales** as the method to compute the *Sales* values in the Values area. Right click on **Sum of Sales** in the table and select **Value Field Settings** to show another dialog for you to change the computation method. The options available include **Count**, **Average**, **Max**, and **Min**, as shown in *Figure A-19d*. Click **OK** when done
- ○ If you prefer, you can change the PivotTable to the classic layout, as is used in Excel 2003. This will allow you to drag and drop the fields directly into the PivotTable itself and also allow more direct changes to the data computation method. To do this, right-click on any cell in the PivotTable and select **PivotTable Options**. In the dialog as shown in *Figure A-19e*, click the **Display** tab and then check **Classic PivotTable layout**. The PivotTable created is shown in *Figure A-20*.
- ○ To add a **PivotChart** after a PivotTable is done, put your cursor anywhere in the data list and then select **Options/PivotChart** from the menu. The PivotChart created is shown in *Figure A-21*.

Figure A-19a

Create PivotTable

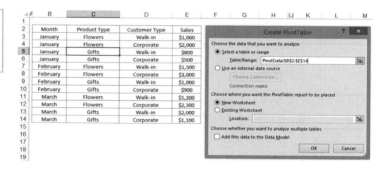

Figure A-19b

PivotTable Field List

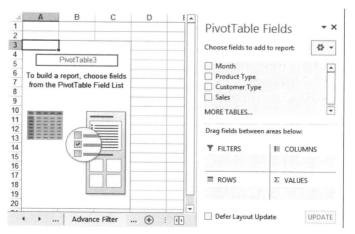

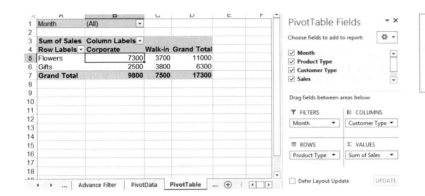

Figure A-19c

Layout for PivotTable

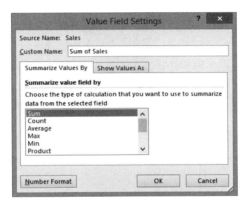

Figure A-19d

Changing the Data Field Computation

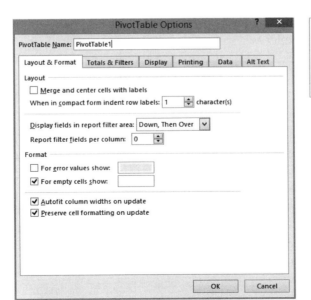

Figure A-19e

Changing to Classic Layout

Figure A-20

PivotTable

	A	B	C	D
1	Month	(All)		
2				
3	**Sum of Sales**	**Column Labels**		
4	**Row Labels**	**Corporate**	**Walk-in**	**Grand Total**
5	Flowers	7300	3700	11000
6	Gifts	2500	3800	6300
7	**Grand Total**	**9800**	**7500**	**17300**

Figure A-21

PivotChart

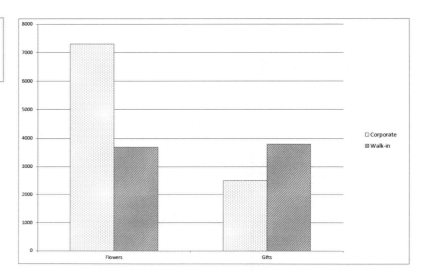

Put your cursor anywhere in your PivotTable and right-click your mouse. The pop-up side menu gives you the options to refresh the data, change refresh intervals, set up column and row totals, and others. You can try working with PivotTable in the *Grand Grocery* exercise in Chapter 8.

Note 12: TARGET AND OPTIMIZATION

Goal Seek

We are all too familiar with computing outputs for given inputs. **Goal Seek** is a spreadsheet operation that allows us to work backwards to find the value of a single input variable that gives the desired value for an output variable. The input variable cell contains only a value, while the output variable cell contains a formula. This inverse operation is done in the background by Excel using iterative calculations, much like what one would do by trial and error but smarter. You therefore do not have to change the formulas in the cells to achieve this. You can access the operation by selecting **Data/Data Tools/What-If Analysis/Goal Seek**.

Consider the same flower shop incurring a fixed cost of $100 and a variable cost of $5 for each flower bouquet sold. Selling price for each bouquet is $8. How many bouquets must this shop sell to break even? To answer this question, let us first list the key relationships among the variables:

- Profit = Total Revenue – Total Cost
- Total Revenue = Unit Price * Number of Units Sold
- Total Cost = Fixed Cost + (Unit Cost * Number of Units Sold)
- To break even, Total Revenue = Total Cost or Profit = 0

As shown in *Figure A-22*, to find the breakeven price, you can use Goal Seek to set the profit in cell F3 to a target value of 0, by changing the number of bouquets sold in cell E3. Goal Seek will compute and leave the breakeven price in cell E3. In this case, we could have easily manipulated the equations to determine the solution directly. However, there will be many other cases where this is not so easy. Even when it is, maintaining two sets of formulas, one in the forward direction and another in reverse, is troublesome.

It is important to note that the underlying Goal Seek algorithm may not converge in its search. Another complication is that there may be more than one solution for the problem posed. The input variable initial value therefore needs to be set appropriately so that the search may end within a reasonable time and find the desired result. To set limits on the search, in case it does not converge fast enough if at all, click **File/Options/Formulas**. In the **Calculation options** panel, set the maximum iterations and maximum change parameter values. If the number of iterations taken by Goal Seek exceeds the specified maximum iterations, the search ends without a solution.

The algorithm ends successfully when the difference between the results of two consecutive iterations is less than the specified maximum change. The algorithm will converge faster when a larger maximum change parameter value is used, at the expense of lower precision in the solution value. You do not normally need to change the default values. These parameters are also applicable to **Iterative Calculations**, which is a topic explored in the *Charity Donation* exercise in Chapter 4.

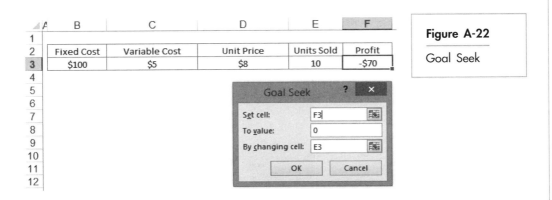

Figure A-22

Goal Seek

Solver

Solver is available as a standard **Add-in** in Excel. It can do the operation of **Goal Seek** and more. First, you can use it to search for the values of many input variables that give the desired value for an output variable. This is an improvement over Goal Seek that permits only one input variable. Next, Solver allows you to find the maximum or minimum value of an output variable (commonly referred to as the *objective function*) subject to the constraints you specify. These constraints can include lower and upper limits on individual input values or their combinations (e.g., budget constraints). Solver only becomes available in Excel after you activate it as an **add-in**. You do this by ticking **Solver Add-in** option in **File/Options/Add-ins/Excel Add-ins/Go**.

Solver uses mathematical programming methods to determine the solution. These include linear programming, nonlinear programming, integer programming, and combinatorial optimization. In all such optimizations, there are five possible result outcomes:

- The solution found is the unique optimal solution.
- The solution found is one of the many local optimal solutions.
- The solution found is a point of inflection, i.e., neither a minima nor a maxima.
- The minimum (maximum) solution found is $-\infty$ $(+\infty)$.
- There are no feasible solutions.

Consider a simple problem faced by a machine shop, as shown in *Figure A-23*. This machine shop is planning to acquire two types of machines. Machine type 1 costs $100 and has a production capacity of 20 units, while machine type 2 costs $150 and has a production capacity of 30 units. If the budget for acquiring these machines is $30,000 and the ratio of machine type 1 to machine type 2 must be less than or equal to 0.75, how many of each machine type should the machine shop purchase in order to maximize its total production capacity?

Figure A-23

Solver

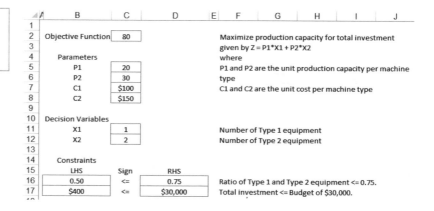

To solve this problem using Solver, we can set up the Excel model as follows:

1. Objective function
    o   This equation defines the objective of the problem, which is to be minimized or maximized.
    o   In this example, cell C2 with the formula =C5*C11+C6*C12 has the *objective function*, computing the total production capacity for the given number of machines. This cell value is to be maximized.
2. Decision variables
    o   These input variables of the model can be binary, integer, or real values.
    o   In this example, they are variables X1 and X2 in cells C11 and C12, for the number of machine type 1 and type 2, respectively.
3. Constraints
    o   These equations specify their left-hand side to be <=, >=, or = to their right-hand side. The right-hand side is usually a resource limit value.
    o   Before you can enter constraints into Solver, you need to set up the left-hand-side and right-hand-side cells to store their values or formulas.
    o   In the above example, there are two constraints. The first is the ratio of machine constraint, where the left-hand-side cell B16 has the formula =C11/C12 and the right-hand-side cell D16 has the value 0.75.
    o   The second is the budget constraint, where the left-hand-side cell B17 has the formula =C7*C11+C8*C12 and the right-hand-side cell D17 has the value $30,000.

Once the model is set up, click **Data/Analysis/Solver**, to activate the **Solver Parameters** dialog as shown in *Figure A-24* and make the following selections:

1. Set **Target Cell** to C2.
2. Select **Max** as the objective criterion.
3. Enter **By Changing Cells** as C11:C12.
4. Add constraint B16:B17 <= D16:D17.
5. Click **Solve**.

If the problem is well defined, the initial values of the decision variables in **By Changing Cells** are reasonable and the number of decision variables and constraints are not exceedingly large, an optimal solution will soon be found.

The termination parameters for the number of iterations and maximum change can be found by clicking **Options** in the **Solver Parameters** dialog. You do not normally need to change their default values. Without going into **Options**, Excel 2010 lets you set unconstrained variables non-negative and select the solving method. The solving methods available include GRG Nonlinear, Simplex LP and Evolutionary.

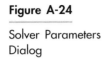

Figure A-24

Solver Parameters Dialog

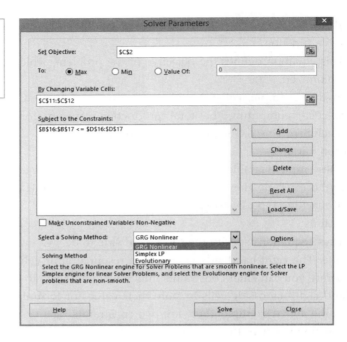

Note 13: DATA ANALYSIS

Analysis Toolpak

Analysis Toolpak is a standard **Add-in** in Excel that supports statistical data analysis. The analysis tools available as shown in Figure A-25 include random number generation, frequency tabulation, test of hypothesis, and analysis of variance. Analysis Toolpak only becomes available in Excel after you activate it as an add-in. You do this by selecting **Analysis Toolpak** in **File/Options/Add-ins/Excel Add-ins/Go**. To access it, select **Data/Data Analysis**. The dialog that appears will be as shown in Figure A-25.

Figure A-25

Data Analysis Dialog

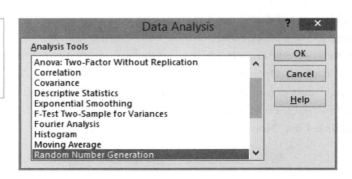

These tools are however computer programs that will take data from your worksheet for their computation and then post the required results back into the worksheet as values. As such, they are static tools and do not work interactively with the rest of the spreadsheet in a dynamic manner. Updates in cell values from changes in data inputs and formula recalculations will not be automatically recomputed by these analysis tools. To compute more dynamic results, you need to use the equivalent Excel functions when they exist. More functions should be added by Excel in future revisions or you may search for add-ins that can provide these functions.

Statistical Functions

The functions in Excel that currently support statistical analysis include **AVERAGE, STDEV, MIN, MAX, PERCENTILE, RANK, INTERCEPT, SLOPE, TREND, GROWTH, RSQ, NORMDIST, EXPONDIST, FDIST, CORREL, CHITEST, CONFIDENCE, ZTEST, TTEST, FTEST**, and **LINEST**. You can call up these functions by clicking the *fx* button in the **Formula** bar and select the **Statistical** category. You can refer to **Help** in Excel to examine in detail how they work.

The most complex function in this list is probably **LINEST**. Array function LINEST(*knownY's, knownX's, [const], [stats]*) returns the statistics that describe the *least squares method* for fitting a straight line to the given data set comprising *knownY's* and *knownX's*. It is called an array function because it returns results, not in a single cell but, in a range of cells. If the optional variable *const* is TRUE or omitted, the intercept value is computed. Otherwise, the intercept value is assumed to be 0. If the optional *stats* is TRUE, four additional rows of statistics are computed. If FALSE or omitted, then only the coefficients and the intercept of the fitted straight line are computed.

The example in *Figure A-26* illustrates the use of LINEST. The formula for range H3:K7 is {=LINEST(E3:E14,B3:D14,,TRUE)}. To key in the formula, first select all the cells that are to display the results. If *stats* is FALSE or omitted, this means one row and number of X's plus 1 (for the Y) columns are to be selected. If *stats* is TRUE, this means 5 rows and number of X's plus 1 (for the Y) columns are to be selected. Key the formula

	B	C	D	E		G	H	I	J	K	L	
1												
2	X1	X2	X3	Y			Coeff3	Coeff2	Coeff1	Intercept		
3	1	1	1	$1,000		Slope =	383.33	-783.33	287.50	1466.67	= Intercept	
4	1	1	2	$2,000		Std Error =	353.92	353.92	216.73	884.80	= Std Error of Intercept	
5	1	2	1	$800		R² =	0.4947	613.01	#N/A	#N/A	= Std Error of MSFT	
6	1	2	2	$500		F stats =	2.6105	8	#N/A	#N/A	= Degree of Freedom	
7	2	1	1	$1,500		SS_pq =	2942917	3006250	#N/A	#N/A	= SSE = Residual sum of errors	
8	2	1	2	$3,000								
9	2	2	1	$1,000								
10	2	2	2	$900								
11	3	1	1	$1,200								
12	3	1	2	$2,300								
13	3	2	1	$2,000								
14	3	2	2	$1,100								

Figure A-26

LINEST Statistics

=LINEST(E3:E14,B3:D14,,TRUE), without the { } brackets and then key **Shift + Ctrl + Enter**. Brackets { } are provided automatically by Excel to indicate that it is an array function (that is, with Shift + Ctrl + Enter applied).

It is interesting to note that the **DataTable** operation is depicted by Excel as an array function. If you put your cursor in any result cell in a DataTable, you will find displayed in the **Formula** bar the formula {=Table(*rowInputCell, colInputCell*)}, with the distinctive { } brackets. It is however not possible to invoke the DataTable as a function, just as it can be done for LINEST. The only way to call a DataTable is to use the Excel menu and enter inputs into the DataTable dialog.

Array Formulas

Array formulas do not have to involve array functions. They all have the distinctive { } brackets, which arise after you type in the formula with **Shift + Ctrl + Enter**, instead of the usual **Enter** key. Many interesting computations can be done as array formulas and they usually give spreadsheet models that are more compact. If you understand array formulas, such models may in fact be easier to comprehend. *Figure A-27* shows two ways for computing the errors of forecasting variable Y using a linearly fitted equation given by the coefficients and intercept values from *Figure A-26*.

Cell G17 gives the average absolute deviations, comparing each value in cells E3:E14 with the corresponding forecast in G3:G14. Similarly, G18 gives the maximum absolute deviation. The same results can be found in cells G21 and G22. The formula for cell G21 is {=AVERAGE(ABS($E$3:$E$14−$G$3:$G$14))} and for cell G22 is {=MAX(ABS($E$3:$E$14−$G$3:$G$14))}. These formulas do not reference the values in

Figure A-27

Array Formulas

	X1	X2	X3	Y		Forecast	Absolute Deviation
2	X1	X2	X3	Y		Forecast	Absolute Deviation
3	1	1	1	$1,000		$1,354	$354
4	1	1	2	$2,000		$1,738	$263
5	1	2	1	$800		$571	$229
6	1	2	2	$500		$954	$454
7	2	1	1	$1,500		$1,642	$142
8	2	1	2	$3,000		$2,025	$975
9	2	2	1	$1,000		$858	$142
10	2	2	2	$900		$1,242	$342
11	3	1	1	$1,200		$1,929	$729
12	3	1	2	$2,300		$2,313	$13
13	3	2	1	$2,000		$1,146	$854
14	3	2	2	$1,100		$1,529	$429

Mean Absolute Deviation	$410	=AVERAGE($H$3:$H$14)
Maximum Absolute Deviation	$975	=MAX($H$3:$H$14)

Array Formulas

Mean Absolute Deviation	$410	{=AVERAGE(ABS($E$3:$E$14−$G$3:$G$14))}
Maximum Absolute Deviation	$975	{=MAX(ABS($E$3:$E$14−$G$3:$G$14))}

cells H3:H14 and therefore do not need them to be computed if these array formulas are used instead of those in cells G17 and G18.

Even though both G21 and G22 are single cells, array formulas have to be used because of the calculations involved. Let us examine these formulas in detail. The first computation step in these formulas is $E$3:$E$14–$G$3:$G$14, which means $E$3–$G$3, $E$4–$G$4, ..., and $E$14–$G$14. These 12 values form an array, on which we next apply the **ABS** function to find absolute differences. The results are collectively still an array. The functions **AVERAGE** or **MAX** are then applied on this array. In general, array formulas involve array subcomputation results or array functions and can, but do not necessarily need to, have array results.

Note 14: EXCEL 2010 VS. EXCEL 2003 In case you are still using Excel 2003 or older versions of Excel and considering migrating to Excel 2010 or newer versions, here is a quick summary comparing Excel 2010 to Excel 2003. First, the worksheet in Excel 2010, as in Excel 2007, is now much larger with 1,048,576 rows and 16,384 columns (A to XFD). It can handle more than the 1 GB memory limit in Excel 2003, constrained only by the memory allocated by your computer operating system.

Other than larger memory, some features are also extended. For example, cells can now have **Conditional Formatting** beyond the previous three conditions. There are many more new and easy-to-use features like **Data Bars**, **Color Scales**, and **Icon Sets**. There is also now a **Rules Manager** that allows you to manage the conditional formatting of the cells in the worksheet all at once. The IF function can now be nested up to 63 levels, much more than the 7-level limit in Excel 2003 and earlier versions. **COUNTIF**, which allows only one criteria range and criteria pair, has an extended version called **COUNTIFS**. This new function can cater up to 127 criteria range and criteria pairs. There are also the **SUMIFS, AVERAGEIF, AVERAGEIFS,** and other new functions.

The main difference between the Excel versions is the menu system, which has been reorganized. The **File** tab in the extreme top-left corner now provides access to **New**, **Open**, **Save**, **Print**, and other file management tools. Author's name and organization information are entered in **Info/Properties**. Note that **F1** is still the **Help** key. **Help** can also be accessed by clicking the **?** icon in the top-right corner of the menu. Above the File tab is the **Quick Access** toolbar, where you can put the icons of the tools you frequently use but are not available in the main menu. Placed there by default are **Save, Undo**, and **Redo**.

Instead of vertical drop-down menus to the main menu items as in Excel 2003, Excel 2010 has made the main menu items into tabs in the **Ribbon**, which organize the tools in groups horizontally. The **Home** and **Page Layout** tabs, the first and third tabs, cover most of the cell and worksheet formatting work.

The second **Insert** tab has the **PivotTable, Pictures, Charts, Hyperlinks**, and **Text** groups of tools, all largely related graphics features. **Formulas** is a whole menu item (tab) by itself, focusing mostly on cell calculation features. Listed here are also the **Define Names, Formula Auditing**, and **Calculation** tools. Data access from external sources and **Data Sort, Filter, Validation**, and **Analysis** tools are in the **Data** tab.

In the **Data Tools** group of the Data tab, there is a **What-If Analysis** button. **Scenario Manager, Goal Seek**, and **Data Table** now reside somewhat obscurely here. **Solver** is now grouped with **Data Analysis Tools** in the **Analysis** group, the last in this tab. This group is only present if it had first been added. To add **Solver**, click File tab, then **Options** (at the bottom) and **Add-ins** option group. In the **Manage** box, select **Excel Add-ins** and click **Go**. Check **Solver**. You might as well at the same time tick **Analysis Toolpak**, and then click **OK**.

Comments and **Protection** features are now under the **Review** tab. **Custom Views**, worksheet gridlines and header options, window split, freeze and zoom, and access to macros are now in the **View** tab. More useful and interesting features can be added. For example, to use text-to-speech commands, you need to get to **Quick Access Toolbar**. To do this, click the **Customize Quick Access Toolbar** icon, which is just next to **Quick Access Toolbar**. Click **More Commands**. In the **Choose** commands from list, select **All Commands**. Scroll down to find **Speak Cells**, click **Add**, and click **OK**.

Many of the option settings previously found in **Tools/Options** of the main menu in Excel 2003 are now more remotely placed in **File** tab. The settings there have to be initialized to your preference, at least once after installing Excel. To do this in Excel 2010, click **File/Options**. For Excel 2010 users, macros are now found in the View tab. The **Developer** tab is by default turned off. To make the Developer tab appear, select **File/Option/Customize Ribbon**. In the right panel, check the **Developer** box.

Now, review other option groups carefully, one at a time. Here are some more suggestions. In **Formula**, set workbook calculation to **Automatic** and disable **Iterative Calculation**. In **Proofing**, set the language dictionary to your preferred language. In **Save**, set your preferred **Auto Recovery** time intervals and file locations. Next in **Trust**, click **Trust Center Settings** and then **Macro Settings**. Select the option to show the message bar when active contents have been blocked.

Finally, you can open Excel 2003 files (named with extensions xls, xlt, and xla) in Excel 2010. After working on them, Excel 2010 will by default still save them in their original format. A new workbook started in Excel 2010 will on the other hand by default be saved in the Excel 2007 format (named with extensions xlsx, xlsm, xltx, xltm, or xlam). It can still be **Save As** into a file of one of the earlier formats. You may encounter some incompatibility difficulties working in Excel 2010 when the workbooks are in Excel 2003 format. A particular one to note is that when you use Excel 2010 features that do not exist in Excel 2003, the changes may not be saved. Therefore, you will soon want to convert your current Excel files to the new Excel 2007 format.

A special point to note in the file format migration is that while all **xls** files can be **Saved As** to become **xlsx** files, those with macros will have their macros stripped away. To retain the codes, you will have to convert workbooks with macros into **xlsm** files, with **m** for macro. Similarly, Excel template files with macros should be saved as **xltm** files. By definition, all Excel **Add-in** files have macros and thus they have to be **xlam** files. This thus explains the larger collection of new extensions in the format introduced with Excel 2007.

Note 15: MIGRATING TO LIBREOFFICE CALC

Calc is the spreadsheet in LibreOffice (LO). LibreOffice branched from OpenOffice.org (OOo; now renamed OpenOffice or OO in short), and thus retains most of its features and functionalities. It has a user-interface practically the same as that of Excel 2003:

Here are a few minor differences between Excel and LO Calc 4:

- **Align**, **Group**, **Flip**, and other graphics manipulation tools found in Excel 2003's **Drawing Toolbar** are in the **Format** menu. **Snap to grid** is found in **Tools/Options/ LibreOffice Calc/Grid**.

- **Conditional Formatting** in Calc is similar to Excel 2003's. Calc uses **Formatting Styles** and you need to create the style if you are not using the standard ones.

- Arguments in Excel functions are separated by commas; the ones in OO Calc 3 are separated by semi-colons. LO Calc 4 allows you to set the separator, which by default is now a comma.

- **Formula Auditing** is called **Detective** in Calc.

- **PivotTable** in Excel is called **DataPilot** in OO Calc3. In LO Calc 4, it has the same name as in Excel.

- **Solver** is directly available in Calc, but the tool is possibly not as rich or mature as the **add-in** in Excel.

- The equivalent **macro** language in Calc is LibreOffice **Basic** (updated from **StarBasic and** OOo **Basic**) that, like **Visual Basic** (VB) used in Excel, is derived from the same underlying **BASIC** programming language. It however uses a different object library to access spreadsheet components. **VBA** codes are ported over automatically when Excel files are opened as LO Basic codes in Calc.

- LibreOffice will insert an additional `Option VBASupport 1` line at the start of each module. This enables your Excel VBA codes to run in the LO Basic environment. However, not all the spreadsheet features can be manipulated in LO Basic yet. The good news is that **Solver** can be called in LO Basic to automate model optimization.

- To give a sense of the differences in the macro codes, here is an example of the same program written in the two languages:

```
Sub VBA_Example()
  Range("B3").Select
  Range("B3") = "Hello"
End Sub

Sub LOBasic_Example()
  oSheet = ThisComponent.CurrentController.ActiveSheet
  oCell = oSheet.getCellRangeByName("B3")
  ThisComponent.CurrentController.select(oCell)
  oCell.String = "Hello"
End Sub
```

APPENDIX

B

Visual Basic for Application

INTRODUCTION

Visual Basic for Application (or **VBA** in short) is the accompanying programming interface that is tightly coupled with Excel to perform more advanced automation. It has as its backbone the **Visual Basic** (VB) programming language and added elements to permit it to interact with the component objects of Excel (and also other applications in the MS Office suite). BASIC is the name of the programming language, and not that it is easy or elementary. To access the **Integrated Development Environment** (IDE), select **Developer/ Visual Basic** (or **Tools/Macro/Visual Basic Editor** in Excel 2003), or simply key **Alt + F11**. The IDE of Excel 2007 to Excel 2013 is the same as that of Excel 2003. There is therefore only one appendix reference for all recent Excel versions. Where needed, version-specific comments will be made.

Once invoked, a separate application window as shown in *Figure B-1* will be displayed.

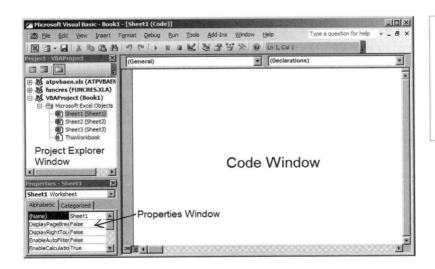

Figure B-1

Visual Basic Editor and Integrated Development Environment

Let us now review the elements of the IDE:

- In the top-left corner, you will see a **Project Explorer** window that displays a tree diagram of all the opened Excel files (now referred to as **Projects**). Within each project, there are **Excel Objects** such as **Workbook** and **Worksheet**, **Excel Add-ins**, **UserForm**, **Module**, and **Class Module**.

- To the right, you will see the **Code Window**. This displays the macro code in your active **Excel Object**, **UserForm**, or **Module**. It is a good practice to put codes related to each object in the object when it is not shared with others.

- In the bottom-left corner, you will see a **Properties** window. This allows you to set the properties of the selected object. For example, we can change the name of a **Worksheet** or the caption of a **UserForm**. This name is not the same as the name of the worksheet in the spreadsheet application. This window, and others, can be opened by selecting **View** in the menu. It is best to maximize the Code Window and close all other windows except the Project Explorer.

- In the **Debug** and **Run** items of the menu, there are features that you can use to support your macro development work. The first is **Compile**. As you amend your code, you may make syntax or "grammatical" mistakes in using VBA. Just select **Debug/Compile** to request the IDE to compile your code and surface the syntax errors. The IDE also highlights syntax errors made as you type your code.

- The IDE provides an **Object Browser** as a reference for programmers. Click **Object Browser** to list all the objects at your disposal. You can click on each object class and see the members (i.e., properties, methods, and events associated with them). If you click on an object class or one of its members and then key **F1**, the syntax notes and use examples will appear in a **Help Window**. Similarly, as you review or type your macro code, you can select a key word and key F1 to get help on it.

- To run your macro, select **Run/Run Macro** from the menu or just click the **Run** button. This will run the macro your cursor is currently at in a VBA module. If you run into an error, you need to click **Reset** before you can run another macro again.

- Before you run the macro you have written or edited, it will be wise to step through it first. This is to run the macro one line at a time, as if in slow motion. To do this, select **Debug/Step Into** or just key **F8**. A marker on the left of the code and the line highlighted in yellow indicate which code line it is at.

- A macro may call another macro. If you step into a line with a macro call, it will take you into the called macro. You can skip this line when you come to it by selecting **Debug/Step Over** or keying **Shift + F8** to stay in your current macro. After you are satisfied with your code review and testing, you can select **Debug/Step Out** or key **Ctrl + Shift + F8** to run the remaining lines of code and finish the test run.

- To run multiple lines of code, faster than one step at a time, you can introduce breakpoints to it. Move your cursor to a critical line of code and select **Debug/Toggle BreakPoint** or key **F9**. You can continue to mark as many breakpoints as you desire. You can switch them off by repeating the same steps. With breakpoints introduced, when you run your code, it will pause at the next breakpoint.

- The values of the variables in your macro change as you process the code, in compliance with the processing it is supposed to do. To better understand what is happening in your code, you would want to watch the variable during each stage of the processing. Select a variable that you want to watch and select **Debug/Quick Watch** or key **Shift + F9**. You can keep doing this for as many variables as you like, one at a time.

- In the bottom-right corner of the IDE, you will find the **Watch Window**. As you run or step through your macro, the variables and their current values will be displayed there.

- When you edit and test your macro, remember to use the **Save** button often to save your work. Sometimes, for example, when the macro runs into an infinite loop and crashes the IDE, all of your work may be irrecoverably lost.

FURTHER REFERENCES

- Dalton, 2007. *Financial Applications using Excel Add-in Development in C/C++*, Second edition, Wiley Finance.
- Frye, Freeze, and Buckingham, 2004. *MS Excel 2003 Programming: Inside Out*, Microsoft Press.
- Green, Bullen, Martins, and Johnson, 1999. *Excel 2000 VBA: Programming Reference*, Wrox.
- Leong, 2014. Excel VBA Web Resources
  - http://isotope.unisim.edu.sg/users/tyleong/SpreadsheetModeling.htm#VBA
  - http://dl.dropboxusercontent.com/u/19228704/SpreadsheetModeling.htm#VBA
- Microsoft Office Developer site
  - http://msdn.microsoft.com/en-us/office
- Walkenbach, 2013. *Excel VBA Programming for Dummies*, Third edition, Wiley.

EXCEL VBA PRIMER

For non-VB programmers, macro recording is the fastest way to perform simple automation within Excel. It is the simplest form of VBA programming in that you do not need to know how to write a single line of code. The codes can be automatically created. All you have to do is to record your keyboard and mouse actions as you work on a spreadsheet. The saved sequence of commands representing the executed keystrokes and mouse movement is a macro. It is also alternatively called a program, though this is generally codes that are directly written by a programmer. The recorded macro will be coded as a **Sub procedure** (or better known as subroutine) in a **Module**. The actions, once recorded, can be repeated by running the macro.

However, in many cases, superfluous garbage codes are recorded as well. There are also some actions that cannot be coded by recording alone. Therefore, simple editing is sometimes needed to make the recorded macro work better. We will cover more on VBA programming in later sections when we discuss about editing and writing the codes. For now, it is sufficient to know that macro recording is an extremely convenient way to capture VB codes that interact with Excel, saving users the need to think hard about how to code these spreadsheet actions.

Nothing beats learning from interesting and practical examples. There are many examples of them in the exercises and tools in this book. Look out for those Excel 2007 (and later versions) workbooks with the *xlsm* extension in their file names. Particularly worth an extra mention are the completed projects and tools in *Chapter 9*, especially the *Useful Macros* tool.

NOTES

Note 16: MACRO RECORDING   Let us now do a simple macro recording and then attempt to read and understand the codes created.

Example: Record a macro to do automatic copying and pasting of values

1. In a new workbook, select **Developer/Record Macro** (or **Tools/Macro/Record new macro . . .** in Excel 2003).
2. A **Record Macro** dialog box as shown in *Figure B-2* will appear. Enter the macro name of your choice, assign a shortcut key (if needed), select where to store the macro (the default location being the current workbook), and finally enter a short description. For this example, we will accept all the given defaults.
3. Click **OK**. Once it is clicked, whatever actions you do with your mouse or keyboard, such as selecting a cell or scrolling up and down the worksheet, will be recorded as codes. [In Excel 2003, a small **Stop Recording** dialog (or toolbar) will appear when macro recording starts. It has two buttons, the **Stop Recording** button on the left and the **Relative Reference** button on the right. You should never click the dialog-close (**X**) button in the upper right-hand corner as this will make the dialog box disappear. If you ever make that mistake, you can recover the dialog box by selecting from the main menu **View/Toolbars**, and then select **Stop Recording**.]
4. Deactivate the **Use Relative References** button if it is activated, select cells B2:B5. Right-click and select **Copy** in the pop-up side menu (as shown in *Figure B-3*).
5. Select cell C2 (by either clicking with the mouse or keying the right-arrow on the keyboard), right-click, and then select **Paste**.
6. Click the **Stop Recording** button to end the process.

Once recorded, the macro can be used over and over again. To run the macro, select **Developer/Macros** (or **Tools/Macro/Macros...** in Excel 2003) or key **Alt + F8** and select the macro to run.

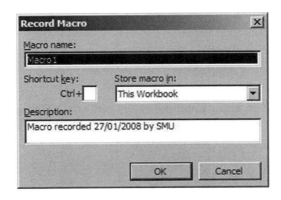

Figure B-2

Macro
Recording Dialog

Figure B-3

Step 4 of Macro Recording

Figure B-4

Codes for Macro1

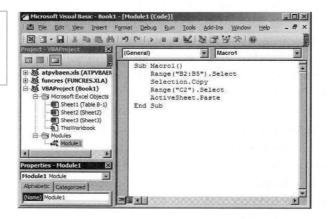

Next, let us review and understand the codes you have recorded.

1. Key **Alt + F11** to launch the **VB Editor** (VBE) interface.

2. Select **Module1** and **Macro1** to show the codes in the **Code Window**, as shown in *Figure B-4*.

3. The codes begin with `Sub Macro1( )` and end with `End Sub`. These mark the beginning and the end of the subroutine.

4. Within the subroutine,

   a. Line 1 = Cell range B2:B5 is selected.

   b. Line 2 = The selection is copied.

   c. Line 3 = Cell C2 is selected.

   d. Line 4 = The copied selection is pasted with its upper-left corner in the selected cell in the active sheet.

Notice how easy it is to understand the codes generated. One way to speed up your learning of the VBA code and macro recording is to have the Excel and VBE windows opened side by side when you next record your macro. See how each line of code is recorded with each action you do in the Excel window. As an additional check, you can reverse the process and step through the code, making it run one line at a time to watch its action played out on the worksheet. To do this, put your cursor in the subroutine code and select from the VB Editor main menu **Debug/Step Into** (or key **F8**). Keep keying F8 to see how the highlight moves from one line of the code to another as the code is run one step at a time.

Absolute and Relative Referencing

We have covered absolute and relative cell referencing in *Note 3* of Appendix A. When you copy and paste a spreadsheet formula from one cell to another, it automatically adjusts the cell references in the formula unless they have been made **Absolute** using the $ sign. There is a similar concept in macro recording. You should try to keep the **Use Relative References** button deactivated as soon as it is not required so that cell referencing will be absolute by default. What this means is that every selection of a cell would refer to that cell and is not interpreted as some relative movement from the last active cell. You can record the same macro as in the earlier example, but this time, select cell B2 before recording the macro and activate the Use Relative References button in the beginning of the macro (and thereafter remember to set it back). Study the difference between the two approaches.

1. Select **Developer/Record Macro** (or **Tools/Macro/Record new macro...** in Excel 2003).
2. In the dialog box as shown in *Figure B-2*, enter *Macro2* as the macro name, and leave the other inputs as default values.
3. Click **OK**.
4. Activate the **Use Relative References** button. Once activated, you will see an orange shaded border surrounding the button.
5. Select cells B2:B5, right-click, and select **Copy**.
6. Select cell B2 and key the right-arrow on the keyboard. Right-click, select **Paste** from the side menu.
7. Deactivate **Use Relative References**.
8. Click **Stop Recording** to end the process.

   Let us read the codes for Macro2 as shown in *Figure B-5*.

   - Line 1 = A column of four cells from the current active cell is selected. Since cell B2 was selected before the macro was recorded, this means cells B2:B5 is selected. A1:A4 reference here is with respect to the active cell as the origin A1 cell.
   - Line 2 = The selection is copied.
   - Line 3 = A relative offset of zero row down and one column to the right from the active cell (cell B2 in our case) is selected. A1 here denotes only one cell is selected. Movements up and to the left are recorded as negative argument values in `Offset`.
   - Line 4 = The copied selection is pasted into the selected cell.

Figure B-5

Codes for
Macro2

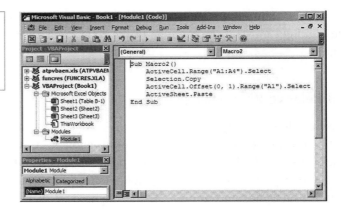

Relative referencing provides greater flexibility as new active cells (to be selected before the macro is run) can be any cell in any worksheet. For this demonstrated macro, it means that we can copy and paste any column of four cells to its immediate right.

Quick Tip 1

- After each copy and paste sequence of operations, Excel leaves behind highlighted cell range selections and dotted box outlines in the worksheet. It is a good housekeeping practice to end your macro with the cursor placed in the appropriate cell and clear away all such unwarranted distractions. In the spreadsheet, just point your mouse to the end cell location and key **Esc**.
- The corresponding macro statements at the end of your Sub are as follows:

```
Range("A1").Select
Application.CutCopyMode = False
```

Note 17: VISUAL BASIC GRAMMAR   So far all the programming we have attempted is by macro recording, letting Excel automatically generate the codes. In order to perform more complex automation, we need to understand the VBA language a little more so that we can directly modify and add lines of code.

Visual Basic for Application is an "object-like," though not fully, object-oriented programming language. Thus it is useful to first understand the hierarchy of objects to better use the properties, methods, and events of the objects. The hierarchy of Excel objects is given as follows:

```
Applications ———┬——— Worksheet Function
                ├——— Add-in
                └——— Workbooks ———┬——— Charts
                                   └——— Sheets ———┬——— Range
                                                   └——— Cells
```

Properties

Each object has its own set of **Properties** that describes it. Some of the properties of the **Range** object include row height, column width, and font.

You can set the width of columns A to E to 10 using the code below:

```
Range("A:E").ColumnWidth = 10
```

In general, any property can be set using the syntax below:

```
Object.Property = Value
```

Methods

Each object also has its own associated set of **Methods,** which are actions that can be performed on it. For example, one of the methods for the **Range** object is **ClearContents**. You can clear the contents of a selected range E4:G7 using the code below:

```
Range("E4:G7").ClearContents
```

In general, any method can be activated using the syntax below:

```
Object.Method
```

Quick Tip 1_____

VBA programming is quite user-friendly. It provides coding help as you type in the code. After you have entered the dot (".") following the object name, a drop-down list will appear as shown in *Figure B-6*, listing all the available properties and methods associated with this object.

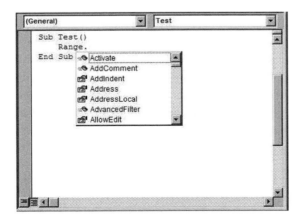

Figure B-6

Drop-down List for Object

When an Excel object (e.g., cell range), is referenced in VBA, this object, unless explicitly coded, is assumed to be in the currently active Excel container (e.g., the active workbook and active worksheet). Therefore, it would suffice to write

```
numCars = Range("C7").Value
```

If you want to be sure that you will be in the right workbook and sheet when the macro is activated, activate and select them first, as shown below:

```
Workbooks("Book1").Activate
Sheets("Sheet1").Activate
numCars = Range("C7")
```

Notice that we have dropped the .Value part since VBA will assume that you are interested in the cell value when that part is missing.

You may need to remember first the active workbook, sheet, and cell, and return there after you are done so that it would not affect other macros. This is done as follows:

```
strActiveDoc = ActiveWorkbook.Name
strActiveSheet = ActiveSheet.Name
strActiveCell = ActiveCell.Address

'The earlier three lines of code here. ----

Workbooks(strActiveDoc).Activate
Sheets(strActiveSheet).Activate
Range(strActiveCell).Select
```

It may be more efficient not to have to move the cursor around the workbooks and sheets and directly work with Excel objects as follows:

```
numCars = Workbooks("Book1").Sheets("Sheet1").Range("C7")
```

Quick Tip 2

The ' sign is the shorthand for REM, the remark or comment key word. All statements that appear after the sign or the keyword will be regarded as mere comments and not code. You can sprinkle your macro with comments to make it easier to understand and read. The other best practice is to indent lines when they are part of another programming structure. In this case, you can see that all statements between Sub and End Sub are indented to show that they are part of the subroutine. You can observe how they are used in other examples later in the chapter.

Similarly, when you record macros, values can only be transferred from one set of cells to another using **Copy** and **PasteSpecial** as shown in *Note 16*. When you edit the macro, rewrite it in VBA to work directly with Excel objects as shown below.

```
dataArray = Range("B2").Resize(4, 1)
Range("C2").Resize(4, 1) = dataArray
```

The above transfers values between two cell ranges. When there are only single cells involved, the code is even simpler:

```
Range("C2").Value = Range("B2").Value
```

Other than transferring data values between cells, you can set formulas in any cell in the spreadsheet as demonstrated below:

```
Range("A12").Formula = "=SUM(A2:A11)"
```

When the choice of cell uses depends on other values, use the **Cells** or **Offset** VBA functions as follows:

```
r = 1 : c = 2
Range("F1").Value = Cells(r, c).Value
Range("F2").Value = Range("A7").Cells(r, c).Value
Range("F3").Value = Range("A7").Offset(r, c).Value
```

The colon (:) is used to separate two statements so that they can be put on a single line. Conversely, the underscore (_) can be used to break a long code statement into separate rows for easier reading. The last three lines above will give different results: `Cells(1,2)` refers to cell B1, `Range("A7").Cells(1,2)` refers to cell B7, and `Range("A7").Offset(1,2)` refers to cell C8.

Sub and Function Procedures

A **Sub** procedure (or subroutine) is a set of codes which when executed performs a series of spreadsheet actions. Each recorded macro is a Sub. You will now learn how to write one. Insert a new **Module** by selecting **Insert/Module** from the VB Editor main menu. Click into the code window and type the following:

```
Sub SayHi( )
  MsgBox("Hi!")
End Sub
```

This is a simple Sub to prompt a greeting. To run it in VB Editor, just put your cursor in the Sub and select **Run/Run Macro** from its main menu (or key **F5**). There is also a **Run Macro** button in the **Standard toolbar** in VB Editor that you can use. Having fun yet?

A **Function** procedure is also a set of codes. However, its primary purpose is to return a result computed with the inputs offered to it. You may have used some of the given spreadsheet functions like **AVERAGE** and **SUM**, and soon you will be able to create more useful functions of your own. Let us begin by writing a simple function to compute the cube root of a number. In order for the function to return the computed value when the function is used, the result variable must bear the function's name, which in this case is *CubeRoot*.

In an empty space in the module you have just inserted, type in the following:

```
Function CubeRoot(number)
  CubeRoot = number^(1/3)
End Function
```

With this done, you can use it in the worksheet. Key in formula =CubeRoot(8) into a cell and see the number 2 appearing in it. All worksheets in the same workbook can use this function. The function you have created can also be used by other Sub and Function procedures in your workbook.

Though a Sub procedure does not directly return computed results, data values can be passed indirectly to and from it through the variable arguments specified within the brackets next to its name, or cells in the worksheets. A subroutine with arguments can only be called by another subroutine and not run from Excel directly as a macro since there is no way to pass the argument values to it that way. We will leave this as a future topic for you to explore on your own.

Variables and Declaration

In many programming software languages, variables to hold values, whether entered or computed, need to be defined first. Each variable must be of a data type, namely integer, real, text, Boolean, array, or object. VBA does not force us to declare all variables before use. Instead, it automatically creates a **Variant** variable type for each variable with type not declared. Although convenient, this implies that more memory storage is set aside for such variables. This bad programming practice is strongly discouraged.

To declare a variable to be of a certain data type, you use the following syntax:

```
Dim variableName As dataType
```

The full list of various data types and their details are given below:

Data Type	Storage Size	Range Values
Byte	1 byte	0 to 255
Boolean	2 bytes	True or False
Integer	2 bytes	–32,768 to 32,767
Long	4 bytes	–2,147,483,648 to 2,147,483,647
Single	4 bytes	–3.402823E38 to –1.401298E-45 for negative values; 1.401298E-45 to 3.402823E38 for positive values
Double	8 bytes	–1.79769313486231E308 to –4.94065645841247E-324 for negative values; 4.94065645841247E-324 to 1.79769313486232E308 for positive values
Currency	8 bytes	–922,337,203,685,477.5808 to 922,337,203,685,477.5807
Decimal	14 bytes	+/–79,228,162,514,264,337,593,543,950,335 with no decimal point; +/–7.9228162514264337593543950335 with 28 places to the right of the decimal; smallest nonzero number is +/–0.0000000000000000000000000001
Date	8 bytes	1 January 0100 to 31 December 9999
Object	4 bytes	Any object reference
String (fixed length)	Length of string	1 to approximately 65,400
String (variable length)	10 bytes + string length	0 to approximately 2 billion
Variant (with numbers)	16 bytes	Any numerical value up to the range of a double
Variant (with characters)	22 bytes + string length	Same range as a variable string length

Source: Table adapted from Microsoft™ Visual Basic 6.3 software, *Help Menu*, Data Summary Table.

Here are some general rules you should follow when declaring variables.

- A variable declared in a procedure is only meaningful for that procedure (i.e., as a a **Local** variable). Another variable of the same name declared within another procedure will be recognized as a different local variable applicable to that procedure only.
- Variables that are to be shared by all procedures within a module should be declared before the first procedure in the module.
- Variables that are shared by procedures in all modules and sheets in a project should be declared using **Public** in place of **Dim**. The declaration should be made before the first procedure in any module in the project. Sometimes, the **Const** keyword is also added after Public to declare the variable as unchanging and permit a value to be assigned to it at the declaration.

Quick Tip 3

- To force yourself to declare all variables used, put `Option Explicit` as the first statement at the very top of your module. With this, VBE will prompt an error whenever an undeclared variable is present.
- Always choose the most suitable data type, one that uses the smallest number of bytes for the variable.

Here is a simple example to help you understand better.

```
Public x as Integer
Public Const gravity as Single = 9.8
Dim y as Long

Sub Mysub()
  Dim z as Single
  Static k as Integer
  k = k + 1
  . . .
End Sub
```

- *x* is declared as an integer variable using the Public keyword and can therefore be used by procedures in all modules.
- *gravity* is declared using the Public Const keywords as a constant parameter, with the value of 9.8 and can be used by procedures in all modules.

- *y* can be used by all procedures within this module because *y* is declared before the first procedure in the module.
- *z* can only be used within procedure *Mysub*.
- *k* is a static variable declared within the procedure, which means that it will retain its value even when current call of the procedure ends. This value is then used by the same procedure the next time it is called. This is useful, for example, when you need to track the number of times the procedure is run.

Quick Tip 4
_____

For a typical declaration statement like `Dim p, q, r As Integer`, only *r* is declared as an integer, while *p* and *q* are variants. This is a common mistake among BASIC programmers.

_____

Declaring Arrays

An array, more commonly known as a matrix, is a group of variables sharing a common name. Arrays can be one-dimensional or multi-dimensional.

An example of a one-dimensional array declared to store the identification number of 200 compact disks is:

```
Dim CD_ID(1 to 200) As Integer
```

An example of a two-dimensional array declared to store the identification number of 1,000 compact disks is:

```
Dim CD_ID(1 to 10, 1 to 100) As integer
```

An array may be declared as a dynamic array which does not have a preset size. Its size can be set later in the procedure using the **ReDim** statement. A simple example is given below:

```
Dim MyArray( ) As Single
Dim ASize As Integer
ASize = Range("A1").Value
ReDim MyArray(ASize)
```

In the above, *MyArray* is first declared with no size specified. Its size is read from cell A1. This array is then sized according to the value in cell A1.

Note 18: MORE PROGRAMMING   Up until this point, you can write simple VBA programs in which all the lines of code are sequentially executed. However, there will be many instances where we would like the program to skip some steps or go directly to one set of steps or another, on satisfying or not satisfying a test condition, respectively. Here are some examples of the most useful ones.

The **GoTo** statement is used when you wish the program to go directly to the start of another block of codes. An example is given below:

```
Sub GotoDemo()
  Rating = InputBox("Enter rating (1 or 2): ")
  If Rating = 1 Then GoTo Ans1
  MsgBox("You have entered 2.")
  Exit Sub
Ans1:
  MsgBox ("You have entered 1.")
End Sub
```

Ans1 here is the label of a line location and it must be suffixed by the : sign. Serious programmers dislike using the GoTo statement because it makes the program unstructured and therefore difficult to follow.

If-Then-Else is one of the most useful statements, which allows the program to execute alternative codes depending on whether the test condition results in a TRUE or FALSE. If the result is TRUE, the codes following **Then** (up to the line containing the **Else** keyword if it exists, or up to **End If** if it does not) will be executed. Otherwise, the codes in the lines following **Else** (up to **End If**) will be executed.

```
If testCondition Then
  doSomethingWhenTrue
Else
  doSomethingWhenFalse
End If
```

An example is given below:

```
Sub IfThenElseDemo()
  Rating = InputBox("Enter rating (1 or 2): ")
  If rating = 1 Then
    MsgBox ("You have entered 1.")
  Else
    MsgBox ("You have entered 2.")
  End If
End Sub
```

Select-Case is useful when the test condition can result in more than two alternatives, thus requiring more paths for the codes to continue the operation.

```
Select Case variableName
  Case value1
    Statement set 1
  Case value2
    Statement set 2
  Case value3
    Statement set 3
End Select
```

An example is given below:

```
Sub SelectCaseDemo()
  Rating = InputBox("Enter rating 1, 2 or 3:")
  Select Case Rating
  Case 1
    MsgBox ("You have entered 1.")
    etc …
  Case 2
    MsgBox ("You have entered 2.")
    etc …
  Case 3
    MsgBox ("You have entered 3.")
    etc …
  End Select
End Sub
```

When you need the program to loop through a set of codes for some number of times, the **For-Next** statement will be very handy. The looping is controlled by a *counter* that will go from a *start* number to an *end* number, increasing by a *stepSize* after each execution of the loop. When not declared, the default step size is 1.

```
For counter = start to end [Step stepSize]
  statements …
Next counter
```

See the example given below:

```
Sub ForNextDemo()
  Dim j As Integer
  For j = 1 to 10
    MsgBox("Hi")
  Next j
End Sub
```

The program above displays the message "Hi" for 10 times, using j as the counter.

A **Do-While** statement is useful when you need the program to loop through a set of codes until a test condition returns a FALSE. Do-While can be used in two slightly different methods.

Method 1: This method tests the condition first, and executes the statement when the condition is tested TRUE. The program ends immediately when the test condition results in a FALSE.

```
Do While testCondition
  statements ...
Loop
```

Method 2: This alternative method executes the statement first, and then tests the condition. Only when the condition is tested TRUE will the next iteration be executed. Similarly, the program ends when the test condition returns a FALSE. The main difference is that the codes in the loop in method 2 will be executed at least once, whereas this may be by-passed completely in method 1.

```
Do
  statements ...
Loop While testCondition
```

The corresponding examples are as follows:

```
Sub DoWhileDemoMethod1()
  Dim j As Integer
    j = 1
  Do While j < 10
    MsgBox ("Hi")
    j = j + 1
  Loop
End Sub
```

Method 2:

```
Sub DoWhileDemoMethod2()
  Dim j As Integer
    j = 1
  Do
    MsgBox ("Hi")
    j = j + 1
  Loop While j < 10
End Sub
```

A **Do-Until** statement is similar to a Do-While statement except the former executes the codes until the test condition becomes TRUE. Again, there are two methods to program a Do-Until statement.

Method 1: This method tests the condition first and executes the codes when the test condition returns a FALSE. The program ends when the test condition returns a TRUE.

Do Until *testCondition*
   statements …
Loop

Method 2: This method executes the codes once and then tests the condition. The program continues to loop as long as the condition returns a FALSE, and ends when it returns a TRUE.

```
Do
  statements …
Loop Until testCondition
```

Their corresponding examples are given below.

```
Sub DoUntilDemoMethod1()
  Dim j As Integer
    j = 1
  Do Until j = 10
    MsgBox ("Hi")
    j = j + 1
  Loop
End Sub

Sub DoUntilDemoMethod2()
  Dim j As Integer
    j = 1
  Do
    MsgBox ("Hi")
    j = j + 1
  Loop Until j = 10
End Sub
```

Quick Tip 1
_____

- Your computer screen may flicker during the running of a macro by virtue of its speed.
- To reduce the flicker and also to speed up the macro, stop Excel from updating the screen by putting `Application.ScreenUpdating = False` as one of the first statements in your Sub.
- You can reinstate the default option by putting `Application.Screen Updating= True` as one of the last statements in your Sub.
- It is very important to reinstate `Application.ScreenUpdating = True` at some point before the macro stop running and you are back in the spreadsheet. In Excel 2007 and later versions especially, it will most likely affect the responsiveness of your spreadsheet. Calculations and Conditional Formatting in particular will not be updated with new inputs.

Note 19: SOLVER AND ADD-INS   **Add-in** functions and operations are contained in workbooks, each typically denoted in Excel by extensions *.xla* or *.xlam*. For example, **Solver** operations are in workbooks *Solver.xla* or *Solver.xlam*. An add-in is only available after it has been activated. This is done by selecting **File/Options/Add-ins**, choose **Excel Add-ins** in the **Manage** box, and click **Go**. In Excel 2003, select **Tools/Add-ins** and in Excel 2007, select **Office/Excel Options/Add-ins/Excel Add-ins/Go.** Do similar steps for other (later or Mac) Excel versions.

Activating an add-in only allows it to run in the spreadsheet. Macros recorded with add-in operations may not work. For example, Solver operations will not run in the macros, unless in addition the *Solver.xla* file is referenced for the project in the Visual Basic Editor. This is done by selecting in **Tools/Reference** and then ticking the check box for Solver. You may have to browse for it if it is not there in the selection list. The file is usually found in **c:\Program Files\Microsoft Office\Office 12\Library\Solver**. The file to link to is *Solver.xlam* and not *Solver.dll*. For Excel 2003, the folder is *Office 11* instead and the file is *Solver.xla*. Again, do similar steps for other Excel versions.

Quick Tip 1
_____

- Some spreadsheet operations will prompt dialog boxes for you to select your response. To avoid such incidences during a macro run, choose the default option and add the following statement to your Sub before the statement that causes the pop-up:

      `Application.DisplayAlert = True`

- It is a good practice to set it back to the default option by putting the same statement, with `True` replaced by `False`, at the next earliest possibility.

Note 20: AUTOMATIC PROCEDURES AND EVENTS

Event handler procedures are programs that are activated by interactive actions or events. Every object has their associated events, such as **Change**, **Activate**, **BeforeRightClick**, and **SelectionChange**.

Follow the steps below to create an event handler procedure.

1. Go to **VB Editor** and select the object from **Project Explorer**.
2. Click **View Code**. From the code window of the selected object, select the desired event from the small drop-down window in the upper right-hand corner.
3. A **Sub** procedure will be automatically created and all you need to do is write the codes within it, referring to the input variables as defined (if any). Refer to *Figure B-7*.

For example, to automatically execute a macro whenever an Excel workbook is opened, you can add a **Sub Workbook_Open** procedure in **ThisWorkbook**. An example of the macro codes that you can put in the Sub is shown below:

```
Private Sub Workbook_Open()
    Sheets("Home").Select
    Range("A1").Select
End Sub
```

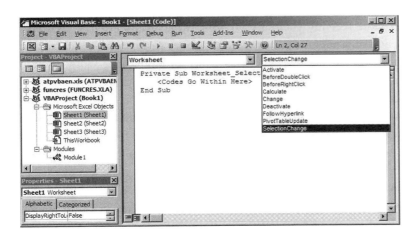

Figure B-7

Event Handler Procedure

Note 21: RUN-TIME ERROR HANDLING

Imagine that you wrote a simple subroutine to compute the square root of a user-input value. In order to ensure that the user has entered a positive value, you need to test the input value before executing the computation. You test by checking if the value is positive and if it is numeric. Alternatively, you can use a general error handling statement to trap all possible errors whenever they occur.

```
Sub SquareRootDemo()
  On Error Goto BadEntry
  Num = InputBox ("Enter a value: ")
  If Num = "" Then Exit Sub
  ActiveCell.Value = Sqrt(Num)
  Exit Sub
BadEntry:
  MsgBox ("Make sure you enter a positive numeric value")
End Sub
```

This example allows the subroutine to proceed straight to the error message whenever the user input threatens to trigger a computation error. The Exit Sub statement jumps to the end of the subroutine when it successfully completes its computation.

> **Note 22: SPREADSHEET PROGRAMMING APPROACH** There are really four approaches to programming a spreadsheet. The first is to use only spreadsheet functions and features (this topic is covered in Appendix A). Since its inception, spreadsheet application software has come a long way. Features that were once only available in programming languages are now present and regularly used in spreadsheets. The basic ones permit one variable (as represented by a cell) to take values from other variables, use of **If-Then-Else** logical branching, and multiple-stage computations with relative cell referencing. More recently, there are random variables, iterative or recursive computations, lookups, and automated computation (i.e., loops in the form of **DataTable** operations). Working on a spreadsheet workbook is really programming work, though many do not see it as such.

The second approach is to record mouse and keyboard actions as macros, and run these macros as automated steps in the spreadsheet operations. The steps are visible to the user by default, though it can be masked to speed up operations. All the calculations are done in the sheets and so the user can vividly review the interactions between variables.

The third approach is to extend the abilities of macros by adding VBA codes to do what mouse and keyboard actions on the worksheets cannot achieve. In addition, the recorded macros can be tidied up and made more efficient, for example, by removing worksheet selections, cell selections, and copy-paste operations, replacing them with codes that work directly with Excel objects.

The fourth and final approach is to write subroutines and functions using the VBA language, with minimal use of spreadsheet features, other than to read data and write results. This is no different than normal computer programming, except now the worksheets become data storage and reporting pages. The computations are all done in the lines of VBA codes and therefore the user must be able to read the computer language to understand, debug, and maintain the codes.

We prefer the third approach since the "computer program" in spreadsheets plus macros is already extremely powerful. On top of that, it is transparent and dynamic. This means that you can build a spreadsheet model with nontechnical people and its results are immediately responsive to changes in input values. Transparency, dynamism, and ease of use are the key strengths of spreadsheets; no other analytical software comes close to matching spreadsheets. No other software would be as readily accessible to novices and experts alike for situational exploration and problem discovery. And to beat that, the work done in these first steps can be further extended into user-friendly solutions, data and solution analyses, and management reports.

INDEX